Refugees of the Nazi period have attracted considerable attention from scholars. Albert Einstein, Thomas Mann, and Hannah Arendt, among others, are famous examples. In contrast, little is known about the daily lives of more typical refugees, their experiences in exile and emigration, their sorrows and their underlying strength. This volume shows how refugee women endured during the Nazi period, underscores their important role in the survival of their families, and explores the meaning of exile and emigration for their future lives and careers. *Between Sorrow and Strength* unites essays by noted scholars in the field and eyewitness reports from contemporaries who relate their actual experiences. This combination is particularly well suited to reveal a gender perspective on the history of Jewish as well as non-Jewish emigration from Europe during the Nazi era.

PUBLICATIONS OF THE GERMAN HISTORICAL INSTITUTE
WASHINGTON, D.C.

Edited by Detlef Junker
with the assistance of Daniel S. Mattern

Between Sorrow and Strength

THE GERMAN HISTORICAL INSTITUTE, WASHINGTON, D.C.

The German Historical Institute is a center for advanced study and research whose purpose is to provide a permanent basis for scholarly cooperation between historians from the Federal Republic of Germany and the United States. The Institute conducts, promotes, and supports research into both American and German political, social, economic, and cultural history, into transatlantic migration, especially in the nineteenth and twentieth centuries, and into the history of international relations, with special emphasis on the roles played by the United States and Germany.

Other books in the series

Hartmut Lehmann and James Sheehan, editors, *An Interrupted Past: German-Speaking Refugee Historians in the United States after 1933*

Carol Fink, Axel Frohn, and Jürgen Heideking, editors, *Genoa, Rapallo, and European Reconstruction in 1922*

David Clay Large, editor, *Contending with Hitler: Varieties of German Resistance in the Third Reich*

Larry Eugene Jones and James Retallack, editors, *Elections, Mass Politics, and Social Change in Modern Germany*

Hartmut Lehmann and Guenther Roth, editors, *Weber's Protestant Ethic: Origins, Evidence, Contexts*

Catherine Epstein, *A Past Renewed: A Catalog of German-Speaking Refugee Historians in the United States after 1933*

Hartmut Lehmann and James Van Horn Melton, editors, *Paths of Continuity: Central European Historiography from the 1930s to the 1950s*

Jeffry M. Diefendorf, Axel Frohn, and Hermann-Josef Rupieper, editors, *American Policy and the Reconstruction of West Germany, 1945–1955*

Henry Geitz, Jürgen Heideking, and Jürgen Herbst, editors, *German Influences on Education in the United States to 1917*

Peter Graf Kielmansegg, Horst Mewes, and Elisabeth Glaser-Schmidt, editors, *Hannah Arendt and Leo Strauss: German Emigrés and American Political Thought after World War II*

R. Po-chia Hsia and Hartmut Lehmann, editors, *In and Out of the Ghetto: Jewish–Gentile Relations in Late Medieval and Early Modern Germany*

Between Sorrow
and Strength

WOMEN REFUGEES OF THE NAZI PERIOD

Edited by

SIBYLLE QUACK

GERMAN HISTORICAL INSTITUTE
Washington, D.C.
and

 CAMBRIDGE
UNIVERSITY PRESS

Published by the Press Syndicate of the University of Cambridge
The Pitt Building, Trumpington Street, Cambridge CB2 1RP
40 West 20th Street, New York, NY 10011–4211, USA
10 Stamford Road, Oakleigh, Melbourne 3166, Australia

First published 1995

Printed in the United States of America

Library of Congress Cataloging-in-Publication Data
Between sorrow and strength : women refugees of the Nazi period /
edited by Sibylle Quack.
p.   cm. – (Publications of the German Historical Institute)
Papers presented at a conference held in November 1991 at the
German Historical Institute in Washington, D.C.
Includes index.
ISBN 0-521-47081-1
1. Women refugees – Europe – History – 20th century – Congresses.
2. Refugees – Europe – History – 20th century – Congresses.   3. Europe –
Emigration and immigration – History – 20th century – Congresses.
4. Women refugees – United States – History – 20th century – Congresses.
5. Refugees – United States – History – 20th century – Congresses.
I. Quack, Sibylle, 1951– .   II. Series.
HV640.4.E8B48   1994
362.87'082 – dc20   94-22866
                                          CIP

A catalog record for this book is available from the British Library.

ISBN 0-521-47081-1 Hardback

Contents

v

PART TWO: REFUGE IN THE UNITED STATES

A. COMMUNITY AND INSTITUTIONS

B. OCCUPATIONS OF WOMEN EMIGRES

Preface

This volume would not have been possible without the advice, encouragement, and cooperation of many individuals. First, I would like to thank all the authors for their contributions. As participants in the conference "Women in the Emigration after 1933," which took place at the German Historical Institute in Washington, D.C., in November 1991, they intensively researched, thoughtfully discussed, and passionately debated this multifaceted subject and helped to transform this collective project into a book.

The idea for the conference and for this volume emerged from many discussions with my friends Marion Kaplan and Renate Bridenthal. For their intellectual and moral support, I am especially grateful.

Hartmut Lehmann of the German Historical Institute, Washington, D.C., Fred Grubel and Robert Jacobs of the Leo Baeck Institute (New York), Dieter Dettke and Carola Weil of the Washington office of the Friedrich Ebert Foundation all supported the organization of the original conference. In addition, Professor Lehmann and the German Historical Institute made possible the publication of this volume by Cambridge University Press.

I am very much indebted to my former colleague at the German Historical Institute, Daniel S. Mattern. His editing skills and his patience were decisive in the process of publishing this volume. With him, large transcontinental correspondence on the book was always a pleasure. I also want to gratefully acknowledge the cooperation and editorial assistance of Anita Kassof.

I am most grateful to Eleanor Alexander, Rachel Cohn, Illo Heppner, Wilma Iggers, Elizabeth Marum Lunau, Susanne Miller, Eva Neisser, and Gabriele Schiff for sharing their personal experiences.

Last but not least, I would like to thank my son Sebastian Anselm, who moved with me from Germany to the United States and back again. During the past five years, he has not only patiently endured my preoccupation with this subject but also expanded my view on how children from a different culture are able to adapt to a new country. I want to express my deepest love and gratitude to him.

This volume is dedicated to the memory of Susanne Herz, née Simon, from Berlin, who was forced into exile during the Nazi period and emigrated to the United States. My interest in the fate of German–Jewish women began sixteen years ago when I met Susanne Herz and she shared her life story with me. She had been a constant source of inspiration and encouragement and a loving friend until her death in December 1994.

December 1994   Sibylle Quack
Bonn, Germany

Contributors

Note: This list does not contain those individuals who contributed eyewitness reports to this volume. Their biographical information can be found at the beginning of each of their respective chapters.

Mitchell G. Ash is an associate professor of history at the University of Iowa, where he teaches modern German history and the history of modern science. He has taught at Harvard University, at the universities in Mainz and Göttingen, and at the Freie Universität Berlin. His current research interests include the history of modern psychology, émigré German-speaking scientists after 1933, and scientific and political culture in postwar Germany. His book *Holism and the Quest of Objectivity: Gestalt Psychology in German Culture* is forthcoming.

Marion Berghahn is executive editor of Berghahn Books, Providence, R.I. A social anthropologist by training, and formerly a lecturer at the universities of East Anglia and Warwick, she is the author of *Images of Africa in Black American Literature* (1978), *Continental Britons: German–Jewish Refugees from Nazi Germany* (1984), and most recently *German–Jewish Refugees in England: The Ambiguities of Assimilation* (1988).

Catherine Epstein is currently completing her Ph.D. at Harvard University, where she is a graduate associate at the Center for European Studies. From 1987 to 1990 she was a research associate at the German Historical Institute, Washington, D.C.

Peter Gay is Sterling Professor of History, Emeritus, at Yale University. He is the author of nearly twenty books, the editor of seven collections, and the translator of works by Voltaire and Cassirer. The third volume in his series on *The Bourgeois Experience: Victoria to Freud* is called *The Cultivation of Hatred* (1993). He is currently working on a fourth volume on the inner life of the bourgeoisie that will be called *The Naked Heart.*

Atina Grossmann is an assistant professor of history at Columbia University. She is the author of *Reforming Sex: The German Movement for Birth Control and Abortion Reform, 1920–1950* (1995) and co-editor with Renate Bridenthal and Marion Kaplan of *When Biology Became Destiny: Women in Weimar and Nazi Germany* (1984). She is currently working on *Maternity and Modernity: New Women in Germany 1920 to 1950* and is particularly interested in population policy and sexual politics in the period after 1945.

Jack Jacobs is associate professor of government at John Jay College, the City University of New York. He has published widely on the nexus of Jews, socialism, and anti-Semitism. Most recently, he has written *On Socialists and "The Jewish Question" after Marx* (1992).

Marion Kaplan is a professor of modern European history at Queens College and the Graduate Center of the City University of New York. Her research and writing interests include the history of Jews in Germany and the history of European women. She has written *The Making of the Jewish Middle Class: Women, Family, and Identity in Imperial Germany* (1991) and *The Jewish Feminist Movement in Germany: The Campaigns of the Jüdischer Frauenbund, 1904–1938* (1979). She has also edited *The Marriage Bargain: Women and Dowries in European History* and has co-edited *When Biology Became Destiny: Women in Weimar and Nazi Germany*.

David Kranzler is a retired historian who taught for several years at the City University of New York. He has published widely on the Holocaust and contributed three articles to the *Encyclopedia of the Holocaust* (1990). His book *Japanese, Nazis, and Jews: The Jewish Refugee Community of Shanghai, 1938–1945* (1976) has been reprinted twice and was recently translated into Chinese. A revised edition is forthcoming. Currently, he is completing a book entitled *The Greatest Hero of the Holocaust* (forthcoming).

Linda G. Kuzmack is visiting associate professor of Jewish history at Baltimore Hebrew University, and president of Learning and Memories, an education and history consulting group. Formerly director of oral history at the U.S. Holocaust Memorial Museum, she teaches and writes on the Holocaust and on Jewish and women's history. She is the author of *The Hate Business: Antisemitism in America* (forthcoming), *Woman's Cause: The Jewish Woman's Movement in England and the United State, 1881–1933* (1990), as well as other books and articles. Among her projects is a high school curriculum with video testimonies, *To Save a Life: Christian Rescuers and Jewish Survivors during the Holocaust* (1994).

Ursula Langkau-Alex is currently senior research fellow at the Internationaal Instituut voor Sociale Geschiedenis in Amsterdam. She is the author of *Volksfront für Deutschland? Vorgeschichte und Gründung des "Ausschusses zur Vorbereitung einer deutschen Volksfront," 1933–1936* (1977). Her other publications, in German, Dutch, French, and English, include studies of emigration from German-speaking countries after 1933 and of European labor history more generally.

Steven M. Lowenstein is the Levine Professor of Modern Jewish History at the University of Judaism in Los Angeles. He is the author of *Frankfurt on the Hudson: The German Jewish Community of Washington Heights, 1933–1983* (1989) and *The Berlin Jewish Community, 1770–1830: Enlightenment, Family, and Crisis* (1993), as well as numerous articles on German–Jewish social history.

Frank Mecklenburg is archivist at the Leo Baeck Institute in New York City. His research has focused on emigration history, the history of postwar Germany, and the history of Jews in Germany after 1933. With Manfred Stassen he has co-edited *German Essays on Socialism in the Nineteenth Century* (1990) and with Ernst C. Stiefel, *Deutsche emigrierte Juristen in den USA* (1991). He has also translated Ernst Bloch's *The Utopian Function of Art and Literature: Selected Essays* (1988).

Katherine Morris is currently visiting assistant professor of German at the University of North Carolina at Chapel Hill. Her forthcoming books include *Jewish Women's Odyssey of Exile and Holocaust: Fleeing Germany for Brazil*, an anthology of German–Jewish women's autobiographies, as well as *Escape Through the Balkans*, the translation of the autobiography of Irene Gruenbaum, who was a German–Jewish refugee in the Balkans during World War II. She is the author of "Balkan Exile: The Autobiography of Irene Gruenbaum," *Leo Baeck Yearbook* (1991), and "Probleme emigrierter Frauen im brasilianischen Exil," in *Deutschsprachiges Exil in Lateinamerika, 1933–1945* (1993).

Sibylle Quack currently works for the German Federal Press and Information Office (*Bundespresseamt*) in Bonn. She also teaches at the Universität zu Köln. She is the author of *Geistig Frei und Niemandes Knecht: Paul Levi – Rosa Luxemburg* (1986) and *Zuflucht Amerika: Zur Sozialgeschichte der Emigration deutsch-jüdischer Frauen in die USA, 1933–1945* (1995).

Guy Stern is a professor of German language and literature at Wayne State University and a fellow of the Leo Baeck Institute. He is the author of *War, Weimar, and Literature: The Story of the Neue Merkur* (1971), *Alfred Neumann* (1979), and *Literatur im Exil* (1990). He has also written numerous articles on eighteenth- and twentieth-century German literature. A festschrift, entitled *Exile and Enlightenment,* appeared in 1987. He is recipient of the Federal Republic of Germany's *Grosse Verdienstkreuz* and the Goethe Medal.

Brigitte V. Sumann is a Ph.D. candidate at Wayne State University. With Guy Stern, she has published "William Pachner, a Painter from Prague, Vienna, and Florida," in A. Stephan, ed. *Exil Literatur und die Künste nach 1933* (1990) and "Mit Zeichenstift und Farbe gegen den Hitler-Staat: William Pachners politische Illustrationen in amerikanischen Zeitschriften," *Exil-Forschung: Jahrbuch* (1989).

Rita Thalmann is a professor of history at the Université de Paris VII and has written many articles and a book on German émigrés to France during the 1930s.

Christl Wickert is currently *wissenschaftliche Mitarbeiterin* in the Institut für Geschichtswissenschaft at the Technische Universität Berlin. Currently, she is working on the resistance and persecution of women during the Nazi era. She has published on the political participation of women in the Kaiserreich and during the Weimar Republic and on left-wing intellectuals in the 1920s

Joachim Wieler is professor of social work at the Fachhochschule Erfurt. Trained in the United States and at the Technische Universität Berlin, he formerly taught at the Evangelische Fachhochschule Darmstadt. He has published numerous studies on the history of social work in Germany, including *Erinnerung eines zerstörten Lebensabend: Alice Salomon während der NS-Zeit* (1987).

Introduction

SIDYLLE QUACK

"It all depended on whom you met after your arrival."[1] These words, written by Hertha Leab, a German–Jewish woman who had fled Nazi Germany for the United States in 1938, show the importance of outside help given refugees, whether by private individuals, fellow immigrants, relatives, or refugee aid organizations. Hertha Leab, a cosmetician from Berlin, did not find such help: With unfriendly, even hostile relatives and no assistance from any organization, she and her family struggled for a long time with illnesses, isolation, and desperation. With great tenacity, Leab finally succeeded in selling one of her products to other women refugees. With time, her cosmetics became well known among a wider range of customers. Despite all the hardships, including several nervous breakdowns, she made it possible for her family to survive.

The case of Hertha Leab, thoroughly documented in the archives of the Leo Baeck Institute in New York, is a good example of the problems of refugee women of the Nazi period. Traditionally, the history of European refugees of the 1930s and 1940s has been associated with the image of the famous or "illustrious immigrant," usually a man.[2] Most studies in this field emphasize the lives and experiences of men and do not focus on the lives of refugee women.[3]

In November 1991 the German Historical Institute in Washington,

---

1 Letter from Hertha Leab to Dr. Taterka, Feb. 12, 1956, in Hertha Leab (Liebeskind) Collection, box 7, folder 6, Leo Baeck Institute, New York. Translated by author.

2 Laura Fermi uses this term in her study on refugee academics: *Illustrious Immigrants: the Intellectual Migration from Europe, 1930–41* (Chicago, 1968).

3 Most material on women can be found in the studies of Maurice Davie, *Refugees in America. Report of the Committee for the Study of Recent Immigration from Europe* (New York and London, 1947) and Ruth Neubauer, *Differential Adjustment of Adult Immigrants and Their Children to American Groups. The Americanization of a Selected Group of Jewish Immigrants of 1933–1944* (New York, 1966). During the past 15 years, there has been a growing number of studies on émigré women writers. For an

1

D.C., organized a conference on "Women in the Emigration After 1933." Its purpose was to take a new look at the social history of Jewish and non-Jewish emigration and immigration after 1933, focusing specifically on the lives of women. For three days, anthropologists, historians, and political scientists, as well as contemporary eyewitnesses, discussed and analyzed the life stories of women refugees during the Nazi period. The participants explored how gender affected women refugees' opportunities for work and how it shaped their emotional world. In addition, the conferees studied the impact of exile, emigration, and immigration on refugee women's future lives and career patterns. Reports of eyewitnesses were introduced into the scholarly debate and contributed to very lively discussions in all sessions. The encounter between researchers from the United States and Europe – among them several children of German–Jewish emigrants – and members of the older generation of eyewitnesses created a unique setting for reconsidering the results of historical research.

The papers read at the conference, presented in this volume, broaden considerably our view of the history of refugees from Europe after 1933. Starting with Marion Kaplan's prefatory essay and ending with an epilogue by Peter Gay, the volume contains two main parts. Essays and reports in the first part document the worldwide search for refuge. The authors discuss the situation of women émigrés in France (Rita Thalmann and Elizabeth Marum Lunau), England (Marion Berghahn and Susanne Miller), Palestine (Rachel Cohn), the Netherlands (Ursula Langkau-Alex), Canada (Wilma Iggers), Shanghai (David Kranzler and Illo Heppner), and Brazil (Katherine Morris and Eleanor Alexander).

Altogether, the contributions – scholarly essays and eyewitness reports – provide us with a rich variety of fascinating experiences, feelings, and attitudes of émigré women seeking refuge in different parts of the world. Each author describes the difficult living conditions that refugees faced and how women refugees were able to adapt to various types of hardships. They did so by actively cultivating solidarity among themselves, coping with unsettling and degrading situations, and comforting their husbands and other family members.

These essays contain many diverse experiences, revealing "different worlds," as one participant of the conference put it. They show that the category *women* of itself does not mean that all women refugees had the

extended bibliography on the subject see *Frauen und Exil: Zwischen Anpassung und Selbstbehauptung,* a special issue of *Exilforschung* 11 (Munich, 1993), 239–77.

same experiences. It is important to differentiate among women with regard to age, marital status, number of children, when they left Germany, whether they could take anything with them, their professions (if any), their religious backgrounds, and their political opinions.

The eyewitness reports are unique documents of individual experiences and stand for themselves. In their directness and closeness to the events in question, they are highly valuable sources; they also prove the multifaceted picture of this emigration. Thus, this volume shows in an unusual way, "not only the records of women's past but also their own 'voice.' "[4] We are fortunate to have the voices of those who are at the center of the historical investigation combined here with the fruits of scholarly research. To provide the reader with the context for these reports, I have located the biographical information for the eyewitnesses at the beginning of each of their respective chapters.

Immigration to the United States is the theme of the second part of this book. Essays on women in the German–Jewish immigrant community (Steven Lowenstein), in refugee help organizations (Gabriele Schiff, Linda Kuzmack, and Jack Jacobs), and in various occupations and professions provide a detailed picture of refugee women's social activities, work patterns, and expectations. Atina Grossmann reports on women refugee physicians, Mitchell Ash on psychologists and psychoanalysts, Joachim Wieler on social workers, Frank Mecklenburg on lawyers, Catherine Epstein on historians, Christl Wickert on politicians, and Guy Stern and Brigitte V. Sumann on writers. In concentrating on the life stories, educational backgrounds, and career opportunities of female refugee academics – as well as the disruptions caused by emigration and immigration – the authors have done pioneering work.

We are especially grateful to be able to include Eva Neisser's eyewitness report on her work at chicken farms in Vineland, New Jersey. We would have liked additional reports and essays from refugee women who worked in nonacademic fields, such as textiles, offices, sales, nursing, or domestic service. Much more research needs to be done in these areas. We hope that this volume will inspire other historians to investigate these challenging subjects.

Most of the essays in this volume apply the methods of gender history, enabling us to make important distinctions between men and women refugees and to discover the relationships between gender, ethnicity, social

---

4 Karen Offen, Ruth Roach Pierson, and Jane Randall have used this expression in their introduction to *Writing Women's History. International Perspectives* (Bloomington and Indianapolis, 1991), xxxi.

status, class, and other important factors. Did men and women perceive their situations differently? Did their attitudes, feelings, and reactions to the needs and challenges of persecution, emigration, and immigration differ, and if so, how? Did they cope differently? As Peter Gay states in his epilogue, reading these essays and eyewitness reports is like "putting together the pieces of a sizable and complex mosaic with more and more pieces in place . . . to glimpse the outlines of the portrait . . . of the refugee woman."

In her contribution, Marion Kaplan analyzes the increasingly difficult situation of the Jewish population in Germany during the years from 1933 to 1939. She points out gender differences in the family and discusses how Jewish women tried to create an atmosphere of normalcy in a highly abnormal and threatening environment. Kaplan argues that women had to absorb much of the family's stress and as a result were the ones who pressed hardest for emigration. Nevertheless, although many Jewish women recognized from an early date the necessity of emigrating, for large numbers of these women leaving Germany was in fact very difficult. Overall, it seems that fewer women than men were actually able to do so.

Kaplan offers a number of compelling reasons for this phenomenon, including the fact that the employment situation for men and women within the struggling Jewish community was different. For example, women, especially young women, could still find jobs in the Jewish sector of the German economy. In addition, Kaplan writes, many women did not leave Germany because they had to care for elderly parents or relatives and were expected to stay. Moreover, Jewish parents and organizations were afraid to let single girls or women emigrate alone. Thus, Jewish women from Nazi Germany were much more reluctant than men to emigrate. The lower rate of female emigration during those years caused a growing disproportion of women to men in the German–Jewish population – a disproportion already apparent before 1933 that was mainly a result of the large number of Jewish soldiers who had been killed in World War I. Ultimately, more women than men, particularly elderly women, remained behind and perished in the Holocaust.[5]

Several factors influenced Jewish women's decisions to leave Germany or stay behind, including personal and public attitudes toward emigration,

---

5   See also Marion Kaplan's article, "Jewish Women in Nazi Germany: Daily Life, Daily Struggles, 1933–1939," *Feminist Studies* 16, no. 3 (1990): 598. Rita Thalmann writes in her book, *Frauen im Dritten Reich* (Frankfurt/Main and Berlin, 1987), 229, that among the Austrian and German Jews deported to concentration camps almost two-thirds were women.

family situation, age, economic position within the Jewish community, and Nazi policies. Gender-based immigration regulations of the various countries also played a role in whether or not women were able to escape the Nazi terror.[6]

Beginning in 1937, the United States started to surpass Palestine as the destination of the largest number of German refugees. The approximately 130,000 German and Austrian refugees who immigrated to the United States during the Nazi period included more women than men. Between 1934 and 1944, 53 percent of all adult émigrés from Germany were women, and 47 percent were men.[7] One reason for the preponderance of women

6   As part of any future research agenda, scholars should gather immigration statistics of different countries of emigration and analyze them according to gender. For example, immigration statistics for Palestine, which took the most refugees from Germany between 1933 and 1936, show 52 percent men and 48 percent women. See David Gurevich, Aaron Gertz, and Roberto Bachi, *The Jewish Population of Palestine. Immigration, Demographic Structure, and National Growth,* Dept. of Statistics of the Jewish Agency for Palestine (Jerusalem, 1944), 27. Clearly, the immigration policies – as to who received an immigration certificate, for example – of the British Mandate government and the Jewish Agency for Palestine were, in part, based on gender. Single mothers and their children were excluded, and, at least during the first few years, fewer certificates were issued to girls than to boys. According to an article in the contemporary press, the reason for this policy was the fear of a surplus of women. Later on, the number of certificates given to girls rose, and in 1936 the League of Jewish Women, which had been critical of the process, called it an "almost balanced relation between male and female juvenile émigrés." See "Palästina als Einwanderungsland," *Blätter des Jüdischen Frauenbunds,* Dec. 1936: 36. But, as statistics show, equity in immigration for men and women was never fully reached.

7   Statistics from the U.S. Immigration and Naturalization Service provide us with demographic characteristics of the group, including data on their marital status and their age. They show that during the early years of emigration, between 1933 and 1936, the proportion of unmarried and younger women from Germany who entered the United States was much higher than in later years. In 1935 and 1936, when comparatively few individuals from Germany immigrated to the United States, unmarried women even outnumbered married women. But from 1937 onward, when the United States became the main destination for refugees, the number of married women émigrés rapidly increased. Of all female immigrants from Germany in 1936, single women comprised 47.6 percent of the total; married women, 41.8 percent. But by 1940, the percentage of single women had dropped to 21.5 percent, whereas that for married women had risen to 65.2 percent. Although figures on male refugees show a similar development, the marital structure of men and women differed because of the greater number of divorced or widowed women. With the overall increase in refugees, the age structure of the whole group changed as more and more older women and men immigrated. In 1941 the percentage of women over forty-five outnumbered the middle group (ages sixteen to forty-four). This trend was even more so in the case of men. That same year, the percentage over sixty years was 18.5 percent for women and 25 percent for men.

Contemporary immigration statistics dealing with the occupational structure of the refugees unfortunately were not gender-based. Considering the high rate of old people among the refugees, it is not surprising that the group of those who said they had no gainful occupation was very high, more than half. Women who had been housewives prior to emigration, and children, also belonged to that group. By and large, the immigrant occupational structure mirrored that of the Jewish population in Germany: a middle-class group with a high percentage of skilled workers, clerks, those engaged in commerce, and professionals.

All numbers are calculated from unpublished data provided by the Immigration and Naturalization

was that immigration regulations in the United States favored married women and children.[8] In addition, the growing pressure on the Jewish population in Germany accelerated the emigration of whole families. With increasing urgency, the Jewish community itself realized that single women, too, should emigrate in greater numbers.[9]

The economic situation facing German–Jewish women after their arrival in the United States was extremely difficult. On the one hand, the country was still struggling to throw off the effects of the Great Depression; on the other hand, most refugees, especially those who could leave Germany only in the later years, brought with them no visible means of support. Refugee aid organizations, such as the National Refugee Service (NRS), the Hebrew Sheltering and Immigrant Aid Society (HIAS), the National Council of Jewish Women, and the American Jewish Joint Distribution Committee (JDC), thus played a critical role in settling refugees. These and other organizations helped refugees financially and advised them in visa matters and in finding a job, an apartment, a doctor, or a school. Women were vital to the operation and activities of all these organizations. The activities of only three organizations are discussed in this volume, and although not necessarily representative, they illustrate the variety of groups that helped the refugees: the large National Council of Jewish Women, which had existed before 1933; a small organization founded in the 1930s by the American Jewish labor movement; and a self-help agency founded by refugees.

For those refugee women who had been housewives in Germany, emigration made it necessary for the first time in their lives to take up work outside the home. Coming to America during the Depression years, these women shared hard economic times with many American women. They were likewise thrown into poorly paid jobs, lost their identity as housewives, were separated from their children, and had few opportunities to choose their own work. They also had to adjust to a new country and culture, and thus were torn by the need to adapt to the new surroundings

Service in Washington, D.C. A gender-based analysis of these data is available in Sibylle Quack *Zuflucht Amerika: Zur Sozialgeschichte der Emigration deutsch-jüdischer Frauen in die USA, 1933–1945* (1995).

8   For a general discussion of immigration regulations, quota laws, and how they influenced the immigration of women to the United States, see Donna Gabaccia, "Women of the Mass Migration: From Minority to Majority, 1820–1930," a paper read at the conference "Continental European Migration and Transcontinental Migration to North America. A Comparative Perspective," Bremerhaven, Germany, Aug. 15–18, 1991. See also Gertrude D. Krichefsky, "Relation of the Quota Law to General Characteristics of Immigrants," *Immigration and Naturalization Service, Monthly Review* 3, no. 6 (1946): 265–70.

9   See, for example, the article "Mehr Frauen für die Auswanderung!" *C.V.–Zeitung*, no. 3 (Jan. 1938): 5.

and the desire to look back to Europe, where family members and friends were in mortal danger and needed their help. Many of the refugee women developed strengths despite their great sorrow; they played a decisive role in getting themselves and their families situated. The difficulties they faced and the high price they paid are related in memoirs, autobiographies, and interviews, of which the essays in this volume make extensive use.

But not all émigré women were former housewives. Many of them had been employed before emigration, either in Germany or in other countries where they had awaited their American visas. Although it was hard for refugee women to find anything better than menial employment, many succeeded in improving their job situation in a very short time. According to a survey from 1946, 48 percent of all women refugees from Europe were gainfully employed. Of these, 11.4 percent worked in unskilled and service jobs, compared to 32.7 percent of employed American women. Twenty-eight percent of employed women refugees worked at skilled jobs or held clerical positions. Semiskilled workers – that is, factory operators, dress-makers, and saleswomen – made up 25.1 percent of the total. The percentage of professionals, 18 percent, was especially high when compared with that of American women, 13.2 percent.[10]

The essays that discuss professional women refugees show how gender – among other important factors in their lives such as age, marital status, and the number of offspring – influenced refugee women's career chances, working conditions, and their adjustment to American life or to American academia. Professional women shared many of the problems experienced by other immigrant women: the struggle of working mothers, including the need to find good daycare; the double and sometimes triple burden on women's shoulders during the first years after arrival; the interruption – or dissolution – of their careers when they had to work as cleaning women, domestic servants, or private nurses. Many refugee women looked to other fields of work or found niches in their own or related areas of expertise, sometimes creating jobs not only for themselves but also for other immi-grants. Social work was one of the fields to which many refugee women who had been trained as teachers, doctors, psychologists, or therapists turned. But, as some of these essays demonstrate, despite the tendency to change their professions, quite a few refugee women succeeded in contin-uing their professional occupations.

Many middle-class refugee families strove to avoid financial dependence on refugee aid organizations or relatives. But it seems that women more

10 Davie, *Refugees in America*, 40.

than men were prisoners of this attitude. The ability and flexibility needed
to preserve the family's income in the short term meant that they had time
neither to find suitable positions for themselves nor to prepare the ground
for their own professional adjustments. Social workers reinforced the existing tendency of women to sacrifice their personal goals for the good of
the family by emphasizing the need for refugee men to adjust first.

Many, but not all, refugee men tried desperately to find a job in other
fields or at lower professional levels not in their academic specialities. But
often, social workers could not help them. The reasons for this lay in the
continuing effects of a depressed economy as well as in the reluctance on
the part of social workers to place a middle-class man in a menial job. A
contemporary article described, for example, a German–Jewish businessman
as a "dignified, statesman-like looking man with iron gray hair and a special
knowledge of finance – German finance" who tried unsuccessfully to find
a job – any job. "Silently, we Americans thought," the article's author
wrote, "what employer would feel comfortable giving orders to a middle-
class office boy who looks like a combination of Paul McNutt and a college
president?"[11]

Meanwhile, the wife, not so favorably characterized as an "untrained,
middle-aged woman in not very robust health," took care of older people,
mended clothes, baby-sat, and read to blind people. This situation changed
after the husband found part-time jobs in his field and, despite being poorly
paid, made more money than his "frail wife had earned." The story ends:
"With a poignant relief which all who know them shared he began once
more to be the provider of funds while his wife went back to homemak-
ing." It occurred to the writer of this article that "perhaps this purgatory
of waiting lasted just long enough to finish his acquisition of English and
his wontedness to American ways."[12]

As the quotation from Hertha Leab with which we began suggests, during the first years it was important to get help from fellow immigrants,
Americans, relatives, or organizations. The essays in this collection extensively document the private and institutional help given these refugees. In
interviews, refugee women talked about their experiences; they did not fail
to mention people who had helped them to adjust, to get back into an
academic or other job, to find employment for their husbands, and schools
and kindergartens for their children. The women were sometimes pro-

11   See Dorothy Canfield Fisher, "Meet Two Families," in *Pilgrims in Our Times*, reprinted from
     Survey Graphic (April 1946) by the National Refugee Service, New York.
12   Fisher, "Meet Two Families," 3.

moted even in such hostile environments as medicine, where being a woman *and* a refugee was especially disadvantageous.

As Atina Grossmann relates in her essay, for Alice Nauen, a refugee physician from Germany, it was absolutely critical to find a sympathetic female mentor, a pediatrician who was willing to let a refugee join her practice, or to find a women's college to which she could take her young son for care while she worked. These and other stories highlight the importance of individual or institutional support.

In urban neighborhoods and refugee communities, women played a significant role in establishing communication among refugees, neighbors, and other mothers. Together they went shopping, looked for schools, kindergartens, and jobs, made contacts, learned the language and customs. Like other immigrant women in America, they felt the need to restructure the household, to build up "survival networks," to learn English as fast as possible, and to adjust to the new culture, all while retaining tradition and familiar customs.[13] Thus, they played an important part in the acculturation process of their groups. And although we have to consider a great variety of experiences and to differentiate according to age, knowledge of English, religion, and so on, one commonalty emerges: Refugee women were better able to cope than refugee men were.

What accounts for such a conclusion? Was it because women had played a more subordinate role in their country of origin, had less to lose, and therefore had fewer problems with a change, especially a deterioration, in their status? Was it because they did not identify themselves exclusively as professionals? Was it because their identity as mothers or daughters was more significant for them than their occupations? Or was it because, at the very least, their gender roles were something they could hold onto, whereas men identified with and derived their status from work, their native country, and values specific to a certain culture? Was that why men found it difficult to regroup and rebound in exile? Anthropologist Margaret Mead wrote in 1932 in *Changing Culture of an Indian Tribe*:

[T]he breakdown of culture is almost always a more vital concern to the men than to the women. The old religion, the old social values, the old bravery, and the old vanities may be taken away . . . but the women must continue to bear and nurture children. . . . It is impossible to strip her life of meaning as completely as the life of men can be stripped.[14]

13 See Dolores M. Martimer and Roy S. Bryce-Laporte, eds., *Female Immigration to the United States: Caribbean, Latin American, and African Experiences* (Washington, D.C., 1981), 360.
14 Margaret Mead, *Changing Culture of an Indian Tribe* (New York, 1932), 318.

Although these lines were written for another culture – a different world – they have resonance for the refugee men and women who were forced out of their middle-class European culture by the Nazis.

Most of the essays in this collection are based on individual life stories or are themselves life stories. All these stories are unique, and, as Heinrich Heine has written: "Unter jedem Grabstein liegt eine Weltgeschichte" (under every tombstone lies a history of the world). As historians and political scientists, the authors of the scholarly essays have searched for patterns and trends and have tried to generalize. A challenge for future research lies in the comparison of these refugee groups. As much as their particular German–Jewish experience needs to be emphasized and their immigration experience included in the history of Jewish women, it is also important to compare commonalties with and differences from other refugee movements in America and throughout the world.

Jewish Women in Nazi Germany
Before Emigration

MARION KAPLAN

INTRODUCTION

"We were so German," "we were so assimilated," "we were so middle class" – these are the refrains one reads over and over again in the memoirs of German Jews who try to explain to us (and to themselves) what their lives were like before Nazi barbarism overpowered them. They stress how normal their lives were, how bourgeois their habits and attitudes. German Jews – a predominantly middle-class group comprising less than 1 percent of the German population – had welcomed their legal emancipation in the second half of the nineteenth century and lived in a relatively comfortable, secure environment until 1933. Between 1933 and 1939, however, they saw their economic livelihoods imperiled and their social integration dissolved. Inexorably, they were engulfed in the maelstrom that led to the Holocaust: impoverishment and ostracism for most; emigration for many; hiding for a handful; and ghettoization, forced labor, and extermination for the rest.[1]

The calamity that hit German Jews affected them as Jews first, but Jewish women had gender-specific experiences as well. In addition to suffering the persecution that afflicted all Jews, Jewish women also had the burden of keeping their households and communities together. A gender analysis of the situation of Jews in Germany suggests that racism and persecution as well as survival strategies meant something different for women than for men – in both practical and psychological terms.

This essay explores the increasingly difficult daily lives of Jewish middle-class women and the work of their main organization, the League of Jewish Women (Jüdischer Frauenbund, or JFB), in prewar Nazi Germany. By

---

1 About 235,000 out of the approximately 525,000 Jews in Germany managed to emigrate. Not all of these people, however, escaped. Many were caught up in the Nazi net cast over Europe.

11

focusing on the 1930s, we can locate the intensification of persecution and its effects on women and their families in a time when few dreamed that developments would end in anything like Auschwitz. In fact, this period is often neglected; either the earlier, more hopeful era of the Weimar Republic (1918–33) or the later, shocking years of genocide are more usually emphasized. But the intermediate era – the fascistization of daily life, when victims had to learn to cope while others looked on (or past), when even relationships among ordinary Germans were coarsened – is often far more instructive politically. Moreover, exploring the daily lives of Jews challenges the myths of political innocence with which so many Germans today surround their accounts of "daily life in Nazi Germany."[2] Most important for our purpose, gender specificity can be illustrated more clearly for these years than for later ones. Gender differences are also apparent in the desire to emigrate and in actual emigration patterns, another topic of concern here. Finally, a brief look at Jewish women's organizations shows how women responded collectively to increasing persecution.

The focus is on housewives and mothers, largely because they are the ones who left the most memoirs. Still, they made up a large portion of the female community. In their twenties, thirties, and forties, these women had embarked upon marriage, created families, and, sometimes, started careers. Like the vast majority of Jews, they experienced the impending catastrophe from their situation as ethnically or religiously Jewish and politically liberal citizens, increasingly shocked by the abrogation of the rights and liberties they once had taken for granted. Other women receive less attention here: Rarely did those who intermarried, who remained in Germany after the war broke out, or who died leave memoirs behind, at least memoirs that are accessible today. Of those who managed to escape, single women and the elderly are underrepresented in memoir collections.[3] Finally, memoir collections are often found in Jewish libraries and archives. Hence, writers who were more self-consciously Jewish might have deposited them there, possibly creating a sample of Jews who were slightly less integrated into German society than the actual range of women's situations.[4]

2   See Mary Nolan, "The Historikerstreit and Social History," *New German Critique* 44 (1988): 51–80.
3   Single women may not have had the motivation to write memoirs (since memoirs are often intended as family histories for future generations), and age may have impinged on the desire or ability of the elderly to write their stories.
4   People who were, or who considered themselves to be, on the edges of the Jewish community – such as women who intermarried or whose ethnic, or religious identities or both were superseded by political loyalties – were less likely to donate their materials to Jewish organizations.

Overview of German–Jewish Community

In 1933, 500,000 people were registered as Jews in Germany (excluding those who had officially left Judaism), or about 0.77 percent of the population. Seventy percent lived in large cities with populations over 100,000 (whereas half of non-Jews lived in places with under 10,000 inhabitants), and a third (144,000) lived in Berlin, where they made up close to 4 percent of the population. Like every minority, the Jewish minority had a career profile that differed significantly from that of the general population. Historically prohibited from a variety of economic endeavors, almost 62 percent of Jews (compared with 18 percent of non-Jews) worked in business and commerce. They were underrepresented in agricultural careers, where less than 2 percent of Jews (but 29 percent of other Germans) were employed. The employment of Jewish women had gradually increased to 27 percent by 1933, but it was still less than that of non-Jewish women (34 percent). Of those who worked, over one-third were salaried employees; about one-fifth were assistants in family enterprises (*mithelfende Familienangehörige*); another one-fifth were self-employed (this could include a large business or a tiny one); and about one-tenth were workers (mostly in industry but often in the offices rather than on the factory floor).[5]

The socioeconomic position of Jews was overwhelmingly middle class, although the inflation of the early 1920s and the Great Depression had definitely set them back. More and more women had to assist or support their families – a trend that intensified in the Nazi period – and more and more Jews had to rely on financial aid from the Jewish communities.[6] In addition, almost one in five Jews in Germany was a refugee from eastern Europe. Most of these *Ostjuden,* as they were called, eked out humble existences as industrial workers, minor artisans, or peddlers. Among this group there was a larger proportion of women in paid employment than among those who were not refugees.

In comparison with non-Jewish women, Jewish women generally had smaller families and more education. They were less likely to work outside the home and more likely to have household help. Although married Jewish women devoted themselves to their families, parents expected their un-

---

5 The breakdown is for Prussia in 1925 but is also representative of Germany as a whole. *Israelitisches Familienblatt* (hereafter cited as *IF*), Feb. 23, 1933, no. 8: 9.
6 Monika Richarz, ed., *Jüdisches Leben in Deutschland,* vol. 3: *Selbstzeugnisse zur Sozialgeschichte, 1918–1945* (Stuttgart, 1982), Introduction. See also Erich Rosenthal, "Trends of the Jewish Population in Germany, 1910–1939," *Jewish Social Studies* 6 (1944): 233–73.

married daughters to study for a career. Many – seven times as many as Christian women – went to a university.[7] As we shall see, after 1933 career development was increasingly obstructed, just as wage earning became more urgent.

During the Weimar Republic, strictly religious education and practices were on the decline and mixed marriages on the rise.[8] In the large cities, marriage to Christians was becoming so common – especially among Jewish men – that some Jewish leaders actually feared the complete fusion of their community into German society by the end of the twentieth century.[9] Jews eagerly joined nonsectarian organizations. For example, the Jewish feminist movement (League of Jewish Women) belonged to the German bourgeois feminist movement from 1908 until 1933, and individual Jewish women were prominent members of German women's organizations. Jews felt a deep allegiance to the ideals of German civilization as they understood them – the liberal values of tolerance, humanism, and reason of the German Enlightenment. They enjoyed general acceptance in the worlds of art and culture, participated in center and moderate Left politics, and excelled in the "free" professions of medicine and law. Possibly as many as one-third of all women doctors in the Weimar Republic were Jewish.[10]

Although Jews adapted to the social, political, or cultural styles of their surroundings, "[quoting] Goethe [at] every meal," most also preserved a sense of ethnic solidarity and religious cohesion.[11] They did so through organizing religious or secular Jewish groups and through maintaining traditional holiday celebrations in the family. Jewish women's organizations in particular fostered a sense of Jewish identity, including religious identity, throughout the Weimar years. Thus, the interest by women's organizations in their Jewish heritage during the Nazi period was not a sudden shift; it was an intensification of a trend already well under way. Finally, a small Zionist movement, although failing to make significant inroads into the assimilationist commitments of most German Jews, sharpened Jewish self-consciousness.[12]

7   Marion Kaplan, *The Jewish Feminist Movement in Germany. The Campaigns of the Jüdischer Frauenbund, 1904–1938* (Greenport, Conn., 1979), 193, note 31.
8   Richarz, *Jüdisches Leben,* 15. Twenty out of 100 marriages were mixed in 1930, but conversions were down in comparison with the Imperial era.
9   Karl Schleunes, *The Twisted Road to Auschwitz: Nazi Policy toward German Jews, 1933–1939* (Urbana, Ill., 1970), 7. For gender-specific intermarriage statistics, see Usiel O. Schmelz, "Die demographische Entwicklung der Juden in Deutschland von der Mitte des 19. Jahrhunderts bis 1933," *Zeitschrift für Bevölkerungswissenschaft* 8, no. 1 (1982): 42, 52–3.
10 This is my estimate based on the number of Jewish female medical students before the war. Jews had received the right to become judges, diplomats, and civil servants only in 1918.
11 George L. Mosse, *German Jews Beyond Judaism* (Bloomington, Ind., 1985), 14.
12 Donald Niewyk, *The Jews in Weimar Germany* (Baton Rouge, La., 1980), 164.

Jewish cohesion was also a response to a pervasive anti-Semitism with roots in Imperial Germany (1871–1918). Virtually all Jews knew of anti-Semites or of an anti-Semitic incident directed against someone in their immediate circle of friends or relatives. The mission of one of the largest Jewish organizations in Germany, the Central Union of German Citizens of the Jewish Faith, founded in 1893, was to fight anti-Semitism politically and judicially and to strengthen Jewish and German consciousness within the Jewish communities as well. The loss of World War I and postwar political and economic instability magnified anti-Jewish passions. To the radical Right and its diverse followers, Jews became the scapegoats for all social and economic ills. Even more common and widespread was what Donald Niewyk has called "moderate anti-Semitism, that vague sense of unease about Jews that stopped far short of wanting to harm them but that may have helped to neutralize whatever aversion Germans might otherwise have felt for the Nazis."[13] This atmosphere could be found in churches, universities, political parties, and the government as well as in relationships between Jews and other Germans.

Even those Jewish women who worked closely with other German women commented on the distance between the groups: "We lived among each other, sat together in the same school room, attended university together, met each other at social events – and were complete strangers."[14] There were exceptions, close and lasting friendships that extended until deportation or even until today, but for the vast majority of Jews, their tenuous friendships with other Germans dissolved as the Nazi terror grew.

THE LIVES OF JEWISH WOMEN IN PUBLIC AND PRIVATE

Social Ostracism

With the Nazi seizure of power in January 1933, Jews as individuals had to begin to struggle for daily survival and Jewish organizations had to gear themselves up for providing unprecedented and massive economic, social, and cultural aid. Jews were forced into an era of "dissimilation" – a process of separation and then segregation – that took about six years, gradually gathering speed and thoroughness. A brief outline of this interim, before

13 Niewyk, 80.
14 Niewyk, 93–4.

the deportations and genocide, provides necessary background for understanding the variety of Jewish responses.

Soon after taking power, the Nazis scheduled an official boycott of Jewish businesses and professional establishments for April 1. On that day storm troopers stood in front of Jewish stores, threatening and exhorting shoppers to "buy German." As unofficial boycotts continued, the Nazis enacted discriminatory legislation. The "April Laws" of 1933 provided for the expulsion of Jews from the civil service, legal and medical professions, and postprimary schools and universities. This "legal" attack reached its peak in late 1935 with the "Law for the Protection of German Blood and Honor," or Nuremberg Laws, which forbade sexual intercourse or intermarriage between Jews and "Aryans" (perceived as "pure" Germans) and made it unlawful for a Jew to employ an Aryan domestic servant under the age of forty-five. These laws were followed by more than 400 pieces of anti-Jewish legislation promulgated by the Nazis between 1933 and 1939.[15] The last stage before outright and organized violence was "aryanization," the attempt to drive Jews from the economy. Proceeding fitfully throughout 1936 and 1937, aryanization speeded up in 1938 and 1939 to the point at which the economy could be considered *judenrein* (free of Jews). Persecutions reached a new level of intensity in 1938, culminating in the November Pogrom, commonly called "Crystal Night." This milestone claimed the lives of at least 100 Jews; destroyed more than 1,000 synagogues and countless homes and shops. More than 30,000 Jewish men were incarcerated in concentration camps.

Despite what appears in hindsight to be the increasing speed and clarity of persecution, Nazi policy followed what one historian described as a "twisted road to Auschwitz."[16] Contradictory pronouncements, regional variations, conflicting satrapies, lack of coordination at the top, and the attempt to appear moderate to other nations gave contemporaries profoundly mixed signals. It was only after the pogrom that most Jews were finally convinced of their peril. At every stage, some Jews thought and others hoped that the government would cease its persecutions. As the Jewish community moved from a relatively porous relationship with the surrounding society to a severely encapsulated one, many believed they could make peace with the new circumstances. Even after the Nuremberg Laws, for example, the central organization of Jews was willing to see them

---

15   Joseph Walk, *Das Sonderrecht für Juden im NS–Staat* (Heidelberg, 1981); Schleunes, 109.
16   Schleunes.

as a "tolerable arrangement" and to work for a modus vivendi with the Nazi state.[17]

As dissimilation intensified, the concept of "normal" became increasingly elastic. This was a complicated process. For some there was the longing to make life "normal" within the ever-narrowing boundaries drawn by the Nazis. Women in particular, I would suggest, attempted to create an atmosphere of normalcy within the family. For others there was a denial of what they saw happening. For many there was a combination of both at the same time: the desire and need to believe that they could remain in their homeland, even under new and trying conditions. Today historians of daily life in Nazi Germany are attempting to capture the double character of normality and terror, the effects on its citizens of both a normal bureaucratic state and an exceptional state. This double character is all the more pronounced – and more complicated – for its victims, whose perceptions of the conflicting signals were colored by their anxieties but also by their hopes.[18]

Life for German–Jewish women often changed dramatically with the beginning of the new regime. One of the first signs of a "new era" (even before one lost a job or one's husband, father, or brother did) was the dissociation of former friends. One woman reported that she had enjoyed getting together with friends from her hometown in a café once a month:

Since the Nazis came to power, I hadn't taken part in these gatherings. I didn't want to cause difficulties for my friends as a result of my [Jewish] presence.

One day she met one of her friends:

She tried to convince me that they were all still my friends, so I decided to go to the next meeting. . . . I couldn't sleep at all the night before the gathering. I was worried about my Christian friends, but I was also worried about myself. . . . I knew I would observe them very carefully. I would notice even a shadow of their discomfort at my entry. . . . But, I didn't have to read their eyes or note a change in their tone. The empty table in the booth where we had always met spoke loudly and clearly. . . . But, I couldn't blame them. Why should they have risked the loss of their jobs only to prove to me that Jews could still have friends in Germany?[19]

Not all Germans abandoned their Jewish friends. In fact, it was often precisely an experience of loyalty – the friend who came by ostentatiously, the former classmate who went out of her way to shake hands with a Jewish

---

17 Schleunes, 126.
18 Nolan, "Historikerstreit."
19 Richarz, *Jüdisches Leben*, 233; all quotations from this book have been translated by the author.

woman in a crowded store,[20] or the "sympathy purchases" after the April boycott[21] – that gave Jews mixed messages, letting some deceive themselves into staying on. Furthermore, in the early years, Jews experienced only isolated local ostracism or attacks that were often based on economic rivalries and resentments rather than on purely racial grounds.[22]

But the government intended to completely isolate Jews and "after some months of a regime of terror, fidelity and friendship had lost their meaning, and fear and treachery had replaced them."[23] Moreover, the Nazis could count on grass-roots enthusiasm. Well before the Nazis prohibited friendly contacts with Jews, gossip and denunciations discouraged such associations. Based on Gestapo (Secret State Police) files, Robert Gellately has observed: ". . . an extraordinary degree and variety of accommodation . . . to the regime's doctrines on race. Friendships and business relationships going back many years were broken off."[24] Of interest here is not only the fear of terror but also the often zealous autosurveillance by the Germans themselves. This had an effect on Jews, too. For example, in a small Rhineland town in late 1933, a Christian woman went to visit her Jewish friend. When she arrived at the door, her friend looked at her in horror: "For God's sake, Frieda, leave, don't come in, we are already being watched." With tears in their eyes, they turned away from each other.[25] Thus, companionship with non-Jews became the rare exception. Jews felt as if they were becoming society's lepers.

20 See the memoirs of Liselotte Kahn, Leo Baeck Institute (hereafter cited as LBI), 16. About her classmate's behavior, Kahn noted: "This I considered already a heroic deed in 1933."
21 Hans Mommsen and Dieter Obst, "Die Reaktion der deutschen Bevölkerung auf die Verfolgung der Juden, 1933–1943," in Hans Mommsen, ed., *Herrschaftsalltag im Dritten Reich* (Düsseldorf, 1988), 374–8.
22 Michael H. Kater, "Everyday Anti-Semitism in Prewar Nazi Germany: The Popular Bases," *Yad Vashem Studies* 16 (1984): 129–59.
23 Monika Richarz, ed., *Jewish Life in Germany: Memoirs from Three Centuries* (Bloomington, Ind., 1991), 352.
24 In April 1935, Nazi Party members were forbidden from having personal relationships with Jews, unless in the line of duty. Still, even Nazi Party members kept business ties to Jews throughout 1935 and some until even as late as 1938 (see Mommsen and Obst, 387, 430–1). Friendships with Jews were not officially a crime for non-party members until November 1941, but local laws frequently forced Germans to break all relations with Jews much earlier (see Mommsen and Obst, 428–9). For more on denunciations, the "key link between the police and the people in Nazi Germany, [which made] the terror system work," see Robert Gellately, "The Gestapo and German Society: Political Denunciation in the Gestapo Case Files," *Journal of Modern History* 60, no. 4 (1988): 664, 669, 673–4, 677. Gellately pointed out the centrality of gossip to the functioning of the Nazi terror system in "Terror System, Racial Persecution and Resistance in Nazi Germany: Remarks on the Historiography," a paper presented to the GDR–USA Symposium on Nazi Terror and Resistance, Princeton, N.J., May 4–6, 1989. See also his *The Gestapo and German Society: Enforcing Racial Policy 1933–1945* (New York, 1990).
25 Francis Henry, *Victims and Neighbors: A Small Town in Nazi Germany Remembered* (South Hadley, Mass., 1984), 92.

Loss of friends was accompanied by general social ostracism. The Gestapo and the courts used charges of friendship and, more seriously, "race defilement," "to discipline (or 'educate') society at large about the importance of the race issue . . . but beyond that, . . . to adjust all opinions to bring them into line with Nazi teachings."[26] By 1936 the Nazis had "brought off a deepening of the gap" between Jews and other Germans, and companionship with non-Jews became the rare exception.[27]

Loss of friends was accompanied by general social ostracism. Officials, neighbors, even the mail man looked past or through Jews as they crossed paths at the local market or in the corridors. I suspect that the loss of friends and the decline of sociability in the neighborhood affected Jewish women more than it did men, because women were more integrated into and dependent upon the community and neighborhood. They were more accustomed to neighborly exchanges and courtesies. Their lives negotiated the interface between family and community. Highly organized and active in communal, volunteer, or women's organizations, women suffered when they were ostracized. Moreover, women probably had more frequent contacts with the state than did men. They had more meetings with such state agents as post office and railroad clerks, social workers, and, for mothers in particular, teachers. Men saw less of neighbors to begin with and had less time to engage in communal or volunteer activities. Also, although men now suffered the loss of even a modicum of courtesy at work, they were more used to competition and a certain degree of conflict in their everyday work life.[28]

The pain of being the object of a general, hateful taboo affected most Jews long before the actual violence began. One woman recalled that when she traveled on the tram on the day of the April 1933 boycott, she felt self-conscious about being Jewish and feared that the people next to her might move away from her if they guessed her true identity.[29] Another woman wrote:

Anxiety accompanied me wherever I went: if I had to talk to shop attendants I'd be afraid they would be hostile to me as soon as they discovered I was Jewish; when I waited for the tram, I always thought the conductor wouldn't stop for me if he knew I was Jewish. . . . I waited for such events all the time and this anxiety tormented me unceasingly. Long before the Nazis forbade it, I had stopped going

---

26 Gellately, "Political Denunciation," 677.
27 SOPADE report quoted by Peter Pulzer in a lecture on the anniversaries of the annexation of Austria and of Crystal Night, Harvard Center for European Studies, April 14, 1989. SOPADE was the name of the Social Democratic Party in exile.
28 The author wishes to thank Peter Pulzer for this insight.
29 Memoirs of Hanna Bergas, LBI, 1.

to movies or the theater, because I simply couldn't stand being around people who hated us.[30]

   To make matters worse, Jewish friends provided little respite. Most Jews, even those who had made genuine friendships with non-Jewish Germans, maintained a circle of Jewish friends and colleagues. But in the strained circumstances affecting the entire Jewish community, shadows hovered over social evenings with Jewish friends. "When one met in Jewish company, it meant mostly that there was not the slightest relaxation, because every last person had either his own unpleasant experience or some sort of ill tidings to report from somewhere else."[31] Moreover, when groups of Jews gathered in private homes, they feared that they were being watched by suspicious neighbors or, worse, the Gestapo. One writer describes the panic that broke out at a birthday party in January 1940 when two police showed up to check why the light was on during a black out. "The eyes of the women . . . showed how cruelly one was once again torn from the illusion of a normal middle-class existence. . . . That more and more each day the Jew was becoming fair game was the devastating realization that underscored every experience of this kind."[32] In this particular case, the policeman himself seems to have been embarrassed by the dread his visit caused and left without further ado.

Economic Strangulation

Rapidly, more concrete dislocations began seriously to affect women. The loss of jobs – their own, their husbands' and fathers' – threatened economic well-being. In early April 1933 a teacher reported:

Briefly before 8:00 A.M., when I arrived at the school building . . . the principal, saying "Good morning" in his customary, friendly way, stopped me, and asked me to come to his room. . . . When we were seated, he said, in a serious, embarrassed tone of voice, he had orders to ask me not to go into my classroom. I probably knew, he said, that I was not permitted to teach anymore at a German school. I did know, but was it to happen so abruptly? . . . Mr. B. was extremely sorry, he assured me . . . I collected myself . . . I also collected my belongings. . . . There was nobody . . . to say goodbye to, because everybody else had gone to the classroom. . . . I rode home . . . in the afternoon . . . colleagues, pupils, their mothers came, some in a sad mood, others angry with their country, lovely bouquets of flowers, large and small, in their arms. In the evening, the little house was full of fragrance

30   Richarz, *Jüdisches Leben*, 232.
31   Richarz, *Jewish Life*, 402.
32   Richarz, *Jewish Life*, 405.

and colors, like for a funeral, I thought; and indeed, this was the funeral of my time teaching at a German public school.[33]

Immediately after the "April Laws" about half of Jewish judges and prosecutors and almost a third of Jewish lawyers lost their jobs. A fourth of Jewish doctors lost their German National Health Insurance (*Krankenkasse*) affiliation.[34] In September the Nazis excluded Jews from the Chambers of Culture and from the worlds of art, film, music, literature, and journalism, areas in which they had been disproportionately active. Restrictions, official and unofficial harassment, and economic boycotts all increased in their frequency and fervor. As a result, many Jewish businesses, particularly small ones, were forced to shut down or sell out.

Unemployment began to plague the Jewish community. In 1933 about two-thirds of Jewish salaried employees worked in Jewish businesses and firms. With the disappearance of many Jewish firms, joblessness among Jewish employees became rampant. By the spring of 1933 nearly one-third of Jewish clerks – compared to one-fifth of the non-Jewish ones – were looking for jobs.[35] Because more than half (53 percent) of employed Jewish women worked in business and commerce, largely as family assistants (22 percent) and salaried employees (40 percent), they lost their jobs when family businesses and Jewish shops closed down.[36] Furthermore, Jewish sources estimated that three-quarters of Jewish women in business and trade were affected by the discriminatory laws and the early anti-Jewish boycotts.[37] By April 1938, over 60 percent of all Jewish businesses no longer existed, and Jewish social workers were trying to help 60,000 unemployed people. Furthermore, those businesses that lingered on tended to be either at the very top (a few banks and financial institutions) or at the bottom (independent artisans).[38] Women rarely worked in either.

Women's economic future looked bleak. The exclusion of Jews from German universities and institutions of higher learning restricted employment possibilities. Even new admissions to trade and vocational schools were limited to 1.5 percent "non-Aryans."[39] By mid-1935 the apprenticeship office for Jewish girls reported that every second young woman ap-

33   Memoirs of Hanna Bergas, LBI, 2.
34   Schleunes, 109.
35   Rosenthal, "Trends," 262.
36   *Blätter des Jüdischen Frauenbundes* (hereafter cited as *BJFB*) 1 (1934): 7; *IF*, Feb. 23, 1933, no. 8: 9; *Jüdische Wohlfahrtspflege und Sozialpolitik* [Berlin] (hereafter cited as *JWS*), no. 2 (1931): 77–8.
37   *BJFB*, March 1935: 2. By 1936, many areas of small business, particularly those associated with agriculture, were declared *judenrein* or "free of Jews." Schleunes, 145.
38   Avraham Barkai, "Der wirtschaftliche Existenzkampf der Juden im Dritten Reich, 1933–1938," in Arnold Paucker, ed., *The Jews in Nazi Germany, 1933–1943* (Tübingen, 1986), 156–7.
39   *BJFB*, March 1935: 4.

plying aimed to be a seamstress.[40] Before 1933, these same young women would have looked forward to business or professional careers. By 1937, when young women had shifted their focus to jobs useful in countries of emigration, 24 percent of graduates from Jewish schools planned to learn a craft, largely preferring tailoring (20 percent). Sixteen percent trained for domestic service, 13 percent for commerce, and 12 percent for social work.[41] Also, Jewish community welfare organizations often gave preferential treatment to boys seeking career training. In the first six months of 1937, Jewish organizations reported that far more boys than girls were receiving subsidies for career training or retraining.[42] The newsletter of the Jewish feminist movement announced that one provincial welfare office had given subsidies to seventy-two boys and ten girls.[43] And, lest girls harbor unrealistic notions about continuing at a university abroad, they were warned "that Jewish girls in and out of Germany have almost no chance to study [at the university]. The few scholarships available are only for young men and it is luck . . . if a girl gets to study."[44]

Migration: Setting Up New Lives and Leaving Old Friends Behind

As the situation for Jews in Germany worsened, an internal migration took place. Economic strangulation occurred most quickly in small towns, where often more than 80 percent of the Jewish population was left destitute.[45] Furthermore, Jews attempted to escape from the personal hostility of villages and smaller towns by seeking the anonymity and, hence, relative safety of large cities. Thus, the Jewish population was in constant flux. For those left behind, the loneliness was of "such a degree and so sudden . . . as had never before been experienced even in Jewish history." Even the most intimate family and friendship circles shrank and those who remained did not offer solace to the lonely, for they too were suffering. One newspaper article concluded: "We must learn how to endure loneliness."[46] In an article on

40 *BJFB*, May 1935: 5.
41 *BJFB*, Feb. 1937: 2–3.
42 *Informationsblätter*, Aug./Oct. 1937: 59–60. At that time 863 people (546 men and 317 women) received some support, that is, 63 percent of the recipients were male.
43 *BJFB*, March 1938, 3.
44 *CV–Zeitung*, March 3, 1938: 6. The article was written by Hannah Karminski of the *Jüdischer Frauenbund*.
45 David Kramer, "Jewish Welfare Work under the Impact of Pauperisation," in Pauker, ed., *The Jews in Nazi Germany*, 183.
46 "Erlebnis der Einsamkeit," *CV–Zeitung*, March 10, 1938: 3.

the same subject, a woman described the feeling of leaving a woman friend as "dying a little" (*Partir c'est mourir un peu!*).[47]

Female friendships depend on entirely different conditions than male friendships. There is something sisterly . . . the basis is reliability and harmony of feelings, thoughts, and actions. . . . Parting from a friend! Last hour together. Suitcases and crates are packed, the furniture stored, the apartment, where we celebrated happy days or quiet evenings, stands empty and . . . appears almost hostile. . . . Will we elderly people ever see each other again? . . . Will friendship last . . . ? Letters – what can they say! Parting from a friend! A personal story from an individual fate but also a community fate for us Jews; for who does not feel . . . this tear, this shock . . . during separation, emigration, departure! Partir c'est mourir un peu![48]

Women who moved their families had to adjust their household to a new urban environment and deteriorating political circumstances and still try to maintain a relatively stable family life. There was little time to pine for those left behind. Women who stayed in big cities participated as never before in social welfare work within Jewish communities and Jewish women's organizations to integrate the steady stream of newcomers. Women often did this while preparing their own families for emigration.

Stress and Stress Management in the Family

To meet new and mounting economic hardships, Jewish housewives tried, when possible, to prepare less expensive meals, to make home and clothing repairs themselves, and to make do with less help around the house. The Nuremberg Laws (when "Aryan" household help was severely restricted in Jewish homes) left Jewish women to their own devices in running a household with greater problems, in shopping for food in increasingly hostile stores, and in doing these tasks with evershrinking resources.

The pain of their children, who often faced anti-Semitism more immediately than did their parents from classmates and teachers in German public schools, disturbed both women and men profoundly as parents, but women learned of and dealt with their children's distress more directly than did men. When children came home from school, their mothers heard the latest stories and had to respond. Mothers also supervised their children's homework. Imagine the contradictory emotions of a Jewish mother who was reassured to learn that her son had sung patriotic songs, said "Heil Hitler" to the teacher, and received praise for his laudatory essay about Hitler: ". . . [his] gross political miseducation at school would keep [him]

---

47 "Abschied von einer Freundin," *IF*, June 25, 1936.
48 Ibid.

out of trouble." About a year later the same child, now enrolled in a Jewish school, wrote a story about Jewish resistance as a Mother's Day gift for his mother. Upon reading it, she was frightened: "[his] political awakening . . . could lead to trouble for the whole family."[49] Principals summoned mothers to pick up their children when they were expelled from school, and these mothers then sought new schools for their children.[50] Mothers were usually the ones whom teachers phoned when children were to be excluded from class events. One mother reported that her children were not allowed to participate in any special event:

My daughter cried, not because she couldn't go to the theater . . . she cried, because she was ostracized from the group, as though she wasn't good enough for her classmates. . . . I believe that the Nazi teacher was ashamed of herself now and then, when she looked into the sad eyes of my little daughter, because she phoned me several times and asked that I not send the child to school on the days when something enjoyable had been planned for the children.[51]

On Mother's Day, Jewish children had to take part in the school festivities but were not allowed to sing along. When the Jewish children protested, their teachers responded: "I know that you have a mother too, but she is only a Jewish mother."[52]

This kind of harassment provoked many families to enroll their children in Jewish schools. Still, about half of Jewish children between the ages of six and fourteen remained in the public elementary schools, subject to torment by teachers and other children, until November 1938, when the Nazis barred their attendance.

Between 1934 and 1939 about 18,000 Jewish children left Nazi Germany for safer havens on what were called "transports of children" (*Kindertransporte*). Immediately after the November Pogrom, with husbands in concentration camps, it was mothers who made the excruciating decisions to send their children abroad.[53] About 8,000 children went to England, 3,400 to Palestine,[54] and the rest to other European countries and the United States.[55] There they received foster care (or, in the case of Palestine, lived

49 Steve J. Heims, ed., *Passages from Berlin* (South Berwick, Mass., 1987), 73–6.
50 Memoirs of Erna Segal, LBI, 78–9.
51 Richarz, *Jüdisches Leben,* 234.
52 Ibid.
53 Rita R. Thalmann, "Jüdische Frauen nach dem Pogrom 1938," in Paucker, ed., *The Jews in Nazi Germany,* 297.
54 Jehuda Reinharz, "Hashomer Hazair in Nazi Germany," in ibid., 334.
55 Herbert Strauss, "Jewish Emigration from Germany: Nazi Policies and Jewish Responses," *Leo Baeck Institute Yearbook* (1980): 328.

on kibbutzim or in children's homes) until their parents could join them. Many parents never made it.

"Children turn into letters" was a phrase expressing the despair of parents who remained behind. The loss of daily intimacy with their children affected parents, but again, mothers most immediately. And, for those increasingly nervous and frightened children who stayed on – the children's transports, like other exits, never were sufficient – parents watched their opportunities dwindle. By the early war years, Jewish children found it difficult to play freely in the fresh air. The Nazis banned Jews from the parks and forests, and even small groups of children were no longer allowed to play in outdoor yards. They were permitted to play only in – and to maintain – the Jewish cemeteries.[56]

Women's organizations urged women to preserve the "moral strength to survive" and looked to Biblical heroines for role models.[57] In the face of progressively worsening living conditions, it was women who were supposed to "make things work." It became apparent increasingly that Biblical role models would not suffice in providing Jewish women with either the courage or the help they needed. Jewish newspapers began to deal more openly (and honestly?) with the issues plaguing families, particularly women. For example, as families moved into smaller apartments, or as others took in boarders to make ends meet, tighter living quarters caused strain. The League of Jewish Women noted this but characteristically urged women to absorb it:

It is the duty . . . of the Jewish woman to regulate the schedule and the organization of the household so that everyone is satisfied. She has to give her husband, the head of the household, the necessary time to be alone to relax. . . . She has to adjust without being subordinate. This is more necessary than ever, given today's living arrangements. Then, living together, even with many people in tight circumstances, will bring about that kind of communal feeling that will bring peace to the household.[58]

Among issues causing stress, cooking seemed to take a preeminent role because of tight budgets, limited household help, and the difficulties of acquiring kosher meat. Housewives were advised to consider vegetarian menus because they were cheaper and healthier. Although meat might be easier to prepare, demanding less time, women were told that "good will is an important assistant in a vegetarian kitchen,"[59] and newspapers printed

56 Richarz, *Jüdisches Leben,* 378.
57 *BJFB,* Feb. 1935: 12.
58 *BJFB,* July 1938: 13.
59 *IF,* June 25, 1936.

vegetarian menus and recipes for their readers.[60] After the Nuremberg Laws, which forbade the hiring of "Aryan" household help under the age of forty-five, a further obstacle for Jewish housewives accustomed to some help, the *Central Verein Zeitung* ran articles entitled "Everyone Learns to Cook" and "Even Peter Cooks."[61] Highlighting cooking as a fine art, one writer compared food preparation to math, chemistry, botany, and zoology and warned against the demons lurking in stoves, on sharp knives, and in every pot. One woman, who had just begun to manage her own household in the past eight days, admitted:

Previously I had always thought it somewhat difficult to translate Shakespeare into German . . . but today I know this is child's play compared to a five pound roast beef and a grill. I'd rather memorize several French irregular verbs (in the subjunctive!) than let myself in for the uncertain adventure of a roast goose.[62]

These articles emphasized how children, particularly daughters, could help their mothers.[63] They suggested introducing work as fun, giving children, especially small ones, permission to help out and warned against demanding too much. "Daughter exchanges," another innovation to help overworked mothers, provided a half year's training without pay to two young women who switched households. Ostensibly both girls would receive an apprenticeship and both mothers some help.[64] It is unclear how many girls if any took advantage of these exchanges.

At a time when everyone had to pitch in, authoritarian behavior was frowned upon, even that of the "head of the family." The justification, "that it has always been this way," was no longer good enough. One writer noted that it stemmed from a time when "men and fathers were overvalued in comparison to women and wives."[65] Thus, male privilege was questioned, if not overtly challenged, because authoritarian behavior was seen as crippling to children, making them incapable of performance. That it was questioned at all, however, indicates some shift in the perception of roles and rightful authority.

Nevertheless, husbands were expected to pitch in only minimally. The League of Jewish Women, for example, suggested that since women felt called upon to do more and more for their families and more and more

60   *IF*, Feb. 27, 1936; *CV–Zeitung*, Feb. 24, 1938: 17.
61   *IF*, March 19, 1936; *CV–Zeitung*, Feb. 27, 1936.
62   *CV–Zeitung*, April 23, 1936.
63   "Junge Mädels lernen der Mutter helfen," *CV–Zeitung*, April 9, 1936; "Häusliche Erziehung," *IF*, May 21, 1936.
64   *IF*, March 19, 1936.
65   *IF*, March 21, 1936.

often became the sole support of families, men should begin to do some housework too.[66] Timidly it reminded its members:

It won't always be avoidable, that our men will have to take part of the household duties, as is customary in North American homes. It is necessary to get together and talk about our resistance to this—a resistance found more in women than in men . . . in order to overcome it [67]

More commonly, husbands were requested to limit their expectations. For example, one writer praised her husband for suggesting that they eat in the kitchen two nights a week, saving her the extra trouble of setting up, serving in, and clearing the dining room.[68] The writer viewed this concession as generous and a way of "simplifying" the household now that the servant had left. Moreover, husbands were urged to restrain their criticisms if the meals were not what they used to be; to try praising their wives once in a while; to close their eyes to some imperfections: "A husband must also adapt. . . . We demand no sacrifices from husbands – only some consideration and . . . adjusting to the changed circumstances!"[69]

Thus, gender privilege within the family was barely modulated. Whereas writers urged a complete reevaluation of the class privilege formerly permitted the leisured middle-class girl in light of her mother's increasing burdens, they continued to allow husbands their leisure at home. Although economic conditions had changed profoundly, with women carrying their full share of the burden, gender hierarchy remained. Why this was so is not difficult to explain: "We must be clear that work for married women is only and may only be an expedient in an emergency. . . ."[70] By proclaiming the crisis nature of women's new position, Jews, both male and female, could hope for better times and ignore the even more unsettling issue of male/female roles in the midst of turmoil.

To lighten women's load, newspapers ceaselessly urged housewives to organize, streamline, and cut back on household tasks. The *Central Verein Zeitung,* for example, introduced Frank Gilbreth, the American efficiency expert, to its women readers and suggested that because their circumstances had drastically changed, his advice would be useful. Articles offered Gilbreth's guidance regarding kitchen design, that is, ways of making a smaller kitchen into a practical workspace. They included pointers on how to save steps and hand motions, how to complete two tasks at once (such as watch-

66 *BJFB*, Oct. 1938: 14.
67 *BJFB*, Oct. 1938: 4.
68 *IF*, May 19, 1938: 19.
69 Ibid.
70 *IF*, July 14, 1938: 12.

ing children and cooking), and how to prevent exhaustion. Authors emphasized that the success of a particular meal was not simply in its execution but in whether the housewife had preserved her energy. If she had exhausted herself, the meal had failed.[71] One such article, "The Question of Aptitude in the Household," gingerly maintained that books on household reform particularly recommended "group work" and that even though it might be hard to imagine a man in the kitchen (*Kann man sich in manchen Familien überhaupt einen Mann in der Küche vorstellen?*) group work completed tasks more quickly, more efficiently, and was often a source of "cheerfulness and animation."[72] Probably most practically, the article warned against unnecessary work, the kind that some women continued to do – according to this writer – long after their circumstances had changed dramatically.[73] As late as 1938 women could continue to read articles suggesting that they purchase time- or energy-saving kitchen utensils.[74]

Advice columns urged women to hire daily or hourly help when possible.[75] In what must have been desperation, leaders urged that young men be hired to help in the household. While leaving gender roles intact within the family, male helpers solved two simultaneous problems: relieving housewives and lowering unemployment for men. Although they could not be expected to do all the housework, they could certainly lend a hand. Men and women were reminded that the most important tasks in a household were often performed by men (e.g., cooks and butlers); that men had learned the rudiments of cooking, sewing, and cleaning as students, soldiers, and bachelors; and that men in North American households (allegedly) did a multitude of tasks from the most lofty to the most humble.[76] Despite such suggestions, very few housewives hired young men to help out.[77]

Rationalizing the household or hiring unconventional helpers was at best a partial answer to the stresses and strains felt by women and families. After the Nuremberg Laws came into effect, articles addressed overworked, overwrought mothers. With titles like "Mommy, do you have time for me?" they pleaded with mothers not to neglect their small children in their overcrowded day.[78] After cooking and cleaning, articles suggested that women

---

71 *CV–Zeitung*, April 23, 1936.
72 *CV–Zeitung*, May 27, 1936.
73 Ibid.
74 *CV–Zeitung*, March 17, 1938: 11.
75 *IF*, March 19, 1936.
76 *IF*, March 26, 1936.
77 Illo L. Heppner told me that her mother hired a young male helper who seems to have done everything wrong. Conversation at the German Historical Institute, Washington, D.C., Dec. 1991. Also, see the memoirs of Elizabeth Bab, LBI, 179.
78 "Mutti, hast du Zeit für mich?" *CV–Zeitung*, Feb. 27, 1936.

might want to turn to darning and repairing torn clothing. Then, they might try to help their husbands and consult with their children on school work. There would be little time left for the youngest, but mothers should not overlook their needs either. "The baby-sitter is by far not my mother," thinks the little girl. Half a year later stories featured even more tension and strain. "Mommy is so nervous!" depicted a tense housewife whose small children were depressed as a result of her anxiety. She scolded them for small misdemeanors. Her husband, also overtired and overworked, tried to smooth things over when he came home. Eventually, she discussed her overreactions with him and he suggested that she should try to control herself (*nimm dich, wenn es irgend geht, zusammen . . .*).[79] The happy outcome of this story was that "although, she, like many of our mothers today, has a huge amount of unaccustomed work to complete every day and actually has every reason to be nervous," she controlled herself and after a few weeks her child recognized "mother, you haven't been so nervous in a while."

Obviously, these articles document the stress rather than the solution. It is hard to imagine that training daughters, streamlining work, taking on extra tasks, and repressing nervousness actually helped anyone. But then again, maybe exertion and repression did help. In August 1938 an editor summed up the theme of letters to a Jewish newspaper written by women who worked both outside and inside the home as: " 'You have to do it' is the eleventh commandment for all of us now."[80] Perhaps following through on this commandment did help.

Women frequently took responsibility not only for the physical double burden but also for the psychological work necessary to raise the spirits of their children and husbands and to tide the family over until better times. As late as February 1938, one woman entitled an article she wrote in a newspaper, "Why so solemn?" She urged her women readers to "laugh again, regain humor again! Don't let suffocating air in, or chase it away!" Reminding Jewish women that they had traditionally been the ones to light the candles, she urged them once again to brighten their homes.[81] These expectations even affected Jewish women whose husbands were "Aryan" and, therefore, safe. One woman who lived in constant dread of what could happen to her mother (before she admitted to herself that she, too, was in danger) restrained herself from sharing her worries with her husband. She confided to her diary: "I can't burden my husband . . . with my family

79 "Mutti ist so nervös!" *CV–Zeitung,* Sept. 16, 1936.
80 *CV–Zeitung,* Aug. 25, 1938: 8.
81 *IF,* Feb. 17, 1938: 16.

problems."[82] This heightened sense of familial obligation, which was fostered by community and friends, was certainly an extra burden but also, perhaps, a source of solace and strength. Suffering a nervous breakdown around the time of the November Pogrom, one woman wrote:

> . . . no doctor could help me. . . . I also was struck by a dangerous case of asthma, the attacks came ever more frequently and seriously. . . . Everyone tried to convince me that I alone had to be able to overcome my fear and desperation in order to help my family in these terrible times instead of lying there so helpless. They insisted on the urgency of this to such an extent that I finally gathered all my strength in the hopes of finding a way out of Germany.[83]

Of course, all of women's efforts could not save some families from dissolution. The Nazi regime challenged existing marriage and familial relations. The Nuremberg Laws were only the beginning of a series of court decisions regarding family life, such as intermarriages, divorce, adoption, and foster care. In 1936 Jewish papers reported that in an *Eheanfechtungsprozess* (a court proceeding to contest a marriage) the *Reichsgericht* (supreme court of the Reich) decided a spouse could contest a marriage on the basis that the other's racial heritage was unclear.[84] Moreover, divorces between Aryan and non-Aryan spouses grew, although most marriages remained intact and the evidence here is largely anecdotal. Gershom Scholem related the story of his aunt, a physician, who married a non-Jewish colleague in 1911. He noted:

> The big test came in 1933. After a while my uncle discovered, following a marriage of more than twenty years, that he was an "Aryan" and asked my aunt Käthe to release him so he could marry a German. Thus my aunt was later taken to the ghetto of Theresienstadt, where she died.[85]

The new laws threatened family ties between parents and children as well. "Aryan" foster children could be taken from families if even one parent was Jewish. Moreover, the courts had declared that "it was unacceptable from a national socialist viewpoint" for a "non-Aryan" child to be brought up among Aryan foster parents "in an environment in which it does not racially belong."[86] Furthermore, after the Nuremberg Laws, adoptions of "racially" different children were no longer permitted.

82 Diary of Erna Becker-Kohen, LBI, 4.
83 Memoirs of Erna Segal, LBI, 93–4. She and her husband and two children were unable to escape; three of them survived underground in Berlin.
84 *IF*, Feb. 27, 1936. In this case it was a man contesting the marriage because of his wife's uncertain lineage.
85 Gershom Scholem, *From Berlin to Jerusalem. Memories of My Youth* (New York, 1988), 30.
86 *IF*, April 23, 1936.

Family stress, referred to in newspaper articles, confirmed in oral interviews, and intensified by racial laws, often overlapped with new job or vocational retraining for women. Many Jewish women who had never worked outside the home before now turned to the job market. Some did not have to look far afield for jobs. They worked for husbands who, facing economic decline, had to let paid help go. Not unlike their grandmothers, these women helped out in their husbands' shops, offices, and practices. One article commented, "We find relatively few families in which the wife does not work in some way to earn a living," and noted that women were also the sole support of many a family.[87] Praising women's flexibility and versatility, the writer continued that this was particularly the case once women emigrated: "My wife got a job relatively quickly, while I. . . ."

Finding a job in new circumstances, particularly for women who had never worked outside the home before, could be demoralizing. First, one had to assess one's abilities in midlife – abilities that were often little more than a typical girl's education and no marketable skills. Job ads, employment offices, friends and acquaintances held out little hope. Middle-class Jewish women frequently met the surprised responses: "A woman like you?"; "It should be easy for her"; "A woman like you should be able to advise and help herself." These phrases often placed the responsibility on women themselves, who were already frightened, nervous, and uncertain. Rather than help and empathy, women received the message that they should not be having the problems that faced them or that they would manage on their own.[88]

Discouragement notwithstanding, statistics indicate that women eagerly sought opportunities to train for new careers and retrain where old careers no longer provided employment. They appeared "more versatile and adaptable," and had "fewer inhibitions" than men, were amenable to changing their lives to fit the times, and were willing to enter retraining programs at older ages than were men. In Berlin, for example, of those seeking career retraining, 51 percent of women and only 26 percent of men were over the age of thirty (of these, 15 percent of the women and 8 percent of the men were over forty). Leaders of the Berlin community noted that retraining for women was less costly, took less time (three to six months for women compared to about one year for men), and that although most women sought retraining from previous jobs in sales or office work, women had more background that related to their new work (such as sewing or

---

87 *IF,* Jan. 13, 1938: 13–14; also see *IF,* July 14, 1938: 12.
88 *CV–Zeitung,* June 25, 1936.

housework, one presumes) and that gave them a head start in retraining for jobs as seamstresses, milliners, or domestic workers. Moreover, jobs were available for young women.[89]

Even though many had lost jobs in commercial fields, younger women (under the age of thirty-five) could find comparable jobs as other Jews began to emigrate. Also, the demand for help quickly picked up in the expanding Jewish social service sector and – after the Nuremberg Laws – in Jewish households. In Berlin, for example, Jewish employment services were more successful in placing women than in placing men.[90] In fact, one could speak of a shortage of Jewish household helpers, particularly in small towns,[91] and an even more serious scarcity of nurses in Jewish hospitals and homes. The latter caused the main Jewish social service agency to promote and support nurses' training.[92]

As the job market changed, so did the opportunities for young people, which was another factor in increasing family stress. Children were forced to reevaluate their options: in other words, to change their former career plans with all the pain and disappointment that entailed. Parents and children often clashed regarding the vision each had of the children's plans for the future. This seems particularly to have been the case between girls and their parents. One school survey (1935) indicated that girls preferred jobs in offices or with children (such as kindergarten teacher), whereas parents thought they should become seamstresses or work in some form of household setting. Parents were more likely to go along with boys' choices of crafts or agricultural training, useful, for example, in Palestine. This tension must have been that much greater among girls who had high school educations compared to those who attended only *Volksschule* and, therefore, had lower expectations from the start.[93] Moreover, the choices available to girls were more limited – if one excludes housework – than those open to boys. Welfare organizations suggested sewing-related jobs, such as knitting, tailoring, or making clothing decorations, whereas boys could consider many more options, including becoming painters, billboard designers, upholsterers, shoemakers, dyers, tailors, or skilled industrial workers.[94]

To make matters worse, it seems that parents preferred to keep girls at

89 *JWS*, 1933/34: 118–21.
90 *IF*, March 19, 1936.
91 *IF*, May 21, 1936.
92 The agency was the *Zentralwohlfahrtsstelle* (Central Welfare Bureau) of the *Reichsvertretung der deutschen Juden* (Central Organization of German Jews). *BJFB*, Oct. 1938: 14.
93 *IF*, July 14, 1938: 12.
94 *JWS*, 1937: 140–3.

home, either to shelter them from unpleasant work or to help out around the house. Jewish papers urged families to provide some household training for their daughters. In an article entitled "That, my daughter does not need!" (*Das hat meine Tochter nicht nötig!*), the writer described a young woman who had left her training program because she had been treated like a servant. The article reprimanded the mother's attitude, pointing out that the young woman need not "put on airs," that the more she knew, the better off she would be.[95]

The old-fashioned idea that girls would not require a career because they would marry lingered on even as that fantasy became more and more inconsistent with reality. We can only surmise that some young girls felt protected by such parental decisions and that others were no doubt seriously frustrated, their anxiety spurred by their lack of any kind of training that could prepare them for emigration. In July 1936 the emigration preparatory career training school at Gross-Breesen could not fill its girls' section but had to turn down 400 boys.[96]

Perhaps the difficulties of family life or of finding a job in midlife caused or permitted a new appreciation of single women. The women's page of the *Israelitisches Familienblatt,* for example, praised the women's movement for rescuing women just forty years earlier from the terror of having to find a beau within three dance seasons or from the misery of spinsterhood and likely poverty. The writer opined that a new generation had emerged, "independent, in freely chosen work." Moreover, although single women might forgo marital comradeship and motherhood, they enjoyed more freedom to meet people in all walks of life and choose their own friends, see more of the world, pursue their intellectual interests without limits, and develop themselves independently. Alluding to the then-current situation, the writer speculated that some married women might envy the single woman who could choose her own path independently.[97] Although the lifestyles of single women might appeal to harried housewives, the situation from the other side of the fence was, in fact, not really so green. As already mentioned, the disproportion between the number of Jewish women and men continued to grow so that newspapers wrote of an increase in surplus

95   *IF,* Feb. 17, 1938: 16.
96   Werner T. Angress, "Jüdische Jugend zwischen national-sozialistischer Verfolgung und jüdischer Wiedergeburt," in Paucker, ed., *Jews in Nazi Germany,* 219. It may be that Eastern European Jewish women took greater advantage of these career programs than did German–Jewish women, a function of the more precarious economic situation of the former. Trude Maurer, "Ausländische Juden in Deutschland, 1933–39," in Paucker, ed., *Jews in Nazi Germany,* 205.
97   *IF,* Feb. 27, 1936.

Jewish women of marriage age that spiraled upward by the emigration of young Jewish males.[98]

WOMEN AND EMIGRATION: PERCEPTION AND REALITIES

The Desire to Flee

Emigration, which became more and more crucial as time wore on, was skewed toward men. Yet, women usually saw the danger signals first and urged their husbands to leave Germany. One women's memoir noted that, in a discussion among friends about a doctor who had just fled in the spring of 1935, most of the men in the room condemned him.

The women protested strongly: they found that it took more courage to go than to stay. . . . "Why should we stay here and wait for our eventual ruin? Isn't it better to go and to build up a new existence somewhere else, before our strength is exhausted by the constant physical and psychic pressure? Isn't the future of our children more important than a completely senseless holding out?" All the women, without exception, shared this opinion . . . , while the men, more or less passionately, spoke against it. Also, on the way home, I discussed this with my husband. Like all other men, he simply couldn't imagine how one could leave one's beloved homeland and the duties that fill a man's life. "Could you really give that all up?" The tone of his voice told me how upset he was at the mere thought of this. "I could," I said, without hesitating a second.[99]

The different attitudes of men and women described here seem to reflect a gender-specific reaction remarked upon by sociologists and psychologists: In dangerous situations, men tend to "stand their ground," whereas women avoid conflict, preferring flight as a strategy.

A more important reason why women were more amenable to emigration than their husbands is that women were less tied to the public worlds of jobs or businesses. Women were, as Claudia Koonz has pointed out, less assimilated than men into the economy and culture.[100] The daughter of a wealthy businessman commented, "When the Nazis appeared on the scene, he was too reluctant to consolidate everything and leave Germany. He may

98 Ibid.
99 Richarz, *Jüdisches Leben*, 237.
100 Claudia Koonz, "Courage and Choice among German-Jewish Women and Men," in Paucker, ed., *Jews in Nazi Germany*, 285; see also Koonz, *Mothers in the Fatherland: Women, the Family, and Nazi Politics* (New York, 1987), chap. 10.

have been a bit too attached to his status, as well as his possessions."[101] Although their decision to leave Germany was as fraught with practical consequences as that of their husbands (since they, too, would face the uncertainties and poverty associated with emigration), women did not have to tear themselves away from their life's work, whether it was a business or professional practice, whether patients, clients, or colleagues. But even business or career women were apparently less reluctant than their spouses to leave. One wife, a wealthy manufacturer whose husband managed her inherited business, wanted to pack their bags and flee immediately in 1933. In contrast, he refused to leave the business behind. Although the wife could not convince her husband that they should flee, she insisted that they both learn a trade that would be useful abroad. After his arrest and release from a concentration camp in November 1938, they managed to escape to Shanghai, where their new skills helped them to survive.[102] In short, because of men's primary identity with their work, they often felt trapped into staying. Women, whose identity was more family-oriented, struggled to preserve what was central to them by fleeing with it.

Men and women led relatively distinct lives, and they often interpreted daily events differently. Although less integrated than men into work and culture, women were more integrated into their community. As noted earlier, there were the daily pleasantries with neighbors, regular exchanges with the grocer and baker, occasional visits to the school, attendance at concerts or local lectures, and, often, participation in local women's organizations. Raised to be sensitive to interpersonal behavior and social situations, women's social antennae were more finely tuned than those of their husbands. They registered the increasing hostility of their immediate surroundings, unmitigated by a promising business prospect, a deep feeling for German culture (as experienced by their more educated husbands), or the patriotism of husbands who had fought in World War I. Women's constant contacts with their own and other people's children and with the community probably alerted them to the warning signals that come through interpersonal relations – and they took those signals very seriously. Men, in contrast, scrutinized and analyzed the confusing legal and economic decrees and the often contradictory public utterances of the Nazis. Men mediated

---

101   Memoirs of Marianne Berel, "Family Fragments," LBI, 16.
102   Lecture by Evelyn Rubin, her daughter, at Queens College, Dec. 1988. Also, see *The Long Island Jewish Week,* Nov. 19, 1978, vol. 188, no. 25. This points in a different direction from Claudia Koonz, who suggested that women with strong business ties judged the situation much as men did. Koonz, *Mothers in the Fatherland,* 364.

their experiences through newspapers and broadcasts. Politics may have remained more abstract to them, whereas women's "business" – their neighbors, direct everyday contacts, the minutiae (and significance) of ordinary details – brought politics home.

That men and women often assessed the dangers differently reflected their different contacts and frames of reference. But decisions seem to have been made by husbands – or circumstances.[103] The widespread assumption that women lacked political acumen, because of their primary role in the private and domestic sphere rather than the public and political one, gave their warnings less credibility in the eyes of their husbands. Thus, one woman's prophecies of doom met with her husband's amusement: "He laughed at me and argued that such an insane dictatorship could not last long . . . he was so certain that there would be a positive outcome." Even after their seven-year-old son was beaten up at school, her husband was still optimistic.[104]

Some of the men who did not take their wives' warnings seriously were those who had received reprieves from the exclusionary decrees of April 1933 (although the reprieves proved to be temporary). In 1933 President Hindenburg interceded to protect those Jewish civil servants, lawyers, doctors, and teachers who had fought in World War I or whose father or son had served or who had been hired for their posts before 1918. The wives of these men typically could not convince their husbands that they were in danger. For example, Hindenburg's move restored one severely wounded veteran's faith in Germany. He would keep his job as a jurist, so he could not take seriously the idea of emigrating with four small children.[105] One woman, who argued with her husband in vain to leave Germany, noted that she was "powerless against his optimism . . . he constantly fell back on the argument that he had been at the front in World War I."[106] Carol Gilligan's psychological theories may apply here: Men tended to view their situation in terms of abstract rights, women in terms of actual affiliations and relationships.[107]

---

103 This does not mean that wives took no initiatives, but the ultimate decision seems to have rested with the husband. In early 1938, for example, Ilse Strauss's mother "applied to the American authorities for a quota number without my father's knowledge; the hopeless number of 33,243 was allocated. It was a last desperate act and Papa did not even choke with anger anymore." Her parents and young brother were deported and killed. Memoirs of Ilse Strauss, LBI, B32/54, chap. 8, 44.
104 Memoirs of Erna Segal, LBI, 45–7, 61.
105 Memoirs of Charlotte Hamburger, LBI, 40–1.
106 Memoirs of Erna Segal, LBI, 45–6, 61.
107 Carol Gilligan, *In a Different Voice: Psychological Theory and Women's Development* (Cambridge, Mass., 1982).

Not only were men inclined to trust their own political perceptions more than those of their wives, but their role and status as breadwinner and head of household may also have contributed to their hesitancy to emigrate. One housewife described her attempt to convince her husband to flee:

A woman sometimes has a sixth sense. . . . I said to my husband, "You know, I think we will have to leave." He said, "No, you won't have a six-room apartment and two servants if we do that." But I said, "Okay, then I'll have a one-room flat with you. But I want to be safe."

Despite his reluctance to leave, she studied English and learned practical trades for emigration, including sewing furs, making chocolates, and doing industrial ironing. After his arrest and subsequent release by the Gestapo, the couple left Germany and she supported the family in Australia.[108]

Women's subordinate status in the public world and their focus on the household may have made them more amenable to the kinds of work they would have to perform in places of refuge. In England and the United States, for example, refugee wives frequently "made do" for the duration, working as domestic servants, whereas husbands attempted to reestablish their business or professional careers. When husbands became butlers and wives maids, the husband often experienced a loss of status more intensely. A daughter described how her mother, formerly a housewife and pianist, cheerfully and successfully took on the role of maid, whereas her father, formerly a chief accountant in a bank, failed as a butler and barely passed as a gardener.[109] Even when both sexes fulfilled their refugee roles well, women seemed less status conscious than men. Perhaps women did not experience the descent from employing a servant to becoming one to the same degree as men because their public status had always been derived from their father or husband anyway.

A combination of events usually led to the final decision to leave. For one woman, who wrote that every Jewish person "knew a decent German" and recalled that many Jews thought "the radical Nazi laws would never be carried out because they did not match the moderate character of the German people," the decision was induced by the abuse her husband and children faced and by the difficulties of running a household after the Nuremberg Laws.[110]

For those who had not yet made a decision, the violence of the November Pogrom definitely tipped the balance toward emigration. The pogrom

---

108   John Foster, ed., *Community of Fate: Memoirs of German Jews in Melbourne* (Sydney, 1986), 28–30.
109   Lore Segal, *Other People's Houses* (New York, 1958).
110   Memoirs of Charlotte Hamburger, LBI, 41, 46.

provided another example of the contradictory behavior of Germans toward Jews – the mixture of rampant viciousness with occasional kindness. As mobs attacked and burned Jewish homes, businesses, and synagogues, one woman recalled the events as follows:

While I was sweeping up some of the debris, I noticed another mob of hoodlums, among them women. They were armed with axes as they approached . . . [and] proceeded to ransack the entire house. . . . Everyone who could have given us shelter was in a similar situation. Then I thought of Anna K., the former parlor maid. . . . Soon we were on our way in hope that there would be some straw bed in her barn. . . . She had two such beds, but we would have to leave early the next day, . . . because her brother had become a member of the SA [*Sturmabteilung* or storm troopers].[111]

Whereas up to this point the number of Jewish emigrants per year had fluctuated between 21,000 (1935) and 40,000 (1938), it became a mass flight reaching 78,000 in 1939.[112]

This is not to imply that the writing was always clearly on the wall. That conclusion emerges largely with the advantages of hindsight. In the 1930s Nazi "deception and cynical dishonesty served the purpose of tranquilizing the Jewish community."[113] More significant, perceptions by Jews of their predicament were not the only factor affecting emigration. A major obstacle to mass emigration lay in the occupational and age structure of the Jewish community – middle-aged and elderly business people who would face grave difficulties in resettling. Most important, the restrictions of foreign countries against immigrants prevented escape. In July 1938 the thirty-two nations assembled at the Evian Conference "regretted" that they could not take in more Jews. The *New York Herald Tribune* concluded: "Powers Slam Doors Against German Jews."[114] A final obstacle to emigration was simply lack of luck, for most would-be emigrants did not have the good luck of having relatives or friends abroad who could sponsor their admission into a country of refuge.

Why Women Stayed Behind

A gender analysis of the desire to emigrate highlights women's different expectations, priorities, and perceptions. It does not follow, however, that

111 *LBI News*, no. 56 (Summer/Fall 1988): 4–5.
112 Statistics come from Richarz, *Jüdisches Leben*, 53.
113 Herbert Strauss, "Jewish Autonomy within the Limits of National Socialist Policy: The Communities and the Reichsvertretung," in Paucker, ed., *Jews in Nazi Germany*, 126. See also Schleunes for the confusing plethora of decrees and exceptions.
114 Rita Thalmann and Emmanuel Feinermann, *Crystal Night* (London and New York, 1974), 22.

more women than men actually left. In fact, the opposite seems to be the case. Fewer women than men left Germany. Why was this so?

There were still compelling reasons to stay, although life became increasingly difficult. First, women, especially young women, could still find jobs in the Jewish sector of the German economy more easily than could men.[115] As Jews were expelled from German social welfare programs, the social service sector within the Jewish communities grew. This Jewish sector hired young women for domestic, welfare, or educational jobs as social workers, nurses, administrators in hospitals or homes, and teachers or administrators in home economics schools.[116]

Whereas the employment situation of Jewish women helped to keep them in Germany, that of men helped get the men out. Some husbands or sons had business connections abroad that facilitated their immediate flight, and others emigrated alone to establish themselves and then send for their families. Women's organizations agreed that wives should not "hinder" husbands from emigrating alone if there was no alternative. They argued, however, that it was often no cheaper for men to emigrate without their wives. A single man still had to pay nearly as much for rent, meals, and laundry service as if a wife ran the household. Besides, women could earn the extra income necessary to establish the family or act as breadwinners "at first." Most important, they stressed that women were necessary because they gave men support and advice.[117]

Another compelling reason that more women remained behind was the fact that before the war, men faced more immediate, physical danger than women did and were forced to flee promptly. In a strange twist of fortune, the men interred in concentration camps during the November Pogrom were released only upon showing proof of their ability to depart from Germany immediately. Families – mostly wives and mothers – strained every resource to provide the documentation to free these men and send them on their way. Furthermore, as more and more sons left, daughters remained as the sole caretakers for elderly parents. One female commentator noted that she knew of "a whole slew of young women who can't think of em-

---

115 *JWS*, 1937: 7–13, 27.
116 Home care assistants (*Pflegerinnen*) were recruited among women who were previously sales personnel, independent business people, nurses' aides, artists, kindergarten teachers, and housewives. *JWS*, 1937: 78–81. Avraham Barkai has discovered that some Jews protested against Jewish women who worked in the social service sector of the Jewish communities as "double earners" (women whose husbands also had jobs). Also, he has found letters to the editor of the *CV–Zeitung* – the newsletter of the Central Union of German Citizens of the Jewish Faith – proposing that these women should become domestics in order to let older and more experienced men who needed jobs take their places. Barkai, "Existenzkampf," 163.
117 *BJFB*, Dec. 1936: 5.

igration because they don't know who might care for their elderly mother in the interim, before they could start sending her money. In the same families, the sons went their way without any thought."[118]

By 1936 the League of Jewish Women saw cause for serious concern regarding the "special problem of the emigration of women which is often partly overlooked and not correctly understood."[119] Not only did it seem to the League that far fewer women than men were leaving but also that if the trend continued, it feared Jewish men of marriageable age would live abroad and would intermarry while Jewish women would stay behind in Germany with no chance at all of marrying. The League reminded parents of their "responsibility to free their daughters too."[120] [even if daughters] "feel stronger psychological ties to their families than sons do, [which] probably lies in the female psyche."[121]

Still, by as late as January 1938, the Hilfsverein, one of the main emigration organizations, announced that "up to now, Jewish emigration . . . indicated a severe surplus of men." Blaming this on the "nature" of women to feel closer to family and home and on that of men to tend toward greater adventuresomeness, the Hilfsverein echoed the League of Jewish Women in warning that Jewish women would no longer find marriage partners in Germany and that Jewish men would either intermarry abroad or marry Jews of a different culture, making the marriage more precarious. The Hilfsverein suggested that couples marry before emigrating, encouraged women to prepare themselves as household helpers, and promised that women's emigration would become a priority.[122] Yet, only two months later the Hilfsverein announced it would expedite the emigration of only those young women who could prove they had a minimal competence in household skills and who were willing to work as domestics abroad.[123]

That some women and men took the advice to marry, or came upon

---

118   *BJFB*, April 1937: 5. A daughter recalled urging her parents to leave Germany after she experienced anti-Semitism in school: "Uppermost in my mother's mind was that she would not leave her mother behind alone . . ." Memoirs of Ruth Glaser, LBI, 18. See also Erika Guetermann, "Das Photographien Album," in her memoirs, LBI, for another example of a woman who would not leave her parents and was later killed by the Nazis.

119   *BJFB*, Dec. 1936: 1. Also, among Eastern European Jews who returned east between 1934 and 1937, the majority were male even though almost half of them were married. Maurer, "Ausländische Juden," 204.

120   *BJFB*, April 1937: 10.

121   *BJFB*, Dec. 1936: 1.

122   *CV–Zeitung*, Jan. 20, 1938: 5. Statistics are hard to come by. The *American Jewish Year Book* for 1938 indicated that during 1936–7, 54 percent of Jewish immigrants to the United States were male and 46 percent were female (three-fifths of the entire Jewish immigration was from Germany). *IF*, Oct. 27, 1938.

123   *CV–Zeitung*, March 3, 1938: 6. This article was written by Hannah Karminski, who also encouraged women to take household preparation seriously.

the idea on their own, can be seen from marriage ads in Jewish newspapers for 1936. Ads for spouses frequently included the requirement that the future spouse be amenable to emigration. For example, one woman advertised that she sought a "marriage partner . . . with the possibility of emigration," and another ad gave the value of a woman's dowry in Swiss francs. A businessman offered a "pretty, healthy, and young woman" the opportunity to join him in settling in Palestine.[124] By 1938 almost every ad announced the desire or ability to emigrate: Those with "affidavit in hand" were probably those most sought after.[125]

In addition, it looks as though fewer women than men received support from Jewish organizations in order to emigrate. The number of émigrés supported by the emigration section (*Wanderungsausschuss*) of the Central Organization of Jews in Germany (*Reichsvertretung der Juden in Deutschland*) in 1937 was 7,313 (the Hilfsverein supported 5,762 and the Palestine Bureau of the Jewish Agency [Palästina-Amt] supported 1,551). This broke down to approximately 4,161 men and 3,041 women. Of the women going to places other than Palestine, 40 percent had no occupation and 15 percent claimed to be domestics.[126]

Moreover, young women and their families were often reluctant to consider Palestine and the kibbutz as an alternative for daughters. One survey of graduating classes from several Jewish schools in late 1935 showed that 47 percent of the boys and only 30 percent of the girls considered Palestine as a destination.[127] And those who actually wound up in Palestine, according to other surveys, seemed to prefer the cities. The majority of German–Jewish girls and young women did not take advantage of available positions on kibbutzim or in agricultural training centers. They preferred jobs as cooks or milliners (better jobs, in such fields as social work, kindergarten teaching, and nursing, were much harder to find).[128]

Although emigration consultants encouraged young women to take up the adventures of kibbutz life, articles appearing on Palestine, often written by committed Zionists, must have given the women pause. In one such presentation, the (male) author described a situation in which eight young

124 *IF,* March 5, 1936.
125 *IF,* Oct. 13, 1938: 16.
126 *Informationsblätter,* Jan./Feb. 1938: 6–7. The *Hilfsverein* supported 3,250 men (56.4%) and 2,512 women (43.5%). The Palestine Bureau supported 911 men (63%) and 529 women (36.7%); 111 people were not categorized as male or female. These are all approximate figures because about 16 percent of the *Hilfsverein* émigrés and 16 percent of those heading for Palestine did not require financial support but are included in the overall statistics.
127 These surveys were of 130 students graduating from Jewish *Volksschulen* and a higher school in Frankfurt/Main, Oct. 1935. *JWS,* 1935: 188.
128 *JWS,* 1933–4: 169.

women cared for fifty-five young men. Besides cooking, they washed "mountains" of laundry, darned hundreds of socks, and sewed ripped clothing, working long days and into the night. But even more was expected of them. They were to do the emotional housework as well:

A friendly word at the right time will bring a young man who once had a dozen shirts of his own and has now noticed that his last carefully maintained shirt has been taken by another to his senses. . . . Whether the kibbutz thrives lies in the hands of the girls! They have to mother one, be a comrade to the other . . . and have the endlessly difficult task of always remaining in a good mood, always smiling and being friendly.[129]

A woman responded by arguing that young men should learn to control themselves and not "bellow" as though they were heads of household (!) and that only together could men and women build good will. She added that women needed far better preparatory training for their strenuous assignments.[130] Such exchanges, plus the numerous news items regarding Arab–Jewish discord and the appeals to women to assuage anger and to teach conciliation to their children regarding the Middle East, doubtless left most young women looking elsewhere for refuge.[131] Statistics for the first half of 1937 indicate, for example, that of those taking advantage of Zionist retraining programs,[132] only 32 percent were female.[133]

The growing disproportion of Jewish women in the German–Jewish population also resulted from the fact that there were more Jewish women than men in Germany to begin with. Thus, to stay even, a greater absolute number of women would have had to emigrate. In 1933, 52.3 percent of Jews were women, a result of such factors as male casualties during World War I and more conversions and exogamy among Jewish men. The slow rate of female emigration meant that the female proportion of the Jewish population rose from 52.4 percent in 1933 to 57.5 percent by 1939.[134] Because many of the young had emigrated by 1935, the percentage of elderly Jews – among them a large number of widows – also increased proportionately. In 1933 there had already been 1,400 women to 1,000 men over the age of 65.[135] By October 1938, 11,000 elderly Jewish women were in need of Winter Relief (*Winterhilfe*).[136] In short, in slightly less than

129   *IF,* Jan. 16, 1936.
130   Ibid.
131   *IF,* June 25, 1936.
132   Hachaluz, Habonim, and Makkabi Hazair.
133   *Informationsblätter,* Aug./Oct. 1937: 60.
134   Richarz, *Jüdisches Leben,* 49.
135   Rosenthal, "Trends," 248.
136   *BJFB,* Oct. 1938: 4.

eight years, two-thirds of German Jews emigrated (many to European countries where they were later caught up in the Nazi net), leaving a disproportionate number of the elderly and of women.[137] Jewish newspapers took note of this fact with touching articles about elderly women whose children had emigrated, whose living quarters were far smaller than they were accustomed to, whose help had disappeared, whose finances were meager. Thrown together, sometimes in old-age homes, sometimes as paying guests in the homes of other Jews, these women passed their days in memories of better times. Financial worries plagued them, but they were even more tormented by not knowing their children's exact whereabouts or circumstances. They comforted each other, a "community of old people, who supported, . . . and consoled each other."[138]

The statistics, memoirs, and interviews all give the impression that the Nazis, whose propaganda trumpeted the threat of Jewish men as rapists, thieves, and crooks, murdered a very high percentage of elderly Jewish women.[139]

Women's Organizations

Jewish women's organizations, the League of Jewish women in particular, tried to alleviate the worsening condition of all Jews, giving special attention to the plight of women. Whereas from its inception in 1904, the League had focused on feminist issues of concern to Jewish women, between 1933 and its demise in 1938, the League took part in a battle for survival along with other Jewish organizations. This endeavor had several aims: (1) to keep communal organizations intact and to maintain Jewish customs and traditions; (2) to help needy Jews; and (3) to prepare people for emigration. The remainder of this chapter briefly sketches these attempts.

With the Nazi seizure of power, the League began to work closely with the Central Organization of Jews in Germany and its welfare bureau (*Zentralausschuss für Hilfe und Aufbau*).[140] As the Jewish community continued to

---

137 Richarz, *Jüdisches Leben*, 61.
138 *IF*, Jan. 16, 1936.
139 Of the German-speaking Jews deported to the Lodz Ghetto in 1941, 81 percent were over the age of 50 and 60 percent were women. Of the 4,000 Berlin Jews in that transport, 94 percent were over sixty. Avraham Barkai, "Between East and West: Jews from Germany in the Lodz Ghetto," *Yad Vashem Studies* 16 (1984): 282–3. See *JWS* (1937): 96–7, for statistics on the German Reich; *JWS* (1937): 161–3 (Hessen–Nassau); and *JWS* (1937): 200–1 (Königsberg). Also, see the Memoirs of "Tante Emma" in the M. Grünewald collection, LBI. When the last Jews of her small town were deported, it was "almost only elderly women," 31.
140 Rita Thalmann notes that the male-led *Reichsvertretung* never acknowledged the important work of the League, agreeing only in April 1938 to have one woman recommended by the League on

draw closer together under the pressure from outside, the League also strengthened its ties to other Jewish women's organizations and to the Jewish youth movement. Furthermore, it founded new chapters and welcomed new members. When, for example, professional women's organizations were Nazified in the process called *Gleichschaltung* (coordination) and Jewish women were thrown out, the League set up its own groups for Jewish career women. In Berlin, the League's Professional Women's Group grew so large that it consisted of nine subgroups, including nursery school teachers, youth group leaders, doctors, gym teachers, arts and crafts instructors, and groups interested in pedagogy.[141] A letter written by one of these new members noted:

As everything crumbled around us, as our professional groups were dissolved, as we lost our jobs, the League invited all professional women. Soon, various groups were formed to give everyone the opportunity to meet with professional colleagues and to attend professionally interesting lectures.[142]

Typically, the women's organization also looked after members' morale. It instituted neighborhood evenings, "so that women of different professions living in one neighborhood could meet . . . to come together both intellectually and spiritually in a small circle."[143] One woman reported: "The first evening was unforgettable. Everyone introduced themselves by name and profession, skimmed over their education, hiring, and job, and – disintegration. . . . Then we spoke of our adjustment to our current lives."[144]

Unwilling to accept cultural deprivation, Jews resisted their exclusion from German cultural life by creating their own. German Jews continued to appreciate German music and the Enlightenment classics in their own theaters and auditoriums. This included holding concerts and public lectures on secular topics in the synagogues.[145] They also promoted Jewish education, opening two Jewish continuing education centers in 1934.[146] The League of Jewish Women sponsored cultural activities, such as reading circles, lectures, and a newsletter, that were primarily concerned with Jewish

---

its board. However, unlike the representatives from other major Jewish organizations on the board, this woman would not represent the League but only herself. "Jüdische Frauen," 296.

141 *BJFB*, Jan. 1935: 10.
142 *BJFB*, Dec. 1935: 13.
143 Ibid.
144 Ibid.
145 Jonathan J. Helfand, "*Halakhah* and the Holocaust: Historical Perspectives," in R. Braham, ed., *Perspectives on the Holocaust* (Boston, 1983).
146 See Herbert Freeden, "Kultur 'nur für Juden': 'Kulturkampf' in der jüdischen Presse in Nazideutschland," in Pauker, ed., *Jews in Nazi Germany*.

custom, history, and religion. In Bochum, for example, women studied *Mishna*.[147] In Gelsenkirchen, forty-five to fifty participants formed a study group called "A Path Through the Jewish Year."[148] In Munich, they studied the weekly Torah section, attended a Bible course, and heard guest lectures on the era of Jewish emancipation.[149] Women in Königsberg participated in a lecture series on the Bible.[150] And in Cologne, a study group met to discuss Jewish newspapers and the philosophy of Martin Buber.[151] Local League groups also organized traveling libraries (like those in Rhineland and Westphalia), concerts, and exhibits of Jewish women artists.[152]

Local sections of the League also, but more rarely, discussed general topics relating to cultural issues and women. As late as January 1935 the Berlin chapter discussed "Recent Literature on the Woman Question." In these early years of Nazi rule, Jewish women, like Jewish men, refused to give up their dual identities as Germans and as Jews. As they turned more and more to Jewish learning and culture, they upheld their version of German culture, both enlightened and liberal, against the barbarism they saw around them. The leaders of the League of Jewish Women reaffirmed their allegiance to the women's movement, seeing themselves as "trustees of the German women's movement in its purest, most spiritual, social-ethical, unpolitical form." Bertha Pappenheim, the founder of the League, refused to yield her German heritage, insisting that:

Being a German, a woman, and a Jew are three duties that can strain an individual to the utmost, but also three sources of . . . vitality. They do not extinguish each other, in fact, they strengthen and enrich each other.[153]

The League knew that people whose social and economic conditions had declined so rapidly needed psychological and material support. One creative way to resist demoralization was to publish a cookbook, which helped to solve a nutritional dilemma for Jews who had difficulty buying kosher meat after Hitler forbade ritual slaughtering. It went through four editions in its first year (1935). When the Nuremberg Laws excluded Jews from the German Winter Relief, the League participated in a Jewish Winter Relief program. In numerous cities, its members helped to collect money, cloth-

147   *BJFB*, May 1935: 10.
148   *BJFB*, Feb. 1935: 5.
149   *BJFB*, Feb. 1935: 12; *Jüdischer Rundschau*, March 14, 1935, no. 11: 18.
150   *BJFB*, Jan. 1935: 10.
151   Ibid.
152   *BJFB*, Feb. 1935: 5; *BJFB*, May 1935: 10.
153   "Aus der Welt der Frau," *Jüdische Rundschau*, Feb. 14, 1935, 18.

ing, and fuel. In Berlin, eighteen collecting depots sent about 30,000 care packages to needy families every month.[154]

As more and more Jews lost their jobs and businesses (at the end of 1936, about 20 percent were on welfare and another 20 to 25 percent were living off the capital they had received from the sale of their businesses), the League tried to help Jewish women and their families adjust to lower living standards.[155] Its local chapters offered courses in cooking, baking, darning, ironing, knitting, tailoring, sewing, first aid instruction, and household repairs. In Bochum, for example, one branch organized four evenings with the theme of "Self Help."[156] In various cities, the League set up communal kitchens, small play groups for children whose mothers needed to do part-time work, and discussion sessions where women could talk about their problems and receive practical and moral support.[157] In Munich, 130 women regularly attended such *Hausfrau* afternoons.[158]

The League also expanded its child care facilities (which included a lunch program, a home, and a rest home for children), its rest home for working women, and its support of the retired women and widows groups. Furthermore, it increased its subsidies for needy women who had to take recuperative vacations or visit a health spa. In October 1938 the League's newsletter recommended setting up communal apartments as a way of stemming the housing shortage and caring for the Jewish elderly.[159] Aware of a growing need among men as well, the League instituted home economics courses for boys, opened one of its homes for the aged to "older gentlemen," and offered places in its Berlin dormitory (formerly for women students) for "also possibly young men."[160]

Repeatedly, the newsletter underlined the essential role of women in providing persecuted families with a peaceful home environment. The League took for granted the notion that women were the ones who preserved the family's equilibrium. It assumed that women would persevere in their usual role of providing optimism and sustenance. In turn, it helped

---

154 *BJFB*, Feb. 1935: 11; *BJFB*, Nov. 1935: 6; *BJFB*, Jan. 1936: 6. Seventy-five thousand Jews received Winter Help in January 1936. These included mixed marriages where the head of household was Jewish, and foreign Jews. For the large cities, the figures were: Berlin, 25,258 people; 20 percent of the Jews in Breslau, or 4,001 people; and 13 percent of the Jews in Frankfurt/Main, or 3,409 people. *IF*, Jan. 16, 1936: 1.

155 Barkai, "Existenzkampf," 164; Kramer, "Welfare Work," 183.

156 These were divided into classes on the care of linens and clothing, the home tool chest, thrifty and practical cooking, the home first-aid and pharmacy kit. *BJFB*, Feb. 1935: 4, 11; *BJFB*, May 1935: 10.

157 *BJFB*, Dec. 1935: 6.

158 *BJFB*, Feb. 1935: 12.

159 *BJFB*, Oct. 1938: 4.

160 *BJFB*, Jan. 1935: 9; *BJFB*, Feb. 1935: 11; *BJFB*, Oct. 1937: 13.

women with practical, emotional, and intellectual advice when they could no longer face the misery around them.[161]

The last important effort of the League of Jewish Women involved preparing women for emigration. At first, the organization did not support emigration. After the Nuremberg Laws, however, it intensified its efforts to train girls for agriculture, domestic service, and crafts – careers in demand in Palestine and other countries of destination.[162] By 1936 the League's newsletter and counseling centers focused extensively on the question of emigration. They discussed practical problems, cultural differences, and the legal status of women in such faraway places as Paraguay, Shanghai, and New York. Furthermore, the organization intended to organize its members abroad so that they could extend aid to newly arrived refugees. Yet, as already mentioned, the League remained dissatisfied with the rate at which women emigrated.[163]

After the November Pogrom, the League was ordered dissolved. Its treasury and institutions were absorbed into the Central Organization of Jews in Germany. Its leaders joined the staff of that organization. Although many of these women had opportunities to emigrate (many had accompanied children out of the country, only to return), they chose to continue their work for the Jewish community. Their duties became more difficult and depressing. In July 1942 Hannah Karminski, former executive secretary of the League, wrote to a friend: "This work can no longer give any satisfaction. It hardly has anything to do with what we understood 'social work' to mean . . . but, because one continues to work with people, once in a while there are moments in which being here seems to make sense."[164] Most of these women were deported in 1942 and became victims of Hitler's war against the Jews.

German–Jewish women had lived in familiar, comfortable surroundings until these had turned hostile and murderous, like a grotesque dream. They coped in a gender-specific way. Their roles as housewives and mothers sharpened their alertness to danger, helping some plan for the future. Oth-

---

161   Ella Werner Collection, LBI, collection no. 3079, folder 22.
162   Affiliates provided a variety of training: Crafts were taught in the home economics schools in Breslau, Frankfurt/Main, and Hamburg; tailoring was taught in Hamburg and Cologne; infant nursing was taught at Neu-Isenburg and in Frankfurt/Main; teacher's aide training was available in Frankfurt/Main; courses for governesses took place in Cologne; technical teachers' training was provided in the Jewish Home Economics School, Frankfurt/Main. The main Home Economics School of the League of Jewish Women at Wolfratshausen expanded all of its courses. *BJFB,* March 1938: 3.
163   *BJFB,* June 1936; *BJFB,* Dec. 1936.
164   "Letters from Berlin," *Leo Baeck Institute Year Book* 2 (1957): 312.

ers, confronted with the increasing dreadfulness of daily life, uncompre-
hending children, escalating deprivation and anxiety, and the loss of
yesterday's friends, gathered their families about them and tried to manage
as best they could. They were able to resist complete despondency through
family and social networks. They had to manage the proverbial double
burden of employment and housework, and indeed a triple burden when
one adds escalating emotional caretaking. In addition, many volunteered to
work for women's organizations. These organizations attempted to alleviate
some of the practical and psychological stress within a community suddenly
impoverished, ostracized, and sundered by the emigration of its loved ones.
In the limited time and space allotted them and with the restricted means
at their disposal, women's organizations encouraged job retraining, emigration, and self-help, while attempting to boost morale and a positive
Jewish consciousness. Neither organizations nor individuals were able to
withstand the force of state persecution and terror, and ultimately, the annihilation of the Jewish community in Germany.

PART ONE

A Global Search for Refuge

1

Jewish Women Exiled in France
After 1933

RITA THALMANN

The history of the émigrés from the Third Reich living in France was a
taboo subject for many years. Thus, research on the subject was delayed
until the end of the 1970s. Part of the documentation is either stored in
French archives, where it is not yet accessible, or has been altogether lost.
I shall therefore use the written and oral source material collected to date,
as well as my own experience as the survivor of one of these families in
exile, to present three main aspects of the topic.[1] These are the demograph-
ics of the émigrés from Nazi Germany, particularly Jewish émigrés living
in France; their residence status and living conditions up to 1938, the year
of crisis; and finally the various stages of persecution by the French and
Germans during the war and occupation.

Because "German–Jewish Women in Exile" was the central topic of the
Washington conference, "Women in the Emigration after 1933," referred
to in the Introduction, some clarification as to methodology is called for.
First, the history of Jewish women in exile, just as the history of women in
general, should not be treated as an appendix to but rather as an integral
part of a historiography that for centuries has been falsified by silence and
omissions. Second, the special situation of women – in all aspects – can
be explained only when seen within the context of the historic events of
the period, namely, the exile. Third, the term "German–Jewish women"
is problematic because many Jewish émigrés from the Reich were not
German nationals. They nevertheless shared the same fate most of the time.
Also, many of the German–Jewish émigrés had lost their German citizenship
de jure or de facto even before they were all deprived of it officially in
November 1941, either because they had been expatriated individually or

1 Françoise Kreissler, "Orientation bibliographique," Colloque international *Réfugiés et immigrés
d'Europe centrale dans le mouvement antifasciste et la Résistance en France (1933–1945)*, IHTP et Université Paris 8 (Paris, 1986): 8–20, 22–27.

51

because their expired papers had not been renewed and were replaced by identity cards for refugees from Germany. These documents were recognized by six member states of the League of Nations, including France, but only if the refugees had entered the country before August 5, 1936. This restriction made it difficult for those who had immigrated at a later date to obtain a permit of residence.[2] Fourth, a few examples must suffice to point out the variety and complexity of the individual person's fate.

EMIGRÉS FROM THE REICH LIVING IN FRANCE: NUMBERS AND COMPOSITION

For the reasons mentioned, there are only partial data or estimates available on the numbers and characteristics of the refugees from the Reich because these were constantly changing.[3] Between 1933 and 1940, roughly 55,000 people fled the Reich for France, including those who fled from the Saarland in 1935 and from annexed Austria in 1938. Among them were also those from the Reich (1937 borders) who fled following the November Pogrom of 1938, those who a little later fled Czechoslovakia before the *Wehrmacht* marched into Prague, and those who fled Italy before Jewish status was introduced. Finally, the total also included those who came to France during the first year of the war, after the *Wehrmacht* had invaded Belgium, Holland, and Luxembourg. Only about half of these refugees obtained a temporary or longer-term residence permit. The others stayed on illegally or emigrated overseas as long as this remained possible. With a ratio of 515 foreigners per 10,000 inhabitants, France was considered to be the leading country of immigration throughout the interwar period (even ahead of the United States with its ratio of only 492 per 10,000). But émigrés from the Reich, who on the average represented less than 1 percent of the foreigners, soon met with distrust and rejection not only by the authorities but also by large sections of the population who felt threatened by the current economic and political crises.

Nonetheless, according to reports of the London Conference on Refugees and the League of Nation's High Commissioner for Refugees, in 1933

---

2 Barbara Vormeier, "Dokumentation zur französischen Emigrationspolitik (1933–1944)," in Hanna Schramm, *Menschen in Gurs: Erinnerungen an ein französisches Internierungslager (1940–41)* (Worms, 1977), 157–384.

3 Rita Thalmann, "L'immigration allemande et l'opinion publique en France de 1933 à 1936," in CNRS, ed., *La France et l'Allemagne 1932–1936* (Paris, 1980), 149–72; and Rita Thalmann, "Die Aufnahme der deutschen Emigranten in Frankreich von 1933 bis zum Kriegsausbruch 1939," in Jacques Grandjonc, ed., *Deutsche Emigranten in Frankreich – Französische Emigranten in Deutschland 1865–1945* (Paris and Munich, 1983), 122–38.

25,000 émigrés, or about 40 percent of the first wave of refugees, chose France as their place of refuge. Refugees chose France because they felt either that this was a country of liberty and equality or that it was the best "waiting room" available until the hoped-for early collapse of the Nazi regime. Statistics of the Paris police headquarters dated July 8, 1933, show that among the 7,195 émigrés from the Reich who had arrived in Paris, only 150 were non-Jews and that more than half of these refugees were professionals – merchants, teachers, artisans, and so on – who suffered from the depression that had hit France later than Germany but that lasted much longer. The distribution by sex was not indicated. But from Marion Kaplan's study on the situation of the Jewish women in the Third Reich, among others, we know that they emigrated to a much lesser extent than did German–Jewish men. Jewish women emigrated in fewer numbers either because they were single and did not have the courage to go abroad without the necessary financial means and connections or because they did not want to abandon sick, helpless people, or because they were living in mixed marriages. These facts regarding the exiles in France are confirmed by the October 1934 report of the French Committee for Assisting the Victims of Anti-Semitism Who Fled Germany (*Comité National de Secours aux Refugies Allemands Victimes de l'Antisemitisme*) to the High Commissioner for Refugees. In this report, the only officially recognized Jewish relief organization in France declared to have already helped 8,000 men, 5,000 women, and 1,000 children. Moreover, a 1935 survey by the French authorities shows that of the 58,867 Germans living at that time in France, 24,867 were women and girls. About half of the Germans residing in France were not refugees, however, and some were even Nazi supporters.

Combined with increasing pressure from abroad and tension on the domestic front – France witnessed fourteen governments between 1933 and 1939 – the high level of immigration to France had the effect that Jewish refugees from the Reich were labeled not only as Jews but also as *Boches* (the usual term of abuse for Germans). They were thus far less welcome than foreigners traditionally were and found it particularly difficult to establish themselves. This, however, did not apply to the children who settled in fast, thanks to the strong integrating force of the French school system.

It is probably not by chance that many children of Jewish émigrés were saved with the help of French institutions and individuals.[4] In my own case, a chain of female solidarity, starting with the schoolmistresses of the École communale in Dijon, aided my integration. Later on, Marcelle Pardé, prin-

---

4 Sabine Zeitoun, *Ces enfants qu'il fallait sauver* (Paris, 1989).

cipal of the girls' school in Dijon, along with some teachers, helped me to evade arrest. During the war, Madame Pardé was a Résistance liaison officer for American intelligence. After a mission to Turkey she was denounced, arrested, and deported to Ravensbrück, where she perished together with her secretary, Simone Plessis. My best non-Jewish friend from high school days, Madeleine Jeantet-Morris, was the daughter of one of my first female grade school teachers in Dijon, with whose family I often stayed as a guest. When we had to leave behind our very sick mother, it was Madeleine who took care of her until she died. Even though she got married in 1945 in the United States, where she still lives as a retired university professor, we still meet every year during summer vacation.

RESIDENCE STATUS AND LIVING CONDITIONS BETWEEN 1933 AND 1938

Because most émigrés from the Reich, whether alone or with their families, had left Hitler's Germany in a hurry with few belongings and limited financial means, the most pressing need was to find an inexpensive place to live and a job. Without a job there was no hope of obtaining a permit of residence for an extended period. By 1933 about 2,000 refugees had settled in Alsace-Lorraine, either because people spoke German there or because these refugees had relatives in nearby Switzerland, where they were not allowed to stay, as was the case with my family. Of these refugees, 1,800 did not have French relatives and were expelled to the French interior only six months later. The main reasons given for this measure were that the chamber of commerce had protested against the competition of foreigners living in France and the French government's fear that the presence of the émigrés in the border region could adversely affect the already strained relations with Hitler's Germany. From that point on, émigrés from the Reich were prohibited from living in the eastern border region. Thus, together with about ten other families we wound up in Dijon, where some unmarried refugees, mostly students, had already arrived earlier. There was, however, not one unmarried woman refugee in Dijon and probably none in other provincial towns either, where the lack of connections and sufficient knowledge of language and customs would have made it nearly impossible to settle permanently.

On the coast of the Mediterranean between Marseilles and Toulon two artist colonies developed around the German–Jewish and non-Jewish artists who had been living there before 1933.[5] They included the painter Leo

---

5   Jacques Grandjonc and Theresia Grundtner, eds., *Zones d'ombres 1933–1944. Exil et internement d'Allemands et d'Autrichiens dans le sud-est de la France* (Aix-en-Provence, 1990).

Marschütz and his companion Anna Kraus, the writer Julius Meier-Graefe and his wife, the Berlin painter Anne-Marie Epstein, who later married the writer Hermann Broch and was able to flee to the United States, thanks to the personal intervention of Eleanor Roosevelt. She is now living in the South of France again. Most of the refugees were married couples, such as Marta and Lion Feuchtwanger and Paul-Albert Krantz-Noth and his wife Elena Fels. The latter succeeded in having her mother Bessy as well as her sister come from Berlin before the war broke out. Also there were the essayist Lucia Fels and her husband the writer Schmidt-Ellrich; the fashion designer Ellen Gerstel with her future husband, the Nuremberg couturier who was the brother of Hanni Gerstel-Stein; and Gerstel-Stein's second husband, the Protestant writer Jochen Klepper, who could not make up his mind whether or not to emigrate.[6] In 1942 Hanni Gerstel-Stein, Jochen Klepper, and Hanni's youngest sister Renate committed suicide in Berlin-Nikolassee. Hilde Stiel, who in the South of France met and made friends with Franz and Alma (Mahler) Werfel and the visiting families of Thomas and Heinrich Mann, was the companion of the painter Erich Klossowski. Even though most of the 5,000 entry permits requested from the United States for the Jewish children threatened with deportation were granted too late — only 313 arrived in time — it was thanks to the representative of the Emergency Rescue Committee, Varian Fry,[7] and the Hebrew Immigration Aid Society of America (HICEM) that most of the émigrés living in these artists' colonies were able to flee to safety in the United States.

Unmarried women thought they would have a better chance in metropolitan Paris. Privileged women who had connections and could to some extent adapt easily, got by. Hannah Arendt, for instance, worked from 1933 until she fled to the United States in 1940 at the Agency for the Emigration of Jewish Children to Palestine. Gerda Pohorylles, alias Taro (1910–37), a politically engaged woman who was arrested as a Jewish Young Communist, escaped to Paris in 1933 and made a living by selling newspapers and by working as a fashion model. She then learned photography from her companion, the press photographer André Friedmann, alias Robert Capa, and went with him as a photo journalist for French magazines to the front lines of the Spanish Civil War, where she was fatally wounded in July 1937.

The painter Doris Kahane (1920–76) also traveled to Spain and from there was able to join her mother, who had fled to Paris. Once in Paris, Doris worked as a cleaning woman and nanny. In 1940, being an "enemy alien," she was sent to an internment camp but was able to escape. She

---

6   Jochen Klepper, *Unter dem Schatten deiner Flügel. Aus den Tagebüchern 1932–1942* (Stuttgart, 1956); also Rita Thalmann, *Jochen Klepper, ein Leben zwischen Idyllen und Katastrophen* (Munich, 1977).
7   Varian Fry, *Surrender on Demand* (New York, 1945).

joined the Résistance in southern France, was arrested as late as 1944 by the Sicherheitspolizei–Sicherheitsdienst der SS or SIPO–SD (Security Police–Security Service of the SS) in Marseilles, was taken to Drancy but avoided deportation because Paris was just then being liberated. The pictures relating to this period, which she painted after she resettled in the German Democratic Republic (GDR), bear witness to the intense sufferings she endured, which probably contributed to her early death.

The Jewish and communist writer Anna Seghers and the dissident Ruth Fischer managed to keep afloat by writing articles for the press in exile until they succeeded in escaping – Anna to Mexico, Ruth to New York City.

Giséle Freund, now nearly eighty years old and a former student at the celebrated Frankfurt School, had no idea that the only object of value that she took along with her when she fled to Paris in 1933 was her Leica camera. It not only assured her survival but also allowed her to become a photographer of the rich and famous. In 1981 she took the official photograph of President Mitterrand that may be seen in all offices of the French Republic. She married a Frenchman and thus was able to obtain French citizenship within a short time. Thanks to her connections, she succeeded in having some well-known writers, such as Walter Benjamin, Siegfried Kracauer, and John Rewald, released from internment camp. She herself received an invitation from Victoria Ocampo, who was director of a literary journal in Buenos Aires, and was thus able to escape to Argentina, where she remained until the end of the war. She then returned to Paris, where she still lives.

The life of the film and art historian Lotte Eisner (1896–1983) took an even more unexpected turn. When the Goebbels press published threats mentioning her name, she left Germany in a hurry with only a suitcase and traveled to Paris, where her sister, married to a French colonel, was living in the elegant suburb of Neuilly. Was it a sign of alienation or of insensitivity that her brother-in-law greeted her with, "Hi, dear Lotte, I am sure you are coming for a vacation." Because of this she did not move into the sumptuous apartment of her relatives but into a shabby room in the Latin Quarter. She lived there until 1940 in a colorful community of artists, keeping afloat with odd jobs. It was there that she met, among others, the movie expert Henri Langlois. She was interned in Gurs but escaped to the South of France where she married an elderly Frenchman as a means of camouflage. Then she met Henri Langlois again on a remote farm where he had hidden his film archives from the occupying power. After the war she was one of the co-founders of the *Cinémathèque française* and a recognized movie expert. It is probably no coincidence that until her death she lived in the same elegant suburb – albeit in a rear building – where she had been received with so little sympathy when she arrived as an émigré.

Although these individuals escaped safely, we must not forget that the material and emotional hardship of life in exile was particularly depressing for those who could find neither a decent place to stay nor any help. In the short period from June to August 1933, as reported by the French police, six émigrés from the Reich committed suicide in Paris, among them three women: the young journalists Rose Kasper and Gudrun Herzog, and Mrs. Freymuth with her husband. Before the war such an extreme solution was rare; even so, it was chosen more often by men than by women. Still, in their isolation the only escape from despair for most of them was to meet with their companions in misfortune. The police who were in charge of watching the refugees complained about these meetings. A 1933 report on the café beat, for instance, states: "The female element is represented by students and artists or so-called artists and it may be assumed with near-certainty that there are many floozies among them who in this way recover their former German clients." These observers refused to understand that unmarried women, who most of the time had to work as cleaning women, knitters, seamstresses, typists, nannies, or assistant teachers in order to make a living for themselves and, as was often the case, for unemployed or elderly relatives, sought relaxation or news or advice in such friendly surroundings. Hence, the impression that these women were bent on prostitution.

It is typical, however, of the mentality prevailing at the time that women were not represented in émigré political organizations. For example, no women sat on the board of the Fédération des Émigrés d'Allemagne en France, founded in 1935. Women were also absent from the Committee for Refugees from Germany, which was formed by the Popular Front government of Léon Blum in 1936. In the mostly bourgeois milieu of the émigrés from the Reich living in France, women carried the double burden of running a household and helping to earn money for the family. In addition, women also participated in the social and cultural activities of this milieu. Even in the Committee for the Creation of a German Popular Front in France the only woman was the social democrat Anna Siemsen. French women, in contrast, played a leading role in the national and international relief organizations for émigrés. The Quaker Germaine Mellon in the Society of Friends, Madeleine Barrot from the Protestant organization Commission Inter-Mouvements auprès des Evacués (CIMADE), and Gabrielle Duchêne, who represented the French section of the Women's League for Peace and Freedom all exemplified such activity.

As a byproduct of the war scare of 1938, the French considered the refugees to be either warmongers or Hitler's spies, which made the refugees' isolation even more complete. Their French co-religionists, who in the first few years had helped them financially but since then had rarely uttered a word or made a gesture of sympathy, let alone make friendly contact, reproached the refugees for their supposed lack of discretion and adaptation to their new environment. That same year the Israelite Consistory published "Rules of Behavior" for the refugees' benefit, and the Daladier government, formed after the Popular Front's collapse, restricted even more drastically the residence rules and living conditions for foreigners. Disregarding the right of asylum that refugees had already been granted, the government subjected them to the same strict controls it imposed on followers of the Third Reich.

STAGES OF PERSECUTION BETWEEN 1939 AND 1944

Beginning in the fall of 1938, French officials drew up lists of suspect individuals. On the basis of these lists, the French began to intern émigrés and Hitler's agents in the same camps, six months before the outbreak of war. About 100 women were sent either to the Parisian prison La Petite Roquette or to Camp Rieucros (in southwestern France), the latter having been set up in March 1939. Using the categories of the camp commanders, the inmates in December of that year consisted of: 10 "criminals," 135 "political suspects," and 104 other women who had invalid papers or who were accused of "disreputable conduct" or "prostitution." Whereas at the beginning probably few émigrés could be found among the inmates, by 1941 things had changed and 453 emigrant women and 39 children under fourteen years of age were interned in the camp. A few were released because they had secured the necessary emigration papers.

A second wave of arrests started with the beginning of the war. It is not true, however, that during this wave "numerous women in exile were arrested in an action under the cover of night and fog," as recently stated by a young German historian.[8] Such unverified statements, which tend to use the terminology and methods of the Nazi regime, may contribute, though inadvertently, to a relativized view of the crimes of the Third Reich, a trend that we see spreading today. The fact is that in September 1939 all male émigrés aged 17 to 50 (later 65) coming from the Reich, including Austrians, were interned. The total number was 12,000, of which most were Jews but which also included Nazis. A few months later about 5,000

---

8   Gabriele Mittag, ed., *Deutsche Emigrantinnen im französischen Exil. Mit einem Vorwort von Giséle Freund* (Berlin, 1990–1).

mostly Jewish émigrés were transferred to the paramilitary labor service (*Prestataires*). My father was among them.

On May 12, 1940, a third order of internment was issued that applied also to single and married childless emigrant women between 17 and 65 years of age. In Paris these mostly Jewish women were ordered to assemble at the Vélodrome d'Hiver, a sports stadium, with a two-day food supply, a mess kit, and luggage weighing less than 30 kilos. From there they were taken to internment camps in southern France. The first convoy carried 2,364 women and arrived in Gurs on May 23, 1940. Meanwhile, emigrant women with children who had been left behind now had to flee from the invading *Wehrmacht* and the bombers, as did most of the population of northern and eastern France. They had to make their way to central and southern France, sleeping in barns and forests until they could find a reasonably safe home.

The rapid defeat of France, the German occupation of two-thirds of the territory, and the proclamation of the reactionary authoritarian government of Pétain were followed by a harsh repression that would last four years. Affected were all those, whether Frenchmen, foreigners, or stateless persons, who were considered "enemies of the new system of government."[9] Jewish émigrés, who under paragraph nineteen of the armistice could be extradited to the occupying power, were exposed to the double jeopardy of persecution by the occupying power and also by the French government.

The first French order concerning the status of Jews was published on October 3, followed by the internment decree of October 4, 1940. By issuing a first decree on September 27, the occupying power prohibited Jews, even residents, from entering or returning to the occupied zone. It also made registration mandatory and ordered that Jewish shops and businesses be identified and given a trustee. Under the "policy of collaboration" the Pétain government ordered that Jews be excluded not only from public service and the media but, beginning in June 1941, also from all business. The French government also called for a census of all the Jews still living in the unoccupied zone and for the creation of a General Commissioner's Office for Jewish Affairs with powers covering the entire territory of France. As a result of these measures, the more than 10,000 Jewish immigrants from the Reich who had already been interned by February 1941 in unoccupied parts of the country, including the 6,500 Jews who had been deported to Gurs from Baden and the Palatinate, not only were now living in despair but in the summer of 1942 were also turned over to the Germans for

9   Rita Thalmann, *La Mise au pas. Idéologie et stratégie sécuritaire dans la France occupée* (Paris, 1991).

deportation to the East.[10] And even Jewish immigrant women with children, who up to the defeat had remained relatively unaffected, were now kept in mandatory residences or in "camps for reuniting families."

The twenty-five Jewish and non-Jewish organizations in France, mainly the CIMADE, the Quakers, the Secours Suisse, and the Jewish Organization to Help the Children (*l'Oeuvre de Secours aux Enfants,* or OSE), united in November 1940 to form the Nêmes Relief Committee.[11] With the help of Jewish and non-Jewish volunteer social workers who stayed in the camps, this committee managed to alleviate some of the despair as well as to free more than 4,000 children held there. With funds from the American Jewish Joint Distribution Committee (JDC) they were able to place these children and those rescued from other camps in homes, convents, or with local families and to provide them with false papers. Subsequently, they were able, albeit illegally, to get them to Switzerland or to Spain and eventually to Palestine.

I wish to mention a few of the women in exile who in spite of their own desperate situations participated in the rescue of about 6,000 Jewish children. Elizabeth Hirsch, who risked her life to take children to Spain with the help of the Jewish resistance, was among them. And the young Marianne Cohn accompanied illegal transports of children to Switzerland. She was arrested but refused to be liberated by the Résistance without the children who had been entrusted to her. The children were finally rescued, but the body of Marianne Cohn, badly mutilated by the Nazi henchmen, was found in a remote part of the French border region. The Jews still living in the occupied zone had no defense against deportation after March 1942. To its everlasting disgrace, the Pétain government, under the pretext of saving the "French Israelites" from unoccupied France (until November 1942), turned over to the SIPO–SD about 10,000 foreign and "stateless" Jews. Included were children whom the Germans had not even requested. Whether unmarried, with children, family, or separated from their interned husbands or companions, women had to obtain false papers at the risk of being denounced or caught in a raid, and they had to rely on the help of individuals or organizations.

Nevertheless, a large section of the population and the Catholic hierarchy, which supported Pétain and his regime as the savior of the country and had more or less tacitly acquiesced to the anti-Jewish measures taken during the first two years after the defeat of France, were outraged when they witnessed the atrocious scenes that occurred in the summer of 1942. They saw how the French police in the unoccupied zone rounded up Jews and carted them away in the most barbaric and brutal manner. Contrary to what happened in other occupied countries, this form of popular protest or act of resistance is why nearly 75 percent of the Jews living in France ultimately escaped deportation.

However, among the roughly 75,000 Jews who were sent to extermination camps, not only as a result of the Vichy policy of collaboration but also because the Scandinavian countries, Switzerland, and the United States were not prepared to receive these people, were about 9,000 German-speaking émigrés from the Reich (roughly 7,000 from Germany and 2,000 from Austria). According to my calculations, which are based on Barbara Vormeier's listing of 7,010 deportees whose names, places, and dates of birth have become known, among the deportees were 2,649 German-born women and girls (nearly 48 percent) and 456 Austrian-born women and girls (nearly 32 percent).[12] This difference can be explained by the fact that émigrés from Austria came from diverse social backgrounds and were better able to adapt to the life of illegal residents. Since the end of the war, many of the survivors of the internment camps, the deportation, and the "final solution" have died. Some, among them Lotte Eisner and Lotte Schwarz, have written their memoirs.[13] The former even made a movie. Tilly Spiegel, the young Austrian communist involved in the extremely dangerous "German work"[14] of the Résistance, was unable to publish more than a small brochure on the subject because no one showed much interest.[15] She again lives in Vienna. Others, like Ruth Aris-Fabian,[16] who lost her citizenship as early as 1935 because of her illegal activity in the Socialist Workers' Party (*Sozialistische Arbeiterpartei,* or SAPD) and who is now more than eighty years old, are still taking care of the old people's home in a Paris suburb that was founded by La Solidarité, an émigré organization of refugees from the Reich. For most of the surviving women, in addition to grieving for families and friends who were mur-

12   Barbara Vormeier, *The Deportation of German and Austrian Jews from France. 1942–1944* (Paris, 1980).
13   Lotte H. Eisner, *Ich hatte einst ein schönes Vaterland. Memoiren* (Heidelberg, 1984); Lotte Schwarz, *Je veux vivre jusqu'a ma mort* (Paris, 1979).
14   "German work" included activities such as the distributing of tracts within German military installations to encourage desertion, meeting with soldiers to obtain information, and organizing sabotage in factories working for the Nazi war machine.
15   Tilly Spiegel, *Frauen und Mädchen im österreichischen Widerstand* (Vienna, 1967).
16   Ruth Fabian and C. Coulmas, *Die deutsche Emigration in Frankreich 1933* (Munich, 1978).

dered, there is the awareness that they asserted themselves during the years of misery and persecution and experienced the full meaning of solidarity. They learned that without solidarity the equality of all human beings cannot be achieved.

2

Arrival at Camp de Gurs

An Eyewitness Report

ELIZABETH MARUM LUNAU

Elizabeth Marum Lunau was born in Karlsruhe in 1910 to Ludwig Marum and Johanna Benedick. Her father, a Social Democratic member of the Reichstag of Jewish descent, was arrested in March 1933 and assassinated a year later. Her mother and younger sister emigrated to Paris soon after Ludwig Marum's death. In 1936 Elizabeth emigrated to France where, the following year, she married Heinz Lunau in Paris. She was interned in Camp de Gurs from May to July 1940, then lived with a friend in St. Tropez until she was able to emigrate to the United States in September 1941. In the United States, she made her career in the hotel industry as a director of housekeeping. After her retirement in 1976, she published a compilation of the letters her father wrote while he was in a concentration camp. She is currently editing the letters her family wrote in France between 1939 and 1941. This report was written in 1991.

THE TRIP TO GURS

One morning in the middle of June we prisoners in the Camp de Hyères were told to pack our belongings and assemble in the yard.[1] On June 10, 1940, Italy had declared war on France and promptly bombarded Toulon, the large French naval port. Hyères was just a few miles from Toulon, and for us, locked in a garage, it felt as if the bombs were coming down right on top of us. The army must have felt the same and decided to move us.

We, about sixty women and some children, were standing in the yard, trembling and scared. We were not told where we would be taken and this uncertainty was frightening. There were some emotional moments. Made-

---

The editor wishes to thank Elizabeth Marum Lunau for annotating her account.

1   Hyères (Var) is a small seaport in southeast France near Toulon. For a description of the internment camp there, see Marta Feuchtwanger, *Nur eine Frau* (Langen, 1983), 276. She describes Camp de Gurs on pages 273 through 281. Not all of her memories correspond to mine, but since I wrote mine down shortly after being liberated and she forty years later, I am inclined to trust my own memories.

63

moiselle Fehr fainted. Hielde Stieler became hysterical and was left behind.[2]
The train passed through beautiful country, but no one felt much like enjoying this beauty. All I remember of that train ride is that the train stopped
somewhere in open country, and we heard that enemy planes were over-
head and attacking nearby. Finally, in the late afternoon, the train stopped
in a small station and we were told to get off. The sign read Oloron, but
we did not know where Oloron might be. We were loaded on two open
trucks, standing so close to each other that we kept each other from falling.
Townspeople must have been told that we were Germans and they yelled
at us, calling us names. I thought of my father, who had been transported
from prison to concentration camp in an open truck in 1933 and had been
yelled at by the populace.[3]

Finally, the trucks turned off the road and into a vast place where low
wooden barracks could be seen on either side of the service road, barbed
wire fences surrounding everything.[4] As the trucks rolled along, women
came running to the fences staring at us. "This is the end of the world," I
thought. "This is desolation, never will I escape from here." At the same
time I had a feeling of seeing a movie with pictures of people behind barbed
wire, a déjà vu perhaps, inspired by pictures I had seen of other prisoners
in other times.

The trucks stopped. We were herded into an area that I later learned was
Ilot I.[5] We were separated and pushed into two barracks. When we entered
our barrack, we saw a long space with a group of women at each end and,
between them, nothing but empty wooden floor planks. These women
looked like peasants, kerchiefs covering their heads, and they were wearing
dark print dresses. They were weeping, moaning, and rocking back and
forth, and they took no particular notice of us. We stood between the two
groups; there was nothing to sit down on. These women were Italians and
Poles, and we could not understand one another.

We were tired, hungry, and frightened. Somebody yelled from outside
to come and get mattresses. I immediately went with two or three others.

2 For mention of Hielde Stieler, see Jeanpierre Guindon, "Sanary-sur-Mer, capitale mondiale de la
   littérature allemande," in Jacques Grandjonc and Theresia Grundtner, eds., *Zone d'ombres: Exil et
   internement d'Allemands et d'Autrichiens dans le sud-est de la France* (Aix-en-Provence, 1990), 35, 40,
   42–3.

3 My father, Ludwig Marum (1882–1934), Social Democratic member of the Reichstag, was carried
   with six other comrades from prison to concentration camp Kislau on an open police truck and
   humiliated by the populace. See *Ludwig Marum, Brief aus dem Konzentrationslager Kislau*, ed. Elizabeth
   Marum Lunau and Jorg Schadt (Karlsruhe, 1984), 127.

4 For a description of Camp de Gurs, see Hanna Schramm and Barbara Vormeier, *Menschen in Gurs:
   Erinnerungen an ein französische Internierungslager 1940–1941* (Worms, 1977); translated from German
   by Irène Petit as *Vivre à Gurs. Un Camp de concentration français 1940–41* (Paris, 1979).

5 A block of barracks.

It was a relief to be able to do something. We were given straw bags and blankets from a storeroom, which we laid in the empty spaces between the Italians and Poles. We stretched out, some of us wept, some whispered. It was dark now, and we fell asleep.

The next morning we saw where we were, found the others from Hyères, and found an empty barrack into which we all moved together: one long aisle, on each side space for thirty straw bags. For breakfast two people had to go to the so-called kitchen, an open space covered with corrugated metal. Big, black kettles sat over an open fire. One person was given a large pot filled with dark liquid. Bread was distributed at 11:00 A.M. – one pound of French bread for twenty-four hours. We began to arrange our belongings. There were nails hit in by other prisoners, and the building beams formed narrow shelves on which we could put a cup and a plate. Our little suitcases had to serve both as tables and as headrests.

The camp was a desolate place, a vast treeless plain with no grass. Far away, hills could be seen when the weather was clear.[6] There was a latrine. One walked up wooden steps to a row of holes; far below were large metal pots. These were picked up once a day, replaced by empty ones, and carried away on a small railroad that surrounded the entire camp. This was one of the few services provided by French employees.

When it rained, which was often, the ground turned into a sea of mud. One had to walk with feet in mud up to the ankles. Often the mud sucked the shoes off our feet, and we had to fish for the precious shoes. The steps of the latrine became caked with mud, and elderly people especially were not able to go up.

DEPARTURE FROM CAMP DE GURS

On July 18, 1940, I was liberated from the Camp de Gurs. At the gate I saw Inge, our friend from Paris, but we were in a hurry to leave and did not take time to talk. A young Austrian girl, Berta Katz, joined me, and we walked from the gate to the road, carrying our little suitcases. We had been told to wait on the road for a bus that would take us to the train station at Oloron. There was already a crowd of other liberated women and children waiting. What finally came was not a bus but an open truck, and all the panicked women pushed to scramble up into the truck. I was never good in crowds and, seeing what was going on, I decided not to try. I told Berta that I was going to walk. She came with me. We walked and

6   The Pyrenees.

walked and our suitcases became heavier and heavier. After some time a military pickup truck passed us and stopped. A colonel and his driver were the occupants. The colonel asked where we were going and offered to take us to Oloron.

I had the address of Tonia, who lived in Oloron because her husband had been a fighter in Spain, and then a refugee from Spain, and finally a prisoner in Gurs.[7] Tonia and her friend, Fanny, shared a tiny apartment, and Tonia had a baby boy. The two women shared one bed and let Berta and me sleep in the second bed. After months of sleeping on straw, this seemed an incredible luxury! The next morning, after breakfast, we said good-bye and went to the railway station, where we got a train to Pau (Pyrénées Atlantiques). Our liberation papers served as tickets. In the train compartment were three soldiers and the two of us. The soldiers asked whether we could play *belote,* a popular French card game. "Yes," I said, and joined as their fourth player. I played well and they respected my game. They trotted out their food supplies for lunch and shared them with us: French bread, goat cheese, and red wine. It was the most delicious lunch I ever ate.

In Pau Berta left us. She wanted to go farther north. The soldiers and I wanted to go to Toulouse (Haute-Garonne) and Marseilles (Bouches-du-Rhône). We did get a train to Toulouse and arrived there while it was still daylight. An indescribable sight awaited us. The station and the platforms were filled with people and baggage. Every inch was occupied. There were refugees from the North, soldiers from everywhere, foreign legionnaires, women and children, and bundles.[8] My soldiers, who by now had adopted me totally and protected me, wanted to find something to eat in the station. However, all had been sold out long ago. So we joined the crowd, sat down on the platform, and waited for a train. After hours, a train came and it was announced that it was for military personnel only. I was afraid to board it. My soldiers said they were not going without me. They lifted me through a train window into a compartment, and one pulled me from inside. We rolled all night and slept leaning against each other, too tired and hungry to stay awake. We woke up around Nîmes (Gard) or Arles (Bouches-du-Rhône), and only then did a conductor come to check our papers. He looked at mine and nodded. Since we were so near Marseilles, he must

7 Tonia Lechtmann, born in Poland in 1918, today lives in Tel Aviv. She lived in Oloron so that she could be near her husband, Sioma Lechtmann, who was interned in Gurs. He perished at Auschwitz. See Hermann Langbein, *Die Stärkeren* (Vienna, 1949).
8 The northern two-thirds of France was occupied by Germany according to the terms of the Franco-German armistice of June 22, 1940. Thousands of refugees fled southward ahead of the German invasion.

have thought it not worthwhile to make a fuss. Also, I was the only woman on the train with hundreds of soldiers. We arrived in Marseilles early in the morning and kissed goodbye.

I made my way to the Vieux Port, sat down on one of the café terraces, and ordered coffee. The waitress put a basket with fresh croissants on the table. Sitting in the sun, enjoying the life of the harbor, I ate them all and asked for more. Only two days ago I had had "breakfast" in Barrack 20, a brown liquid and a piece of dry bread, saved overnight. Now, the most ordinary things seemed to me the cause for great enjoyment.

The reason I stayed in Marseilles was the letter I had received in Gurs from my husband, in which he told me that he was in Casablanca and had no identity papers. I wanted to try to get copies of his military papers. I asked my way to military headquarters, and once in the building, I repeated my story from office to office until finally someone was willing to talk to me. The files from Manosque (Basses-Alpes), where he had been stationed first, had been sent to Paris, I was told, and before Paris was occupied by the Germans, were evacuated to "somewhere." Nobody knew where.[9] But I was given the name and private address of the commanding officer of Manosque and advised to write to him.

Frustrated and tired, I walked the long way back to the train station. I had been told in the morning that there would be a train for Toulon at 8:00 P.M. Now I found that the train would not leave until midnight. I sat on my little suitcase, which I had already retrieved, and cried. Suddenly the happy feeling of being free had left me. I was tired and hot and hungry and disappointed about not having gotten papers for my husband. The prospect of having to wait four or five hours in that crowded station overwhelmed me. I had almost no money, not even enough to buy a cup of coffee.

The hours passed and, at last, I was on the train to Toulon, where I was told I could change for Saint Raphael (Var). On the platform in Toulon I asked the train dispatcher where the waiting room was. He looked at me and said under no circumstances could I go into the waiting room. It was full of a hundred *Spahis,* black African soldiers. I guess he thought putting me into the waiting room was like throwing meat into a lion's cage. He took my suitcase and walked me across the rails to the stationmaster. They decided to put me in the package room. They carried a bench from the platform for me and told me they would wake me in time for the train.

By now it was past 2:00 A.M., and I fell asleep immediately lying on the bench. A strong light shining in my eyes woke me up. It was the flashlight

9 June 13, 1940.

of a military policeman who, of course, was surprised to find a sleeping young woman in the package room. I answered his questions and he left, after having made a pass at me. The next time I woke I found the train dispatcher with his hand on my breast. I sat up and he let me go. He sat on the other end of the bench and when he heard where I came from and that I was a German–Jewish refugee, he began telling me about de Gaulle, about radio from England, about a second French government in Africa. Thus, in the middle of the night in a dark station baggage room in Toulon, I heard about de Gaulle and what had been going on in the world.

Now I was on the train to Saint Raphael. When I saw the train stopping in Sanary (Var), I suddenly decided to get out and visit my friends from Gurs who lived there.[10] When I grabbed my suitcase from the rack, the handle stayed in my hand, the suitcase on the rack. People helped me out, and the station people tied a cord around it. This is how I arrived at Maja Caden's house.[11] The whole group was sitting at a table for lunch. They greeted me with a great "hello" and made me eat. After lunch they decided I should stay a couple of days and rest. They took me to Ruth Hermann, who had not been in camp because she had a baby. Ruth lived in a tiny house, but she had a second bed where I could sleep.[12] She was a friend of the writer, Friedrich Wolf,[13] who was at that time in le Vernet,[14] as was my brother.[15]

---

10   At that time, Sanary was a small fishing port. See Jeanpierre Guindon in *Zone d'ombres;* René Schickele, *Die Witwe Bosca* (Berlin, 1933) also contains a description of Sanary. Many German artists and writers took refuge there, and several described Sanary in their memoirs.

11   Née Mosse, wife of Gert Caden. See André Fontaine, "Les peintures murales des Milles [1940]," in *Zone d'ombres,* 287; Fontaine, *Le Camp d'Etrangers des Milles 1939–1943* (Aix-en-Provence, 1989).

12   See Fontaine in *Le Camp d'Etrangers,* 109. He describes her as a friend of Friedrich Wolf.

13   Friedrich Wolf (1888–1953), German playwright and author. He joined the Communist Party in 1928, and in 1933 emigrated first to Switzerland and then to France. He left France in 1941 for the Soviet Union, where he worked as a radio propagandist until the end of the war. From 1949 to 1951 he was the German Democratic Republic's ambassador to Warsaw.

14   In the Pyrenees, near Pamiers, le Vernet was a camp for those whom the French government considered "undesirable."

15   Hans Marum (1913–1979).

3

Women Emigrés in England

MARION BERGHAHN

The topic of refugees, women or men, invariably arouses considerable interest. But this interest stands in inverse relationship to the knowledge people tend to have about refugees. Even refugees themselves often have no more than a vague understanding of their situation. This was certainly true when I started my own research, with which I had practically entered virgin ground way back in the late 1970s. In the meantime, to be sure, more empirical data have been collected, as is witnessed by the proceedings of the first major conference on "German-speaking Jews in the United Kingdom," published in 1991.[1] However, as that volume also shows, a lot of the work carried out in this field does not go beyond a catalog of German–Jewish "achievements" or a description of political developments. What is now needed, it seems to me, is a better understanding of the underlying processes of migration and its impact on the German–Jewish community as a whole and on its individual members in England and elsewhere. Let me therefore begin by raising a couple of points of a more theoretical nature that affect refugees in general before I examine women refugees in England in particular.

First of all, however, I would like to outline briefly the empirical basis for my observations. About 250 people were approached originally in a random way.[2] About 180 of these were interviewed in the stricter sense. These respondents were divided into three main categories: representing the first (80 respondents), second (68 respondents), and third (32 respondents) generations. Those born up to 1920 were regarded as first generation. The second generation were those born between 1920 and 1945, and the third generation were those born after the war. The main consideration in

---

1 Julius Carlebach et al., eds., *Second Chance. Two Centuries of German-speaking Jews in the United Kingdom* (Tübingen, 1991).
2 The study, upon which this chapter is based, was first published by Macmillan as *The Ambiguities of Assimilation. German–Jewish Refugees from Nazi Germany* (London, 1984) and appeared in paperback as *Continental Britons. German–Jewish Refugees from Nazi Germany* (Oxford and New York, 1988).

establishing these categories was the stage within the life cycle that the respondents had reached at the time of emigration. It was assumed that it would make a significant difference to the attitudes of individuals whether they had left Germany and settled in England as an adult or as a child, or whether they were born in England after the war and brought up in a changed political climate and within a primarily English environment. The interviews were informal; they were not based on firmly structured questionnaires. Instead, a catalogue of questions was used as a guideline to give the conversation some direction. These interviews were supplemented by group sessions, which some respondents had arranged to allow me to discuss some of my questions with a larger number of people, and by participant observation at many events within the German–Jewish community. Important information was furthermore gleaned from numerous memoirs, autobiographical fiction, and publications of various German–Jewish organizations, apart from the relevant secondary literature.

The refugees from Germany living in England today are first and foremost of Jewish origin. There were also quite a few non-Jews among the original refugees. Most of these returned to Germany after the war, as did quite a few Jews who had left Germany primarily for political reasons and who returned to help rebuild a better, preferably socialist, Germany. Those Jews who stayed in England had been forced to leave their homeland on account of Nazi racism; had they not been Jewish, many of them would no doubt have stayed and, just like other Germans, have come to some kind of arrangement with the Nazi regime. Certainly quite a few among my respondents admitted this much openly. Some even went so far as to claim, as one of them put it: "My father used to say, thank God we are Jews. We would have made very good Nazis otherwise." This may have been an extreme even if by no means isolated statement because the majority of German Jews were leaning toward the left-liberal parties. Nevertheless, it is not too farfetched to assume that given the choice most German Jews would have stayed in Germany and would not have emigrated, with all the hardships and uncertainties that this involved. The fact that they were forced to leave was particularly hurtful for many refugees and impeded or even prevented reconciliation with Germany later on. It deeply colored their relationship with Germany and all things German as well as their perceptions of themselves and their relationship with the host society, in this case England. This will be discussed later in greater detail.

Similarly, one often finds that the history of German Jews, more so than that of other Jewish communities, is judged on the basis of the observer's feelings about Germans and Germany's relationship with its Jews rather than on the basis of dispassionate analysis. In other words, German history in general and the behavior and attitudes of German Jews in particular are often seen, especially by other Jews, in terms of what should have been rather than what actually happened. A good example is the continuing debate on the German–Jewish symbiosis. Quite a few students of German–Jewish history find it very difficult to accept this notion and prefer to define the relationship as a dialogue and in terms that express distance between Germans and Jews: "Weil nicht sein kann, was nicht sein darf" (because what cannot be, may not be). On closer inspection it becomes clear that this position is based on an argument from hindsight developed after the experience of the Nazi era, and it conveniently overlooks the fact that the 1930s were not typical of Jewish life in Germany. It ignores the fact that no other Jewish community in Europe had been as deeply rooted in its majority society as the German Jews, who were the only group – until the 1930s – never to have been completely expelled from their territory in 1,500 years. There would thus appear to be problems with a position that perceives and judges the history of Germany's Jews predominantly in light of the catastrophic end, the Holocaust, and that criticizes German Jews for having ignored the signs which, according to this view, had all along been pointing toward the bitter end.

Against the dialogue view of German–Jewish history, I reiterate and uphold the hypothesis, which I also consider crucial for an understanding of the situation of women refugees in England, that German Jews had developed what has been called the first hyphenated ethnic identity. This mix of German and Jewish elements set them apart from the Germans as well as other Jews in Europe. Even after three generations, these mixed cultural traits are still discernible to a surprising degree.

As a result of the ambiguity that marks the attitudes of German Jews toward Germany, their "step-homeland," any mention of ethnic peculiarities in terms of being non English obviously made quite a number of the older refugees uncomfortable. Members of the younger generation, in contrast, proved in the interviews to be quite unperturbed in this respect. Whereas the latter expressed a largely positive attitude toward ethnic differentiation in respect of the English, the older refugees were still marked by the experience of persecution they had suffered. After all, their cultural differentiation had served the Nazis as a pretext for denying them "elementary rights, including the right to life itself."[3]

---

3 Larry D. Nachman, "The Question of the Jews: A Study in Culture," *Salmagundi* 15 (Spring/Summer 1979): 179ff.

This brings me to a further basic point. Assimilation, although a key concept in Jewish, in particular German–Jewish, history is at the same time one that is the least understood. This is partly because both lay persons and professional historians use this term very loosely and frequently without realizing that it is a concept borrowed from the social sciences, where it is fairly strictly defined. This is not to say that social scientists have reached agreement as to the exact meaning of assimilation. Nevertheless, a large body of literature exists that analyzes assimilation, acculturation, and ethnicity, in which one finds hardly a trace in works on Jewish history. Instead, a popular and, as is common with popular concepts, often normative rather than precise analytical notion predominates. Thus, the historical examination of the process of assimilation becomes combined with moralizing judgments as to whether it was "good" or "bad," and in all too many cases assimilation is considered bad.

No less unhelpful, assimilation is closely linked in many studies with religion, and a people's degree of assimilation is defined according to the type and intensity of religious observance or lack of it, ultimately leading to the erroneous conclusion that the more "nonreligious" a person, the more "un-Jewish" and "German" he or she is or was considered to be; and the more Orthodox, the more "Jewish."

However, none of these received notions were confirmed by my respondents. Their responses indicated that the question of Jewish identity is far more complex. It became apparent that the strength of Jewish consciousness varied but that it did not correspond to the degree of religious belief or observance by the individual. In fact, the depth of a Jewish or, rather, German–Jewish (continental) group consciousness was surprising, especially in the light of another paradigm of German–Jewish history, namely, that of the reputedly extreme assimilationist tendencies of German Jewry. Logically, one would have to expect a similar degree of acculturation to the English environment, which the empirical material did not, however, confirm. To be sure, some acculturation did take place, especially among the younger people but only in subtle ways that have been explored elsewhere. Generally speaking, what my material shows is that processes of assimilation are far more complex and ethnic cultures far more persistent than the historical literature on the German Jews would lead us to believe.

The problem is that this literature tends to share the traditional view that assimilation is inevitable when ethnic groups live in close proximity to each other, as, for example, when a minority is surrounded by a culturally different majority. Until recently it was considered equally inevitable that it was only a matter of time before the minority would be culturally absorbed

by the majority. This conclusion is based on the simplistic view that geographical and social isolation have been the critical factors in sustaining
cultural diversity. This view, in turn, led to the conclusion that cultures
cannot survive if geographical and social divisions disappear and minority
cultures merge into the culture of the majority – a process once regarded
as desirable. The experience of the 1930s and 1940s, however, triggered a
reversal of this view.[4]

Where this position goes astray is that it defines "culture" exclusively in
terms of institutions, customs, and traditions, particularly religious ones, that
is, in terms of clearly identifiable elements. Add to this the previously mentioned conviction that geographical isolation was a precondition of the
survival of cultures and that cultures disintegrated when the boundaries
disappeared, and one is left with a concept of culture that cannot adequately
deal with the situation in multiethnic societies in which there are no geographical divisions between ethnic groups and which are marked "by a high
degree of cultural erosion."[5] As a result, although institutions and customs
may have a diminishing significance, individuals have nonetheless shown a
remarkable "emotional attachment to the ethnic group."[6] Social scientists
have therefore attempted to redefine culture in terms that do more justice
to this striking phenomenon.

It is now generally accepted that patterns of behavior, attitudes, and value
systems are more important than concrete customs and institutions in determining a person's ethnicity. As standards of value and behavior are shaped
virtually from birth by the child's upbringing and education, they form so
integral a part of a person's nature that most people hardly ever become
fully aware of them. They therefore remain largely beyond their control.
In other words, perceptions strongly influence people's interaction with the
world around them. In the context of our topic, this means that we should
not expect to find members of a minority integrating elements of the majority culture unchanged into their own culture. Instead, they interpret
them in the light of their own cultural background and then assimilate them
to their existing cultural heritage.

Seen in this light, assimilation has to be defined as the opposite of how
it has been used by historians of German Jewry (that is, as the adaptation
of a minority culture to the culture of the majority). It is not a one-
dimensional process. Assimilation in the sense of re-interpretation means

---

4 For a more detailed discussion of this question, see Berghahn, *Continental Britons,* esp. chaps. 1
 and 2.
5 A. L. Epstein, *Ethos and Identity* (London, 1978), x.
6 Nathan Glazer and Daniel P. Moynihan, eds., *Beyond the Melting Pot* (Cambridge, Mass., 1963), 8.

the interaction between the new and the old, leading to a fusion of old and new cultural elements and resulting in a new combination that is identical with neither. Applied to the specific case of the German Jews it means that, since emancipation, if not before, an ethnicity has developed combining Jewish and German elements in an original way and representing a unique ethnicity that is not identical with either culture.

The same would, of course, apply to the German–Jewish refugees in England, where one would have to expect a fusion of German–Jewish and English cultural traits over time, again creating a new ethnicity. Nevertheless, it may be too soon to identify the specific character of this new culture. At present, the German–Jewish or "continental"–Jewish characteristics remain more clearly recognizable than those of an Anglo-Jewish culture. In fact, this process can be expected to be quite drawn out because the refugees who emigrated to England instead of to the United States encountered a very homogeneous society, one marked by sharply delineated boundaries of class and status but held together by a pervasive sense of "Englishness."

Many German–Jewish refugees went through phases during which they tried to be more English than the English. They tried to adopt at least the outward signs of "Englishness," in the hope of becoming more acceptable to the majority. This was not a result of an "assimilationist tendency" but had mainly to do with the difficult situation they found themselves in: They had been expelled by the country they had considered their home. This filled them with bitterness and the wish to dissociate themselves from Germany. Moreover, they were now living in a country at war with Germany, where anything German was detested. No wonder they tried to hide their German traits and exchange them for "Englishness." But England not being an immigrant society, they soon found that it is impossible to become English overnight; one has to be born into English society to be fully accepted as English. In Franz Neumann's words: "Much as I (and all the others) loved England, her society was too homogeneous and too solid, her opportunities (particularly under conditions of unemployment) too narrow, her politics not too agreeable. One could, so I felt, never quite become an Englishman."

This also explains why not a few refugees moved on to the United States or Israel – two immigrant societies. Some of those who stayed in England never stopped striving for acceptance, even becoming emotionally disturbed and having to undergo medical or psychotherapeutic treatment. An interesting case is that of a refugee of the second generation whom I met only recently. She told me that she had tried terribly hard when she was younger to adopt a perfect English accent, with considerable success. (Several refugees had attended elocution classes for the same reason.) She now regrets having lost her German accent; had she kept it, so she explained, she would not have to pretend anymore who she is not, namely, not English-born. People would know immediately who she is: a refugee from Germany.

Nevertheless, most refugees accepted these realities. They did not take elocution classes and gave up striving for absorption. In fact, they learned to appreciate the positive side of nonacceptance. As I was told more than once: "The English leave you alone." It was a telling insight, generally gained through a long learning process that in the early years of emigration had caused much pain.

But it was not just the question of coping emotionally with being confronted by a relatively closed society. The highly restrictive immigration regulations made it extremely difficult for refugees to rebuild their businesses or professional lives and thus at least to improve their economic prospects, their economic and social integration. Right from the beginning, the British government pursued a rigorously selective admissions policy. As early as April 1933, it was decided at a cabinet meeting to

try and secure for this country prominent Jews who were being expelled from Germany and who had achieved distinction whether in pure science, applied science, such as medicine or technical industry, music or art. This would not only obtain for this country the advantage of their knowledge and experience, but would also create a very favourable impression in the world, particularly if our hospitality were offered with some warmth.[7]

As a result, only scholars who had achieved a certain reputation and business owners who were prepared to start up enterprises in the so-called special or depressed areas (for only those goods, however, that previously had been imported) were given work and resident permits. Later on, the concept of usefulness was extended to domestic servants from which refugee women in particular benefited and who were thus able to enter England in larger numbers, especially in 1938. England's official attitude, significantly enough, was that it was a "country of transit, not of settlement for the purpose of work, except in individual selected cases. . . . But the limitations [of employment] have been very strict."[8] The situation did not improve until the early 1940s when restrictions on work were generally lifted because of the need for more labor in British industry. Naturalization was granted only after World War II.

During these early and extremely difficult years women played a crucial

7 A. J. Sherman, *Island Refuge: Britain and Refugees from the Third Reich, 1933–1939* (London, 1973), 32.
8 John Hope Simpson, *Refugees: A Review of the Situation since September 1938* (London, 1939), 68–9.

role in the survival of their families and the establishment of a German–
Jewish community in England. As the *Blätter des Jüdischen Frauenbundes*
pointed out as early as December 1936, women proved to be more adaptable than men. Although men had upon entry to the country promised to
accept any work, however menial, a high percentage of them was unable
to face working for little pay at low-skill jobs. They often sat at home idle,
succumbing to feelings of despair and depression. On the whole, women
were more flexible and ready to grasp whatever opportunity offered itself
to boost the meager family income. It mattered less to them that most jobs
were badly paid and in many cases also illegal without a work permit. For
many years, refugees, except for those who fulfilled certain criteria, were
refused work permits.

As is well known, German–Jewish refugees came from predominantly
middle-class backgrounds and in Germany had been highly upwardly mo-
bile, thanks not least to a well-developed work ethic that traditionally
permeated German and Jewish society and had also become part of the
German–Jewish ethnicity. Because of the restrictive economic and social
measures that the Nazi regime forced upon the Jewish community, women
in particular had started to make adjustments already in Germany to the
changed climate and had lowered their expectations of education, status,
and employment long before emigration. As early as 1936, a survey showed
that only a little more than a tenth of the girls questioned were interested
in getting their *Abitur* (high school leaving examination) and that the number of those who were prepared to accept jobs with a lengthy period of
training had dropped considerably.[9] This meant that even before emigration
quite a few women had begun to consider or to take more menial jobs.
Meanwhile, many women of well-to-do background, who were used to
having servants and cooks at home, had to learn to keep house and to cook.
So, again it was they in particular who had begun to make adjustments in
life-style and attitudes even before emigration.

Yet, however bad the economic situation may have been in Germany,
for the refugees it seemed in some ways worse for them in Britain because
they were anxious to rebuild their shattered lives. They felt humiliated by
being forced to be idle and made dependent on handouts from refugee
organizations. Women's greater readiness to swallow their pride and to
accept whatever opportunity offered itself probably also explains why they
seem to have coped better emotionally. It was they who became the emotional bedrock of the family, who offered comfort to the other members of

9   Herbert Freeden, *The Jewish Press in Nazi Germany* (New York and Oxford, 1993), 147ff.

the family while their husbands lapsed into depression or even committed suicide. Women seized the initiative; they hurried from place to place, consulted refugee organizations about any, even unpaid, job possibilities for their husbands; they sifted the advertisement pages of newspapers. These efforts were not always fully appreciated. Thus, one respondent, after a lot of trouble, at long last succeeded in finding a place at a hospital for her husband, a well-known surgeon. Their married life had come under severe strain because the enforced inactivity had made him very depressed. But to her great disappointment, he refused to accept the position offered to him. As his wife put it: "It was not good enough for him. . . . He did not know how important this job was. He had no idea what you have to do in the world, what you have to accept."

In other cases men did accept jobs for which they were overqualified, and it was their wives who had to give them emotional support to help them accept their lowly position. Women also assisted their husbands practically – for example, in helping them sort and sew buttons for clothing firms or acting as their receptionists or helpers. In a number of cases, women set up new businesses with their husbands and took over after their husbands' often premature death – businesses as varied as hops, furs, or textiles. A great number of women also looked for jobs for themselves and worked as domestics. This allowed them to earn a modest income but also had the advantage of not having to pay for board and lodging. In a few cases men took on the job of butler. But it was mainly women who worked as domestic servants to support themselves and their husbands and children as well. Because many of the women had had cooks and maids in Germany and therefore lacked personal experience in housework, they quickly taught themselves rudimentary skills. Even so, they had to make considerable psychological adjustments. Some took on jobs as cooks or matrons in boarding schools to be near their children who had found a place there – occasionally to the embarrassment of the latter. Some were well treated, but for most this was an unhappy time. It may not have been bad treatment by their employers but merely the humiliating experience of being treated as a domestic by English people who lacked any clear idea of their domestics' background. In England's secluded and stratified society, many employers were unaware of the middle- and upper-middle-class upbringing and self-perception of their "maids." Thus, one respondent "had a horrible job. I got the sack because I stayed in bed when I had the flu, as I would have done in Germany." She was luckier with her next job, which was with a left-wing English lawyer who had bought a big house in the country and employed several refugees.

Understandably, refugee women made strong efforts to get out of the domestic employment situation as soon as possible or to avoid it altogether. Women with families especially developed other means of earning a living. There was often no other choice for them than to "work their way through illegally," as one of them put it. With an astounding degree of imaginativeness and talent for improvisation, they found themselves a variety of odd jobs. One respondent mended the clothes for refugee men whose wives had stayed behind in Germany. Later, she made teddy bears and gas masks that were sold by her husband, a former journalist, who now traveled as her salesman. Others did secretarial work for refugees or took in refugees as lodgers. How precarious this situation could be is well illustrated by the case of Mrs. L. She had come to England on a visitor's permit and first stayed with friends from her hometown. But soon she had to leave because her friends had to accommodate immigrant relatives. She took a room and through contacts found a job as a cleaning woman – of course, without possessing a permit. Since she did not earn enough to pay her rent, she left without notifying her landlord. Afterward she worked for a refugee couple. "It was horrible. They were 150 percent Orthodox, and I had a lot of work; imagine all the dishes on Sabbath." But at least they helped her obtain a work permit. She left once more, took a room with other refugees, and through them found a job with a non-Jewish German refugee couple. Mrs. L. had to look after and sleep in the same room as their dogs. She was so hungry that she ate the dogs' food. She also did some secretarial work for her employer but left when he made sexual advances. After that, she held various secretarial and cleaning jobs.

These few examples show how important the informal refugee community was for individual refugees. Again, it was women who played an important role as pivotal members of their circle of families and friends, thus creating and re-creating networks through which the refugees were able to forge personal, business, and other connections – all vital for the process of reestablishing the community and for the personal reconstitution of the individual. Refugees who had missed out on the early, formative years of the emigration experience and had entered Britain after the war often found it difficult to fit in and feel at home in this community.

A sad example is offered by Mrs. M., who should have emigrated to Montevideo with her mother in 1938. But four weeks before their departure, their permit was declared invalid because Jews were no longer admitted to Uruguay. Her mother subsequently left for Shanghai, and Mrs. M. joined her father in one of the Baltic countries where he had settled after he had divorced Mrs. M.'s mother. In 1940 this area was overrun by the Russians, and she and her father, together with all other Germans living in this area, were interned and sent on a three-week journey in cattle cars to Siberia. Mrs. M. spent the following eleven years in some twenty different labor camps. "Many people died from starvation, but I was young and healthy and therefore survived."

In 1952 Mrs. M. was released and returned to her hometown in Germany, where she tried hard to adjust to the completely different life. But it was difficult, and she found it impossible to earn a living for herself and her child who was born in one of the camps after she had been raped. She was also desperate to be with her mother with whom she had always been very close and whom she had not seen for thirteen years. In the meantime, her mother had left Shanghai because of the Chinese Revolution and gone to Israel, where she hoped to set up a textile business similar to the one she had built up in Shanghai. This time the mother was unsuccessful and therefore joined a cousin in London. The cousin was the only other surviving member of a once large family. Mrs. M.'s mother made another start in England, but the firm did not yield enough income to support her daughter and grandson, too. So Mrs. M. left her child in Germany with relatives and went to Britain on a domestic permit. Here she worked as a domestic in various families but was terribly lonely. Although she and her mother had reestablished their close relationship, Mrs. M. found it difficult to make friends. Because of her past experiences, she did not fit in with existing Jewish, let alone English circles. Finally, she joined a group of young refugees with whom she felt at home and where she met her future husband. Soon after the marriage she sent for her child. Her husband got on very well with his stepson; however "it was one change too many for him. He had loved it in Germany and would have preferred to stay. The child that I knew and the child that he had become in Germany were two different people." He felt like an outsider in England and was extremely lonely. He was teased at school because he was German and also for being Jewish, and he was very unhappy about having "foreign parents." After a few years, he suffered a nervous breakdown from which he only gradually recovered.

It was not only in the informal community that women played a crucial role; they also became actively involved in the formal community, that is, the various refugee organizations such as the Association of Jewish Refugees from Germany and Austria; the Free German League of Culture and its associated centers of artistic and intellectual activities; the Club 43, set up by first-generation refugees; the Hyphen, a meeting place for second-generation German–(Austrian–)Jewish refugees; the Leo Baeck Lodge; and, last but not least, the congregations, especially the large New Liberal Jewish

(Belsize Square) Congregation and the smaller Orthodox "Munk" congregation in Golders Green. The women involved in these institutions were thus continuing the tradition of community care that had been one of the strengths of the Jewish community in Germany for several centuries.

In all these various roles, women were instrumental in securing the survival of the German–Jewish community in a less than hospitable English environment. By transmitting, often unconsciously, German–Jewish cultural traits (which are found not only in specific customs, such as eating habits, but also in attitudes, value systems, etc.), they helped to preserve a German–Jewish ethnicity and identity, thus ensuring continuity in the face of upheaval and disorientation. At the same time, they facilitated the integration of the refugees, especially of the younger generation, into English society through the openness and ease with which most of them entered into social, even if rarely close, relationships with the English.[10] It is with thanks to women refugees that German Jews or Jews from Germany and their children feel reasonably comfortable in England as Jews, even as German Jews, again.

---

10 Respondents commonly differentiated between "English" and "British." Whereas the former excludes most immigrants, the latter is seen as all encompassing and thus able to accommodate the various non-English groups who live in the United Kingdom.

4

England

An Eyewitness Report

SUSANNE MILLER

Born in 1915 in Sofia, Bulgaria, Susanne Miller was raised in Vienna. In 1935 Miller emigrated to England, where she worked with the Internationaler Sozialistischer Kampf-bund *(ISK) and the British Labour Party. After World War II, she went to Germany with her future husband, Willi Eichler. In 1952 she began working for the National Executive Committee of the Social Democratic Party (SPD). She headed the SPD's Historical Commission from its establishment in 1982 until 1990. Miller received her Ph.D. in history in 1963. She subsequently joined the Commission for the History of Parliamentarianism and Political Parties. Together with Heinrich Potthoff, she wrote* A History of German Social Democracy from 1848 to the Present *(1982). She has published widely in the field of German and Austrian labor and political history. This report was written in 1991.*

Perception is determined not only by its object but also by its subject, by the person who perceives, experiences, judges, and remembers his or her observations, impressions, and feelings. I think, therefore, that I should first introduce this person – myself. I wish to state from the outset that my biography, my motives, and my experiences cannot be regarded as typical for women émigrés in England.

I was brought up in Vienna in a rather well-to-do and conservative family of Jewish descent but was christened as a small child and learned practically nothing about the Jewish religion. Born in 1915, I went to the University of Vienna in 1932 to study history, English, and philosophy. I joined the Socialist Students' Union, was more interested in attending political meetings than university lectures, and watched with anguish the agony of the Austrian Social Democratic Party.

In February 1934 parts of the Schutzbund, the paramilitary organization of the Austrian Social Democrats, rose up against the increasing pressure put on left-wing organizations by the clerico-fascist government of Engelbert Dollfuss.[1] After a short, violent fight, the uprising was crushed by government troops. The defeated were persecuted, and many were arrested or put in prison or in concentration camps. Some leaders of the revolt were executed, and left-wing organizations, including the social democratic trade unions, were outlawed. British and American Quakers sent financial aid to Vienna to help the victims and their families. These relief activities were organized by socialists, mainly those belonging to youth organizations, and I took part in them. I had to visit many families, mostly working-class and unemployed, to hand over small sums of money. This was my most important early apprenticeship in politics.

A few months after the events of February 1934, which had turned Austria into a fascist country – although without the extreme racism of the German Nazis – I had a chance to spend some time in England. I had successfully applied for an au pair job in an institution called Bermondsey Settlement, which was owned by Methodists in the East End of London. I was happy about this opportunity to improve my knowledge of the English language, to leave the oppressive atmosphere of Vienna, and to get acquainted with life in a free, democratic country. My duties in the Bermondsey Settlement were connected with the Children's Country Holiday Fund, which sent children from poverty-stricken districts to families in the countryside where they spent holidays. I gained an insight into the social conditions of this part of London, populated mostly by dockworkers, much worse than most of those I saw in the council houses for working-class families in Vienna.

In London, I made contact with British Socialists, and with some of them our friendships lasted until their deaths. But my most important encounter was with German refugees. It influenced my whole life. I met a Jewish couple from Magdeburg, Jenny and Walter Fliess, who were members of a small, extremely active socialist organization called *Internationaler Sozialistischer Kampfbund* (ISK).[2] They had relatives in London who helped them financially so that they could open a vegetarian restaurant in the West End. Thus, Jenny and Walter Fliess found a livelihood for themselves, but their main aim was to earn enough money to support their political group's

---

1 Engelbert Dollfuss (1892–1934) was chancellor of Austria from 1932 to 1934 and leader of the Christian Social Party. In 1933 he disbanded the *Republikanischer Schutzbund*, an Austrian paramilitary organization founded in 1922 in opposition to the right-wing *Heimwehr*. After 1933, the *Schutzbund* went underground until it was finally destroyed in the uprisings of February 1934.

2 The *ISK* (Militant Socialist International), an outgrowth of the *Internationaler Jugendbund* (International League of Youth) was formed in 1926. Its members, who were leftists, played a significant role in the anti-Nazi resistance. See Werner Link, *Die Geschichte des Internationalen Jugend-Bundes (IJB) und des Internationalen Sozialistischen Kampf-Bundes (ISK). Ein Beitrag zur Geschichte der Arbeiterbewegung in der Weimarer Republik und im Dritten Reich* (Meisenheim/Glan, 1964).

resistance work against the Nazis. Their restaurant had a good start, but they had difficulty finding suitable staff, because jobs in the catering trade were badly paid and unpopular. When the refugee restaurant owners met me, I was a strong, healthy, young girl, eager to take part in the struggle against fascism, no matter where or in what capacity. Although I had no idea how to cook, or about any other practical things, they asked me to work with them. Overcoming my own doubts and the strong objection of my parents in Vienna, I left Vienna and its university for good in 1935 and became an employee in the vegetarian restaurant in London. There were some legal difficulties, but somehow I managed to stay.

The restaurant became a flourishing business. Some days it catered to a thousand customers, and in the course of time I became familiar with most jobs that had to be done. It was hard and strenuous work, and during the first years I had hardly any energy left to devote myself to political and intellectual matters. The frustration I sometimes felt was outweighed by my satisfaction in knowing that I could help to make profits that were used for the antifascist struggle both inside Germany and in the centers of socialist exile. Before the annexation of Austria by Hitler in 1938, I visited my family in Vienna several times.[3] After Austria had been incorporated into the Nazi-dominated Reich, I became a genuine refugee, and Great Britain became my country of exile.

At this point I should make a remark about semantics. In England the general term for those who left their own country to live outside the reach of Nazi persecution was "refugees." It had an adequate meaning and connotation. In Germany, however, a differentiation has been made recently, both in academic work and in political discussions, between emigrants and exiles. The distinction between these two words was pointed out by Bertolt Brecht, himself a refugee in several countries, in a poem from which I quote in an English translation:

> I always found the name false which they gave us:
> Emigrants.
> That means those who leave their country. But we
> Did not leave of our own free will
> Choosing another land. Nor did we enter
> Into a land, to stay there, if possible for ever.
> Merely, we fled. We are driven out, banned.
> Not a home, but an exile, shall the land be that took us in.[4]

---

3 March 11–12, 1938.
4 Bertolt Brecht, "Concerning the Label Emigrant" [1937], in John Willet and Ralph Manheim, eds., *Bertolt Brecht Poems 1913–1956,* trans. Stephen Spender (London, 1976), 301.

It would have been difficult to find out, and it never was done, who among the German and Austrian refugees deserved the name "emigrant" according to Brecht's definition. There can be no doubt, however, that many politically and intellectually active antifascists hoped to return to their own country one day to resume the activities they had been forced to give up. Referring again to Brecht, their legitimate name should be "exiles." With them, female and male, I had the most contact, as I had joined the aforementioned organization, which was partly financed by the restaurant in which I worked. But for simplicity's sake, I shall use the general term "refugees."

Before World War II it was very difficult to gain entry to England as a refugee. Restrictions against the influx of undesirable foreigners, against their staying and working in Great Britain, were rigorous, and they were applied efficiently, even mercilessly. There was, however, a loophole in this insurmountable legal wall, and this loophole was used by women. Because Great Britain was very short of domestic servants, one could apply to receive maids from abroad, and a number of families did so. That was the way my sister, several of my friends, and many other German and Austrian women came to England.

Their lot as household servants depended on chance. As far as my personal experience goes, I found that the treatment they received was independent of whether the maid was Jewish, and of whether the family who employed her was Jewish. I knew Jewish girls in Jewish families who were shamelessly exploited. A close friend of mine who had been a student of economics at the Berlin University left Germany as early as possible, being Jewish and a socialist, to work for a rich Jewish family in London. She had to take care of the two-year-old grandchild of her mistress. Thereafter, I stopped believing that all little kids were sweet and lovable. Besides looking after the little girl, my friend had to clean rooms, help in the kitchen, and be at the beck and call of numerous members of the family. When she asked to be relieved of some of these duties to have a little time to rest and recover, she was refused, and she was told that she should be grateful to have work in England, as otherwise she might have been put in prison by Hitler.

It would not be fair to base generalizations on the case of my friend, but her treatment was not a rare exception. I remember how shocked I was when I heard that some of the girls who worked as maids used their afternoons off to sleep because they were completely exhausted. I should add that many of these female refugees who escaped the horrors and dangers of Nazi dictatorship by serving as household maids in Britain had no prior experience in such work. Their inexperience and their loneliness increased their misery. It must be admitted, however, that their employers sometimes had reason to be disappointed and dissatisfied with their refugee maids.

There were, on the other hand, also instances of happy relations between employers and their employees from abroad. I wish to point to one, as it also concerns friends of mine. In this case the new housemaid came from a German working-class family. She had been an active socialist during the Weimar Republic and joined the underground resistance movement after Hitler came to power. When some members of her group were seized by the Gestapo, she fled from Germany and got a job with an English lady in the countryside who was very kind to her. Later, she was employed by the family of a Jewish doctor from Germany who had settled near London. In this family she found much understanding for her situation, she loved the baby who was entrusted to her care, and she could discuss political matters with members of the family. They became and remain friends. Although her experience was not unique, it was by no means the rule.

The outbreak of war changed the situation of the refugees. The restrictions against their accepting employment were lifted, but they had to work in industries or businesses that were essential for the war effort. The restaurant where I worked belonged to this category, and thus the number of German and Austrian refugees working there increased. Although they were labeled "enemy aliens," I never noticed enmity against them on account of their nationality. Our British colleagues took it for granted that we wanted Great Britain and her allies to win the war. And, of course, they were right. But as the "phony war" ended and the German armies went from victory to victory, a certain difference between the attitude of the British people and that of the German refugees became noticeable.[5] Whereas the British never had any doubt that they would ultimately win the war, we refugees were not so sure and were terrified by the idea of what might happen. We expected the worst when the German troops marched through France without meeting any effective resistance.

The fate of England's closest ally naturally also alarmed the British people, but generally they controlled their thoughts and feelings better than we did. During those fateful weeks of the spring and summer of 1940, as one of the waitresses in the restaurant, I could watch the reactions of many people to the dramatic events. Among our customers were some high officials of the Foreign Office. I had just served soup to one of them when he looked at me with despair in his eyes and said, "Paris has fallen."[6] I went to the kitchen

5 The period between September 1939, when Great Britain and France declared war on Germany in response to the invasion of Poland, and May 1940, when fighting broke out in Western Europe.
6 June 13, 1940.

and spread the terrible news. Thereupon a young girl, the daughter of a miner from Yorkshire, started to sing, "Rule Britannia, Britannia rule the waves. . . ." Such a reaction may seem to us today, after more than half a century has passed, ludicrous or absurd. But at the time it happened we took it as a spontaneous and natural expression of genuine patriotic sentiments.

The fall of Paris was a terrible blow to Britain and a turning point in World War II. For us refugees, it meant that we had to prepare ourselves for the possibility – some thought even for the probability – of German troops invading England and German authorities ruling the country with the Gestapo. We knew that German and Austrian refugees, Jewish and non-Jewish, would then be among their first victims. A German doctor, a refugee herself, fulfilled our wishes for pills that would enable us to commit suicide should we be in danger of falling into the hands of the Nazis. I shall never forget the evening when the female members of our group sat together to sew these pills into the shoulders of the jackets of our male comrades. We thought, not quite rationally, that they would be in greater danger than we women. Fortunately, developments made it unnecessary to use these pills.

After the German occupation of France, the great wave of internment of "enemy aliens" set in.[7] Most of the internees were men, but a number of women, some of them good friends of mine, were also interned in camps on the Isle of Man. This treatment of people who had been driven from their country by the Nazis and who had no greater political desire than to contribute to their defeat caused hardship and bitterness among the refugees. But soon we were impressed by the campaigns led by prominent British women and men, especially by some members of Parliament, against the indiscriminate internment. And they were successful. Within about a year all nonfascist internees were released.

In contrast to the prewar years in England, during the war German and Austrian socialists developed public political activities. Some of the women played an important role in planning and organizing them. This was the case in the Austrian Labor Club, in the Union of German Socialist Organizations in Great Britain, in the group of German Trade Unionists, and in an organization called German Educational Reconstruction, which had the cooperation of prominent British personalities. Generally, political and

---

7   British tribunals divided "enemy aliens" into three groups: those to be interned, those who were
    exempt from internment but were subject to certain restrictions, and those who were exempt
    altogether. See Marion Berghahn, *German-Jewish Refugees in England. The Ambiguities of Assimilation*
    (New York, 1984).

national allegiances and loyalties proved to be stronger than understanding and solidarity on the basis of gender. The German socialists were regarded with distrust by the socialists from the Allied countries, and during the war there was no socialist women's organization accepting members of all nationalities. But individual contact between socialists from various countries – between British, "friendly aliens," and "enemy aliens" – did exist, and they were valuable for the men and women concerned, as well as for their postwar relations. Lucy Middleton, who was a member of parliament after the war, and her husband, a former secretary of the Labour Party, were shining examples. They did not discriminate between nationalities and offered their moral support to all of us.[8]

Members of my own political group were lucky to have British friends. They had known a few before they came to England, but they met most during their stay in Great Britain. These friends helped us to get in touch with people and institutions in their country. Mary Saran, formerly Maria Hodann, a social worker and well-known political figure in Berlin, soon became an impressive speaker in many institutions and public meetings.[9] For a time she was the editor of the monthly journal *Socialist Commentary* and was later the secretary of the Women's Group of the Socialist International.[10] I, myself, had an apprenticeship as a political speaker during the war years in London; I was often invited to talk on events in Europe at meetings of the Women's Cooperative Guild, which were held in the afternoon in various parts of London. Although I sometimes arrived there dead tired, having worked since early in the morning, I enjoyed these gatherings. I am sure that I learned from my audience at least as much as its members learned from me.

Toward the end of the war, when Hitler's defeat was in sight, the members of our group made plans for their future work. Women and men alike were determined to contribute to building a democratic society in a united Europe. I had no desire to return to Austria; for personal and political reasons I preferred to go to Germany. In England, during the last war years, I lived and worked with Willi Eichler.[11] Later, once in Germany, we got married. The remarkable measure of equality between men and women in

8 See Lucy Middleton, ed., *Women in the Labour Movement: The British Experience* (London, 1977).
9 See Mary Saran, *Never Give Up: Memoirs* (London, 1976).
10 Mary Saran began editing *Socialist Commentary* in 1942 and held the position for fourteen years. The journal originated as a publication of the Socialist Vanguard group.
11 Willi Eichler (1896–1971), a member of the executive of the *Internationaler Sozialistischer Kampfbund*, is credited with blazing the way for reconstruction of the German Social Democratic Party after World War II. See Sabine Lemke-Müller, *Ethischer Sozialismus und soziale Demokratie. Der politische Weg Willi Eichlers vom ISK zur SPD* (Bonn, 1988); *Willi Eichlers Beiträge zum demokratischen Sozialismus,* ed. Klaus Lompe and Lothar F. Neumann (Berlin and Bonn, 1979).

our group was reflected also by their postwar careers as members of parliament, state officials, political party and trade union representatives, college and university professors, and in other public functions. In this respect, however, our group was more the exception than the rule. Only relatively few women who returned from exile aspired to political or professional careers. Some of the former refugees who had had to fight so hard for their own and their families' existence when abroad were content with the role of housewife and mother once they were back in their own country.

Compared with the refugees from Nazi persecution in most European countries, those in Great Britain were privileged: They did not have to suffer the invasion of Hitler's troops and occupation by his authorities. Emigration and exile were generally easier for women than for men. They adapted themselves more quickly to changed circumstances, had better possibilities of finding jobs, were less concerned with having lost their former status, and often found social contacts and circles of friends.

Exile in England offered the opportunity to live in an environment with democratic traditions and virtues. These had a strong impact on public and private life during the war. They created an atmosphere of courage, dignity, and fairness, unforgettable for all who had the good fortune to experience it.

5

Women Emigrés in Palestine
An Eyewitness Report

RACHEL COHN

Rachel Cohn was born in Hamburg in 1915. She emigrated in 1936 to France, where she married Leo Cohn. The couple spent the most of the war years with the Jewish underground movement. In 1944 Leo Cohn was arrested and sent to Auschwitz. He did not survive. After World War II Rachel Cohn emigrated to Palestine. There, she married Marc-Mordechai Cohn. She received a Master of Library Science degree from the Hebrew University in Jerusalem. In 1963 she was asked to develop and run Jerusalem's first municipal public library, which grew into a system of branch libraries. Since her retirement in 1980, Cohn has worked as a volunteer in various municipal libraries, the Israel Museum, the Hebrew University, and in private collections in Agnon and Tycho. In 1991 she received the title Yakirat Yerushalayim, *distinguished citizen of Jerusalem. She has four children, eighteen grandchildren, and four great-grandchildren, all of whom live in Israel. This report was written in 1991.*

To understand the fate of the Jewish women who left Germany after the Nazis came to power, it is necessary to look at the spiritual climate in which families lived before 1930. I would like to say some words about my parents' home. My parents were born in southern Germany, where their ancestors had lived for several generations. My mother came from a family of teachers. She attended a German elementary school and learned French and embroidering from the nuns in a convent. My father attended the Jewish teachers' seminary in Würzburg. After their marriage, they settled in Hamburg. My parents kept a traditional Jewish home but took part in the secular cultural life of Germany. As a young girl, I was a member of the Friends of the Museum of Art; we visited the theater and the opera, like all good citizens of the Freie Hansestadt Hamburg (free Hanseatic city–state of Hamburg). Upon graduating from the *Jüdische Höhere Töchterschule* (a Jewish secondary school for girls), I studied at a German *Gymnasium,* or secondary school. We took excursions and field trips, visited museums together, and met German writers.

89

I want to add that a great part of the Jewish population increasingly detached itself from Jewish tradition and leaned more and more toward German culture. It was the time of the Weimar Republic. In contrast to the Jews of eastern Europe, who had already thought of and practiced emigration for generations, German Jews felt at home in Germany. I too felt well and at home there.

Suddenly everything changed. On the morning of April 10, 1933, we had our weekly student assembly. When we met around the flag, the principal of our class announced without any preamble that "the Jewish pupils have to leave the school as of today."[1] No word, no protest was heard. We were petrified. Our native country did not want us anymore. We were five girls in the same situation, with one year left until university entrance exams. There was only one solution: the Jewish secondary school for boys, where we passed our examinations in 1934.

I was a member of the Jewish youth movement, Esra,[2] where I had a good friend, Leo, to whom I was engaged.[3] His parents were respected, wealthy business people who had left Germany in 1933 and moved to Paris. In 1936 Leo sent me a student visa and I followed him to Paris, where we married that same year. Leo was one of the leaders of the Jewish Boy Scouts of France and was responsible for the Jewish cultural activities of this youth organization.[4] In 1938 we were sent to Strasbourg, where our eldest daughter, Naomi, was born.

In 1939 World War II broke out. The leaders of the Jewish Boy Scouts felt responsible for their protégés. After the occupation of northern France by the German army,[5] they organized children's homes and agricultural schools for the different age groups.

One evening, Leo and I met with several other counselors around the campfire and decided to emigrate to Palestine after the war. We hoped to

1 On April 25, 1933, Germany passed the "Law Against the Overcrowding of German Schools and Institutions of Higher Learning," placing quotas on the number of "non-Aryan" students permitted to remain enrolled.

2 Esra sponsored Jewish agricultural settlement in Palestine. Founded in Berlin in the second half of the nineteenth century, Esra eventually established branches throughout Germany and with the rise of political Zionism served as the coordinating association for other European Zionist organizations.

3 Leo Cohn (1913–1944?) is credited with reinvigorating the Jewish Boy Scout movement in France after his emigration from Germany.

4 The Jewish Boy Scout movement (*Eclaireurs Israélites*) was established in France in 1923 to foster awareness of Jewish heritage in assimilated French–Jewish boys. In the Nazi period it gained momentum by aiding refugee children.

5 The Franco-German armistice, signed on June 22, 1940, stipulated that the Germans would occupy the northern two-thirds of France, including Paris and the entire Atlantic coast. The French retained nominal independence in the south.

begin new lives there. We drafted and signed a statement of our intent; most of the survivors of this group are in Israel today.

In 1942 the south of France was occupied.[6] Life became dangerous for groups of people living in children's homes. A solution had to be found for every single one in order to save his or her life. All of us lived in the Underground with false identification papers and under false names. Meanwhile, we had two more children. Leo was entrusted with taking a group of young boys over the Spanish border and escorting them from there to Palestine. Leo and I agreed that our children and I would cross the Swiss border illegally and wait for the end of the war in Switzerland. In Palestine we would meet again.

But man proposes and God disposes. When Leo arrived at the train in the Toulouse station, he was arrested by the Gestapo – he had been denounced. He was sent on one of the last transports leaving France for Auschwitz.[7]

After the end of the war in 1945, I returned to France with the children. The Scouts organization offered me a place in one of the children's homes for several months.

Palestine at that time was still under the British Mandate, and to land there you had to get an affidavit from the English authorities.[8] The demand for affidavits was very great, and the total number of legal immigrants was limited. Only a few people managed to secure this document, which was of such great importance. After endless troubles, I finally got the affidavit, and I was able to board a ship with my three children, ages eight, five, and eighteen months.

A Greek ship named *Mataroah* was waiting for us in the harbor of Toulon. We numbered about 600 immigrants from various European countries, a great number of us traveling illegally. Our destination was Haifa. Once there we fell under the supervision of the British police. First, the legal immigrants descended. Then, in a mysterious way, our very documents showed up in the hands of the illegal immigrants so that finally all of us were allowed to disembark.

Now, we thought, we are at our destination; we can begin a new life, put the horrors of the Nazi period behind us. We are in our country and

6 After the Allied landings in North Africa in November 1942, the Germans occupied all of France.
7 Leo Cohn was sent to Auschwitz with a convoy of about 1,300 people on July 31, 1944. See Serge Klarsfeld, *Memorial to the Jews Deported from France* (New York, 1983).
8 The mandate system was established by the Treaty of Versailles after World War I to administer overseas possessions formerly under German or Turkish control. Great Britain was responsible for the administration of Palestine until 1948.

everything will be easy now. But the reality was different. The Jewish Agency had a lot of work to do.[9] Everybody who had family in Palestine had to wait in the reception camp at Athlit until their family came to call for them. I had family: My parents-in-law, the grandparents of my children, lived in Tel Aviv. They welcomed us very cordially, and we stayed with them at first. But of course it was not easy for an elderly couple to care for a woman with three children and no resources.

There were a lot of difficulties to overcome. First was the language, then the unemployment, and last, the longing to create our own home. I knew biblical Hebrew but not the modern colloquial speech. My parents-in-law spoke German, so I could communicate with them without any effort. But the children understood only French and did not have any language in common with their grandparents. In kindergarten and at school, they spoke only Hebrew. Little by little these problems vanished, but the period of transition was very difficult.

There was also the need to earn something. By chance, I heard that the recently opened Tel Aviv opera was looking for choral singers. I liked to sing and had had some musical training. I applied and was accepted. I now met the Palestinian population from the stage.

In addition, I knew the owner of a book shop who was willing to employ me. The salary was not great and was in no way sufficient to support my family. I had to give direction to my life and choose a profession. I tried several ways, including an attempt at life on a kibbutz, but the experiment did not succeed.[10]

Then suddenly I found an unforeseen solution: I met one of Leo's school friends from Hamburg in the street. He had been active in Palestine's public life for several years. He advised me to register in a seminary in Jerusalem to be trained as a teacher and counselor. We anticipated the arrival in Palestine of hundreds of orphans from the European refugee camps. Trained educators were needed. The seminary was a boarding school, where I could stay but the children could not. My eldest daughter lived in my brother-in-law's house. He was a well-known lawyer and later a member of Israel's Supreme Court of Justice. The two little ones were placed in the home of a couple of shoemakers. My stay in the boarding school was paid for by the Jewish Agency. In addition, I got a little bit of money from the Scouts

9   The Jewish Agency, an international organization based in Jerusalem, is the representative of the World Zionist Organization. In the period following World War II, the agency was responsible for helping immigrants to assimilate and settle in Palestine.
10 A kibbutz is a voluntary, collective agricultural community. The first kibbutz was established in Palestine in 1909, and the influx of refugees in the Hitler period and after World War II reinvigorated the movement.

organization in France, and with it I was able to pay the cost of boarding the little ones.

In September 1946, my courses were finished and I was sent to the children's village of the Youth Aliyah (*Aliyat Hanoar*).[11] I was responsible for the eldest group of about twenty girls, fifteen to sixteen years old. The majority of them had survived German concentration camps, where they had lost their parents. Under the circumstances, most of them had not attended school for years and had to be compensated for everything: parentless homes and lost studies. Above all, we had to restore their psychological equilibrium and a little bit of joy in their lives.

That was no easy task; no pedagogue, no philosopher had ever foreseen such a situation. We were on our own to develop new methods. The children were so sad, so anxious, that it seemed a miracle if one of them smiled. Young German–Jewish women worked in the kitchen and in the sewing rooms or were employed as nurses. I had my children with me again.

Meanwhile, the Red Cross had answered my inquiry, but all attempts to locate my husband had been unsuccessful. There was no hope left of ever seeing him again.

The situation in Palestine became more tense. The State of Israel was proclaimed on May 14, 1948.[12] The English had left Palestine, and now the war with the Arabs broke out. The civilian population lived in continual readiness for alarm; during the night we had complete blackouts. In the courtyard of our home we had to dig trenches, and when the sirens howled we had to jump into them. Then came the armistice and we could once again breathe.

In January 1949 I married for the second time. My new husband, Marc, had lived in Paris, where he was a reserve officer in the French army. He had spent five years as a prisoner of war in Germany. We had already known each other a long time. In September 1948 he came to Israel. He had been a lecturer at the University of Paris and the director of the first Jewish lycée in France. In Israel he looked for work, as did every immigrant. At that time, Israel's only university, located in Jerusalem, had about 400 students. High schools were also rare. Finally, Marc found a post teaching in the second-lowest class in one of the local elementary schools in Tiberius. After

---

11 The Youth Aliyah, part of the Zionist movement, was established in 1933 to rescue children from persecution and poverty in Europe and settle them in Palestine, where they were placed in *kibbutzim* or in the organization's children's centers.

12 The State of Israel was proclaimed after the British withdrew in response to the United Nation's decision of November 29, 1947, to dissolve Great Britain's mandate powers and partition Palestine into two independent states, Jewish and Arab.

our marriage, the children and I went to live with him there. I found a
position as a teacher in the same school. Our combined salary was not high
but was sufficient for us to rent a little house on top of the hill. The school
building was directly on the bank of the lake. In the morning, our family
went to school together along a beautiful road. Tiberius was a small old
town, nearly untouched by modern civilization. There were still scorpions
and snakes, and during the night we heard the howling of jackals. The
temperature during the summer months frequently reached 40 degrees cen-
tigrade. At noon the population was often asleep. But people were nice, if
also a bit primitive. Our little pupils helped us to speak Hebrew fluently,
which proved useful to us later on.

The first anniversary of the newborn State of Israel was a historic event.
I remember how the women sat on the streets with their sewing machines
and sewed flags. Altogether it was a most interesting year, but it was clear
to us that there were no opportunities to advance professionally. My husband had to go back to Paris for one school year. And, finally, in September
1950, we found an apartment in Jerusalem, where we still live today.

Now we had arrived at a turning point in our acclimatization. By now,
the situation in the country had changed entirely. The English were no
longer there, and Arab hostilities had temporarily ceased. All of our political
and economic institutions had to be created from scratch. Hundreds of
immigrants arrived every day. We were no longer newcomers, and now
we had to contribute our part to building the country. I had already been
in Israel five years. The language was not difficult anymore. Meanwhile,
my husband had become the director of a lycée in Jerusalem. We had no
trouble registering the children at the school. The young state enacted one
of its first laws, instituting free compulsory education for children up to
fourteen years. I myself had to complete my professional training. I gained
satisfaction from being useful to my country.

The population of Jerusalem was a rather closed society, and it was not
easy to be accepted. When we arrived, we expected everything to be offered
to us on a silver platter, but it was not like that. We got five beds and five
blankets from the Jewish Agency, but that was the only support we received
from public institutions. We had to provide everything else for ourselves.

I registered at the university as a student of geography and prehistory.
Professor Stekelis, my teacher, asked me to arrange the library of the department, which consisted chiefly of books in French. Specialized professional books in Hebrew were rare at the time.

The same year, the university and UNESCO jointly opened a school for librarians.[13] As one of the institute's first students, I earned a master of library science degree. This became my new profession. Shortly afterward, Jerusalem's municipal public library opened, and I was put in charge of developing and running the new project. The system grew with the city, serving both East and West. I was appointed director of municipal libraries. In 1951 my youngest daughter was born. We now have four married children, eighteen grandchildren, and four great-grandchildren, all of whom live in Israel.

In closing, I want to mention that the immigration to Israel differs in several ways from that to other countries. In most states, the population and the governments are somewhat reluctant to accept immigrants, who have difficulty settling down, finding work, and becoming naturalized. In Israel, every newcomer is cordially welcomed. If he chooses, he may become an Israeli citizen without any bureaucratic formalities. He is permitted to work as well.

A Jew is never a stranger in Israel. Collective memories are awakened, and the holy places and biblical history seem familiar. Jewish immigrants from all over the world have the same feeling when they first set foot on Israel's soil.

Of course, Israel also has its more difficult sides: the continuous conflict with the Arabs, the military service of three years for boys and two years for girls, as well as the economic and other problems.

Much patience is necessary and acclimatization requires several years. But, as far as I know, few women from Germany have ever regretted having emigrated to Israel.

---

13   The United Nations Educational, Scientific and Cultural Organization (UNESCO) is an inter-governmental agency of the United Nations established in 1946 to promote peace through international educational collaboration.

6

"Naturally, many things were strange but I could adapt": Women Emigrés in the Netherlands

URSULA LANGKAU-ALEX

I

Of the 534 persons[1] mentioned by name as émigrés to the Netherlands in the three-volume *International Biographical Dictionary of Central European Emigrés, 1933–1945*[2] only thirty-four are female.[3] There were, however, many more women who are not listed. The biographies of the thirty-four women

---

1 In addition to the references given in the footnotes, this chapter is also based on talks, interviews, letters, and a recent survey whose participants will remain anonymous. I am grateful to all the women, some who are now deceased. I would especially like to thank Elisabeth Augustin (Amsterdam), Änne Basch (Cologne), Nelly and Co Dankert (Amsterdam), Gerty Hanemann-Kelemen (Amsterdam), Marianne van Heereman (Amsterdam), Elisabeth Meter (Amsterdam), Laureen Nussbaum (Portland, Oregon), Friedel and Rudi Quast (Bochum), and my younger colleague, historian Barbara Henkes (Groningen). I also listened to Ilse Blumenthal-Weiss and Grete Weil when they gave lectures in Amsterdam and answered questions. Furthermore, I took advantage of Kiki Amsberg, *Naturalisatie Duitschers in Nederland,* radio program in the series "Het Spoor" of the Dutch broadcasting station VPRO, Nov. 6, 1988; Jacob Boas, *Boulevard des Misères: Het verhaal van doorgangskamp Westerbork* (Utrecht, 1988); Miep Gies and Alison Leslie Gold, *Anne Frank Remembered* (New York, 1987); Beatrix Herlemann, *Wilhelm Knoechel* (documentary video film, with Cilly Hansmann, for a West German television station, ca. 1985); Barbara Meter: *De afstand van dichterbij* (movie; Amsterdam, ca. 1985); Eva Schloss, *Herinneringen van een joods meisje, 1938–1945* (Nijmegen, 1989), this was originally called *Eva's Story: A Survivor's Tale by the Step-Sister of Anne Frank* (London, 1988); Heinz Umrath, *Aufs neue Beginnen. Vom Grossbetrieb zur Gewerkschaft, 2* vols. (Bonn, 1986 and 1987); and Louis de Jong, *Het Koninkrijk der Nederlanden in de tweede wereldoorlog,* 14 vols. (The Hague, 1969–[1991]).
2 *Biographisches Handbuch der deutschsprachigen Emigration nach 1933. International Biographical Dictionary of Central European Emigrés 1933–1945,* a project sponsored by Research Foundation for Jewish Immigration, Inc., New York, and the Institut für Zeitgeschichte, Munich, and directed by Herbert A. Strauss and Werner Röder, vol. 1: *Politik, Wirtschaft, Öffentliches Leben;* vol. 2: *The Arts, Sciences, and Literature;* vol. 3: *Index* (Munich, 1980–83).
3 One of these thirty-four women, however, Marie Arning, a former textile worker and member of the *Reichstag* faction of the Social Democratic Party (SPD), apparently lived in Belgium. See Gaby Ullmann, "Ein Leben als SPD-Parteisekretärin und Reichstagsabgeordnete. Die Politikerin Marie Arning," unpublished as part of Projektbericht zum Forschungsprojekt "Exil und Nationalsozialismus," led by Prof. Dr. Heinrich Mohr (Universität Osnabrück, Fachbereich Sprache und Literatur, 1988).

émigrés given in the first two volumes indicate that there were another eighteen women who fled to the Netherlands: their mothers and sisters. When I checked the first sixty-two names of the 500 male émigrés mentioned in the dictionary, I found thirty-four men whose mothers, sisters, wives, or daughters – fifty-four women in total – had also emigrated to the Netherlands. For example, the Social Democrat Karl Kautsky and his wife Luise, who is listed under his name, were followed in the summer of 1938 by the wife of their son Benedikt, who had been interned, and their two daughters. None of these family members appear in the dictionary. Quite another example is that of the historian and social scientist Henry Ehrmann, who emigrated via Czechoslovakia to Paris and then to the United States in 1940. His biography shows that his wife Claire Sachs had lived as an émigré in the Netherlands between 1935 and 1937. She is not listed separately.

In the absence of precise facts, I estimate that of the approximately 30,000 émigrés who set foot in the Netherlands after 1933, and who stayed there for at least two weeks, more than half were female. This approximation is based upon official statistics of refugees, as well as other considerations.[4] Until 1936–37 few serious difficulties had existed for children and younger or older women legally to join their relatives who had fled Germany earlier. But they had to show that the latter were recognized as refugees from Germany, that they received some aid, or that they had managed to establish some sort of living. After the so-called *Anschluss* of Austria to Germany in March 1938, 500 of the estimated 800 émigrés from Austria and Czechoslovakia, who obtained permission to come to the Netherlands despite the official closing of the frontier, were women. Most of these were "human-

4 For statistics, see Dan Michman, "Die Jüdische Emigration und die niederländische Reaktion zwischen 1933 und 1940," in Kathinka Dittrich and Hans Würzner, eds., *Die Niederlande und das deutsche Exil 1933–1940* (Königstein, 1982), 73–87, 74. Ursula Langkau-Alex, *Die Aufnahme der Flüchtlinge aus Deutschland und den deutschsprachigen Gebieten Mitteleuropas in den Niederlanden* (Amsterdam, 1983), manuscript located in Deutsche Bibliothek (Frankfurt/Main), Internationaal Instituut voor Sociale Geschiedenis (Amsterdam) and other libraries; for the Dutch version, see Heinz Schneeweiss, ed., *Kun je woorden verbranden?, redactie en samenstelling* (Rotterdam, 1985), 44–75. Ursula Langkau-Alex, "Karl Kautsky in den Niederlanden," in Hans Würzner, ed., *Österreichische Exilliteratur in den Niederlanden 1934–1940* (Amsterdam, 1986), 39–65. Barbara Henkes, " 'Das Deutschtum in Gefahr': Deutsche Dienstmädchen in den Niederlanden, 1920–1940," in Monika Blaschke and Christiane Harzig, eds., *Frauen wandern aus: Deutsche Emigrantinnen im 19. und 20. Jahrhundert* (Bremen, 1990), 51–63, 59. Barbara Henkes, "Changing Images of German Maids During the Inter-War Period in the Netherlands. From Trusted Help to Traitor in the Nest," in Raphael Samuel and Paul Thompson, eds., *The Myths We Live By* (London and New York, 1990), 225–38, 226. Horst Lademacher, *Geschichte der Niederlande: Politik–Verfassung–Wirtschaft* (Darmstadt, 1983), 417.

itarian cases," that is, their parents, husbands, or fiancés already lived in the Netherlands as distinguished foreign businessmen or even as Dutch citizens. The same phenomenon recurred, though the numbers may have been lower, following the signing of the Four Power Pact in Munich at the end of September 1938, after the occupation of what remained of Czechoslovakia in March 1939, and after the outbreak of World War II. But then, the refugees of German nationality (including, since March 1938, the Aus trians) needed a visa. Early in September 1939, the Dutch government repealed their obligation to furnish visas, even if applicants wanted only to go abroad to other, third countries. In all the foregoing cases, the official granting of refuge or transit depended upon funds that the emigrant(s) had to bring into the country or that relatives or friends in the Netherlands already possessed. In the first years after 1933, even the "political" refugees, who often had carried only a handbag due to the urgency of their escape, had to demonstrate to the Dutch authorities that they had enough money on which to live.

Before 1933, women had come to the Netherlands for professional reasons – for example, as artists of various kinds and, above all, as housemaids who did not want to return to (Greater) Germany. Domestic servants were allowed to immigrate until 1934. In 1939 between 1,500 and 2,000 maids resisted Nazi campaigns to send them home and attempts by the Dutch authorities to send them back in order to find jobs for unemployed, unmarried Dutch women. Despite laws restricting foreign workers, the Ministry of Social Affairs permitted sixty young Jewish women to enter the country in 1938–39 to work in Jewish homes. It is unknown whether these women were trained like those young women of good Jewish families who soon after the *Anschluss* followed the lessons of an Austrian count to qualify as parlor maids in distinguished (Jewish) homes in England.

The category of hidden refugees should be expanded to include women who in the 1920s had come to the Netherlands as children to recover from the postwar misery and famine in Germany and Austria and who had stayed. One example is that of Miep Santrouschitz, who as Miep Gies (she married the Dutchman Jan Gies in 1941) became well known as the preserver of the diaries of Anne Frank, the most famous woman émigré in the Netherlands. This category should also include women who crossed the border illegally or who came as tourists or visited relatives and then stayed on without ever registering with the authorities. Members of the Communist Party and especially women (and men) who worked with the German resistance movement did not legalize their stay for fear of being interned in a Dutch camp or – what would have been even worse – expelled and sent back to Germany. There was one exception: Adelheid Torhorst entered into a fake marriage with a Dutchman and lived in the Netherlands legally. This greatly improved her chances of doing illegal work because foreign communists were persecuted especially harshly by the authorities. Her sister Marie, however, remained in the country illegally.

After the burning of the synagogues and the plundering of houses and businesses belonging to German–Jewish citizens on the night of November 9, 1938, the so-called Crystal Night (*Reichskristallnacht*) and the internment of at least 30,000 Jewish men, 8,000 individuals were granted permission to enter the Netherlands. Jewish parents, mothers whose husbands had been interned, and grandparents often sent their children or grandchildren into the Netherlands in the middle of the night; the *Alijah* Youth Movement and the *Hechaluz* took care of them. These children gathered in special camps where they trained for a future life in Palestine. During the day – even after the occupation – they worked with the Christian peasants in the neighborhood, so long as there was no acute risk of being arrested.

Dutch Jewish organizations obtained permission to organize transports of some 1,000 children, many of them orphans, who came out of Greater Germany. Most of them were transported to England until shortly after the outbreak of the war when the frontiers were closed and transit visas were needed. The last ship sailed to England with seventy-five orphans on May 14, 1940. Seven hundred orphans were placed with Dutch families, most of them Jewish but also Catholic and Protestant families, and in homes where émigré women helped take care of them.[5] In addition, more than 2,000 women and children crossed the Dutch borders illegally, as did 100 men in the following months. All of them got at least a temporary sojourner's permit.

The masses of new refugees were sent to special camps along the coast. There were camps for Protestants, camps for Jews who had been baptized Catholic, camps for mixed Jewish and non-Jewish families, and camps for Orthodox Jews. Men without families were among the first sent in October 1939 to Westerbork, fifty kilometers from the German border. The Dutch government had decreed in February of that year the establishment of this central camp for the growing number of Jewish refugees. Little by little the Dutch police, at first on their own initiative and then on the orders of the

5 Gustel and Heinz Moses, " 'Im Schatten der Feuersäule,' vom Kampf des holländischen Hechaluz," lecture, 1983, in possession of the author of the present chapter. D. Cohen, *Zwervend en dolend. De Joodsche vluchtelingen in Nederland in de jaren 1933–1940. Met een inleiding over de jaren 1900–1933* (Haarlem, 1955), 232–54.

occupying Germans, moved people from the various camps along the coast to Westerbork. Cities and towns were evacuated last, with Amsterdam at the end of the list.

Two further points need to be added to this statistical survey:

1. The Netherlands was a country of transit, although not usually in a positive sense. Of the 30,000 émigrés mentioned, about 26,000 to 27,000 passed through the country. By "passing through" I do not mean only those who voluntarily went to other countries or returned to Germany for family reasons or with the purpose of reinforcing the German resistance movement. I also think of those who were expelled and those who died in the Netherlands. When the German troops invaded the country in May 1940, a considerable number of people committed suicide. I think also of those who were arrested and brought to trial in Germany, who were deported to the concentration and the extermination camps. During this time, about 20,000 émigrés were caught in the Dutch trap. Only about 3,000 refugees came back after the war, and most of them were women. They came out of the Underground as well as from the camps. Some had resided in the country legally, though they lived much of the time in fear or even in real danger.

After the end of the war, however, a new migration began. Several hundred émigrés left the Netherlands forever. They looked for a new life, for better chances overseas, in the United States or in Palestine. Emigrés who had fled for political reasons, democrats, but most especially socialists and communists, went back to Germany to help construct a new society. Wives (sometimes with young children) accompanied their husbands. Some women now crossed the border in an easterly direction to join their husbands who, after having been drafted by the German administration in the Netherlands or picked up in the streets by the *Sicherheitspolizei* (Security Police, called the *Grüne Polizei*, because of their green uniforms) had been forced to join the *Wehrmacht* or even, when deprived of their German citizenship, the *Waffen–SS*. (Jewish men or men who were discovered to be involved in anti-Nazi activities were first sent to camps in the Netherlands and then to concentration and extermination camps – for instance, Mauthausen or Auschwitz. Emigrés who in the years before 1940 had acted against the Nazis but whose activities had remained secret were included among those forced to join the German military.) Still other women followed the wives and children of these involuntary soldiers who had gone back to their parents or other relatives already during the war. Other women could at last exercise their professions in Germany – for instance, teaching. The previously mentioned Adelheid Torhorst advised in the construction of a new school system in the Soviet zone of occupation. Her sister Marie, who had assisted her in the antifascist resistance, became minister of culture and education in Thuringia. The Social Democrat Liesbeth Hennig resumed her municipal work in Gelsenkirchen, from which she had been removed by the National Socialist regime in 1933.[6]

There were other motives for going back to Germany. Much later, the author Grete Weil, whose novel *Tramhalte Beethovenstraat* gives a literary impression of the life and fortunes of the mostly Jewish émigrés who inhabited this new quarter of Amsterdam Zuid (south), expressed not only her own feelings when she explained why she had returned: "I was crushed. Germany was crushed. We belonged together."[7] Her husband had been arrested in Amsterdam and was murdered in 1941 in the Mauthausen concentration camp. Grete Weil herself had spent the years 1943 to 1945 in the Underground.

2. Approximately 23,000 of the 30,000 émigrés who came to the Netherlands had fled Greater Germany because of the Nazi regime's racial policies and the climate of race hatred. In 1941, 15,174 of them were still in the country, a figure that represented more than 10 percent of the entire Jewish population. Another 5 percent of all Jews in the Netherlands had come from countries other than Germany. But quite a few of those who had been persecuted for political or trade union activities were also of Jewish descent. During the German occupation of the Netherlands, they ran a double risk.

Returning to the thirty-four women listed in the *International Biographical Dictionary,* we need to discuss two general problems of method that are not easily resolved. First, the women listed represent only a minority of émigrés: They are the exceptions. They have a name because of their professions, their careers, or because of their extraordinary political or social activities. The average woman émigré is more likely to be found under the names of the men – husbands, fathers, brothers, sons. Second, the list includes women who at the time of their emigration to the Netherlands were children or teenagers. They became known only after they had left the country, through the establishment of careers following studies or some other training. This was the case primarily for women who went to the

6 Rudolf Quast, "Zwischen Amsterdam und Bochum," *Jahrbuch der Ruhr–Universität Bochum* (Bochum, 1974): 83–128, 115.
7 Grete Weil, in reply to the reproach by Konrad Merz, a Dutch-naturalized German emigrant, at the end of a lecture she had given in Amsterdam in 1983. Grete Weil, *Tramhalte Beethovenstraat* (Wiesbaden, 1963).

United States.[8] Nevertheless, because I am convinced that their character and intellect were formed mainly in exile, that is, before arriving in the United States or another permanent home, I am disposed to count all children born between 1918 and 1930 as adults.[9]

II

The following discussion deals with the situation in general and with specific problems that women émigrés from Germany and other parts of Central Europe confronted in the Netherlands. Because no serious research on the subject has been done, my observations are necessarily impressionistic. I concentrate on those problems that émigrés who lived in the Netherlands for a longer period had in common and give examples that emphasize various perspectives or simply highlight individual or social differences. Artists such as Erika Mann and Therese Giese, among others, who came and stayed mainly to tour the country and make public appearances are of no interest here. In comparison with the years before 1933, however, they were now confronted with changed tastes and official admonitions not to insult a certain "friendly statesman." They did not really experience what it was like for the average refugee who wished to settle in the Netherlands at least for a while.[10]

8   Thus, in the third volume of the *International Biographical Dictionary* their names also figure under the United States of America, or one of the other "Countries of Immediate Emigration and Final Settlement."

9   Remarks on discussions during the Washington conference on "Women in the Emigration after 1933," a discussion I had afterward in the Netherlands, and some letters I received made me understand that the age of the émigré and especially the age of the children was much more determinant for the experience of the emigration period and the personal and professional development later on than was gender. So it could happen that three sisters aged six, nine, and twelve when coming to the Netherlands in 1936, developed totally different attitudes and reminiscences. The oldest had great difficulties in becoming a self-confident young woman after being separated from her close friends in Germany and was sent back two classes in school in her new country. The youngest had few difficulties with the new environment. School had just started for her and she became totally acculturated to the new society. The second of the girls, however, adapted herself without totally losing her background. Later on, in the United States, she became a professor of German and Dutch language and philology. (She does not appear at all in the *International Biographical Dictionary*.) Differences in adaptation and acculturation between sisters of different age are also to be seen in the diaries of Anne Frank. Here, I quote from the official revised edition: Rijksinstituut voor Oorlogsdocumentatie, *De dagboeken van Anne Frank* (The Hague, 1986), 195–713.

10 As the references in these notes make clear, studies exist only on intellectual, learned, and artistic individuals, the professions, and on some political organizations and persons. For the artists, whether they undertook promotional tours or tried to stay permanently, see the articles in the chapter "Culturele en kunstzinnige wisselwerkingen," in Kathinka Dittrich, Paul Blom, and Flip Bool, eds., *Berlijn – Amsterdam 1920–1940. Wisselwerkingen* (Amsterdam, 1982), and the communications of Walter Huder, Jacques Kloeters, Kathinka Dittrich, Nico Bredero, Marius Flothuis, and Hans Jaffé, in Dittrich and Würzner, eds., *Die Niederlande und das deutsche Exil;* and Kathinka Dittrich, *Achter het doek. Duitse emigranten in de Nederlandse speelfilm in de jaren dertig* (Munich, 1987).

What were the Netherlands like in the 1930s? The country was (and remains) a constitutional monarchy that since 1890 has been headed by women. The feminist movements succeeded in introducing the eligibility of women in 1918 and women's right to vote in 1919.[11] In spite of those facts, the Netherlands was a country of deep conservatism and male chauvinism. From May 1933 to August 1939 the country was ruled by coalitions of three religious parties: one Roman Catholic and two Protestant. Throughout the period the prime minister was the authoritarian, somewhat aristocratically mannered Hendrik Colijn of the leading Reformed Anti-Revolutionary Party (*gereformeerde Antirevolutionaire Partij*).

Colijn's cabinets promoted bourgeois policies that were not only antisocialist but also established a very thin social security net during the years of economic crisis. In the Netherlands, the economic crisis became serious in the summer of 1931, and it reached its climax in 1933–34, later than in Germany. But the worldwide depression struck the Netherlands even harder and lasted longer than in many other countries. In foreign affairs, the Netherlands traditionally cultivated a policy of strict neutrality; yet its most important trading partner was Germany.[12]

Official policy toward the refugees was determined by some contradictory factors.[13] Because the Dutch at the time maintained deeply rooted appreciation of law and order, they at first welcomed Hitler as the savior of a rotten, anarchic, and Bolshevist Germany. Thus, the "political" refugees were consistently regarded as potential troublemakers. But the fear of a strong, threatening neighbor, namely, Germany, was also growing, especially in light of the growing Dutch National Socialist movement. In the provincial elections of 1935, the National Socialist Movement (*Nationaal-Socialistische Beweging,* or NSB) got nearly 8 percent of the vote. Consequently, the government prohibited émigré political activities, especially

---

11 The first and only woman elected in 1918 was a Social Democrat; in 1921 she was joined by a Liberal; in 1922 seven women were elected; later in the 1920s there were eight women in parliament. They represented the Social Democrats (*Sociaal-Democratische Arbeiderspartij* or SDAP), the Roman Catholic Party (*Rooms-Katholieke Staatspartij*), the Liberal Party, the Liberal Democrats (*Vrijzinnig-Democraten*), and one of the Protestant Reformed Protestant parties, the *Christelijk Historische Unie.* In the 1937 elections, only four women were voted into parliament. See A. E. J. de Vries-Bruins, "Op de politieke bres," in M. G. Schenk, ed., *Vrouwen van Nederland 1898–1948. De vrouw tijdens de regering van Koningin Wilhelmina,* met een woord van hulde door Eleanor Roosevelt (Amsterdam, 1948), 274.

12 Lademacher, *Geschichte der Niederlande,* 324–404. J. L. van Zanden and R. T. Griffiths, *Economische Geschiedenis van Nederland in de 20e eeuw* (Utrecht, 1989), 129–65.

13 Dittrich and Würzner, eds., *Die Niederlande und das deutsche Exil,* here especially Dan Michman and Ursula Langkau-Alex, "Chronologische Uebersicht wichtiger Fakten zur niederländischen Flüchtlingspolitik 1933–1940," 87–90. Bob Moore, *Refugees from Nazi Germany in the Netherlands* (Dordrecht, 1986).

those of socialists and communists. Furthermore, there was the apprehension that, on the one hand, immigrants would enlarge the army of the unemployed, or on the other hand, that they might take the few available jobs. There was even the fear of *Überfremdung* (that is, excessive foreign influence on Dutch society) in light of the many Jewish people coming to the Netherlands. But some Christian mercy remained, for instance, when Prime Minister Colijn, in a radio speech on December 1, 1938, called on the Dutch people to contribute to the national collection for the refugees from Germany, Austria, and the Sudetenland (Czechoslovakia). The new Dutch government, consisting since August 1939 of the *hervormd* Protestant Party (*Christelijk Historische Unie*), the Roman Catholic Party (*Rooms-Katholieke Staatspartij*), and – for the first time – the Social Democratic Party (*Sociaal-democratische Arbeiderspartij*), followed the queen and the royal family to England after the German troops overran the Netherlands in May 1940. Hitler himself installed the Austrian National Socialist Seyss-Inquart as *Reichskommissar der Niederlande* (Reich commissioner of the Netherlands), alongside the military occupying authorities. Within two years, the National Socialists took command of all branches of military, police, and civil administration. The Netherlands were finally coordinated (*gleichgeschaltet*) when the systematic deportation of the Jews in the country began in July 1942. On July 1, 1942, the SS took over the Westerbork camp from Dutch authorities; Westerbork became the "police transit camp" (*polizeiliches Durchgangslager*) for Jews. With Seyss-Inquart's permission, politicians from various political parties had founded the Union of the Netherlands (*Nederlandsche Unie*) in July 1940 in an attempt to overcome the "pillared" (*verzuilde*) structure of Dutch society as well as to find both a new national identity and some political autonomy under the occupation. However, German authorities prohibited the union in December 1941.[14] Only the Jewish Council (*Joodsche Raad*), installed in early February 1941 by order of the occupant authorities to administer the so-called *Arbeitseinsatz* (labor service) of the Jews, remained in operation through October 1943.[15] Until the beginning of the systematic deportations, the Jewish Council tried to save specific Jewish traditions by stimulating new activities in the fields of

---

14 The best English translations of the Dutch terms "zuil(en)," "verzuiling," and "verzuild" are "pillar(s)," "pillared structure," and "pillared," respectively. These terms reflect the structure of the Dutch state, which much like a building was held up by independent societal pillars. Each pillar was hierarchically organized, with its own ideological, religious, and cultural identity as well as means for social control. There was almost no communication among the pillars in between the basement (national territory) and the roof (government, bureaucracy, economy).

15 The role of the *Joodsche Raad* in the deportation of the Jews still is a matter of debate in the Netherlands.

literature, theater, and the sciences. Grete Weil was one of several other émigré men and women who temporarily, until she joined the Underground, was active in it.

This phenomenon of *verzuiling* (pillared structure) has to be explained because it was unique to the Netherlands and did not exist in other countries. Since the end of the nineteenth century, Dutch society had been organized into several "pillars": the Protestant, the Catholic, and, finally, the socialist (social democratic) pillars. In addition to their distinct beliefs or ideologies, they had their own political parties and trade unions, their social, cultural, and even sporting organizations. Each pillar had its own schools, publishing houses, newspapers, and radio stations.[16] Apart from business matters and the political necessities of democracy, very little communication among the pillars was possible. Perhaps one could add another, smaller pillar with a different ethnic as well as religious and cultural character: the Dutch Jews. But there never existed a Jewish political party or a Jewish general school system. Politically, Jewish workers tended to align themselves with the socialists, and the upper-class and middle-class Jews favored the liberals, who had no subcultural organizations.[17]

How were the émigrés received by the Dutch people? How did women and girls experience the country and its society? Furthermore, we need to know what the political and social lives of the émigrés looked like. To this end, a little anecdote, which I read in the memoirs of Elisabeth Augustin, yields an impression of some typical Dutch frames of mind. (This excellent novelist, poet, essayist, and author of radio plays, who writes both in German and in Dutch, unfortunately does not appear in the *Biographical Dictionary*.) Augustin came from a Jewish family. At the end of the 1920s, she joined a local social democratic organization. She left Germany in 1933 at the age of thirty. Her husband, who was half Dutch, half German, had preceded her to the Netherlands to find a house and a source of income.

16 The population of Amsterdam, where most of the émigrés lived until 1938, consisted of 30 percent Catholics, 30 percent Protestants, 10 percent Jews, and 30 percent atheists. In general, children of socialist and other non-Christian, "liberal" parents attended the so-called *openbare scholen* (i.e., schools not bound to any church). The pillared structure of the Dutch society lasted until the 1970s, but even nowadays the school and the media system still exist, though these are much more flexible and transparent. Because the socialists had no schools of their own and because in the 1930s the SDAP opened itself up to Catholics as well as to Protestants, some historians speak of the socialist pillar as an "open" one. See C. H. Wiedijk, *Koos Vorrink. Gezinheid, Veralgemening, Integratie. Een biografische studie (1891–1940)* (Groningen, 1986), esp. 524. Van Zanden and Griffiths, *Economische geschiedenis*, 9–15.

17 The following characterizes Dutch society in the 1930s very well: "A society based on mutual respect but without too much contact or cordiality – that was the Dutch recipe, and the Jews readily conformed." From Herman Vuijsje, "Vermoorde onschuld. Joden in vooroorlogs Nederland," *HP – Haagse Post* (Amsterdam), 1983, 18, 22–31, 24. Translation by the author.

When Augustin first stepped onto Dutch soil at Amsterdam's central train station in early summer 1933, she noticed that some people looked disapprovingly at her and her two little children who excitedly chattered in German. When they stepped into a cab, an elderly lady intentionally passed by, uttering audibly and contemptuously: "Moffen!"[18] *Mof* (*Moffen* is the plural) was, and still is, the abusive name for a German. When the German army violated the neutrality of Belgium and was likely to do the same to the Netherlands during World War I, what had for nearly a century been a nickname or general expression of dislike of German migrant laborers – for instance, peat-cutters from Westphalia – also took on a moral and a political dimension.

The incident at the central train station may be taken as an example of a mixture of prejudice, ignorance, and arrogance on the part of average Dutch men and women in the early 1930s. Of course, there were innumerable examples of friendliness. But until 1941, real solidarity and friendship between Dutch people and émigrés usually happened within a particular pillar. The signatures at the bottom of a letter of congratulation for the first émigré couple to marry in Amsterdam (September 1934) testifies to the existence of friendships between Dutch and German émigrés within the socialist pillar.[19]

Those émigrés who came to the Netherlands in the later 1930s often had the advantage of joining relatives or friends already there. Yet it has to be added that even within the Dutch–Jewish community there was a palpable aversion to their poor sisters and brothers from Eastern Europe. People were afraid of undermining their own economic and social standing and prompting an outbreak of (latent) anti-Semitism. Furthermore, nearly all eyewitness accounts tell of the unwilling, even rude attitude of the Dutch police toward the refugees.

When trying to tell the story of how women émigrés experienced life in the Netherlands, it is important to distinguish between 1933 to May 1940, or even to the end of 1940 and the years after 1941 – when all Jews were registered – to 1945, or even until 1947. As for the period of 1940 to 1941, women's experiences depended upon the way they looked at their personal situation, as well as a few external factors: whether the women, alone or with family, focused on a new life in the Netherlands or overseas or looked toward a return to Germany as soon as National Socialism was over-

---

18 Elisabeth Augustin, *Het patron. Herinneringen* (Amsterdam, 1990), 97.
19 I would like to thank Dr. Rudi Quast and his wife, Friedel, of Bochum, Germany, for sending me a copy of the letter.

thrown.[20] Most of the politically minded refugees belonged to the latter group.

Nevertheless, only a few women found a way to work on or try to work on the undermining of the regime. Whereas we know the names of at least six female members of the Communist Party who worked for the Red Help or served as couriers between émigré and Dutch organizations and resistance circles in Germany, we know little about socialist women.[21]

"Our Dutch female friends were much more involved in political activities than the majority of the wives of our German [social democratic] comrades," writes one of the women I interviewed. In fact, no female émigré appears to have been an active member of the clandestine social democratic groups or of the nonpartisan Central Association of German Emigrants (*Zentralvereinigung deutscher Emigranten*) founded in Amsterdam in early 1937. Prohibited some months later, this organization attempted to assemble the heterogeneous émigrés in order to stimulate solidarity and to function as their united legal representation vis-à-vis the Dutch authorities.[22] Neither Liesbeth Henning, mentioned earlier, nor Martha Tausk, the former International Women's Secretary of the Labor and Socialist International, undertook clandestine activities.

Three observations, however, may explain women's lack of participation. First, most of the wives, fiancées, and girlfriends who followed male social democratic and trade union émigrés to the Netherlands voted for the Social Democratic Party (SPD) but had not officially joined the party. Few active female members of the SPD actually emigrated to the Netherlands. Most of those who wanted to do political work went to countries where such activities were not totally prohibited: Czechoslovakia, France, England, or Sweden. The socialist Irmgard Enderle and her husband, for example, went on to Sweden after having been expelled from the Netherlands in November 1933 because of their political activities.

Second, those few younger women who belonged to the SPD's leftist group, New Beginning (*Neu Beginnen*), worked separately from the social

---

20   It has been suggested that we call the first category "emigrants" and the second "exiles." Since the use or the meaning of these terms differs from country to country (for example, the Dutch language follows the French meaning), I am unable to lend greater precision to these terms here. Both groups have in common the fact that they left Greater Germany – or refused to return – because of the National Socialist regime.

21   Hilde Erxleben, Cilly Hansmann, Jenny Matern, Clara Muth, Adelheid Torhorst, Marie Torhorst. See *International Biographical Dictionary*; Beatrix Herlemann, *Auf verlorenem Posten. Kommunistischer Widerstand im Zweiten Weltkrieg. Die Knöchel-Organisation* (Bonn, 1986).

22   Ursula Langkau-Alex, "Die deutsche sozialdemokratische Emigration in den Niederlanden nach 1933 – Ein Überblick am Beispiel der Stadt Amsterdam," in Dittrich and Würzner, eds., *Die Niederlande und das deutsche Exil*, 90–106, 100–01.

democratic and other socialist circles. They reduced or altogether stopped their courier activities in about 1936–37 because of the many arrests made by the Gestapo. Third, well-known social democratic women generally belonged to an older generation. In 1939 Martha Tausk was already seventy years old when she fled Austria following persecution by the police and the Gestapo, and joined her son in Nijmegen. She contacted, however, old Dutch friends whom she knew from her work, as well as German and Austrian women émigrés. One of her friends was Luise Kautsky, with whom she met regularly.

The even older Luise Kautsky continued to support her husband by writing down his thoughts and memories, conducting research for him in the library, renewing old and fostering new friendships with socialist women and men either through personal contact in Amsterdam or through correspondence. After the death of Karl Kautsky in October 1938, she started to organize his archives in the International Institute of Social History (IISH) and the family documents in her possession. She also prepared Rosa Luxemburg's letters for publication. The loss of the family documents and of the letters of her beloved friend Luxemburg as the result of confiscation by the security police in 1943 grieved Kautsky deeply. She could not foresee that five years later her son Benedikt, who was forced to labor at Auschwitz's Buna-Werke while in December 1944 his mother Luise died five kilometers away at Auschwitz–Birkenau of weakness and a broken heart, would discover both collections among other archive materials of the IISH on two barges near Hanover, Germany.[23]

Apparently, most of the political women did only "female" work: They typed the minutes and the articles written by men and, if needed, did translations; they made coffee and cleaned the meeting room, which in most cases was someone's living room. Naturally, most of these women also listened to what the men discussed and sometimes would take part in the debates.

With this last point, we have already touched upon the external factors alluded to earlier. Two of these concerned the "political" and the "unpolitical" women and men émigrés, especially in the cities. Of course, everybody experienced emigration to the Netherlands individually,[24] but the

23 Ursula Langkau-Alex, "Karl Kautsky in den Niederlanden," in Hans Würzner, ed., *Österreichische Exilliteratur in den Niederlanden 1934–1940,* 49–52.
24 The widowed German writer Georg Hermann took refuge in his beloved Holland in 1933. Hermann, sixty-three years old, was accompanied by his daughter, who was nearly fourteen years old at the time. In light of the political, economic, and social peculiarities of the Netherlands and his own experiences and observations, he generalized in 1937 that only children and teenagers would be able to adapt: "People beyond the age of 20 already have difficulties. For people older than 50

statement of one of my female interviewees covers the general experience of women émigrés whom I either personally met, know through correspondence, or whose reminiscences I have read (although I must confess that their number is not so great): "Naturally, many things were strange, but I could adapt."[25]

First, there were the different customs and ways of daily family life. A characteristic custom all émigrés (including myself, a "semigrant" since 1966) tell about is that when you are invited for tea or coffee, the lady of the house will take your cup, pour the liquid in, add sugar and/or milk, then she will take a painted tin box out of the cupboard, open it, offer you a *koekje* (cookie; in German, *Plätzchen*), say "please, take one," then shut the box and put it back into the cupboard. This mixture of hospitality and typical Dutch thrift has often been misunderstood as a gesture of reserve or even unfriendliness.

A further source of irritation was the habit of Dutch citizens to feel bound to correct foreigners who wanted to settle in the Netherlands in everything that did not correspond to given rules. On the one hand, this repressive tolerance (as we might call it) furthered a willingness on the part of the newcomers to adapt to the new country. On the other hand, expectations that the immigrant must conform to the standards of the host country as soon as possible often met with the stubborn: "Bei uns zu Hause . . ." ("Where we come from . . .").

Another, quite different example of the clash of customs had to do with dinnertime and playtime. In the Netherlands dinner takes place at 6:00 P.M., Dutch children stay inside from about half past five till about half past six or even seven o'clock, depriving emigrant children of their playmates. Emigrant mothers were used to preparing dinner for noon or 1:00 P.M. and called in their children for supper and bedtime at about the time Dutch children would come out again. But these mothers adapted to the changed circumstances as soon as their children had to attend school, for school lasted from nine o'clock in the morning till four o'clock in the afternoon, with only an hour or an hour and a half break in between. Even if the school

it will be rather impossible to grow into a new environment. Old people become entirely lonesome" (*alte Leute verwaisen vollkommen*). Paraphrased and translated by the author. Cited in Laureen Nussbaum, "Verliebt in Holland: Ein wichtiges und wechselndes Verhältnis in Georg Hermanns reifen Jahren," in Sjaak Onderdelinden, ed., *Interbellum und Exil. Liber Amicorum für Hans Würzner. Abschied von der Rijksuniversiteit Leiden* (Amsterdam, 1991), 181–98, 189.

25 Original: "Natürlich war vieles fremd, aber ich war anpassungsfähig." This quotation comes from a response to a questionnaire I distributed to several women who had emigrated to the Netherlands after 1933.

was close by, there was only enough time for a sandwich between morning and afternoon lessons.

During the initial phase, surely many a girl (I never heard of boys) shed bitter tears when their little Dutch school friends did not appear at birthday parties. They had been invited, but their parents – and we may suppose that the mothers were the driving force – did not allow such visits. In general, Dutch and émigré children met only in school and played together on the streets. Because whole newly built blocks of apartments were occupied by emigrants, Dutch families did not always live in the neighborhood. At least this was the case in Amsterdam, where until 1938 most of the emigrants lived. It was very difficult for émigré children to be accepted in Dutch homes. For their part, many girls did not dare accept an invitation to a Dutch birthday party because they felt awkward not yet speaking the language, dressing "German" (for example, wearing a Berchtesgaden-style cardigan), and generally being alien.

Second, for women from abroad the possibilities of finding a job or of developing professional activities were extremely limited. The economic crisis forced the government to cut Dutch women employees from employment rolls as much as possible to maximize places for men. When they married, women had to quit their jobs. The handful of married female teachers and postal and other officials who were still employed were dismissed in the mid-1930s. In those years only 2 percent of married Dutch women practiced a profession or held a paid job outside the house and independently of their husbands' job. Nevertheless, the restrictive measures meshed well with the general middle- and upper-class opinion that women should confine themselves to service jobs such as nursing and housekeeping. It was felt that married women ought to concentrate on their husbands and their children.

In May 1934 a new decree prohibited newly arrived émigrés from Germany from getting a job or from following a technical course of study. Emigré students, especially female students, who had already begun their professional training were forced to abandon their plans. As a result, only women émigrés trained or self-schooled in rare professions (and who were unmarried by choice) had a chance to find legal employment or to be self-employed. Such legal occupations included specialized nurses, physiotherapists, writers, journalists, and translators (for example, Ilse Blumenthal-Weiss), photographers, and artisans.

Erika Oppenheimer, a clinical psychologist, worked as a research assistant at the Wilhelmina Gasthuis in Amsterdam in 1934–35; between 1935 and

1938, she served as the director of the Netherlands' first psychological laboratory, Het Apeldoornsche Bos. Throughout this time she needed additional financial assistance from friends. Women in general received half of what men earned, and émigrés were paid a fraction of what their Dutch colleagues were paid.[26] In 1938 Erika Oppenheimer left the Netherlands and went with her fiancé to the United States, where they were married and where she became the renowned psychologist, Erika Fromm.

The child analyst and psychoanalyst Anny Angel fled Vienna for the Netherlands in 1936. In the following year she married a Dutch colleague, Maurits Katan. Now a Dutch citizen, she trained other analysts at the Psychoanalytic Institute in The Hague, where she remained until 1946. During this time, she served as director of the Child Guidance Clinic. That same year she left with her husband, who as a Jew had lived in the Underground during the time of the deportations, for the United States.[27]

A former teacher told me that an employment bureau had found her a position with a private school run by the Soviet Union's trade mission in the Netherlands. After a year, however, the Dutch government would not extend her work permit because she was not a citizen. She had no choice but to work illegally in order to make a living.

Single women who were not Jewish, Protestant, or Catholic, who did not belong to the SPD or another socialist party or to the KPD (German Communist Party) did not receive a penny from the individual refugee aid committees. As a result, they had to take any illegal job they could find. They worked in textile factories and in laundries. In most cases, they did housekeeping jobs of all kinds. Between 1934 and the end of 1936, approximately 18,000 domestic servants, most of them of German nationality, returned to their native country. Many Dutch households no longer could afford them. Furthermore, in June 1936 the Dutch government outlawed the employment of servants from abroad without permission. Some women quit working because they had married a Dutch citizen. Other émigrés were hired illegally as replacements for the departed German maids. The fact that they were illegal often led employers to lower wages in order to save money.

26 By intervention of the SDAP, Hugo Sinzheimer, a well-known professor of labor law and sociology at the University of Frankfurt/Main until 1933, was appointed professor at the University of Amsterdam. His salary, however, was beneath subsistence level. See Ursula P., "In memoriam Hugo Sinzheimer," in Volker Jacob and Annet van der Voort, eds., *Anne Frank war nicht allein. Lebensgeschichten deutscher Juden in den Niederlanden* (Berlin and Bonn, 1988), 210–20. Langkau-Alex, "Emigration in den Niederlanden nach 1933," in Dittrich and Würzner, eds., *Die Niederlande und das deutsche Exil,* 96.

27 See *International Biographical Dictionary of Central European Emigrés,* 2:345–6 (Erica Fromm), 598 (Anny Katan).

Unemployed émigrés who belonged to one of the community or party organizations – in the latter case, as we have seen, these were mainly men – received six guilders a week for themselves but nothing for their spouses. The aid committees were obliged to treat the émigrés according to the Dutch law of unemployment which, naturally, covered only Dutch citizens. Communists, as far as they did not carry out party functions, got only some pocket money. Most of the weekly sum was paid to the families of Dutch communists who took care of these illegal individuals.

Six guilders a week, however, was not sufficient for a couple to live on, even if they rented the most humble loft and lived very simply. As a result, the women looked for extra work in a system that offered more illegal positions for women than for men. The male partner became a househusband, discussed politics with other émigrés and Dutch friends, and, incidentally, learned Dutch. The Central Organization of German Emigrés offered Dutch courses that were attended it seems mainly by men; no woman I asked had ever heard of it.

Only a few of the highly educated women forced to work illegally had the chance to work privately as a secretary or to work at any other job that somewhat corresponded to their previous training. The teacher I mentioned earlier worked as a housemaid in the homes of middle- and upper-class Dutch and Jewish émigrés. Aside from the fact that the work was hard and monotonous, in the Dutch homes even more than in the émigré ones, she felt humiliated. Their employers had to be addressed as "Madam" (*Mevrouw* or *Gnädige Frau,* respectively), but the housemaids were themselves called by their given names and the informal "you" as if they were stupid little girls. Only at one émigré home was she allowed to join the family at the dinner table, after she had complained of having to take her meal alone in the kitchen, which was located in the basement. After changing homes five or six times, the teacher got an ironing job in a laundry, where she learned to speak Dutch fluently – and even some slang.[28]

A few women émigrés worked in the boardinghouses, the refugee homes, and the vegetarian restaurants managed by their husbands, fiancés, and political friends. Some women naturally helped with the business when their husbands owned the capital resources (or were at times in partnership with a Dutch citizen). Jewish men were often able to get permission to run little shops that sold, for instance, Schachemayer wool or accessories (*Galanteriewaren*); or to operate a wholesale company for

---

28 Friedel Quast, *Die wirtschaftliche und soziale Lage der Frauen im Exil in den Niederlanden nach 1933* (Bochum, 1991), manuscript, 4.

chemicals, medicaments, and materials (as Otto Frank did); or to open a little factory that made, for instance, special paints and lacquers, lady's silk underwear and stockings, or hats. Luxuries were scarcely produced by the sober Dutchmen, yet they were dreamed of by middle- and upper-middle-class Dutch women and men. In the spring of 1937 the Dutch government limited the trading and manufacturing activities of all resident aliens; this measure affected Jewish émigrés above all. Only if they did not compete directly with Dutch businesses and if they promised to employ Dutch citizens did the government grant permission for these enterprises to operate.[29]

During the war, however, when Jewish or politically active husbands were in danger or had already been arrested, did middle- and upper-middle-class non-Jewish wives run a business, provided that no non-Jewish Dutchman could take over. In general, for most women émigrés of the German–Jewish middle and upper classes, the position of being only a housewife was not a problem. They continued – or tried to continue – their earlier life amidst the German and Dutch relatives and friends of their social standing. Middle-class families like the Franks lived in Amsterdam's Rivierenbuurt, a new quarter in the south where all streets were named after rivers. Upper-class émigrés lived in the vicinity of the Beethovenstraat, where the surrounding streets in this new quarter of south Amsterdam were named after composers. The houses had not been built especially for the émigrés, but most Dutch could not afford them in view of the economic recession.

Whereas most male émigrés of the Jewish middle and upper classes became acquainted with the Dutch language in the course of business, their wives picked up phrases from their Dutch maids. They usually stayed at home or visited with friends. Moreover, they missed their former live-in servants in Germany; Dutch servants, besides being only day-maids, generally had a different attitude, lacking the assiduousness (*Beflissenheit*) of their German counterparts.[30] The Parish of the Liberal Jewish Community (*Kerkgenootschap Liberal Joodsche Gemeente*), founded by the émigrés themselves, gave a feeling of solidarity to non-Orthodox Jewish women and men. The Jewish Women's Committee (*Joodsche Vrouwencomité*), a sister organization of the Jewish Refugee Committee (*Joodsche Vluchtelingen Comité*) in Amsterdam, tried to give social and psychological help. The former Cologne

---

29 For the Dutch laws and measures concerning enterprises of foreigners, see D. Cohen, *Zwervend en dolend*, 272–8.

30 A Dutch maid, for instance, never held the coat of her employer when she (or he) was about to go out. See Barbara Henkes, "Changing images of German maids," in Samuel and Thompson, eds., *Myths We Live By*, 235.

social worker Margaret Tietz was a member of the boards of both organizations from 1934 until her departure for Palestine in 1940.[31]

Most of the émigré children learned Dutch rather quickly in the streets and at school, where special courses for the older ones were organized. They often felt superior to their parents and simultaneously ashamed of their parents', especially their mothers', poor Dutch. It was only after the war that most of those Jewish émigré women really learned Dutch, as they settled down and became naturalized citizens. In Amsterdam, the typical *Beethovenstraat* accent and look — as we called it — is now dying out.

For a woman like Elisabeth Augustin, a totally new life began in 1933, because she did not live among the German émigrés. Moreover, she immediately began to write in Dutch. Although she successfully published novels and essays and she and her husband made friends among the Dutch literary and artistic circles, she remembers:

My first seven years in the Netherlands were years of more or less difficult accommodation, years of silly overestimation of my still poor Dutch, years of fits of desperation and uncertainty.[32]

Surely, the women and men who in 1938–39 took refuge in the Netherlands and were gathered early on in camps hardly were likely to think of accommodation. For example, a young female student of languages, who joined her parents and friends in late 1939, fell in love with a Dutchman a few days after her arrival, married him some time later, and had a child in 1942, experienced being an émigré to the Netherlands in yet another way. Moreover, the war, the occupation, and the persecution of the Jews did not leave her any time to think about being an alien among the Dutch Jews.

III

The war period, especially the time of the persecution after 1941 and the systematic deportations of Jews beginning in July 1942, obscured some of the distinctions among emigrated women but much less those between themselves and the Dutch-born Jews.

After the country had been occupied, Dutch and émigré Jewish women of the middle and upper classes, at least in Amsterdam, arranged private lectures and theatrical performances of Jewish émigré artists and intellectuals in their houses.

31 *International Biographical Dictionary,* 1:763.
32 Augustin, *Het patroon,* 97. Translation by the author.

That women émigrés took charge of the family business when their Jewish husbands were arrested or had gone underground has already been
noted. Until the general prohibition of August 1942, the wife of the Protestant pastor Bruno Benfey, a pastor in her own right, took charge of the
baptized Jews at Westerbork after he was prohibited from doing so on
account of his Jewish descent.[33] Although émigré women and men worked
courageously with Dutch resistance groups (for example, transporting illegal
messages and newspapers or even guns and explosives, perhaps in disguise),
in general it was too risky because of their imperfect mastery of the language. In her antifascist activities, Anny Katan, mentioned earlier, took
advantage of her position at the clinic in The Hague.

In the late spring 1943, the Nazis decreed that Jewish women and men
who were married to non-Jews could be exempted from wearing the Star
of David (*Judenstern*) and from deportation if they were infertile or willing
to be sterilized. This decree concerned Dutch and émigrés alike. In general,
women above the age of forty-five could be exempted without having to
undergo the operation. Thus, the seventy-nine-year-old Luise Kautsky was
permitted the right to sit where signboards said, "Prohibited for Jews." It
is not known how many Dutch and émigré women and men hopefully –
and in most cases, ultimately in vain – grasped at that straw. But it is said
that "sterilization" became a normal word even in children's conversations.[34]

At the beginning, Jewish wives and their children from a marriage with
a non-Jew were spared deportation. This, too, affected both Dutch and
émigré women. Also, the experience of going to and living in the Underground was, generally, quite similar for both groups: the fear of getting
discovered, the confinement, the necessity of remaining quiet, the conflicts
between family members and fellow-lodgers (so directly described by Anne
Frank), and the loneliness.[35] Naturally, one needed money to survive in the
Underground; fortunately, most of the helpers were able to nourish the
hidden guest(s) for quite a long period. In the winter of 1944–45, when

33 *International Biographical Dictionary,* 1:50. Langkau-Alex, *Die Aufnahme der Flüchtlinge,* 25–6.
34 J. Presser, *Ondergang. De vervolging en verdelging van het Nederlandse Jodendom 1940–1945,* 2 vols.
    (The Hague, 1965), 1:357–66. On page 366, one document said that until June 15, 1944, of the
    8,610 Jewish partners in mixed marriages, 2,562 had taken the promised advantages out of the
    decree; 1,146 men, most of them after a surgical sterilization, and 1,416 women, most of them
    because of their age. For Luise Kautsky who on August 24, 1944, was arrested by the "Grüne
    Polizei" and in early September was deported from Westerbork via Theresienstadt to Auschwitz.
    See Langkau-Alex, "Karl Kautsky in den Niederlanden," in Würzner, ed., *Österreichische Exillite-
    ratur,* 47–50.
35 See also Helga B., "Untergetaucht," in Volker Jacob and Annet van der Voort, eds., *Anne Frank
    war nicht allein,* 239–45. Almar Tjepkema and Jaap Walvis, eds., *"Ondergedoken." Het ondergrondse
    leven in Nederland tijdens de Tweede Wereldoorlog* (Weesp, 1985).

nearly all people in the occupied Netherlands were starving, the people of the Underground suffered most. It seems that more women than men lost their nerve. They wanted to see the blue sky, to breathe some fresh air, to buy some flowers – and were caught by the police when they came out of hiding.[36]

It is likely that Dutch people had more chances to slip away from being arrested, to find a hiding-place and perhaps a separate one for their children than did émigrés. One reason was their superior knowledge of the country, of its people, the language, and how the society was organized (recall the "pillars"). Nevertheless, Dutch resistance movements and private individuals helped émigrés as much as Dutch citizens (and English soldiers who had been dropped by parachute or whose planes had been shot down over the Netherlands). I even know of one case when a Jewish émigré mother and her baby, born in 1943 (the husband had already been arrested and deported), were hidden by a German woman who had come to the Netherlands with the *Wehrmacht*.[37]

A nunnery, in contrast, was by no means a safe haven, as we know from the fate of the German philosopher and anti-National Socialist Edith Stein. In April 1938 Stein, a descendant of Jews, became Sister Teresia Benedicta a Cruce; after the pogrom of November 1938 she fled from Cologne to the Carmelite Convent Ech in the Netherlands. In August 1942 she was arrested, brought to Westerbork, and some time later deported with her sister Rosa to Auschwitz.[38]

Let me add some remarks on the children entrusted to friends or, as in most cases, to unknown people in the hope of saving their lives. Non-Jewish foster parents were found in all social groups and in all religious and ideological communities. The austere Reformed Protestant peasants proved to be the most generous in this regard. They believed that the Jews were God's chosen people. The most pious foster parents, nonetheless, often tried to educate or to convert the children to their own faith. Yet, it has to be admitted that the boundary between trying to convert and instruction in what was necessary for survival – perhaps a new name and becoming recognized as an authentic member of the family – was rather thin. Great problems often arose when the natural parents and siblings – mostly sisters who had been separated for reasons of security – were reunited after the

36 Franz Loeser, *Sag nicht, du gehst den letzten Weg. Ein deutsches Leben* (Cologne, 1986), 49. Konrad Merz, "Een uur Esther," in Konrad Merz, *De man die niet op Hitler schoot* (Utrecht and Antwerpen, 1979), 29–34.

37 For a story on the difficulties of hiding a baby, see Hans B., "Nachwuchs zu unrechter Zeit," in Jacob and van der Voort, eds., *Anne Frank war nicht allein*, 121–8.

38 *International Biographical Dictionary*, 2:1110.

war: alienation, crises of identity, legal and religious claims.[39] Although I cannot prove it, I believe that in general émigré parents and especially mothers had more difficulties when they were reunited with their children than the Dutch did.

In the first months of the deportations, the émigrés at Westerbork, in comparison with the Dutch people interned, were "privileged," insofar as a number of them had been charged with official functions since the opening of the camp in October 1939. Most of them were men and over time interned Dutchmen were also given official duties; it is hardly surprising, then, that of the 876 survivors who were freed by British troops in April 1945, 464 were male, 309 were female, and 103 were children. In total, only 209 people were from Greater Germany, among them Gerda Kautsky, the daughter-in-law of Karl and Luise Kautsky, and one of Gerda's daughters. Gerda Kautsky's other daughter had survived at the Community of the Society of Friends at Ommen. She had escaped imprisonment after all three had been discovered in January 1945 in the place where they had being hiding since April 1943. But Gerda and her daughter as well as all other non-Dutch persons at Westerbork had to stay at the camp for several more months. Like all Jews, they had been deprived of their citizenship by the Nazis in 1941, and the Dutch government would recognize only its own former citizens. Finally, Gerda Kautsky and her daughters received a permit to go to Switzerland, where they joined Benedikt, the husband and father who had returned, via Buchenwald, from Auschwitz. They left together for the United States.[40]

Most of the émigré women who survived in the Netherlands and those who came back after the war stayed in the country and became naturalized. All these women, including those who returned to their native land or found a new home overseas, feel very much obliged to the Dutch people, but feelings of gratitude are accompanied by critical, even bitter memories.

The direct, personal experience of the Holocaust built at least an inner, silent wall between the survivors of the Underground and the extermination camps and all the others. All survivors were confronted with hate and anti-Semitism on the part of a great many of the Dutch people.[41] The émigrés,

39 Elma Verhey, *Om het joodse kind* (Utrecht, 1991). Max Arian, "Hollands Dagboek" [a week's diary on The First International Gathering of Children Hidden During World War II in New York], in *NRC Handelsblad* (Rotterdam), June 1, 1991, Zaterdags Bijvoegsel, 7. On orphans, see Hans Keilson, unter Mitarbeit von Herman R. Sarphatie, *Sequentielle Traumatisierung bei Kindern. Deskriptivklinische und quantifizierend-statistische follow-up Untersuchung zum Schicksal der jüdischen Kriegswaisen in den Niederlanden* (Stuttgart, 1979).
40 Langkau-Alex, "Karl Kautsky in den Niederlanden," in Würzner, ed., *Oesterreichische Exilliteratur*, 51.
41 Dienke Hondius, *Terugkeer. Antisemitisme in Nederland rond de bevrijding* (The Hague, 1990).

moreover, were told that, now that it was all over, they should leave and go back to where they had come from. A passage in a letter an Austrian émigré wrote to friends in Palestine in November 1945 illustrates some of those elements that constitute the wall of silence:

Here in Holland where I have felt very happy till the deportation, I now feel very alien. All feel alike. The intensified anti-Semitism, the general mood of discontent because of the trying circumstances and shortage are oppressing. I live as if I were on some sort of island with other islanders, and I should like best to withdraw to a less worldly atmosphere. . . . Have you never met a person who has come back from Bergen–Belsen?[42]

Despite these experiences and feelings after the war, most of the Jewish émigrés did not return to what was left of Greater Germany – and to the people there who had let happen the crimes or even had assisted in their commission. Yet the older they become, the more the women émigrés I know long for their native language, for German-speaking theater, for the old places, and for the cooking. One of them wrote to me the following sentence, which seems to speak for the majority: "I went back to see my native place, I love it as ever. But my home is here."

42　Gerty Hanemann-Kelemen to Grete and Leo Perutz, Nov. 8, 1945, in *Leo Perutz 1882–1957. Eine Ausstellung der deutschen Bibliothek Frankfurt am Main* (Vienna and Darmstadt, 1989), 303–5. Translation by the author.

7

Refugee Women from
Czechoslovakia in Canada
An Eyewitness Report

WILMA A. IGGERS

Wilma Iggers was born in Mířkov, Czechoslovakia, in 1921. In 1938 she emigrated with her family to Canada, where she received her B.A. in French and German from McMaster University, Hamilton, Ontario. She received her M.A. and her Ph.D. in Germanic languages and literature from the University of Chicago. She conducted postdoctoral research in Göttingen and has received fellowship assistance for research in the United States, both postwar Germanies, and Czechoslovakia. She has taught at universities throughout the United States and has been a professor at Canisius College since 1975. The author of Die Juden in Böhmen und Mähren *(1986), she has also published and lectured widely in the field of comparative literature. Married in 1948, she has three children. This report was composed in 1991.*

In the fall of 1938, we emigrated to Canada and settled on farms near Hamilton, Ontario.[1] I am offering this story of the immigration from farms in Czechoslovakia to farms in Canada as a corrective: first, to the general notion that Central European Jews were anything but farmers, and second, to the notion prevalent in the publications of the Leo Baeck Institute, that they tended to be *Grossbürger* (upper middle class). My father was the leader of a group of thirty-nine people, mostly relatives, who were Jews and farmers in western Bohemia. Farmers were the largest category of immigrants to Canada. We suspected, and our suspicions were confirmed by the well-documented book, *None Is Too Many: Canada and the Jews of Europe,* by Irving M. Abella and Harold Troper, that the Canadian immigration authorities had hoped to avoid taking in Jews. It does not seem to have occurred to them that there were Jewish farmers.[2]

1 Hamilton is on the western tip of Lake Ontario, about fifty miles southwest of Toronto.
2 Irving M. Abella and Harold Troper, *None Is Too Many: Canada and the Jews of Europe* (New York, 1983).

I should point out here that, because not all were real farmers, my father paired off families so that each pair would include one man who was a farmer and another who owned hard currency (which was, incidentally, illegal in Czechoslovakia) sufficient at least to satisfy the requirement of the Canadian immigration authorities of $1,000 per family. So we, for example, went to a farm together with a young Prague lawyer and his wife and child to live together in the same household. While living with our partners was decidedly fun, this was not so with many of the others, and the families separated as soon as they could. Our lawyer, incidentally, was also the only one in the group who could make himself understood in English.

My parents were in their early forties, which was the average age of the adults in our group. I was seventeen and my sister was fifteen. In Czechoslovakia, we had all been good middle class, *Gutsbesitzer* or *Gutspächter*.[3]

Having arrived in Canada in November, I went to high school in Hamilton right after New Year's, knowing almost no English. Because there had never been a foreigner at the school before, and people had very vague and peculiar expectations of newcomers from Czechoslovakia, my reputation for being a prodigy, of course undeserved, spread quickly, and some time in the spring I received a letter from McMaster University inviting me to become a student there, with a scholarship, regardless of whether or not I passed the senior high school matriculation.[4]

I passed the "matric" and spent part of the summer being very unhappy as a maid in two Toronto homes, and part of it addressing advertising for a chick hatchery, for $10.00 a week. In September, I went to McMaster and stayed with two families in succession, working for my room and board. Both at the university and with the families, I stuck out like a sore thumb.

Later, the owner of the chick hatchery and his wife invited me to live in their house, where my only duty was to teach their reluctant children French. This was a very lucky break. The family later decided that I should be more Canadianized and paid for me to live in the dormitory for the remaining years at McMaster. But not everybody was so fortunate. Another prominent family, who invited my two cousins to stay with them while they attended high school, immediately dismissed their two maids and had the two sixteen-year-old girls do the work for their room and board.

I should also mention the long discussions I had with my host, the gist of which was that since I was not what Canadians perceive as Jewish, I should not insist on saying that I was.

---

3 A *Gutsbesitzer* was the owner of a large farm who usually also ran it; a *Gutspächter* leased a farm and also ran it.
4 McMaster University, Hamilton, Ontario, at that time and until 1957, was governed by the Baptist Convention in Ontario and Quebec.

I majored in honors French and German. By the way, I do not recall any of the refugees being critical about my German major.

Because the university was then Baptist, fundamentalist religion courses and chapel were compulsory; many of the students were related to, or preparing to be, ministers or missionaries. Drinking and smoking were forbidden, as was dancing on campus. I did not miss those types of entertainment but still felt that there was something restrictive about the atmosphere. People did not seem to have a problem with my Jewishness but, rather, with my atheism.

I felt that the Canadians kept more of a distance from one another and from us than I had been used to among the people I knew. But I did have friends, interestingly, I think, among the religious. I actually was most interested in the religion courses, especially in the New Testament, and was constantly amazed by the fact that people at a university in the twentieth century seemed to believe in God and miracles.

Some time in the fall of 1939, my parents received a visit from an official of the Canadian Pacific Railway, representing the Canadian government. He expressed his surprise that I was not working on the farm and explained that all who immigrated as farmers were obliged to farm for at least five years. My father told him that he had not sold me into slavery, and nothing further was done about the matter. The following fall, my sister went to McMaster as well.

In the early days, however, the refugees criticized my going to university. The prevalent attitude was that Jews should have learned their lesson and should aim at mainstream occupations. Therefore, most of those who were in their teens when they arrived became hairdressers, dressmakers, and waitresses, and later married and became housewives. It was only when a few of us began to teach at colleges and universities that our own careers came to be regarded positively. My older male cousins, who were in their early teens when we arrived, became farmers. Among the members of our group who were under the age of ten when we arrived, however, several did go to college.

After us, many other families, Jewish or of Jewish origin, came from Czechoslovakia, and we knew most of them. Some few belonged to non-farming categories of immigrants, namely, so-called capitalists or introducers of needed industries, and a few, friends or wives of Jewish refugees, were not Jewish. Some, being predominantly Czech-speaking, are outside the range of this discussion.

The refugees on the farms lived very frugally. We received some help from local Jews, all of Eastern European origin and much more religiously observant than we were. But we surely did not receive as much help as we would have had we not been strongly urged by the anti-Semitic Canadian authorities not to contact any Jewish organizations. Our not knowing Yiddish and not eating kosher put a barrier between us and the Canadian Jews.

The new life was much more of a change for the women than for the men. The men had always worked for a living, although not with their hands, but the women, with very few exceptions, had never had jobs and, if so, only before marriage. With very few exceptions, they adjusted amazingly well.

In most cases it meant, for the first time, keeping house without maids, and cooking and doing laundry for the hired men as well. Many of the farms had no bathrooms, only outhouses. Some of the women raised chickens and sold eggs and homemade cottage cheese from door to door or at the weekly market in Hamilton, often hitchhiking into town. What problems there were, were mostly connected with two women sharing one household. Essentially, however, things went surprisingly well.

As I found out during the long Canadian summer vacations, it was difficult for those of us not needed in the household to get jobs. Canada still suffered from the tail end of the Depression. Also, for example, I was overqualified for a position at Bell Telephone, and for some sales jobs I had too much of a foreign accent. During the second summer, I worked in two factories in succession, and for a month, together with another of the "Czechopeople," milked thirty cows, cultivated corn and other crops, while my sister was in charge of the henhouse.

I remember two of our women who worked as salespeople at Kresge's. One of them, the very spoiled wife of a Pilsen doctor, whose apartment had been furnished by Adolf Loos, sold buttons.[5] An extreme example was a member of one of the richest families in Czechoslovakia who became a baby nurse before emigrating in her late sixties and then worked very successfully in that profession in Canada. When my mother commented to her on her adjustment to her new life, she just answered, "Ich danke Gott fürs Gehabte" (I thank God for my past fortune).

Among the German-speaking women, I recall only one tragic story. An aunt from Prague, who had suffered from depression before, committed suicide on the farm.

Much of what I have to say, of course, is true of the men in the same way as of the women. For the most part, the refugees continued to associate among themselves, even later when many moved to Hamilton and Toronto. On the farm, they associated with the surrounding farmers. With

5   Adolf Loos (1870–1933) was an Austrian architect and a pioneer of modern architecture.

the exception of the refreshments they served, their social gatherings were similar to those of the Canadian farmers. Besides, there were a few Canadian Jews who befriended us. We found their religiosity as remarkable as I did that of the Baptists at McMaster. And this leads me to the complex topic of how people handled their Jewishness.

With the exception of the Polish Jewish rabbi of our community in Czechoslovakia and his wife, who followed us to Canada, we were what might be called lukewarm Jews, more so than the Jews from Germany I have come to know since then. Our family can stand for the average in going to synagogue on the High Holy Days and on the anniversaries of the deaths of parents. But instead of Hanukkah, we celebrated Christmas, and instead of Passover, Easter. Within our large repertory of jokes, those about the Polish (that is, the Orthodox Jews) played a prominent part.

Against this background, I think it is plausible that many of our people decided to present themselves as gentiles or even to formally convert to a Christian religion, or at least to avoid saying what they were. This was less problematic for those who spoke Czech, who could call themselves Czech, than with the German-speaking refugees who at that time didn't want to identify themselves as Germans, either.

Various additional factors affected this situation. On the one hand, social life in Canada was largely centered around churches and synagogues; on the other hand, we fitted in neither with the Protestants nor with the Eastern European Jews. And in those days when every penny counted, the membership fees in the synagogues were a problem. As one of our women wrote to the Reform synagogue in Hamilton, after receiving a hefty bill for membership, "I can join the United Church for free."

However, as the refugees became more prosperous – and they all did in varying degrees – many became active members of synagogues. With many who earlier had not wanted to be known as Jews, the desire to be part of the group became dominant, and they joined the rest of the crowd in synagogue on special occasions. In the lives of those of the oldest generation still living, synagogue plays much more of a role than it did in Europe.

Many people of my generation married other refugees from the Czech lands, Germany, or Austria. Some married Canadian or American Jews and gentiles. Intermarriages became more frequent in the next generation – with Canadian and European gentiles and with Jews of Eastern European origin.

Again, if I dare to generalize from a very small sample, the direction of the husband's religious orientation generally prevailed over the wife's in our children's generation. I recall the daughter of an originally Jewish, formally Catholic, refugee couple, who married a Catholic and became part of his community. The daughter of our rabbi married an ultra-Orthodox man and became part of that community. One young woman married an Episcopalian and became one herself, that is, she followed her husband's religion. On the other hand, several Canadian gentile women who married sons of Jewish refugees converted to Judaism and became members of synagogues, in several cases very active ones.

In this connection I want to insert a footnote that goes beyond the scope of this report: The same trends are observable as in North America generally. In the generation of our children, people either moved even further away from Judaism or became more observant, even in the cases of Jews married to gentile women who were converts to Judaism.

But let us return to the early years: In the early 1940s my parents moved to Brantford, a town southwest of Hamilton, where my father managed a farm. Brantford had a small, friendly Jewish community into which my parents became fairly well integrated. My mother even became an active member of Hadassah, the existence of which she had never known in Europe.[6] She also became very friendly with the gentile upper crust of Brantford – wives of industrialists, an architect, and what we called *ein Privat Gelehrter* (a scholar without professional affiliation). In addition, she had a third circle, the refugees who came to visit on weekends. She kept a detailed diary with entries such as, "14 zum Mittagessen" (14 for lunch) and "22 zum Kaffee" (22 for coffee). I know of no other refugees who were members of three comparable groups.

In various ways, the women transferred their European lifestyles to Canada. Now without maids, they did their own European-style baking. Especially on weekends, it would have been very embarrassing to be found by drop-in visitors – phoning was very expensive – without having anything home-baked to offer them. Mother even tried to do some baking for sale, but the Canadians were not ready to pay for pastries with such expensive ingredients and were shocked by cakes that contained rum.

For the most part, the immigrants continued to cook as they always had. Vegetables boiled and pulled out of the water were labeled "kanadisch" and were totally out of the question. We were also long recognizable by our European clothes, not only because we could not afford new ones, but also because – well, our word for "in bad taste" was "kanadisch." Again, this has changed greatly in the course of more than five decades. And it is both the refugees and Ontario, most of all Toronto, that have evolved.

6 An international women's Zionist organization, Hadassah was founded in the early twentieth century in the United States. In Israel it sponsors medical training, research, and care, and in the diaspora it raises funds and sponsors Jewish educational activities.

The women of my mother's generation also continued to save up European trousseaus, especially of household linens, for their daughters.

The story of our group is definitely a success story. They are well integrated economically and socially, for the most part to their satisfaction, although they are not indistinguishable from Canadians. The group, organized by women, which still meets annually for a picnic near Hamilton, has been getting smaller in recent years, but gradually grandchildren and even great-grandchildren of the original immigrants have begun to take over.

Many threads of continuity can be traced. In some cases the grandchildren are now farming, and some are in farm-related professions and stand out far above the average Ontario farmers. An aunt of mine, who died a few years ago in her eighties, typifies both the continuity and the change: She, who while in Europe had taken exotic trips, even to Africa, stayed on the farm. Although well enough off to spend part of her winters in Florida, she continued to feed the calves until the end, and to make her European pastries and to play the harmonica as she had in her young days in Czechoslovakia.

As for the cultural orientation of the women, I would say that the oldest, now close to ninety or over, are essentially still what they were when they came: assimilated Central European Jews, still not entirely trusting the Germans, with very few ties to the Czechs in Czechoslovakia, and still not feeling one with the Canadian Jews of Eastern European descent. The latter is what my aunt meant when she was asked about going to a Jewish retirement home in Canada and replied, "Die sind mir zu jüdisch" (They're too Jewish for me). The younger women are, of course, more assimilated to Canada, although they also still associate largely with people of our background. One who immigrated at the age of three is now, fifty-three years later, together with several Canadian women, involved in an innovative enterprise that aims to educate school children about farming. Several are active in ORT, an organization that provides technical training for people in Israel.[7] Referred to as "the Czechs," they have the reputation of being more dependable than "the Canadians" and "the Israelis." The generation after them is probably very much like most Canadians, their interest in Czechoslovakia and their Jewishness being determined by whether life led them to a Jewish or gentile, European or Canadian marriage partner.

The older generation still speaks German among themselves, mine speaks

---

7   ORT (from the Russian, *Obshchestvo Rasprostraneniya Truda sredi Yevreyev*), a society for manual and agricultural work among Jews, was founded in Russia in 1880. After World War II, ORT trained Jewish manual laborers for immigration to Palestine.

predominantly English, and in the generation of our children, with the exception of our own, they hardly speak German anymore.

In many ways, I was reminded of our people when I read Marion Berghahn's book about the refugees in Britain,[8] but there are differences: Our people rejected Germanness to a much lesser extent, hardly having thought of ourselves as Germans before, and we were also much less Jewish religiously. Thus, German refugees in Britain, being for the most part less rural and more observant Jews, would not likely have been caught by incredulous Jewish-Canadian visitors cooking pigs' heads and tails in a big kettle, as members of our group were.

A final question that might be helpful to ask is which country outside of the North American continent they visit. The answer might not be easy to guess: Those of the older generation who traveled at all went to Israel, although in their young days they made fun of Zionism. Those of my generation and younger still mostly visited Israel or more rarely went to places that tourists visit, such as Switzerland. Interestingly, there is little nostalgia for Czechoslovakia. I am definitely the exception, although some went there once or twice, and then mostly focused on the inevitably negative impressions.

I think the successful adjustment of the "Czechopeople" to Canada has a lot to do with their previous history of adaptations, with their special sense of humor with which they put up with the unexpected, but mainly with their expectations. Most of us had almost no idea what to expect in Canada, and in comparison with those we left behind, we felt very, very lucky. I am thinking, by way of contrast, of the people in the German Democratic Republic, who became part of united Germany with expectations supplied by television images of unlimited goods and worldwide travel. For our present purposes, it would not be relevant to speculate if anybody intentionally misled the East Germans, or to contemplate how large-scale unemployment could have been avoided. What I have in mind are the indignant outcries of those who, at the age of forty or fifty, are expected to retrain. Most of them had thought little about what their rules would be. Therefore, having actively to try anything new, outside of accustomed grooves, came as a shock to them. Among us, by contrast, there was remarkably little talk of hardships. Some of us who are becoming the old folks still indulge in reminiscing about paradise lost, but as the number of those born in Canada continues to outgrow the number of surviving immigrants, they are merging more and more into the quilt of Anglo-Canada.

8   Marion Berghahn, *German–Jewish Refugees in England: The Ambiguities of Assimilation* (London, 1984).

8

Women in the Shanghai
Jewish Refugee Community

DAVID KRANZLER

To Shanghai! But you've only three more months to wait before your visa from America comes through. Why go to the Orient? . . . almost took my life last week. Only this news, that one can get easily to Shanghai, kept me from doing it.[1]

During the late 1930s and 1940s, Shanghai became a haven for almost 17,000 German and Austrian as well as some 1,000 Polish–Jewish refugees. The combined total exceeded the number of refugees from the three countries accepted by the British Commonwealth nations of Canada, Australia, New Zealand, South Africa, and India. Of the Central European refugees, women made up about 40 percent of the Germans and less than 10 percent of the Poles. In this chapter, I focus on the Jewish women who underwent this experience.[2]

Women first played a special role in the exodus from Nazism in the aftermath of *Kristallnacht* (November 9–10, 1938), which set off the panic flight of most German Jews. Because only men – approximately 20,000 – were arrested and placed in concentration camps, women became responsible for obtaining a visa to any country willing to accept them and the men. In this way, they could obtain the release of their husbands, fathers, and brothers. But in those days it was very difficult to get a visa. At the Evian Conference of July 1938, the United States resolved to maintain narrow quotas. This act was aped by virtually every other nation. Consequently, these women trudged from one consulate to the next, often in

---

1 Helen Hilsenrad, *Brown Was the Danube* (New York, 1966), 321–2. Cited in David Kranzler, *Japanese, Nazis, and Jews: The Jewish Refugee Community of Shanghai, 1938–1945* (New York, 1976), 25.

2 For the statistics of the refugee population, see Kranzler, 21, 605. For the statistics of immigration to the Caribbean area, see Robert M. Levine, "Rescue in the Circum-Caribbean: Mixed Patterns of Response," a paper read at the Conference of the Latin American Jewish Association, University of Maryland, Oct. 6, 1991.

vain, until they discovered the way to Shanghai. This route was first used by Austrian Jews in August 1938.[3]

Until May 1939, no papers of any kind were required to enter the Japanese sector of the International Settlement in Shanghai. To get their husbands out of the camps, all that these women had to do, therefore, was to obtain ship tickets to Shanghai. Ironically, only luxury liners plied the waters to China and even these were hard to book. Of necessity, the women frequently sold their last pieces of jewelry or other valuables to purchase those expensive, life-saving tickets to East Asia. The reason Japan, which at the time was allied with Nazi Germany, had such a unique position toward Jewish refugees is a long and complicated saga and better told elsewhere.[4]

I

The Shanghai Jewish experience lasted approximately twelve years, which may be divided into five periods, each with its characteristic circumstances and varying effects on the subjects of this essay. The first period was one of painful adjustment. It started in August 1938, when the Sebastian Steiner family set foot in Shanghai, and it ended on December 7, 1941, with the Japanese attack on Pearl Harbor. Adjustment to a completely unfamiliar Asian city, with a depressed economy, a foreign culture and language, and different climate was difficult. The Sino-Japanese hostilities that started in 1937 did nothing to help the situation. Nevertheless, this first period was one of the better ones.[5]

By 1941 one could discern the following economic portrait of the refugees. Members of the most fortunate category, consisting of the 1,000 to 1,500 refugees who became successful businessmen or highly paid professionals, were able to find a niche in Shanghai's economy. They frequently lived in the elegant French Concession, where their apartments had hot and cold running well water and flush toilets. Many of them got started in business with the help of friends and relatives in the United States. A typical example, though on a minor scale, is that of one refugee who opened a thriving secondhand shop selling used clothes and china sent by American relatives. Another refugee purchased one of the typical Hongkew houses

3 For the best general description of *Kristallnacht,* see Rita Thalmann and Emanuel Feuerman, *Crystal Night: 9–10 November 1938* (London, 1974). For the special role of women following this mass pogrom, see taped interviews by this author of Illo Heppner and Elizabeth Van Dyke.
4 See Kranzler, esp. chap. 6.
5 For Sebastian Steiner's family, see Kranzler, 90. The period until Pearl Harbor is covered in chapters 1 to 16.

for the large sum of $200 sent by friends in the United States, which he subdivided and rented out to fellow refugees.[6]

Not quite as economically successful as the first, the next category of about 2,500 refugees rented their own apartments. These consisted of one, or at best, two small rooms, often no more than partitioned sections of formerly larger rooms. About 5,000 to 6,000 lower-salaried employees or small businessmen were still independent enough to live in rented rooms, but they had to obtain their food at one of those hastily built, makeshift refugee camps, ironically called *Heime* (homes). These were established by local relief organizations and financed primarily by the American Jewish Joint Distribution Committee, better known as the Joint. The remaining poorest 2,500 or so of the Jewish refugees were totally dependent on the *Heime* for their food and shelter.[7]

These lines of classification were not hard and fast; people shifted from one category to the next, according to the period and circumstances. Even those totally dependent on relief always had the hope of somehow overcoming their present predicament and moving out. Indeed, for many their dreams came true, but when their situation deteriorated or they were forced to relocate to the ghetto (as is discussed later), they were forced to return. What kept them going was an assumption that their stay in Shanghai was temporary. The United States was the favorite, hoped-for destination – an objective actually achieved before Pearl Harbor by only a handful of refugees.[8]

The second period begins with the opening of the war in the Pacific on December 8, 1941, and concludes with the proclamation of the German-inspired ghetto in Shanghai on February 18, 1943. This era is characterized by a reduced economic base caused by the severing of communications between Shanghai and the United States, as well as the further loss of aid that resulted from the internment of the leaders of the small, wealthy Sephardi community, who were mostly British citizens.[9]

The third and most depressing, trying period was that of the ghetto, from February (or May) 18, 1943, until August 14 (or September 2), 1945, and the end of the war. By forcing the refugees to undergo still another relocation, this time into a small, very dirty and crowded area of Hongkew, and virtually restricting their movement, it dealt the refugees a series of blows, both psychological and economic. Their worst fears were realized,

---

6 Kranzler, chap. 9, esp. 287–93.
7 Ibid.
8 For the *Heime,* see chap. 5.
9 For Pearl Harbor and its aftermath, see Kranzler, chap. 16.

and in their ears rang the warning of a Nazi official, "Never underestimate the long arm of the Gestapo."[10] During this period, most refugees had to sell many of their personal belongings to buy food or to supplement the now very meager allotments dispensed in the *Heime*.[11]

The fourth and best era for the refugees began with the close of the war in the Pacific and the arrival of the U.S. armed forces in September 1945. This era lasted until the 1949 takeover by the Communists. It heralded freedom, restoration of communications with the United States government, businesses, and armed forces, and most important, opened up opportunities for emigration. For those who were unable to find a home in Europe or North America, the establishment of Israel in 1948 was especially crucial. An Israeli Embassy was immediately opened in Shanghai and accepted applications for immigration from all Jews.[12]

The final phase, from 1949 until the early 1950s, took place under Communist rule when the small number of refugees remaining, as well as Sephardic and Russian Jews, slowly made their way out of a tightly ruled, despotic regime that permitted neither livelihood nor exit. It concluded in 1955 with the release by Chou En-lai of all those desiring to leave. The tiny remnant of mostly old people who remained was quietly taken care of by the American Jewish Joint Distribution Committee.[13]

II

Living in Shanghai meant adjusting to a radically different environment, including climate, sanitary and health conditions, culture, and a shrinking economy. For the mostly middle-class and middle-aged refugees, this was quite painful. Most traumatic was the fact that they were thrown out of their highly civilized Germany or Austria, where their families had lived for centuries and had found a comfortable, even prestigious niche, into a totally unfamiliar environment 8,000 miles away, where they were unknown and dependent upon relief for their bare existence. Their former world was now shattered, and their faith in their *Vaterland* was in shambles.[14]

Typical of their incongruous situation is the picture of a long queue of

10   Kranzler, chaps. 17–20, esp. 477.
11   Kranzler, 544–5.
12   Kranzler, 579–82.
13   See interview of Joseph Abraham. His brother Ezekiel Abraham, who was a leader of the Jewish community in Shanghai until 1953, and then in Hong Kong, was the one who contacted David S. Marshall, chief minister of Singapore and fellow Sephardi. Marshall negotiated with Chou En-lai for the release of the last few thousand Jewish and non-Jewish white population from Shanghai.
14   Kranzler, chap. 10.

refugees, still dressed in their good clothes, women in the latest fashions, even in fur coats, waiting with tin cups and plates in hand for their ration of food at the *Heime*.[15] One former resident remembered how her mother and her friends would gather together around a single light bulb, knitting sweaters and dresses for sale in some shops – earning a little money in order to buy margarine for their bread. It also buoyed their spirits, and whereas their husbands wandered about aimlessly, it helped the women make most of the family decisions.[16] Such a situation crushed many a man's spirit. No wonder that some thirty-six refugees, mostly men, committed suicide; it was the women who withstood the traumatic events far better than the men. It was also the women who had to bear the brunt of the added tensions resulting from such circumstances.[17]

Even the more resilient refugees were ill prepared for the semitropical climate of Shanghai, with its humidity, mildew, and torrential rains, and the concomitant diseases, especially forms of dysentery rarely found in the temperate climate of Central Europe. It took a while before the refugees became immune to the milder forms of the diseases and the doctors learned how to treat them. Although the relief committee soon established a refugee hospital, the dearth of medicines and proper food, especially during the leaner years in the ghetto, made the healing process slow and often futile.[18]

III

The climatic implications for the refugee women were harsh and numerous in many aspects. For example, it was a homemaker's nightmare. All fruits and vegetables, as well as drinking water, had to be boiled. Drinking water had to be bought from vendors. Hands had to be constantly washed for fear of contamination, and people were afraid to pick up anything from the floor, at least until they settled down somewhat and became immune to some of the minor diseases that had hit them at first. Shopping was a chore. Not only was there the problem of language in dealing with Chinese vendors (at least until a pidgin English–German made simple dialogue possible), but there were so many new, strange fruits and vegetables to which one had to get accustomed.[19]

15 Kranzler, 134.
16 Interview with Van Dyke.
17 Kranzler, 607. Also interviews with Heppner and Van Dyke. It was natural that since men in Central European societies of the 1920s and 1930s held virtually all the prominent positions, they would be more likely to lose the self-esteem and dignity concomitant with the loss of their jobs. This feeling was exacerbated for those who experienced the concentration camps after *Kristallnacht*.
18 Kranzler, chap. 10.
19 Interviews with Heppner, Van Dyke, and Rachel Hellman.

Except for the fortunate few, the process of cooking was an exercise in frustration. It was usually done on a Japanese hibachi stove. Charcoal briquettes, made up of a combination of coal dust, cinders, ashes, wet straw, and sand made both starting as well as maintaining a fire a tedious process. Because of the heavy smoke the hibachi emitted, most cooking took place outside the home, usually in the lanes, the common back alleys. More than once did women black out inhaling such smoke when cooking indoors during inclement weather.[20]

The lack of habitual comforts, such as flush toilets and hot, running water, which were reserved for the lucky few, made personal hygiene a major hurdle. One young Shanghailander recalled the unique wedding gift presented to her by her father: a tub of hot water for a delicious longed-for bath. The heated water was purchased from a vendor and poured into the tub. This bride was almost late for the ceremony, having luxuriated a little too long in this dream come true.[21]

The scourge of parasitic worms transformed the simple matter of eating bread, rice, cereal, or cheese into a most distasteful and time-consuming chore. Bread had to be sliced almost paper thin and held up to the light to detect and eliminate the ubiquitous worms. Likewise, rice was spread out on a flat surface, and cheese and flour were checked carefully. Bedbugs were constant nocturnal companions and a distinct nuisance, especially in the *Heime,* where the beds were inevitably infested. It became most difficult to decide whether or not to keep the covers on during the hot nights. If one uncovered one's self, the mosquitoes would prevail, and if one was covered, the bedbugs made life miserable.[22]

One young woman recalled how she and her friends spent one night in the *Heim,* where she lived with fifteen girls in a room, tackling this problem. First, they stayed up as late as possible, talking in the garden, which was created by one of the more resourceful refugees. Just when they felt ready to fall asleep, they would rush up to their room and jump under the covers, hoping to outwit the bedbugs by falling asleep instantly. When it was impossible to sleep, they would take the beds apart, separating upper and lower bunks, take them downstairs, and burn out the nests – an extremely unpleasant nighttime activity.[23]

In addition, checking and hand-picking lice from the head, especially for mothers, became a permanent feature of life. Adding to life's difficulties

---

20   Ibid.
21   Interview with Heppner.
22   Interview with Heppner, Van Dyke, and Hellman.
23   Interview with Hellman.

was the vile odor emanating from the "night soil," a euphemism for the contents of the wooden bucket that served as the toilet. The odor permeated the air of the small one-room apartments. Every morning, a Chinese servant would collect and empty these buckets' contents into his cart. He then sold the night soil as fertilizer.[24]

More than 400 children were born in the Shanghai community, and their care was particularly difficult.[25] Under these circumstances, it is difficult for a contemporary American to visualize having to wash a dozen dirty diapers a day in cold water – that is, even if you had the diapers. One usually made them out of old rags. It is true that those who were better off had Chinese amahs (maids) to do this work, but most refugees could not afford even the very low wages the amahs earned. Most problems, though, were a lot worse than washing diapers. For example, one woman recalled how her neighbor's newly born infant got frostbitten while sleeping in his parents' unheated room. Milk for the baby was generally not available – for the Chinese, drinking milk is barbaric – so one used soybean milk as a substitute. Few could afford to buy baby clothes. One borrowed, sewed, and adjusted what was available from friends and neighbors.[26]

Of course, the constant fear of contamination and unknown diseases was a very serious concern for every wife and mother. Under the circumstances, numerous successful attempts were made to alleviate trying conditions. The refugee hospital supplied 12,000 vaccinations per year, which helped what was a difficult situation. Nevertheless, a dearth of many of the necessary medicines, especially during the lean years, resulted in quite a few unnecessary deaths from various diseases.[27]

IV

As a result of being cut off from its economic relations with the great Yangtze River hinterlands following the Sino-Japanese hostilities of 1937, Shanghai's economy stagnated. This meant that business opportunities were scarce and jobs were difficult to find. Most middle-aged refugees were severely disadvantaged, being unable to apply their skills, talents, or experience to Shanghai's economy or civil service. Their wives and teenage daughters had far greater opportunities to find employment in clerical or sales positions. Before Pearl Harbor, some women, especially the younger

24 Kranzler, 120–1.
25 Kranzler, 606.
26 Interviews with Heppner, Van Dyke, and Hellman. Also, see Kranzler, chap. 10.
27 Ibid.

ones, found jobs as nurses or nannies to members of the resident foreign population. Most of them were treated as mere domestic servants, but at least they supplemented their families incomes with some decent food as well as money.[28]

The most envied young woman was one who had found a position as nanny for the family of an American diplomat. They treated her as one of their own – to the point of providing tennis lessons for her along with their children. Some of the women, especially older ones, worked as seamstresses or did sewing at home. Younger women found positions as waitresses or even bar girls, with all of the latter job's implications. Few of these jobs paid well, but the extra money, as we have seen, helped supplement the meager food allotments of the *Heime* or brought home from them.[29]

Although only seven women were registered as official prostitutes, to earn extra money many desperate women and girls plied this oldest profession or entered into a liaison with an unattached male. The fact that there were 3,000 more males than females in the community further encouraged this situation. Frequently, these liaisons took place with the consent of the women's husband or parents. About twenty mothers were desperate enough to raise their standard of living that they willingly sold their newly born babies.[30] One refugee recalled a scene early in the morning in the *Heim* when a couple's daughter returned from her stint as a "lady of the evening." Her parents argued with her about the amount she took in from her night's occupation.[31] Upon their arrival in the States, most of these women, who had resorted to selling themselves out of sheer desperation, reverted to normal middle-class status.[32] During the good times of the post-war stationing of American armed forces in Shanghai, hundreds of women found good jobs with high salaries paid in American dollars, while others earned even more by providing sexual favors for the servicemen. A few young women fell in love with and married American soldiers.[33]

V

Still, to obtain a proper perspective on the Shanghai experience, one should bear in mind that even during the worst ghetto period, it hardly resembled even the early phases of the ghettos created by the Germans in Eastern

28 Kranzler, 281–5. See also interviews with Heppner, Van Dyke, and Hellman.
29 Interview with Van Dyke.
30 Interview with Heppner.
31 Interview with Van Dyke.
32 Ibid.
33 Interviews with Van Dyke and Heppner.

Europe between 1939 and 1941. There was never any random shooting or a systematic policy of starvation carried out by the Japanese authorities. If one did not have to obtain a pass from the mercurial Ghoya or Okura, the authorities did not disturb him or her. The Japanese even permitted the transfer of American relief money for the refugees long before the American government gave its approval to send money to enemy-occupied territory in December 1943.[34]

Even considering the difficult conditions and real hunger for many in Shanghai, especially in the ghetto, the statistics for the total number of fatalities of about 1,500 for a population of 17,000 amounted to thirteen per 1,000. Of course, some years were worse than others. The refugee population, which was primarily middle-aged and older, compared favorably with 1974 Germany's ratio of 11.8 and Austria's 12.6 per 1,000. The point here is not to underrate the hardships sustained by the refugees; rather, it is to pay tribute to the relief in food, medicine, and care provided by the local and American relief organizations, the refugee doctors and nurses, and especially the ingenuity of the refugees themselves.[35]

In sum, throughout the trying period of the Shanghai experience, women in the Jewish expatriate community proved themselves to be strong. They not only shouldered their normal responsibilities under much more difficult circumstances but frequently endured the added burdens usually shared by the husband and father. It was the father who, much more so than the mother, lost his self-assurance and self-esteem, as well as much of his former authority. An incident recalled by one refugee about her mother is illustrative. In Germany, while living a comfortable middle-class existence, she suffered from ulcers. Yet, in Shanghai, under laborious conditions, where she became the breadwinner and had to make most decisions, her ulcers disappeared.[36] In short, we find that the decade or more of the Shanghai Jewish experience, beginning with *Kristallnacht,* created a major change in the secondary role of the German–Jewish wife and mother of the old Central European patriarchal society (in which the husband–father figure was that of authority, prestige, obedience, and honor) to that of the primary figure. In other words, the Shanghai Jewish refugees slowly changed from a wholly patriarchal society to one in which many women in Shanghai achieved a much more independent, if not quite a matriarchal, role.

34 For the period of the ghetto, see Kranzler, chap. 19. For communications with the unoccupied world, see 558–62.
35 Kranzler, 303.
36 Interview with Van Dyke.

9

Shanghai

An Eyewitness Report

ILLO L. HEPPNER

Born in Berlin in 1923, Illo L. Heppner fled with her parents to Shanghai, China, in 1940. Interned by the Japanese occupation forces in 1943 and liberated by American troops in 1945, she worked as a United States War Department civilian for the Shanghai Port Command and the United States Military Advisory Group to Chiang Kai-shek's government in Nanking. She emigrated to the United States in 1947, settled in Indianapolis in 1954, and worked in the real estate department of a major insurance company for twenty-six years. Since her retirement in 1984, Heppner has focused her volunteer activities on helping Russian immigrants to settle, learn English, and acculturate to life in the United States. She is married and has a daughter and three grandchildren. This report was written in 1991.

The subtitle of this book, "Women Refugees of the Nazi Period," has a special meaning for me: I was sixteen years old when I emigrated to Shanghai and a married woman when I left.[1] The Shanghai years were the years during which I was transformed from a teenage girl into a woman.

First, I will give a brief personal background. I was born in Berlin into a thoroughly assimilated family. My father was managing director of a bank, a decorated disabled veteran of World War I, and active in Jewish causes. His family had lived in the same house in Halberstadt since the 1690s.

After my father escaped the roundup of Jews the night of November 9, 1938,[2] he decided not to wait for our American quota number to be called[3]

---

1 Shanghai, a port in the Kiangsu province of eastern China, attracted refugees because no visa was necessary for entry into its International Settlement. See David Kranzler, *Japanese, Nazis, and Jews: The Jewish Refugee Community of Shanghai, 1938–1945* (New York, 1976), 42; and Ernest G. Heppner, *Shanghai Refuge. A Memoir of the World War II Ghetto* (Lincoln, Neb., 1993), 38.

2 On the night of November 9, 1938, the Nazis staged a "spontaneous" pogrom, in which Jewish property was destroyed, synagogues were burnt, and Jews were beaten and arrested. The pretext for the mass violence was the protest shooting of a German official by Herschel Grynszpan, whose parents had been rounded up and expelled to Poland along with 12,000 other Polish Jews living in Germany.

3 In 1921 the United States passed the Quota Act, which limited the number of people permitted to immigrate from a given country in a given year. The combined annual quota for Germany and Austria was 27,370.

but to go to Shanghai temporarily; my mother and I, an only child, would stay in Berlin and meet him later in the United States.

He left in March 1939. On my sixteenth birthday, Germany invaded Poland and we decided not to stay any longer.[4] Since steamship traffic had ceased, the only route to Shanghai was by train via Siberia. We finally were able to leave in May 1940, leaving behind my grandmother, who later died in Theresienstadt.[5]

My Shanghai experience before the ghetto differed substantially from that of those refugees who were taken in cattle trucks to camps and settled in Hongkew.[6] My father met us at the wharf and took us to a furnished apartment he had rented in the International Settlement.[7] We were not dependent on the aid of any committee, for my father had been able to transfer some funds out of Germany before emigration and had started an accounting and tax advisory service. The apartment was small – one room with a tiny sleeping porch, which became my room, a kitchenette and a bath with hot running water, and best of all in the damp and cold winters to come, steam heat. The European type of building was occupied mainly by families of the United States Fourth Marines, then stationed in Shanghai, so I had an opportunity to meet other teenagers and practice American English.

While I was adjusting, my mother had a very difficult time. At forty years of age, she was transplanted from comfortable, familiar surroundings into a foreign environment, separated from her mother, sister, and friends and, although fluent in French, unable to speak more than a few words of English. The apartment came with the part-time services of an amah, a Chinese maid, who would do some of the shopping at the Chinese market for a commission from the merchants. My mother would not leave the apartment by herself and quickly our roles were reversed; it was I who took her shopping and showed her the exciting and fascinating sights of that cosmopolitan city. She would not attempt to socialize with our neighbors. In retrospect I realize that she was severely depressed. And with good reason: Housekeeping and cooking were an enormous challenge. Water had to be boiled even for brushing teeth; fresh milk was not available; vegetables and

---

4 September 1, 1939.
5 Theresienstadt (Terezín), a ghetto established in 1941 in Czechoslovakia, was promoted by the Nazis as a model settlement for Jews. In fact, of the 150,000 Jews who were sent there, thirty-three thousand died of disease as a result of the squalid conditions. Thousands of others were sent to the camps in the east.
6 Hongkew was the Japanese-controlled portion of Shanghai's International Settlement. The majority of the refugees settled in this partially destroyed quarter, where housing was relatively inexpensive. See Heppner, 39.
7 The International Settlement was a part of Shanghai that did not fall under Chinese control. It was governed by a municipal council. See Heppner, 38.

fruits differed from European ones and had to be cooked. Even watermelons were not safe because vendors frequently injected river water into them to make them heavier. The heat in that tiny apartment that first summer was oppressive, with outside temperatures often around 100 degrees and close to 95 percent humidity. Although we had a small electric fan, it didn't help much. We were constantly wet with perspiration. At night, sleeping under mosquito nets, the air was stifling, and the bed sheets were soaking wet a few minutes after lying down. If we did away with the net, the insects would get us immediately and giant flying cockroaches would use us for a landing strip. But the worst was the bedbugs. Although an exterminator came regularly, there was no escape from them. My mother would turn on the light a couple of times each night and, as she termed it, "go hunting," picking them out of the beds one by one. It was as useless as the ineffective spray. Another challenge was finding a job, which wasn't easy for someone my age. Some of the refugee girls worked as nannies to children in the foreign community. Although some were treated like servants, one of my friends worked for an American diplomat's family and was treated like an older daughter. Although her own parents lived in squalor in Hongkew, her life revolved around tennis, riding, and the country club. But being a nanny was not for me. My father had a client who had opened a rare books and art store in the French part of the city. He needed someone to do the office work and help with sales, and that was just the environment I loved. He offered to tutor me in literature and art history and pay a small salary as well. The store occupied half of a Chinese art and curio gallery and its Chinese owner introduced me to the beauties of Chinese art. The noted German writer and art critic Lothar Brieger was a daily visitor to the store.[8] Whenever he lectured at St. John's University, I helped him with English and typed his lectures in my free time.[9] He always insisted on a thorough discussion of the subject, so while working, I also got a private tutoring in the liberal arts.

Meanwhile, I had joined a Jewish youth group and made friends with other Central European teenagers, met and fell in love with Ernest Heppner, the young man who was to become my husband, and managed to have a pretty good time. Things got better for my mother, too. She met other German-speaking refugee women, and my parents once again began to have an active, though very modest, social life. Money was always a problem

---

8 Lothar Brieger (1879–1949) was active in Shanghai's cultural life and was a regular contributor to the German-language refugee newspaper, *Shanghai Morgenpost*.

9 One of the two universities in Shanghai that accepted foreigners, St. John's University, was run by Christian missionaries.

– keeping up with both the office and the apartment rent and having enough left for food was a constant struggle for my father, who had by then depleted our funds. Yet, life settled down to a routine – until Pearl Harbor Day.[10] On the morning of December 8, I was awakened by the sound of explosions; the Japanese were sinking the British gunboat *Peterel* in the harbor. The captain of an American boat surrendered. The American marines and their families had left weeks before, and their apartments were being occupied by Japanese. For those refugees who were not dependent on the American Jewish Joint Distribution Committee (JDC)[11] funds sent from the United States, life, except for the ever-present Japanese military, went on pretty much as usual. But that didn't last. In February 1943 the Japanese issued the Ghetto Proclamation and we had to move to Hongkew.[12]

We managed to find an unfurnished room in a four-room row house. To buy the bare essentials of furniture, we had to sell some of our few belongings to the Chinese and Japanese, who were always ready to buy European goods. The room was roughly 10 feet square, with just enough space for two narrow daybeds on opposite sides, a small table in between, and two small chairs. One wall was occupied by our steamer trunk, a small chest of drawers, and a shelf that held a few dishes and kitchenware. On top of it stood a Chinese stove, a kind of hibachi,[13] which looked like a flower pot with a hole for what, euphemistically, was called charcoal. Actually, it was a mixture of coal dust and river mud that had to be fanned constantly to keep it burning. We did have a one-burner electric plate but not enough electricity to use it with any regularity. At night the table would be lifted on top of the trunk, which created just enough space for a folding cot on which I slept. In the morning, then, the cot would be exchanged for the table. The house had one immeasurable luxury, though – a bathroom shared by "only" eight people, which had not only a cold-water bathtub but also a real flush toilet. Most houses had so-called "honey buckets," which were used by as many as twenty people and emptied once a day by coolies.[14] The ghetto was ruled by a Japanese psychopath by the name of Ghoya, who declared himself "king of the Jews" and alternated

10 The Japanese surprise attack on the United States naval base in Hawaii, December 7, 1941.
11 The American Jewish Joint Distribution Committee (JDC) is a philanthropic organization founded in 1914 by American Jews to offer relief to Jews in wartime. During World War II, the JDC spent more than $78 million on relief and rescue.
12 The Ghetto Proclamation of February 18, 1943, which was issued by the Japanese occupation forces at the instigation of German authorities, required Central European Jews in Shanghai to live within a designated area. See Heppner, 111.
13 A cooking source in which food is exposed to the heat source through a metal grill.
14 Unskilled laborers who usually work for subsistence wages.

physical abuse with occasional favors.[15] I had to confront the "king," shaking in my shoes, when I needed a pass out of the ghetto to go to work. My father had to close his office and again faced the loss of all income. Still, he managed to work out of our room, keeping books for refugee enterprises, often in exchange for food or goods.

For me, the move into the ghetto was more an inconvenience than a disaster. I now lived close to my friends, and among them and my parents I felt secure. For my mother, however, the move was devastating. The lack of privacy, the physical closeness, the worries about where the next meager meal would come from, and the terrible heat caused constant tensions. Quarrels were usual in almost every family. One could always hear people screaming at one another. Living among the Chinese people in the crowded alleys, the constant noise was pervasive. My most vivid memory of these days, aside from always being hungry, is the total lack of silence. Even at night the chatter and the clanging of mah-jongg tiles never ceased.[16]

Summer turned into winter – damp and cold, with no heat at all. I never felt warm, not even in bed under our German down comforters on which we piled whatever would provide additional warmth. I had to give up my job. Standing in line, sometimes for two days, to request the pass out of the ghetto, and the long travel in two crowded buses each way, became too difficult. I kept busy doing some secretarial work for the Jewish Community Association[17] and giving English lessons in exchange for food. There were many opportunities to expand my knowledge: professionals in the arts and sciences were eager to teach us; music and theater groups performed; and there were lectures and discussion groups on many subjects.

In July 1944 my mother contracted bacillary dysentery.[18] There was no medication to be had. The doctors could only stand by helplessly. She died after three days, and my protected world came to a sudden end. She was buried, wrapped in a straw mat that did not quite cover her body, in a shallow grave where ground water could be seen.

So, overnight, I became a homemaker, not only having to deal with my grief and loss but also learning how to make meals from whatever was

15 Ghoya was the tyrannical and erratic ghetto administrator who, with his colleague, Okura, was responsible for issuing passes that enabled the Jews to leave the ghetto temporarily. See Heppner, 115.

16 Mah-jongg is a game of Chinese origin in which tiles are drawn and discarded until one player holds four sets of three tiles and a pair.

17 The Jewish Community Association, or *Jüdische Gemeinde,* was established in Shanghai in October 1938 to address religious, legal, and community issues.

18 An often epidemic intestinal disease, usually spread through contaminated food or water.

available, how to handle that miserable stove with the windows open, even in driving rain, so I would not be overcome by the poisonous fumes. Let me tell you how I cooked rice: First I took a pot and put in the rice. Then I went to the watershop down the street, purchased boiling water to be ladled into the pot, and went home. Then I put the pot on the stove and fanned the so-called coals for five minutes to bring the rice back to boil, and then took the pot off, wrapped it in blankets, and let it sit. The result: undercooked, but edible rice. Another housekeeping chore was washing clothes, and particularly sheets, in cold water with whatever substitute passed as soap.

Let me give you an example of health care: One day one of my recurrent throat infections developed into a serious case of abscessed tonsils, and I had to go into the refugee hospital. The chief surgeon, an old family friend, told me that he had no choice but to lance them. Anesthetic was too precious to be used for such a minor procedure; three nurses held my head and shoulders while the doctor pleaded, "Please try not to spit on me – this gown is sterile and still has to last all day." Then he cut out my tonsils, and I dutifully held the stuff in my mouth until a nurse could provide a pail.

For my father, the added stress of being left a widower at the age of forty-nine proved to be too much. He became overly critical, demanding, and always angry. And my life, along with that of many refugee women, changed to that of a victim.

My boyfriend could not bear to see me in that situation, and although we foresaw no future, we decided to marry. The only room we could find was one for a single person, and my father was persuaded to move there so Ernest could move in with me. Amidst all that misery we wanted our wedding to be special and beautiful. My mother had brought some white curtains from Berlin that didn't fit any windows. My mother-in-law's friend, a Viennese dress designer, made an exquisite wedding gown from them as her wedding present to me. I had my mother's veil, and Ernest wore his tuxedo one more time before he had to sell it. As a wedding gift, I asked my father to buy me enough hot water to take my first warm bath in years. The water was brought to the house by coolies, and I soaked in the tub until it was almost too late to leave for the makeshift synagogue. While we were standing under the *huppah* that beautiful April day in 1945, the air raid alarm sounded.[19] As usual, we were unconcerned because we were sure the Americans wouldn't target the ghetto, and the ceremony went on. Afterward, eighteen family members and close friends celebrated

19   The canopy under which the bride and groom stand in a Jewish wedding ceremony.

with tea and a cake that friends had baked with pooled ingredients. We got presents, too – people brought whatever they could spare: a jar of jam, a sausage, a dinner plate, a towel – but the present I appreciated most was a wet mop someone made from a bamboo pole and rags.

But now I found myself with a new problem: birth control. That was *the* major concern for married women. Not only was the survival rate of babies very low, but the odds of raising a healthy child were dismal under our living conditions. Looking back at the birth control options that were available to us, we were very lucky.

On July 17, 1945, American bombers did target the ghetto.[20] Our street received several hits. The roar of the departing planes was mixed with the screams of injured people lying in the alley. One house was on fire. Along with other women, I grabbed whatever I could and helped to bandage some of the injured and organize the children into a bucket brigade to get water to the men in their futile attempt to contain the fire. Our house escaped, but the roof was partially torn off. From then until the end of the war, we slept under open umbrellas whenever it rained. The bombing raids demolished Ernest's work place and now we had to join the food lines in the camps, lining up for a bowl of thin soup or a *kasha* concoction once a day.[21] The raids continued, the hunger got worse, and all hope for survival was vanishing fast when in early August we heard that an atom bomb had been dropped on Hiroshima and rumors were flying that the war might be over soon.[22] We didn't dare to hope, but one day we awoke to an almost eerie sight: The Japanese military had suddenly disappeared.[23] The war really was over! An American military detachment arrived, along with a representative of the JDC and supplies from the United Nations Relief and Rehabilitation Administration (UNRRA).[24] My weight was down to ninety-four pounds, and the army C-rations tasted like gourmet food. To this day, whenever I'm served fruit cocktail, I remember the time we opened our first tiny can and savored each morsel separately.

With the end of the war, the American forces established their head quarters in Shanghai and needed civilian employees for their operation. My knowledge of English shorthand and typing produced a plum position: secretary to the adjutant general of the Shanghai Port Command. My husband found work, too, and we were soon able to move out of the ghetto.

---

20 One of the targets of the American attack was a Japanese radio station in Hongkew.
21 A mush usually made from buckwheat groats.
22 August 6, 1945.
23 The ghetto was opened on August 30, 1945. On September 9, capitulation terms were signed for the estimated one million Japanese troops stationed in China.
24 Established in 1943, UNRRA offered relief to victims in countries under Nazi occupation.

Later we transferred to Nanking, where we worked as United States War Department civilians for the Joint United States Military Advisory Group to Chiang Kai-shek's government. Living with American service personnel gave us a foretaste of life in the United States, and for the first time since early childhood, we enjoyed some carefree months.

Finally, in June 1947, we received our papers and were able to leave China, together with my father and mother-in-law, for the United States and a second emigration. This one, however, was the beginning of a normal life, and we finally were able to establish a home and a family.

10

German–Jewish Women in Brazil: Autobiography as Cultural History

KATHERINE MORRIS

Many cultural historians are now taking a new look at the significance of gender in literature and history and at how extraordinary events affected ordinary people. The devastation of World War II that shaped transit, exile, Holocaust, and immigration changed the lives of all involved, but one cannot assume that these occurrences affected men and women in the same way. The cultural sphere for women has always been different from that of men, and this has always been true during the turning points of history. The unique way in which German–Jewish women recorded the major upheaval of the century adds perspective to our understanding of the era, specifically the South American exodus to Brazil.

Women's autobiographies describe and explore universal questions of exile and displacement. However, few studies have examined the methodology of such an undertaking. Autobiography as a primary source leads one to question the authenticity of "literature" as history. This is also a focus of the problem: Should autobiographies of this turbulent era be interpreted as literature, as history, or as both fact and fiction? How can one formulate a methodology for gender-based studies of exile and Holocaust memoirs? There is little precedent for a critical assessment of women's exile autobiography. Many critics tend to see autobiography as literature and are often uncomfortable discussing literature as history. More recent works such as Heinemann's *Gender and Destiny* and Young's *Writing and Rewriting the Holocaust* focus on the problems of interpretation regarding the Holocaust, but neither text focuses on exile.[1]

Feminist criticism has broadened our understanding of the definition of literature and canon and has added new depth to the study of women's literature and history. Because of progress made in the realm of feminist

---

1 Marlene E. Heinemann, *Gender and Destiny* (New York, 1986); James E. Young, *Writing and Rewriting the Holocaust* (Bloomington, Ind., 1988).

criticism, what was not considered literature in the traditional sense is being reclassified and reassessed.² This chapter reflects this interest in the study of gender in that it focuses on women's experiences of exile. It is a study of cultural history from a woman's point of view. The women of exile did not fight on the battlefield, nor did they establish new borders as politicians. I am examining history from the point of view of "ordinary" women who were not generals but citizens and victims. This chapter explores exile as seen through the eyes of several German–Jewish women who fled Nazi Germany in the 1930s and immigrated to Brazil.

The distinguishing characteristics of these autobiographies are the context of World War II and its aftermath, the political marginality of the German–Jewish women, and the genre of writing they use to express their experiences as women in Hitler's Third Reich.³ The various relationships of writer and narrator come into play as well. The following is a short discussion of the major focuses of my work: marginality, the plurality of genre, and the cultural aspect of autobiography.

German–Jewish women played a politically marginal role in Hitler's Third Reich in relation to the ruling class of the time. Not only were they far removed from any sort of power in society because of being Jewish but also because of being women. It is important to note how these women viewed themselves and whether or not they saw themselves as marginal. Irene Gruenbaum was well aware of her marginal status and mentioned it on her first page. "Hitler had decided the fate of millions of people, also my fate, because I am a Jew, a child of Jewish parents, and married to a Jew."⁴

The genre of these texts is the literary framework of a life story. Was this form an imitation of male autobiography? What did they consider a "normal" life or a "normal" story? These women's backgrounds were essentially the same in that all of them were literate members of the German–Jewish middle class when they wrote their texts and were fully aware of the autobiographical genre, although most did not refer to their work as autobiographies. All knew they had experienced the unusual because they were Jews in Hitler's Germany. Their writing allows them to make sense of past experiences and weave them into a coherent narrative. In this process, they organize, interpret, and give meaning to their lives.

The first example is the autobiography of Marthe Brill. She was born in

2 Shari Benstock, ed., *The Private Self: Theory and Practice of Women's Autobiographical Writings* (Chapel Hill, N.C., 1988); Sidonie Smith, *A Poetics of Women's Autobiography* (Bloomington, Ind., 1987); Carolyn G. Heilbrun, *Writing a Women's Life* (New York, 1988).
3 Personal Narratives Group, *Interpreting Women's Lives* (Bloomington, Ind., 1989).
4 Irene Gruenbaum, untitled manuscript, 1. Vienna, 1950. Institut des Österreichischen Widerstands.

1894 in Cologne and came from a family of intellectual women. Her mother, Bertha Leiser, was a writer and advocate for women's rights. Both of her parents were Jewish, but having lost her mother as a child, Marthe was not brought up in a religious way. Marthe Brill was a liberal-minded intellectual and interested in everything connected with Judaism, from history to mysticism. She received her Ph.D. in economics shortly before World War I, and during the war she worked for the Weltwirtschaftsinstitut (World Economic Institute) in Hamburg. Because literature and journalism were her main interests, she later wrote articles, short stories, and travel reports for newspapers and was a regular contributor to the *Hamburger Fremdenblatt*.

Der Schmelztiegel is the autobiographical novel in which Marthe Brill tells about her years of wandering, from 1933 to 1939. She relates the story of Sylvia and her daughter Miriam in the form of a *Schlüsselroman* (roman à clef). This form was fashionable at the time and gave Brill the freedom to describe people without having to expose their actual identity in case her book was published. By using this method, the author concentrates on the autobiography as a narrative as well as a historical work. Even though Marthe Brill's story is true, she writes it in the third person and safely distances herself from a tragic and difficult period of her life. Her text, *Der Schmelztiegel,* is organized chronologically, starting with her early life in Hamburg in 1933 and ending with her life in Brazil.

Her daughter, Alice Brill Czapski, is now living in São Paulo. She has also written an autobiographical memoir of her life entitled *Memories from 1933–1945*. In this memoir, she refers to the diary that she wrote at the age of twelve and quotes directly from it. Alice Brill is mentioned here because her autobiography represents two points of view: that of her present persona as a mature woman and that of the young Alice Brill who kept a diary. She also appears in her mother's autobiographical novel *Der Schmelztiegel* as Miriam, the daughter of the pseudonymous Sylvia. In effect, we have three different sources describing Marthe's life in transit and her early years in Brazil.

The story of Sylvia (*Der Schmelztiegel*) is the story of a German–Jewish refugee and the hardships she faces. She is secretary for the newly founded Relief Committee for Jewish Immigrants in São Paulo and describes much of her work there. It is her task to find shelter and jobs for those people who left Germany almost penniless. They are scared and cannot speak Portuguese. Few have practical professions. Being a refugee herself, Sylvia is sympathetic to the plight of these people and knows that they must adapt themselves to new conditions in order to survive.

Looking through the novel, one sees how Marthe Brill describes Sylvia's work for the Relief Committee. People would stream into her office in an endless procession looking for housing and work.

It was sad and comforting at the same time: sad, because the means of help were so shamefully limited. Sylvia soon learned that one can really only help those who are willing to help themselves and who are ready to do anything. . . . Sylvia learned, to her surprise, that women were the easiest to place; they found work in houses and offices, as maids, governesses, and stenographers. In this country, there were not yet many women who worked, and women were needed.[5]

In her autobiography, Alice Brill Czapski also mentions her mother's work. She tells of the problems her mother faced in trying to help refugees. Women seemed to be able to adjust to the difficulties of immigration more easily than men on both the emotional and practical levels. Alice says in her autobiography:

My mother tried her best to help them. Some were inventive and managed to survive, especially the women. Take Mrs. Reichmann, for example. She was the wife of a scholar and mother of a ten-year-old boy. She decided to start a boarding house, rented a nice home, and began to cook, clean up, and wash clothes for her clients. My mother was her first lodger. She was glad to have a room for the two of us and not to have to worry about meals.[6]

Marthe Brill and her daughter Alice contrast sharply with Erich Brill. Marthe married Erich Brill in 1920, the year Alice was born, and divorced him in 1922. He was an artist accustomed to the cosmopolitan atmosphere of Europe and arrived in São Paulo with his daughter in 1934. He stayed in Brazil for several months and made friends with other modern artists but could not get used to the new country. He was restless, unhappy, and politically unaware.

One day he announced he would be leaving for Germany in January 1936. Marthe Brill tried in vain to talk him out of it. She told him that returning refugees were incarcerated, but he didn't believe her. "The Germans are incapable of such behavior. It can't be true, they are a civilized people," he insisted. Nothing could change his mind. He simply said, "I trust my fate." Alice Brill states in her autobiography: "He never stopped to think of me. I felt revolted, I was fifteen at the time."[7]

When he arrived in Hamburg, no one noticed him at first. He enjoyed months of freedom, traveling in Germany and Europe and painting wherever he went. But his time ran out. Alice Brill states: "I think that it must

5   Marthe Brill, *Der Schmelztiegel,* 193. Institut für Zeitgeschichte, Munich.
6   Alice Brill Czapski, *Memories from 1933–1945,* manuscript, São Paulo, Brazil, 1991. Private collection.
7   Czapski, 11.

have finally dawned on him, for his last self-portrait, painted on New Year's Eve 1936/37, has a haunted feeling about it, reminding me of the picture of Dorian Gray."[8] Soon after, he was charged with *Rassenschande,* or race defilement, and imprisoned. He admitted that he had ignored the law and had an Aryan girlfriend. He spent a year in prison and then was sentenced to five years of forced labor.

It was 1946 when Alice learned of her father's fate. Her aunt received an answer to an ad published in *Aufbau,* confirming that after he was released from prison he was forced to join a transport to Riga, where he was interned in a concentration camp. According to a fellow prisoner who escaped, Erich Brill was executed with thousands of others on March 26, 1942.

In *Der Schmelztiegel,* Marthe Brill introduces Erich as the painter Erich Schönberg. She illustrates how National Socialism affected artists and thinkers even in Brazil. Erich was a young German Jew who brought trunks of his own canvases from Europe, unaware when he arrived in Rio de Janeiro that it would not be possible to support himself by painting modern art in South America.

His dream came true. On Avenida Rio Branco, in the center of that city of a million, he exhibited his pictures in the rooms of a German club. A group of National Socialists tried to break up his exhibition. He resisted them, and fought for his rights. "I am a German," he declared angrily. "I have shed blood for Germany; my pictures still hang in the most famous art galleries of Germany." He made his point. Openings, cocktail parties, glowing reviews, a nine-day wonder. . . . Not a single picture was sold. The Germans did not buy because he was a Jew, and the Jews did not visit his exhibition because it was in a German club. How could an artist live![9]

How these German–Jewish women acclimated to Brazil is also the focus of Mirjam Logat's text. She chose to describe her years of exile and immigration in the form of a short story, or *Erzählung,* entitled: *Ich bin ausgewandert.* Her narrative begins with the boycott against the Jews on April 1, 1933, and continues through to her emigration to Brazil and her life in São Paulo. She, like Marthe Brill, tells her tale in the third person. However, unlike many women who wrote autobiographies, she gives herself the pen name of Mirjam Logat. In reality she was Martha Glogauer. She immigrated to São Paulo in December 1933 with her husband and small daughter after her husband had been fired from a good position with A.E.G. He remained sick and unemployed for the rest of his life. Mrs. "Logat" wrote the manuscript for the entire family.

8 Czapski, 13.
9 Brill, *Schmelztiegel,* 231.

We can assume that one of Glogauer's motivations for writing was to expose the problems that all Jewish émigrés had in Brazil. "It describes the life of a woman who has emigrated, it is the personal story of one woman, but at the same time it illustrates the fate of all women in the social upheaval of emigration."[10]

Glogauer states that all Jewish women who immigrated to Brazil had similar problems and solved them in their own individual ways. "All persons, in as far as they are mentioned, are fictional and any identity with real persons is coincidental. The events, however, are based on absolute fact."[11] Again fictional names are used to characterize people and to narrate events that really happened. This device safely distances the author from the narrator and shields the author from exposing the identity of real people.

Despite the fact that the names are fictional, the events are factual. Instead of using the autobiographical first person, Glogauer uses the third person and tells her story through Marion, the main character. There is no way of telling how much of the main character Marion was the author. More important is her use of Marion to represent the fate of all Jewish women and to tell how they managed a different life in Brazil.

As Mirjam Logat, Glogauer speaks of a Jewish relief organization that helped Marion and her husband Peter get started. Gradually after Marion learned Portuguese she became more independent and started her own business, a boarding house set up for Jewish immigrants. She had strong ideas about the role of women in this wave of immigration.

The women always found a way to get ahead, they worked, they slaved, they sacrificed, they defended themselves and they supported the family. Marion, who had observed, heard and experienced so much, knew very well that she was not an isolated case, that she was only one of the many who emigrated and now fought for a new goal. She belonged to the uncounted ones, who with sheer iron will and energy struggled, stuck it out and got ahead.[12]

Notable is the portrait of Marion as "uncounted," a term that minimalizes her importance. Despite the fact that she had overcome many of the obstacles emigrant women faced, she was one of the uncounted ones who had acclimated to a new country and culture. Many of these women prospered, but they remained unnoticed and marginalized in the patriarchal culture of Brazil. The character of Marion puts into relief the character of her husband, Peter, who languished in the new surroundings.

10   Mirjam Logat, *Ich bin ausgewandert,* manuscript, São Paulo, 1990. Private collection.
11   Logat, 1.
12   Logat, 34.

His self-confidence waned, his energy vanished, his hands quivered, his nerves went on strike, and the escape into illness was the excuse for his resistance to responsibility. This developed into total apathy for the world around him. A simple bronchial infection became almost life-threatening because of his lack of will to live. He tottered in this state between sickness and health for decades. Of course, Marion had to take over the affairs of the family.[13]

Women were part of this group of unnamed persons who gradually made their way in a society that was a melting pot of various races and religions. Women who lived in Brazil in the 1930s and 1940s were not part of the male hegemony; they had to survive under circumstances different from those they had been accustomed to in Europe.

Hilde Wiedemann, another writer, does not commence with Brazil but with Germany and the story of her parents and grandparents. As in other autobiographies, we learn about the explicit character of Hilde Wiedemann as a younger woman in the 1930s and 1940s and the implicit character of Hilde Wiedemann writing the story of her life in 1966. First she describes the *act* of writing. In her house in a German colony in the state of Paraná, Brazil, she begins: "The writing room is small, the desk is built in the corner to the right of the window. . . . I open the files and lay some family documents carefully on the table."[14] Wiedemann is well educated and begins an unusual story in an ordinary manner. She does not begin with the story of how she managed a farm in the Brazilian jungle in the 1930s but with the story of her grandparents in Germany.

The autobiographical part of Weidemann's book starts chronologically with her arrival in Santos in 1933, her impressions of São Paulo, her life on a farm in Terra Nova, Paraná, in the south, and Recife, Pernambuco, on the northeast coast of Brazil. She also paints a picture of various places in Brazil where she took vacations with her family. Parts read like a travelogue of Brazil in an era when most of its landscape was still wild and pristine. Wiedemann also discusses the position in Brazil of women and the political situation of Germans and Jews during the war years.

In 1933 São Paulo was still a typical Brazilian city, unlike the burgeoning megalopolis it is today. The general attitude toward women and their role in society was more provincial and much different from the prevalent attitude in Europe at the time.

13 Logat, 25.
14 From the unpublished manuscript of Hilde Wiedemann, *Der Weg ist das Ziel,* chap. 1, EB autogr. 328. Deutsche Bibliothek, Deutsches Exilarchiv, 1933–1945, Frankfurt/Main.

What I noticed above all else at the time was the male dominance, especially on the street. Chatting groups of men stood on every corner. They milled about at the bar counters as well as sat at the marble tables of open-air cafes, where they would close the day's business over coffee. Judging by the men who uninhibitedly stared at my child and me, a single woman walking on her own seemed to be a curiosity.[15]

Wiedemann spent nearly seven years on a farm in a German colony near Castro in Paraná. Her difficult pioneer life in Terra Nova ends with a move to Curitiba in 1939. She explains the Nazi movement in southern Brazil, where there was a strange juxtaposition of German Nazis and Jewish immigrants. Brazil was a frontier that offered asylum for many opponents of the Third Reich, and Hilde Wiedemann was one of the many German–Jews who immigrated there. Brazil attracted 15,000 German–Jews in the 1930s. In 1941 there were 20,000 German–Jewish émigrés in this country.[16] The dominance of Nazis was especially noticeable in Curitiba, the capital of Paraná.

The progress of nazification was more perceptible in Curitiba. There the Germans either belonged to the party, where they were "good Germans," or they were Jews and did not exist at all. There were still a few others who were neither party members nor Jews. They claimed to be Democrats and to be able to express their opinions freely, which is why they were viewed as idiotic eccentrics.[17]

The situation of the German Jews and Nazi sympathizers was further complicated by the anti-Semitic policies of President Getúlio Vargas. His *Estado Novo* was nationalistic and became more and more restrictive for Jews. Given the increasingly stringent immigration policies directed against the large numbers of Jews who came to Brazil in the 1930s (mostly from Germany), one could understand this strange mixture.[18]

When the war broke out, the relations between Brazil and Germany came to a standstill, and the affairs of Hilde Wiedemann and her family became uncertain. They moved north to the more tropical climates of Recife and Salvador. Even in Recife, the effects of the war could be seen. All German men were imprisoned in the city, whether they were sympathizers or opponents of National Socialism. In the first years of the war, internment

---

15   Wiedemann, chap. 24.
16   Wolfgang Frühwald and Wolfgang Schieder, eds., *Leben im Exil* (Hamburg, 1981); Wolfgang Kiessling, *Exil in Lateinamerika* (Leipzig, 1981); Herbert Strauss and Werner Röder, eds., *International Biographical Dictionary of Central European Emigrés, 1933–1945*, 2 vols. (Munich, 1983), 2:22 and 34.
17   Wiedemann, chaps. 42–4.
18   Jeff H. Lesser, "Pawns of the Powerful: Jewish Immigration to Brazil, 1904–1945," Ph.D. diss., New York University, 1989, 219.

camps were set up in all states and in the interior for members of the Axis. The more politically active members, such as the leaders of the Nazi Party and the SS, were imprisoned on a small island in a bay in Rio.[19]

Just as the war changed the Brazilian political situation, it also had an effect on the social situation. Foreign troops in Brazil exposed people to more western ideas. Wiedemann relates what was expected of women in Brazil at the time (1940) and notes their marginal status. She reflects on her experiences as a woman in Recife, where she and her family lived for twenty years, and she comments on the different roles of men and women.

When Wilhelm and I were invited to visit other homes, it was at first difficult for me to be good and associate exclusively with other women. At this time, strict segregation of the sexes was still the norm. The men stood around or found a cool place to sit in the garden, where they discussed business or politics. We women sat on the sofas and in the easy-chairs and talked about illnesses, domestic help, and children.[20]

This separation of the sexes gradually changes with the war. "The war brought the decisive turn in the direction of equality between the sexes."[21] Brazil was on the side of the Allies, and American troops were stationed there. Recife was the residence of 20,000 American marines who brought the American way of life with them. This change in lifestyle gradually began to rub off on the natives. "American women not only went shopping unaccompanied, they even went to the movies alone or stopped to relax at a cafe where they could order ice-cream. Their only escort was the bag full of packages they carried home all by themselves."[22]

Contextually, Hilde Wiedemann was in a much different environment from that of immigrants who went to the United States or to other European countries. She was a woman in a Third World country. Like many of the other German–Jewish women of exile, Hilde Wiedemann was politically astute. Her awareness was certainly enhanced by the extraordinary circumstances she experienced in Germany and Brazil. She assessed the war years, Nazi Germany, and the future of Brazil in a reflective manner. Although the Germans in Brazil were not isolated from the war, not all of them learned of the full consequences until after it was over. Hilde Wiedemann describes in detail how at the end of the war she heard of the destruction of Germany and the annihilation of the Jews. "In addition to the sadness about what had been lost forever in cultural treasures, came the

19 Wiedemann, chap. 48.
20 Wiedemann, chap. 47.
21 Wiedemann, chap. 49.
22 Wiedemann.

shock about the horrors, to which our people had let themselves be de-graded. A people whom we had always loved as respectable and honest."[23]

Trudi Landau (née Trude Joseph) arrived in Brazil in January 1946. Had she not been married at the time, she states, she might have gone to Palestine to join her mother. She went to Brazil because her husband's parents had been there since 1936. The Landaus sent Trudi and her husband the re-quired legal papers and permanent visas. The younger Landaus arrived in the port of Santos on December 31, 1945.

One of the major themes in Landau's work is the concept of identity, of being both German and Jewish. Like many German–Jewish immigrants in Brazil, she at first found the acclimatization to be difficult. Because she could not speak Portuguese or get a job, she was forced to live with her in-laws. She also had a small baby who was born in February 1946. "With a baby, not being able to speak the language of the country, and not knowing the city or having any of my friends around, I felt fairly isolated."[24] Because she had been in exile and transit for years in Europe and had been forced to make it on her own, many of her ideas and customs had changed. This difference between the old and new generations is best illustrated by a comment of her mother-in-law:

One night, when I went to the bathroom, she saw that I used no nightgown in the tropical heat. She was outraged and told me that her husband had never seen her in the nude. . . . My feelings must have been, in a way, the same that soldiers have when they come home after the war. They see with surprise that life at home continues as before with the same frivolities and conventions. Those who stayed at home and did not have their whole existence shaken up cannot understand that soldiers suddenly have other preferences and other ways of judging.[25]

Of great interest here is Trudi's identification with the soldiers who were returning home. This attitude deepens her sense of marginality, because she views things differently from the accepted norm. Even though she had not been a soldier in Europe, she had been exposed to great danger as a Jewish woman escaping Nazi Germany.

Initially, she and her husband were financially dependent on their in-laws. This situation was difficult for Trudi, especially after having been a refugee for so long in Europe. "When I came to Brazil, I felt that everyone else had lived in peace, while I had suffered, lost loved ones, my home, and had faced hardships. I felt that everyone 'owed' me something, at least in

23 Wiedemann, chap. 50.
24 Landau, 22.
25 Landau.

the way of tolerance."[26] Gradually, their monetary situation improved, and one year later they moved to Bom Retiro, a Jewish section of São Paulo that had been inhabited by Eastern European Jews fleeing the pogroms. In 1933 the German Jews fleeing Hitler began to settle in Bom Retiro.

Landau was first employed in Brazil as a secretary for a Swiss firm, where she corresponded in German. After this, she worked for a Belgian firm, where she corresponded in French. Because she was multilingual, she then looked for a job in which she could use her English. Generally, such jobs offered higher salaries. In 1952 she began to work for Braniff International Airways as secretary to the district manager. In this way, she earned money for the family and gradually learned Portuguese in the work place.

She was surrounded by the Jewish community living in Bom Retiro and sent her son to a Jewish kindergarten. She explains what it was like in the early days. "I never had time for idle talk because I was working most of the time, and for a long time I even worked on Saturdays until one o'clock."[27] Many of the German–Jewish women in Brazil worked in offices and started their new lives in such a fashion, because women were needed in the work force.

Landau has been a writer for many years and has always championed basic human rights. Not only has she experienced the horror of the Nazi era on a personal level; she has also written about the political persecution in Brazil during the military regime (1964–79). Her book, *Vlado Herzog-O que faltava contar,* recounts the life of a Jewish journalist who was tortured and murdered by the dictatorship.

The ability to make the best of setbacks and tragedies was characteristic of these women who immigrated to Brazil. All were educated women from the German middle class who had enjoyed certain privileges and freedoms before the Nazis came to power. They moved to Brazil out of necessity and faced the challenges of a new country, culture, and language. Marthe Brill, Alice Brill Czapski, Martha Glogauer, Hilde Wiedemann, and Trudi Landau all describe diverse problems women émigrés faced in Brazil. Whatever norms these women accepted or defied, one cannot dismiss their gender or take it for granted. Through them we get a subjective picture of what life was like for immigrant women during this difficult period. Details of day-to-day life enliven personal views of history.

Gender was not the only issue. Immigration to a Third World country such as Brazil tended to enhance difficulties that might have been easier to

---

26 Landau, 23.
27 Landau, 25a.

overcome in such countries as the United States or Canada. The upheaval of exile and immigration forced women out of their domestic life to a transitional type of existence, and their memoirs reflect this. The women write about aspects of their lives that changed them, and in so doing, they force the reader to think of other issues such as marginality and the body politic. Although history is on the pages, the impetus for writing is for a personal history, an attempt to write the story of a family or a community that has nearly perished. The narratives give us a rare glimpse into the sensitivity and intelligence of German–Jewish women caught in sinister circumstances beyond their control. They offer unique insight into the female experience of war, displacement, and exile. Women's autobiographies do not conform to any expectation of what a woman's life should be. Instead, they offer a rare view into the truth of female experience.

11

A Year in the Brazilian Interior

An Eyewitness Report

ELEANOR ALEXANDER

Born in Berlin in 1913, Eleanor Alexander (née Eyck) was educated at the Auguste Viktoria Realgymnasium. After earning the Abitur *in 1932, she attended medical schools in Berlin and Heidelberg before leaving Germany for Paris in the spring of 1933. The following year she went to London as an au pair and eventually found a job teaching at a girls school. Her stay in Rolandia, Brazil – the focus of this eyewitness account – lasted from the spring of 1936 to the spring of 1937. From there she left for Cambridge, Massachusetts, to marry Paul Alexander. The couple spent the war years in Washington, D.C., where two of their three children were born. The third child was born in Geneva, New York, where Professor Alexander was teaching at Hobart College. Later, he taught at Brandeis, Michigan, and Berkeley. He died in 1977. Eleanor Alexander returned to school in 1961, earning a B.A. (1963) and an M.A. in French literature (1967) at Michigan. After teaching at the University of California Extension in Berkeley from 1968 to 1983, she turned to writing book reviews and essays on French and German literature. Her memoirs,* Stories of My Life, *were published in 1986. She currently lives in Berkeley, California. This report was written in 1992.*

I was teaching French at the Red Gables School in Carlisle, England, when I received an exciting letter. My old friends, Heinrich and Käte Kaphan, had sold their farm in Pomerania and bought land in Brazil. They wrote to ask me to come along as their children's teacher.

I was glad to accept the invitation to start a new life with good friends, in a new world, and to be on my own no longer. I had many fond memories of happy vacations on their farm where Heinrich Kaphan had taught me to ride, a useful skill later in Rolandia.

I had left my home in Berlin in May 1933 after passing my first medical exams and had gone to Paris as an au pair with a Russian family. I soon realized that it would not be possible to continue my medical studies there and decided to accept an au pair job in London, where I had good friends.

A year later I was able to find a position as a French teacher in a girls school – and that is where the good news reached me.

The Kaphans had bought the land in Rolandia from an English company that was building a railroad in the interior. The company purchased the heavy equipment it needed in Germany. This situation created a financial mechanism through which German Jews, who could not take any money out of Germany, could buy land in Brazil with German funds – an exchange of German heavy equipment for Brazilian farmland.

My memory of the day I left Hamburg for Brazil aboard the S.S. *Artigas* is as vivid as if it were only yesterday. My mother and my future mother-in-law saw us off, and when the ship sailed out of the harbor, I thought my heart would break. I was excited and happy to go but anxious about the fate of my family and friends whom I left behind.

We arrived in Santos, Brazil, in June 1936 after an enjoyable three-week boat trip. We took the train to São Paulo, where we were met by friends. We stayed in a boarding house run by a wonderful couple, both refugees from Germany. After a week, Heinrich and Käte Kaphan left for Rolandia to get our house ready. I followed a week later with their three children: Annemarie (12 years old), Klaus (10), and Marianne (6). Not one of us knew a word of Portuguese. The train trip took twenty-four hours, first by sleeper, then on a very dusty, slow train. We arrived in Rolandia, the last stop on the line, in the late afternoon.

Rolandia had been founded as a haven for political and Jewish refugees from Germany, and soon after 1933 the first settlers began to arrive.[1] They were businessmen, professional people, and politicians. Heinrich Kaphan was one of the few farmers in the group. He had farmed not only in Pomerania but also in Romania during World War I. He was able to adjust to the new conditions in a most admirable way and was always willing to give advice to less experienced settlers. Heinrich's help was invaluable, but Käte's influence was just as important. Her charm, kindness, and delightful sense of humor solved many budding crises. What I remember best is her infectious laugh.

Our "house" was really just a box with four interior walls to create four rooms. We gradually settled down and I began my teacher's life in Rolandia.

---

1 More than 150 settlers participated in the Rolandia project. Most were Catholic; among them were prominent members of the German Center Party (*Zentrum*). Some were Protestant, and about ten families were Jewish. The Rolandia project developed from an agricultural settlement founded before Hitler became chancellor into an important refuge for many who were persecuted by the Nazis. See Patrik von zur Mühlen, *Fluchtziel Lateinamerika. Die deutsche Emigration, 1933–1945: politische Aktivitäten und soziokulturelle Integration* (Bonn, 1988), 104–5. About Rolandia in 1936–37, see Eleanor Alexander, *Stories of My Life* (Berkeley, Calif., 1986), 41–69.

"School goes well," I wrote my parents, "things are much easier now because we have the use of two tables – the open sewing machine and the dining room table. We also have a shelf for our school books in the children's room." Soon our social life was very busy, including a steady stream of visitors. This made teaching difficult at times, because every word spoken could be heard in every corner of the house, and the conversations were often far more interesting than the three R's.

We made new friends and renewed old friendships. The Isays, who had been my parents' good friends in Berlin, were our neighbors. They sent their two younger children to my school. The two Hinrichsen brothers, one tall and one short, farmed together, and along with Bismarck and his friend Hoppenstedt (called "Hoppie") were new friends. Young Bismarck was a descendant of the first German chancellor, whose biography my father was then writing.[2] Hoppie's father had known my father in the Democratic Club in Berlin. We got to know the Koch Wesers, also friends of my parents, and at their house we met Mr. Thomas, the director of the English company building the railroad in Paraná.[3] With my help as interpreter, Heinrich and Mr. Thomas hit it off at once and from then on worked well together.

Koch Weser's house was the most elegant; it had a large staff and electricity as well. He had been a justice minister during the Weimar Republic. He and my father had been active in the Democratic Party together. Bebsie Heerdt, who looked after their large garden, was the daughter of friends of Max and Titti Maier, who were also close to my family. I had once met her and her sister Elisabeth at their house in Frankfurt am Main. The Maiers later settled in Rolandia and became neighbors and friends of the Kaphans.

2 Erich Eyck, *Bismarck,* 3 vols. (Zurich, 1941–4; 2nd ed. 1963). A series of lectures given at Balliol College, Oxford, *Bismarck and the German Empire* (London, 1950; reprinted: New York and London, 1964) was translated and published in German as *Bismarck und das deutsche Reich* (Zurich, 1955). It was also translated into Swedish and Italian. Eyck was also the author of *A History of the Weimar Republic* and *Wilhelm II,* as well as several books on English history. Eyck studied law in Berlin and Freiburg, writing his doctoral thesis in history. After finishing his studies, he practiced law in Berlin and from 1915 to 1933 was one of the editors of the *Vossische Zeitung.* He was very active in the German Democratic Party (DDP) and served as an alderman of the city of Berlin from 1928 to 1932. In 1937 he emigrated to England, settling in London and, during the war, in Boars Hill, Oxford. He died in London in 1964 at the age of eighty-five.

3 The politician Erich Koch Weser (1875–1944) studied law and economics at Lausanne, Bonn, Munich, and Berlin. He was a co-founder of the German Democratic Party, a member of the *Nationalversammlung* (1919–20), a Reich minister of the interior (Oct. 1919 to May 1921), vice chancellor (1920), a Reichstag deputy (1920–1930), and chair of the DDP (1924–30). Between June 1928 and April 1929, he served as Reich justice minister. In April 1933 the Nazis closed down his law practice because his mother was Jewish. He emigrated to Rolandia, where he died in 1944. See *International Biographical Dictionary of Central European Emigrés, 1933–1945,* ed. Herbert Strauss and Werner Röder (Munich, 1980), 1:376.

The partnership of these two families was a great success, and their farm, Fazenda Jaú, became a model.

In spite of all our new experiences, the center of our life was always the mail from overseas. Airmail arrived on Thursdays once a week if all went well. It came to Rolandia by bus at five o'clock in the afternoon and was then deposited on a windowsill where everyone could have a go at it. If there was an interesting stamp on a letter, you might never get it.

We wrote long letters to our families every week. I sent my sister in Sydney, Australia, a copy of my letters to my parents, and she saved them. It is these letters that made it possible for me to give the full story of my stay in Rolandia.

My own social life flourished. There were parties for the younger people that I loved. We danced, flirted, talked, drank, and ate a good deal. And then we drove home in the moonlight in a creaky carriage. But the most exciting party was the one that the parents of one of my pupils, Bodo Ranke, gave for me on their land. We celebrated my birthday and my engagement to Paul Alexander, a graduate student in Byzantine history at Harvard University – a long way from life on a farm in Brazil.[4]

I described the party to my parents:

The Hinrichsen brothers and Bebsie came for a duck dinner; it was hot and crowded but lovely. In the afternoon the Hinrichsens, Bebsie, Hoppie, and I rode out to Ranke's land; the others followed in a truck. The short Hinrichsen fell into the stream when he took the horse for a drink. Bebsie and I got wet all over so that our white slacks and blouses had already lost their pristine beauty when we arrived in the best of moods. There was a tent for the children, who were in seventh heaven, and one chair for me as the guest of honor. There was good food and dancing in the evening and a ride home in the moonlight through the woods, which looked mysterious and beautiful. The next morning we canceled school because we all slept late. It had been a long day but one I'll always remember.

Later in October we celebrated the Jewish New Year. We enjoyed the holiday and felt that it was most important to keep up traditions. I wrote to my parents: "It was a simple celebration with a nicely laid table with candles in silver candlesticks, a white tablecloth and flowers, and of course

---

4 Paul Julius Alexander (1910–77) studied law and received his doctorate in 1932 at Hamburg. He emigrated to France in 1933, earned his second law degree at Paris in 1934, and emigrated to the United States in 1935. He studied history at the University of Michigan and at Harvard, where he received his Ph.D. in history in 1940. He was a junior fellow at Dumbarton Oaks from 1941 to 1943 and worked for the OSS from 1943 to the end of the war. After the war, he taught ancient and medieval history at Hobart, Brandeis, Michigan, and Berkeley. He made important contributions to the study of the iconclastic controversy of the eighth and ninth centuries as well as to the study of Byzantine apocalyptic writing between the fourth and sixteenth centuries. See the *International Biographical Dictionary of Central European Emigrés*, 2:17–18.

a splendid meal: asparagus from a can, white bread, chopped liver, sardines, a fruit salad of peaches and pineapple, and cookies with hot toddy."

And a few weeks later I wrote:

We are all busy with preparations for Chanukah. The girls made presents out of old pillowcases and Klaus created a box for the candles with "Chanukah" painted on it in black. Klaus said the Brochah prayer and we all sang the first verse of the Chanukah song and then I read a few words about the holiday.

While we were busy with our new life in town, Heinrich Kaphan spent a great deal of time on his new land, eight miles from Rolandia, on the river Jaú. He often stayed there for several days. At the end of September, the forest was ready for burning, the land was prepared for cultivation, and the first rice seeds were planted. Heinrich found a place high on a hill for the new house, wood was delivered, and the carpenters began to build according to our plans. A pump was installed to supply running water to the house. We were going to have showers! By the middle of November the house had a roof and floors were laid. We ate the first vegetables from our land: watercress, radishes, and lettuce.

Finally, on the fifteenth of January, we moved to our new house. The move was not an easy one. I wrote:

You won't be able to imagine our move. Elfriede (our maid) had stopped coming, three members of the family were sick, it rained continuously and we never could change our clothes because most of our things were packed in boxes and cartons for weeks. Because of the heavy rain our furniture could not get through from São Paulo to Rolandia, but in the end the sun came out and our belongings were put on a truck which moved everything in three trips.

A few weeks later I wrote to my parents:

I wish I could tell you how marvelous it is here, sitting in the library. Looking out of the window I see a large field of soybeans, with the woods behind and a road running along. The land is all cleared and looks most attractive. Out of the window one sees a large field of corn, already three meters high, with the Jaú behind and the hill going up on the other side of the river. The forest is full of flowering bushes, yellow and purple. Peace reigns all around.

I was absolutely delighted to have a room of my own and did not mind at all that it was small. I had a comfortable bed, a table that folded under the window and almost an art gallery: two Rembrandt prints, a Flemish picture from the Metropolitan Museum, and the flute player from the Ludovisi throne in Rome, a gift from Paul. "When I look up at night," I wrote, "out of my window I see a beautiful star, almost green, the trees against the sky, and further away I hear the pump pumping water."

Excited as I was about the new house, my main concern was my school, which was terribly important for me. My schoolroom was splendid, a wonderfully large room with an adjoining verandah and plenty of fresh air. By now I had eight children in my little one-room school. I taught the older ones from 7:30 A.M. to noon, and the two little six-year-olds in the afternoon. Before the start of school, I made the beds, straightened out the children's rooms, then began class with fifteen minutes of exercise every morning. The daily routine made life much easier and more satisfactory for all of us.

Soon we had our first harvest of soybeans, a mill by the stream was almost finished, the cotton was in bloom, and the first step for growing coffee had been taken.

The children worked hard, and I was pleased when Annemarie and Klaus did well in written exams; the reward was Easter holidays. I found teaching the three R's easy, but teaching biology and geography seemed more difficult. In biology we studied the human body, for I still remembered a few things from anatomy classes in medical school. We studied geography by mapping out travel routes all over the world.

One project was particularly close to our hearts: the possibility of training young emigrants from Germany. Jewish organizations had started an agricultural training farm in Gross-Breesen in Silesia to enable young people to go to a new country and begin a useful life.[5] Many were able to go to Palestine and other countries all over the world. A friend of my brother went to live in Kenya, and others went to England or America.

Before we left for Rolandia there had been a good deal of discussion about the possibility of sending some young people to Rolandia to learn farming and to settle there. We built a house for them next to ours, the *Elevenhaus* (trainees' house). In the spring a commission was sent to inspect the farm and the land around it. We were terribly excited and certain that the commission would be so taken with what they saw that they would send some young people right away. Unfortunately, there was so much delay that only one young man was able to come, but he was a wonderful person and I am happy to know that we helped him.

Years later, after a discussion of life in Brazil, two members of the audience came up to me. They had been in Gross-Breesen in the 1930s and

---

5   On Gross-Breesen, see Werner T. Angress, *Generation zwischen Furcht und Hoffnung. Jüdische Jugend im Dritten Reich* (Hamburg, 1985); Angress, "Auswanderungslehrgut Gross-Breesen," *Leo Baeck Institute Yearbook* (1965): 168–87; and Wolf Simon Matsdorf, *No Time to Grow. The Story of the Gross-Breeseners in Australia* (Jerusalem, 1973).

now lived in the United States. It was exciting for me to talk to them about their life in Gross-Breesen and later on in the emigration. The past seemed to come alive again after all these years, a marvelous moment for me. It made me glad again that I had been able to live in Rolandia for a year.

In the spring of 1937 my life in Rolandia was slowly coming to an end. It took an incredible amount of time and effort to collect all the necessary papers. It was a great help that my uncle, a professor at Columbia University, gave me an affidavit, and so I had no difficulty in obtaining my visa.

The last paper I needed was a testimonial from the authorities in Londrina. Heinrich Kaphan and I went to see Mr. Thomas to ask for his help, which he was glad to give, but he added that he could not understand why I did not get married in Rolandia. He called the police, who sent a young man to escort me to the police station, where one policeman spoke German and was able to help me. After long consultations they decided to charge me ten mil for the testimonial. After friendly farewells, I was conducted back to Mr. Thomas's office. My escort impressed on me to be most careful and trust no one but to let the shipping company handle my affairs. I promised to do just that. They were unhappy to hear that only my fiancé lived in the United States and that my parents still lived in Germany. Of course, that was a constant worry and sorrow for us. In the midst of great happiness and achievement that sorrow was always with us. But soon after, we had the good fortune to see our families leave Germany and start a new life.

My last day in Rolandia was May 14, 1937. I was sad and excited at the same time. Fazenda Jaú had become a second home to me, and I had been happier there than at any other time since leaving Germany in May 1933. We decided to have an informal Olympics as a farewell ceremony. The children decorated the schoolroom with all kinds of flowers and wrote delightfully illustrated poems. We were all moved and excited, but Klaus was concerned that the flowers might seem too cheerful! I gave a speech and after that we all had breakfast. Then it was all over and I was off into the unknown.

I traveled to São Paulo to get my visa and had to wait there two weeks until the next boat left for New York. I stayed with two very nice ladies whom I had met during my first stay in the city. I was met in New York by my aunt and Paul, and I stayed for a few days with my uncle and aunt and my cousin Marianne. Paul and I then left for Cambridge, Massachusetts, to begin our new life together. I was very happy.

In one year I had watched virgin forest turned into a busy farm, had seen the planting and harvesting of cotton, rice, and soybeans, the planting of coffee, the beginning of a vegetable garden, and the building of our new house. Perhaps best of all I had been able to help my friends in the difficult first year and had learned a great deal.

I kept in close touch with my friends in Rolandia. I saw the Maiers when they came to New York City, and later they came to visit us in Ann Arbor, Michigan, bringing one of the Koch Wesers's granddaughters along. The Kaphans visited us in Boston, and Klaus's wife came to see us when we lived in Princeton, New Jersey. This was the beginning of a close friendship. She was born in Germany, grew up in Chicago, and moved to Brazil when she married Klaus.

One day at lunch in the Women's Faculty Club at the University of California at Berkeley I had a very interesting discussion with a nun who had lived in Brazil for many years. She told me that so much had changed in Brazil since I had lived there and urged me to go and visit my friends there.

Thus, in the spring of 1973 – thirty-six years after leaving Rolandia – I flew from San Francisco to São Paulo. I arrived on time and while waiting in the incredibly hot customs shed, I got a message that someone was waiting for me. It was Annemarie, who was thirteen when I left and was now married to a Cuban–American businessman. She took me to her lovely and comfortable home that had a swimming pool in the garden. It all seemed like Southern California! In the evening Marianne, who was seven when I saw her last, came to see me with her Italian husband, who had been in the Italian resistance. With Italian dramatic flair, he called me *la professoressa!* We had a marvelous time together, speaking German, Italian, and English. The next morning I flew to Londrina, where I was met by Klaus and his parents.

I would never have recognized Londrina and Rolandia, but the house that we had built in 1936 was unchanged and I felt quite at home. The Maiers now lived five minutes from the Kaphans in a charming house with a verandah full of flowers and hummingbirds. Klaus and his family lived in a modern house on the other side of our house.

The farm was flourishing and very different from the farm I had known. The Kaphans now had cattle and there was coffee growing. The mill by the Jaú was busy, and the coffee was roasted right on the farm. It was delicious. I loved the countryside with its lush green hills that we could see from the verandah. There were many beautiful gardens – all so very different. And I enjoyed the swimming pool, which seemed quite incredible to me, for I still remembered our joy at having a shower in the house.

Social life was busy and delightful. Many friends came to visit and at other times we went around making calls, admiring the prosperous farms. Some old acquaintances had returned to Germany and others had died, but many people still remembered me and everyone told tall tales. The affection of many good friends was heartwarming, but I was happiest when Marianne Kaphan said to me, "You are just the way I remembered you."

One afternoon during my stay, Ruth Kaphan and I went to a field a few miles away that was dotted with three or four little huts. Soon a bus pulled up and women and children tumbled out. They had come to learn to sew, read, and write. There was also a little laboratory to give medical tests. The children played while their mothers learned, and the babies were "stored" in cardboard boxes.

I realized then the enormous change that had taken place in the years I had been away. Käte and I had often gone to visit the wives of the farmers on the land, and not knowing one another's languages, we had smiled and drunk lemonade in cottages that were almost bare. How different they looked now! It was a wonderful afternoon and in many ways the highlight of my stay.

My visit had shown me the progress in Rolandia since 1937. It was good to know that many women had been able to start a new life and at the same time contribute to the well-being of citizens of the country that had taken them in.

PART TWO

Refuge in the United States

A. COMMUNITY AND INSTITUTIONS
B. OCCUPATIONS OF WOMEN EMIGRES

12

Women's Role in the German–Jewish Immigrant Community

STEVEN M. LOWENSTEIN

There is a strong contrast between the impression one gets looking at the role of women in the organized German–Jewish community and the picture that emerges of German–Jewish women's changing position in the immigrant family and the world of work. Studies of German–Jewish immigrant women at work and in the family generally stress the success of women's adjustment and their enhanced position in the family. However, a look at women in public communal life shows a continuation of traditional patriarchal patterns. Women's roles in the synagogues, social clubs, and immigrant organizations that grew up in New York and other large American cities tended to be traditional and behind the scenes. With some notable exceptions, German–Jewish organizations did not break with conservative patterns concerning the place of women.

By their very nature, immigrant organizations tended to have a traditional and conservative cast. In contrast, those immigrants interested in leaving their past ways behind tended to avoid the organized immigrant community and to affiliate with American groups or ideological movements. It follows, then, that the very desire to associate with fellow immigrants and to preserve the customs, language, and belief patterns brought over from Europe was a profoundly conservative act. It was intended to keep the familiar and to ease the transition to the New World rather than to break new ground. For these reasons, the traditional role for women described here will not be typical of the whole German–Jewish immigrant group because it concentrates on the more tradition-minded who joined immigrant organizations.

The traditional nature of women's roles in immigrant congregations and other organizations is not only the result of the traditional nature of immigrant organizations, however. It also comes about because both the German and the Jewish traditions from which the immigrants came tended to be patriarchal in nature. In German society, the father's role in the family was particularly great, and until relatively late, women were restricted in their access to higher education and organizational life.[1] In the Jewish tradition, synagogue life had been mainly the province of men, with women sitting in a partitioned section and playing no role in leading the services. Both the German and the Jewish traditional restrictions on women had been challenged during the nineteenth and early twentieth centuries. Nevertheless, the circles most heavily represented in immigrant congregations – lower-middle-class Jews from small south German towns – were the least likely to have accommodated such challenges.

It would therefore seem at first glance that there is little to discuss about the role of women because it was so restricted. What is more, the place of women, except insofar as it involved changing family and occupational roles, was rarely discussed publicly within the German–Jewish community, and there were few open challenges to the traditional way in which the sexes interrelated. A closer exploration, however, shows that women often did play an important role, sometimes even within the congregational sphere. Their participation, though, was generally behind the scenes and, on the surface at least, did not challenge the male predominance in official communal functions.

Like so much else in the history of the immigrants, the mutual influences of Jewish, German, and American cultures and institutional forms affected gender relations. Both developments in American views of the role of women as well as the specific traits of the immigrant community are reflected in changes in women's activities among the immigrants.[2] In some ways, Americanization gave women an increased role in communal life, but in others, especially within Orthodoxy, it often restricted women in ways that had not previously been expected.

Women appear in two main contexts within the communal structure – as participants in general organizations and within their own specifically female groups. The specifically female groups were often attached to a gen-

---

1 See, for example, Marion A. Kaplan, "Tradition and Transition. The Acculturation, Assimilation and Integration of Jews in Imperial Germany. A Gender Analysis," *Yearbook of the Leo Baeck Institute* 27 (1982): 3–36, esp. 10–11, which deal with the laws limiting women's admission to higher education and to "political" organizations.

2 The influence of the general American community can be seen, for instance, by the fact that in the 1950s, when the domestic role of women was being particularly emphasized and glorified, sisterhood programs were more likely to deal with questions like nutrition, child development, or generational issues. In the 1940s the emphasis was on the more general Jewish situation greatly affecting the immigrants. In the 1960s and thereafter as the community aged rapidly, one notices both an emphasis on issues of generations and senior citizens and a general increase in entertainment programs at the expense of educational ones.

eral or male-dominated group as a ladies' auxiliary or a synagogue sister-hood. Within immigrant organizations not specifically restricted to one gender, the role of women was quite different in synagogues, where it was usually quite limited, and from welfare and charitable organizations, where it was more equal and sometimes dominant.

The immigrant synagogues created by those who came to the United States in the 1930s covered a broad spectrum of ideologies from the strictest of Orthodoxy to a German liberal Judaism only slightly more traditional than American Reform. Because of the approach of traditional Jewish law to the role of women, the more Orthodox congregations, as a matter of principle, were unable to grant women rights that more liberal congregations were at liberty to bestow. Orthodox Judaism prescribed that women sit separately from the men behind a partition (*mechitzah*); it did not permit them to lead the service, be counted for a prayer quorum, or be called to the Torah.

Nevertheless, one cannot completely predict the status of women in an immigrant congregation just by looking at the official ideology of its bylaws. Personal and cultural factors often had as much influence as did ideology and religious law. Many, even of the congregations of the liberal tradition, continued the practice of separate seating of the sexes they had applied in Germany, although they did not place a physical partition between them.[3] In a few liberal synagogues founded by immigrants of the 1930s, there was a mixed choir, but in others, there were only male singers. In the Orthodox synagogues all-male choirs were universal.

Even in matters in which religious law was not clear-cut in excluding women, many of the more traditional immigrant congregations restricted women. In quite a number of the immigrant congregations, there was very broad democracy for men, including broad powers for the annual *Generalversammlung* (general assembly) of male adult members, but women were totally excluded from voting. In others, including some liberal congregations, women were allowed to vote but rarely if ever were chosen for congregational offices. (In the moderately liberal Beth Hillel congregation in Washington Heights, New York City, for instance, no woman has ever served in any of the executive elected offices of the congregation [president, vice president, treasurer, or secretary], though two women served among the sixteen trustees of the congregation in 1976.) In the Reform Hebrew Tabernacle women have served as executive officers but not yet as presi-

---

3   It would seem that there had been relatively little opposition to separate seating in Germany because in most German churches men and women had sat separately.

dents.[4] As far as I can determine, Congregation Habonim is the only German congregation that has had a woman as its president.

The exclusion of women from the honor and prestige of congregational office does not necessarily mean that they were totally without influence, merely that such influence had to be exercised through more informal means. Nor does the greater exclusion from formal power of women in the more Orthodox congregations necessarily mean that active women always opposed Orthodoxy. A good case in point is that of Ruth Suesser Koplowitz of New Hope Congregation in Cincinnati. Koplowitz was not only one of the fourteen founders of this traditionalist congregation but was also one of those most active in trying to strengthen the Orthodox elements within the congregation. This was done mainly in informal ways such as letter writing or offering a donation if the synagogue parking lot was closed on the Sabbath. Ruth Koplowitz's role as a force for tradition was well enough known to be remarked upon in humorous synagogue plays satirizing the congregational leadership. Women could also play a role in a liberal rather than orthodox direction, as happened in the same congregation when several women were influential in inviting Reform Jewish speakers to congregational events.[5]

Protest against the secondary role of women in traditional congregations rarely took explicit form, although one can perhaps detect it in certain indirect ways. Sometimes the deference of women was more apparent than real. A satire of a women's card party in the earlier mentioned New Hope Congregation depicts them as stating, "Which woman is interested in a [synagogue] constitution? This is something for men." They then proceed to criticize various provisions of the document.[6] An even more indirect "protest" against the lack of role in the synagogue is the frequently remarked fact that many women ignored the praying of the men and gossiped among themselves in the women's gallery. The men, who were not averse to gossiping in the synagogue themselves, seemed especially sensitive to the noise coming from the women and tried in vain to put a stop to it.[7]

4 *Festschrift – Congregation Beth Hillel of Washington Heights, New York City* (New York, 1976), 7, 24, and written communication from Rabbi Robert Lehman dated Oct. 7, 1991.
5 Benny Kraut, *German–Jewish Orthodoxy in an Immigrant Synagogue: Cincinnati's New Hope Congregation and the Ambiguities of Ethnic Religion* (New York, 1988), 5, 29, 61, 83, 169, 256–71. Kraut's remarks that the twenty-fifth anniversary banquet program of the congregation states that the congregation was founded by "a mere handful of men without means" ignores Suesser Koplowitz's role as a cofounder (p. 200).
6 Kraut, *German–Jewish Orthodoxy*, 275–76.
7 The alleged tendency of women to gossip in the synagogue more than men has become a staple of Jewish folklore. The tendency of women to discuss recipes or other matters unrelated to the service is sometimes mentioned in women's memoirs as well. See, for example, Marion Kaplan, *The Making of the Jewish Middle Class. Women, Family, and Identity in Imperial Germany* (New York, 1991), 66.

Women were not restricted completely to informal means of making their views known even within the congregations, however. Every immigrant congregation seems to have had a sisterhood, and in most cases the sisterhood's role was an important if circumscribed one. The president of the sisterhood (in direct parallel to the male president of the congregation) was often reelected for term after term and became an important personality in the community. Some, like Alice Oppenheimer of Ahavath Torah in Washington Heights, connected the sisterhood presidency with other offices (Mizrachi chapter chair, editor of the newspaper *The Jewish Way*) to build up a broader arena of influence. In some cases (for instance New Hope Congregation in Cincinnati), the women were a force for unity in a congregation whose men were often divided by religious ideology and petty personal squabbles.[8]

The sisterhoods of the German immigrant congregations had some roots in Germany, where many communities had a *Jüdische Frauenverein* (society of Jewish women), but, as their usual name "sisterhood" indicates, they were heavily influenced by American patterns of synagogue life.[9] In some of the German Orthodox communities, the sisterhood also had a Hebrew name *Chevras Noschim,* a term that implied that it was the female equivalent to the *Chevra Kadisha,* or male burial society. This Hebrew name gave the sisterhood, or at least the part of it that functioned as a burial society, a semisacred status. In at least one immigrant congregation, it was customary for men to give donations both to the burial society and the sisterhood when called to the Torah, although sometimes the amounts given to the sisterhood were smaller.[10]

The functions of the sisterhood tended to group into four categories: socialization, charity, education, and providing food for certain synagogue functions. Sisterhoods met regularly for all types of social events, including

8   On Alice Oppenheimer, see oral history interview with her at Research Foundation for Jewish Research in Herbert A. Strauss, ed., *Jewish Immigrants of the Nazi Period in the U.S.A.* (New York, 1986), vol. 3, pt. 1: 90, interview 166. See also *Jewish Way,* esp. Feb./March 1954, June 1955, and March 1957. On the New Hope sisterhood Kraut remarks, "Interestingly, religious tensions were mitigated within New Hope's highly organized and socially effective sisterhood, in which ethnic sociability transcended religious differences" (p. 33).

9   On the sisterhood in American Jewish life, see Jenna Weissman Joselit, "The Special Sphere of the Middle-Class American Jewish Woman: The Synagogue Sisterhood, 1890–1940," in Jack Wertheimer, ed., *The American Synagogue: A Sanctuary Transformed* (New York, 1987), 206–30. The synagogue sisterhood seems to have been an innovation of Americanized synagogues of the late nineteenth century.

10 Congregation Shaare Hatikvah in Washington Heights, New York City. It is interesting that when a rabbi with no German background was hired by the congregation, he tried (without success) to change the Hebrew title from "Chevras Noschim" (women's confraternity) to "Ezras Noschim" (women's aid) presumably because in the East European Orthodox tradition, the term "Chevra" (confraternity) applied only to men's sacred societies.

card parties, teas, luncheons, and the ubiquitous *Gemütliches Beisammensein mit Kaffee und Kuchen* (social gathering with coffee and cake). On occasion, the social events were mixed with cultural events when a film of Jewish or general interest was seen or a musical performance took place. In many congregations, sisterhood events were very well attended – sometimes better attended than male-oriented events were. Some congregations had male equivalents of the sisterhood entitled *Herrenabend* (men's clubs), but these were only rarely as successful or active as the women's events.[11] In some Orthodox synagogues, the only men's organization was the burial society, which did indeed have an annual banquet but few social events.

In the largest and strictest of all German Orthodox synagogues, K'hal Adath Jeshurun (Breuer's), it was the very exclusion of women from the religious duty of intensive Torah study that enabled them to have the broadest cultural and social programs within the synagogue. The Breuer sisterhood sponsored many lectures, films, plays, and skits and even an annual outing to the promenade concerts of the Philharmonic, all events of the type men were expected to be too busy for.[12]

In general the social get-togethers of synagogue sisterhoods played an important role in fostering unity and in preserving some of the informal

---

11 Attendance figures for various congregational events are given in the bulletin of Congregation Ohav Sholaum of Washington Heights–Inwood. Some relative figures chosen at random are: Oct. 30, 1949: extraordinary congregational meeting, 68 in attendance; traditional Hoschana Rabba learning, 45; Parent Teachers Association, 44; sisterhood lecture, 60; sisterhood, Israeli films, 120; general meeting of men's club, 40 – "a surprisingly large audience"; Men's Club, close to 100 at Tu Bischvat party with film; men's club lecture on personality and marriage, 30; at the fifth anniversary dinner of men's club, 70; at sisterhood lecture on Southern Rhodesia, 65; at first social affair of sisterhood in new synagogue, 70 (March 1951); 130 at sisterhood Lag Ba'omer evening, "eine Rekordziffer"; Hebrew school graduation, 150. *Ohav Sholaum News* 7/6 (Dec. 1949); 8/1 (Jan./Feb. 1950); 9/2 (March/April 1951); 9/4 (July/Aug. 1951). The first *Herrenabend* at Congregation Beth Hillel was announced for January 1950. It was designed so that the male members could get to know one another and make and renew friendships. The program was to include *Gesellschaftspiele* (games), cards, sandwiches, and drinks. They were to be held every other week. It would seem from the synagogue bulletin that the men's gatherings lasted for less than a year, although at first they were very popular. Similar indications that the women's auxiliary had more lively activities than did the more prestigious and powerful main men's organization is reported by Claudia Prestel for the German B'nai B'rith, "Weibliche Rollenzuweisung in jüdischen Organisationen. Das Beispiel des Bnei Briss," *Bulletin des Leo Baeck Instituts* 85 (1990): 77, note 55.

12 *Mitteilungen. Organ der K'hal Adath Jeshurun* announces the following activities of the sisterhood for April/May 1968: lecture by the congregational rabbi on Rabbi Akiba Eger (a nineteenth-century rabbi); a Purim party with a parody based on the Broadway show "Oliver" and donations for the Beth Esther homes; the Purim party of the Golden Age club; a lecture on Passover laws by the congregational rabbi, and a Bible class by Marc Breuer. The same issue announced that the sisterhood had tickets for the Promenade concerts at Lincoln Center and that the Ladies Auxiliary and Parent Teacher Association of the Yeshiva Rabbi Samson Raphael Hirsch (under congregational auspices) would hold its spring luncheon. Meetings of a previous year included a play, a magician, a "musical journey," a lecture by an Orthodox magazine editor, a lecture on career opportunities for Jewish women (by a rabbi), and a number of lectures on Jewish history.

elements of the immigrant culture, but this importance was almost never acknowledged. In addition, there was sometimes a cultural gap between the older women who usually dominated the sisterhoods and the younger generation. Sometimes, especially in the 1950s, attempts were made to create special activities or even separate organizations for the younger set of the sisterhood. In other congregations, American born or educated women simply did not attend sisterhood functions, partly because the sisterhoods frequently retained the German language much longer than did the official congregations as a whole.[13]

The charitable side of sisterhood activities had especially great significance in the early years of immigration. In those years, sisterhoods aided newcomers in various ways and gave mutual advice and support on the difficult questions of family adjustment. One sisterhood even organized a *Kleiderkammer* (clothes closet), which gathered and gave away used clothes for needy immigrants. Other women's groups gave aid to the war effort by knitting for the Red Cross, sending food packages to soldiers and internees, and providing other traditional women's aid activities.[14] After World War II, the importance of the charitable activities of the sisterhoods declined somewhat as need within the community decreased. It was often reduced to fund raising for worthy causes through raffles, bazaars, and other means. Some of these causes, such as Women's Social Service for Israel, were gender-based.[15]

Many of the meetings of synagogue sisterhoods were educational in nature: a lecture, a film, a cultural event or concert, or a discussion of a theme of interest. In Orthodox synagogues there was often a women's religion class (ladies' *shiur*) that generally covered some religious topic or text in a less systematic way than did the similar and more numerous men's study groups. The lecturers at sisterhood meetings came from a broad spectrum. In almost all groups they included both men (frequently the congregation's rabbi) and women (including outside speakers with distinguished records in social work, academia, or as eyewitnesses to the tragic events of the war). Sometimes the topics were geared specifically toward women (famous Jewish women, the role of the woman in Judaism, issues of child raising, women's careers) and sometimes toward more general themes. Although

---

13   On the attempt to create an organization for the "younger set of the sisterhood," see *Beth Hillel Bulletin* 131 (Jan. 1956) and 134 (April/May 1956). See also *Mitteilungen der Congregation Shaare Hatikvah* 27 (Dec. 1949). On the avoidance of the sisterhood by the native born, see Kraut, *German–Jewish Orthodoxy*, 189–90.

14   On the *Kleiderkammer*, see *Jewish Way*, Feb./March 1954; *Mitteilungen der Congregation Gates of Hope* (later Shaare Hatikvah – Washington Heights) includes information on *Strickabende* (evenings of knitting) for the Red Cross and for displaced persons in 1 (Dec. 1944), 2 (Jan. 1945), and 10 (Feb. 1946).

15   Some sisterhoods also organized visits to old-age homes and other institutions.

undoubtedly there may have been a somewhat paternalistic attitude by some of the male speakers, the functions were generally considered of importance within the congregation and were often described at length in congregational bulletins.

Besides these functions, which were exclusively or predominantly female in their audience, there were other events in which the men and women in the synagogue joined together for social events. Sometimes the men's club or sisterhood would invite spouses of members to a banquet or other social event. Most German–Jewish congregations, even sometimes the most extremely Orthodox among them, had at least some mixed social events (in contrast to right-wing Orthodox synagogues of Eastern European background). Even groups from which women were excluded, such as the male choirs, included spouses in their social events and outings. There were also internal synagogue organizations – Hebrew school parents associations, couples' clubs, young people's clubs, and so on – in which men and women participated on a seemingly equal footing.[16]

At some of the mixed events, however, the presence of women meant that they were expected to prepare and serve the food for the event.[17] There is much evidence that this expectation was shared by men and women. Americanization did not change this fact. So, when in the late 1950s, several Orthodox and Conservative congregations created informal youth services to meet on Sunday mornings on the pattern of American synagogues, they assumed that the teenage boys would put on tefillin and lead services and the girls would then serve breakfast.[18]

It would seem that men were as anxious as women to see the creation of sisterhoods and other separate women's groups. At least one synagogue

16 In Beth Hillel and Ohav Sholaum, two German congregations in Washington Heights, there were Young People's Leagues. In Ohav Sholaum there was also a Parent Teacher Association of the Hebrew School. In Shaare Hatikvah there was a PTA as well as a Mr. and Mrs. Club and, in later years, a Golden Age Club (*Yachdov*). In the Parent Teacher Association it is noticeable that at first the leaders of the organization were mainly men but that later women played an increasing role in the leadership.

17 Later, as the communities became more prosperous, food was provided by paid caterers. In most cases in the German–Jewish immigrant community, both the caterers and their serving personnel were women. In some congregations, the women of the sisterhood also provided refreshments for youth activities, including occasional ice cream parties as well as the annual distribution of candy and chocolate on Simchath Torah. Women also served food at certain men's religious events such as the annual *Hoshana Rabba* and *Shavuot* learning vigils. In at least one German Orthodox congregation in recent years they have also served (but not eaten at) the traditional third meal of the Sabbath [Shalosh Sudos]. See Steven Lowenstein, *Frankfurt on the Hudson. The German–Jewish Community of Washington Heights, 1933–1983. Its Structure and Culture* (Detroit, 1989), 285, note 45.

18 Women were also about equally likely as men to participate as amateur or professional entertainers at synagogue social events (except among the stricter of the Orthodox who excluded women singers). In some congregations, probably mainly non-Orthodox, women were also lecturers at general congregational events or meetings of the men's club.

sisterhood was founded at a meeting called by a man.[19] Other organizations had active women's auxiliaries. Most surprising of these was the very active women's auxiliary of the Jewish Veterans Association, whose male members had all served in the German army in World War I. Even such an organization, whose raison d'être would seem so masculine, felt the need for a women's group. The auxiliary had its own modest funds and held meetings and entertainment of its own. Its longtime leader, the entertainer Erna Fenchel, was treated as an important figure by the organization as a whole.[20] The Leo Baeck Institute, which had a women's auxiliary that performed fund-raising, socializing, and cultural activities similar to those of synagogue sisterhoods, is another surprising example of this organizational phenomenon.[21] Some important immigrant organizations had parallel, though not necessarily completely equal, male and female branches – for instance the Leo Baeck Lodge and Leo Baeck Chapter of the B'nai B'rith. Here they followed the same pattern as the overall American Jewish parent body.[22]

Many of the institutions set up by German–Jewish immigrants of the 1930s did not have an explicit gender character. Most of what were considered the major German–Jewish organizations – American Federation of Jews from Central Europe, New World Club (and its famous newspaper *Aufbau*), Leo Baeck Institute – tended to have a mainly male leadership. There was one type of organization, however, in which the role of women

19 Kraut, *German–Jewish Orthodoxy*, 223-4, records that Dr. Leo Tietz, president of the New Hope congregation, called a meeting of the female members and spouses of male members of the congregation on March 20, 1941, to establish a women's burial society. The women voted unanimously to create an all encompassing sisterhood out of which *chevrah* (burial society) would emerge. Kraut continues, "There was no question that the sisterhood was considered subordinate to the congregational functions controlled by the men, nor that they were not expected to partake in congregational governance. Still, the New Hope sisterhood over the years proved to be an extremely dedicated, effective force in supporting the congregation, adding a much needed and appreciated social dimension to congregational activities."

20 See *Mitteilungen der Immigrant Jewish War Veterans, 1942–1945,* which frequently describes activities of the Ladies' Auxiliary. In January 1951 the organization still had 281 surviving veterans and 83 members of the Ladies' Auxiliary. Both men and women attended the annual general meetings (see organizational minutes of the Jewish Veterans Association in the Leo Baeck Institute archives). In 1963 the main veteran's association had assets of $1,327; the death benefits fund had $15,022, the Ladies' Auxiliary had $413, and the men's *Hilfskasse* (collection) had $218. The bulletin of Beth Hillel congregation describes the memorial service for Erna Fenchel in its Dec. 1957/Jan. 1958 issue.

21 The women's auxiliary of the Leo Baeck Institute has only very recently gone out of existence (oral communication from Robert Jacobs). Another example of the existence of separate women's institutions was the fact that the (mixed-sex) Prospect Unity Club advertised that its club headquarters acquired in 1938 included a *Damenzimmer* (room for the ladies).

22 Separate female auxiliaries had already existed in the German lodges of the B'nai B'rith. In the post–World War I period, the question of admitting women to full membership was a matter of considerable controversy. Though the issue was frequently raised, the more conservative forces that wished to keep women in separate organizations were victorious. See Claudia Prestel, "Weibliche Rollenzuweisung," 51–80.

was often greater than that of men – the social service organization. To an extent women's role may be the result of the expectation that had become traditional, at least since the nineteenth century, that acts of charity and kindness were the role of women. Another influence may be the fact that social work was one of the few professional fields among German Jews in which women were present in large numbers.[23]

Whatever the causes, women played a very important role in some of the chief German-Jewish national welfare organizations such as Selfhelp as well as more local institutions such as the Immigrant Mutual Aid Society of Boston. Women worked in such organizations both as volunteers and as paid professionals. The functions of Selfhelp, whether as employment agency for domestic help, providing homemakers for the elderly, or counseling, often served a mainly female clientele, employed mainly female professional staff, or appealed to interests traditionally considered feminine. The full story of Selfhelp is told elsewhere in this volume. In the first decade of immigration, women were also predominant in providing daycare and preschool training within the community, either as a business or through organizations such as Help and Reconstruction.[24] In more recent years, women have been chief administrators at a number of complex facilities for the elderly created by immigrant organizations, among them Margaret Tietz at Newark House and Hansi Baruch Pollack at the Kissena Boulevard Apartments, both in New York City.[25]

Some energetic women created institutions and programs more or less on their own initiative although they worked with established organizations. A good example of such a person is Irma Tyson, who, besides having served as president of the Leo Baeck Chapter of B'nai B'rith, created an arts and crafts center for seniors in Washington Heights, New York, in the early 1960s. She also founded a coed youth group, dozens of neighborhood groups of women (men's neighborhood groups, she said, never succeeded), and, finally in the 1980s, she directed a German discussion group at the YMHA of Washington Heights to which a regular audience of 100 to 200

---

23 See Kaplan, *Making of the Jewish Middle Class,* 192–227, for a thoroughgoing discussion of the function and role of Jewish women's organizations in Germany and the pioneering role of Jewish women in the creation of the social work profession.

24 In Help Reconstruction most of the officers were men but many, though not all of those involved in running the kindergartens, were women. Oral history information on Help and Reconstruction is referred to in Strauss, vol. 5: 45, 46, 126, 127, and 128, and vol. 3, pt. 1: interviews 10, 52, 56, 86, 136, 157, and 213. Among the early commercial kindergartens (all led by women) were: Washington Heights Nursery and Play School – Bella Marx – April 1937; Amerikanisch-Deutscher Kindergarten – Selma Kahn Gruenstein – Nov. 1938; Alice Wertheimer's Progressive Kindergarten – Oct. 1939 (information from advertisements in the *Aufbau*).

25 Herbert A. Strauss, ed., *Jewish Immigrants of the Nazi Period in the U.S.A.* (New York, 1986), 5: 289–301, contains transcripts of oral history interviews with both Tietz and Pollack.

came. In all these events her personality set the tone for the event. She had strong opinions about her mission and did not wish her groups to be merely social. They were meant to have a substantive program.[26]

Within the Orthodox community, too, women played a larger role in social service organizations than elsewhere. The *Gemilluth Chessed,* chief Orthodox social service agency established in Washington Heights, was founded by four men and a woman who continued to play an important role in the organization.[27] Its Palisade Garden Home in New Jersey had a female administrator. In the very Orthodox Breuer community, it was the sisterhood which ran the Golden Age Club under the leadership of Hanna Jacobowitz.[28]

Perhaps even more influential, at least in recent years, is Elisabeth Wurzburger, executive director of the Jewish Community Council (JCC) of Washington Heights and Inwood. Although nominally a roof organization representing all Washington Heights Jewish organizations, the council is heavily influenced by the Breuer community. Elisabeth Wurzburger, whose father Dr. Raphael Moeller had been president of the Breuer congregation for almost forty years, controls most of the day-to-day activities of the council. Her role as administrator does not merely mean overseeing a host of social welfare organizations but is political as well. The JCC is the chief organization working to preserve the Jewish stake in the changing ethnic composition of Washington Heights. It is Elisabeth Wurzburger, alongside the male lay leaders of the council, who represents Washington Heights Jewry to local administrative and political bodies. Although the Orthodox synagogue to which she belongs automatically excludes her from congregational office, it seems to have no difficulty in accepting her as a leader of a powerful organization representing all of Washington Heights Jewry. It would be difficult to imagine a woman in an equally powerful position in similarly right-wing Orthodox groups of East European Jews in Brooklyn.

Other extremely Orthodox German–Jewish organizations, such as the Agudath Israel chapter of Washington Heights, also tend to be much less likely to separate the sexes at meetings and social events than are the Agudath chapters of East European origin. However, as the extremely Orthodox became Americanized (that is, came under the influence of East

---

26   Interview by author with Irma Tyson from July 21, 1983, and interview with her by Research Foundation for Jewish Immigration. See Strauss, *Jewish Immigration of the Nazi Period,* vol. 3, pt. 1: 126–7, interview 232.

27   The founders were Mrs. Rosenstock, and Messrs. Hagenbruch, Kirschner, Fred May, and Berthold Nussbaum.

28   In Congregation Beth Hillel, too, the club for older members ("Family Club") was founded by a woman – Erna Heilbronn. See *Festschrift,* 23, and *Beth Hillel Bulletin* 138 (Nov./Dec. 1956).

European Orthodoxy), formerly more flexible attitudes toward mixed social events, coeducational schools and public entertainment, and teaching by women were reversed and became less liberal.

As this very brief survey of women's roles in the community has shown, women have had a public role only in certain specific and rather restricted environments and were generally left to show their influence behind the scenes and indirectly. In some areas, such as social service organizations and political representation, women seem to have had increasing influence over time. In others, especially within the Orthodox community, restrictions on women seem to have increased rather than decreased.[29]

The contrast between the continued conservative attitude toward women's roles in many immigrant institutions and the changes in their roles in the "real life" arenas of family and employment requires explanation. One part of the explanation may relate to the function of immigrant organizations as a whole. These, like other minority organizations, often served as refuges from the struggles, humiliations, and difficulties of day-to-day life. Especially in the early years of immigration, when economic life was difficult, family relations were strained by women's greater chance of finding employment, and familiar patterns were upset, the immigrant clubs and congregations served as enclaves in which things were "as they should be." In these refuges from the storm of life, traditional male prestige, the natural use of the German language, the preservation of beloved traditions both sacred and secular, were the rule. If men had to accept the unaccustomed independence and even dominance of women at work and in the home (especially in the early years), they could still bask in the deference they received in their immigrant organizations. As we have seen, the dominance of men in those organizations was often not as great as it seemed on the surface. Women often deferred to men in organizational life but still exercised influence behind the scenes. Within the organizations, at least, women used traditional means to attain influence without directly challenging the patriarchal organizational patterns most of them preserved. In that way, perhaps, men were able to preserve a sense of psychological equilibrium when their position outside the immigrant institutions was being challenged, and women were able to avoid being excluded totally from all influence.[30]

---

29 It remains to be investigated to what extent the role of women in the German–Jewish immigrant community is distinctive and to what extent it reflects more general trends in American and American Jewish society. Many of the patterns described here, especially concerning synagogue sisterhoods and women's auxiliaries, probably differ only slightly from those of their counterparts in immigrant and native American Jewish institutions.

30 For a discussion of how the B'nai B'rith in Germany may have fulfilled similar functions as a male refuge from troubled times, see Prestel, "Weibliche Rollenzuweisung," 72.

There is one final aspect of the role of women in the community, especially in recent years, that must be discussed: the increased demographic prominence of women. As the community as a whole grows older, the actuarial fact that women tend to live longer than men has created a community in which the female population is becoming an increasing majority. In the early 1980s three separate samples of German–Jewish populations in Washington Heights revealed that women were anywhere from 53.5 percent to 61.2 percent of the total.[31] A large proportion of the surviving German–Jewish community now consists of widows, some of whom are in old age facilities but most of them living on their own with an independence many had not known before. As the role of the surviving German–Jewish organizations decreases, the aging German–Jewish community is in some ways more of a female society than ever before in its history.

31 In 1981 K'hal Adath Jeshurun had 759 male members and 873 female ones (53.5%). In 1982 Congregation Shaare Hatikvah had 268 male members and 422 female ones (61.2%). My own mail survey of three Washington Heights congregations in 1983–4 showed the families (heads of family and spouse only) or respondents contained 305 males and 466 females (60.4%).

13

"Listen sensitively and act spontaneously – but skillfully": Selfhelp

An Eyewitness Report

GABRIELE SCHIFF

Gabriele Schiff was born in Hamburg in 1914 and received her high school education in Germany. She came to the United States in 1938, where she received a BA from Swarthmore College and an MSW from the Pennsylvania School of Social Work. She earned her CSW in New York. Schiff served as the secretary to the refugee section of the American Friends Service Committee in Philadelphia and was a social worker for the Springfield State Hospital for the Juvenile Court in New York. After World War II, she spent three years in the displaced persons camps in Europe as a medical and clinical social worker. Upon her return to the United States, she worked as a supervisor with several refugee organizations. Since 1959 Schiff has worked with Selfhelp Community Services, New York City, in various capacities and currently serves as the agency's deputy director. Today, she makes her home in New York. This report was taken from notes and finalized in 1991.

Selfhelp has been part of my life for thirty-two years, and we still have not gotten tired of each other. Some people have done well-documented studies that explore this social agency's past and present. I can add to this only an eyewitness report demonstrating how a social agency can grow and change, adapt and adjust, and still be loyal to the concept on which it was based.

Selfhelp for Emigrés from Germany was founded in 1936 by émigrés from that country, but it was supported by a group of Quakers and also received support from some outstanding personalities connected with the New School for Social Research, or as it was then called by most people, the "University in Exile."[1] I met Selfhelp's first president, Professor Paul

---

1 The New School for Social Research was founded in 1919 by a group that included Thorstein Veblen, James Harvey Robinson, Charles A. Beard, and Alvin Johnson, to encourage open scholarly debate. Its Graduate Faculty of Political and Social Science, established in 1933, became widely known as the University in Exile.

Tillich, long before I had any connection with Selfhelp.[2] We met in 1938 when I was working for the Friends Service Committee in Philadelphia, helping to organize the Quakers' refugee section.[3] At this time avenues in Germany that were completely closed to Jews were open to Quakers. With American affidavits of support, one could rescue prisoners, political or racial, from concentration camps. Professor Tillich's speech explaining the concept of *agape,* which is more than charity, and his challenge, "to listen sensitively and act spontaneously, but skillfully," captured me then. It has been and still is today, the leitmotif of Selfhelp. However, it took twenty years for me to complete my American education and three years of work in displaced persons camps in Europe before I joined Selfhelp, which was by then called Selfhelp for Emigrés from Central Europe. The change in title is significant. First, there were the newcomers from Germany, and after the war, what was left of Central European Jewry. Selfhelp has always been ready to meet the needs of the day and to assist the group in need of assistance.

It was founded by people who knew what it was all about and, therefore, helper and client understood each other. They had in common not only language but also the mutual past and the joint struggle to create a better tomorrow. At all times, Selfhelp was infused with the spirit and intellectual influence of former teachers like Gertrud Bäumer,[4] Alice Salomon,[5] and Bertha Pappenheim.[6] They inspired the deeply felt tradition of noblesse oblige. This explains how Selfhelp came into being with very little money (charging only fifty cents for membership, for example) and on a volunteer basis. Volunteerism was the lifeblood of the early Selfhelp, and it was the women who carried the main burden.

There is an interesting phenomenon to be noted: On the whole – and of course with exceptions – it was the women who carried the family through, always reminding me of the grandmother in John Steinbeck's *The Grapes of Wrath* or characters in Scholem Aleichem's stories.[7] Many of the men in the

---

2 Paul Tillich (1886–1965) was a Protestant philosopher and teacher. Adamantly opposed to Nazism, Tillich came to the United States from his native Silesia in 1933. He remained active in the refugee cause in the United States.

3 The American Friends Service Committee was established in 1917 by the Religious Society of Friends of the United States to offer relief and reconstruction to war-torn Europe.

4 Gertrud Bäumer (1873–1954) was a leader of the feminist movement in Germany.

5 Alice Salomon (1872–1948), an educator and economist born in Berlin, actively encouraged women's professional participation in the field of social work.

6 Bertha Pappenheim (1859–1936) was born in Vienna to a wealthy Orthodox family. She became a social worker and a leader of the German–Jewish feminist movement.

7 Sholem Aleichem (1859–1916), Yiddish author and humorist.

early emigration were professionals and had to study again. The women had one skill that the volunteers of Selfhelp recognized as salable: They were good housewives. And so the profession of homemaker was born, elevating women from glorified maid to semiprofessional status. Because of his cultural background, it was much more difficult for the German man to accept serving others. First, the women helped with their own group. Then, the American social agencies "borrowed" our homemakers and even paid for their services! Later, Selfhelp developed home care services citywide, glad to share their experience and expertise with the city that had been so good to them. And Selfhelp always realized that both the client and the employee are, in a sense, clients. Both deserve a listening ear and a helping hand.

Selfhelp grew from small beginnings. A tiny office, a secretary who helped as a volunteer, and a small group of about twenty women working as counseling and placement volunteers. Money was in short supply, but shared experience, a listening ear, advice, and helpful hints were always available. And people were given time; the volunteers knew that the clients were bursting with recent experiences. Intuitively, the volunteers understood the healing quality of the shared experience. This was, I believe, one way in which Selfhelp differed from American agencies, whose workers had much less time and had to work with a waiting list. Although American-based agencies were extremely helpful, Selfhelp's clients needed something extra, a special, almost intangible component. Let me illustrate with a little anecdote that, shall we say, happened somewhere in the United States.

The case worker was highly professional and goal-directed, the client an elderly rabbi in traditional garb. The worker tried to persuade the client that he had to adjust and adapt, explaining the meaning of the new country. The client listened, watched the worker, and thought, "Poor young lady: no wedding band, no husband, has to work for a living." The American concept of "casework" is not necessarily an export article that is understood by all immigrants. In my work with displaced persons, I have seen how difficult it often is for the European man to accept the woman in such an authoritarian role as caseworker or counselor. The women may not agree with their advisors, but they are able to refrain from expressing disapproval when politically inadvisable. The need for "macho" caused quite a few difficulties in the beginning. On the other hand, women's belongings, their dishes and carpets, were extremely meaningful to them, and quite frequently they waited too long to leave their European homes because they simply could not part with their lifestyles and possessions.

But back to the early years of Selfhelp. Our main business was providing domestic jobs, averaging about fifty a month. There was at that time no competition from public home-care agencies. It sometimes seems as if Self-help invented the concept of home care when the time was ripe for it. Using home care constructively was a stroke of genius. One of our best baby nurses was a woman who had been a successful lawyer in Europe. There were also husband and wife teams who worked as couples. Some of them eventually owned restaurants. In one way, this immigration differs from others, because there was absolutely no going back. It was a completely involuntary immigration, and people had no choice but to sink or swim.

The counseling service worked, literally, day and night, seeing approximately 600 clients a week; the big organizations saw almost 1,000 a day. By today's standards, such a load would be unthinkable, but during those years, the unthinkable ruled the day.

One of Selfhelp's outstanding characteristics was and still is its extreme flexibility. If there is a need, it must be met. As one of Selfhelp's presidents said, "Define the need, tell me how you plan to meet it, we will find the money." One such need resulted in the creation of a "vacation spa." Clients had to deal with the hot summers in New York. These were, after all, "P.A." (pre–air conditioner) times. Most clients were hard working and needed, but could not afford, a break. But the American idea of camping was alien to their background. They thought more in terms of Carlsbad or Baden. So, Selfhelp rented a hotel. It was self-service, but it had a coffee hour in the afternoon and music at night. Somehow, it was a little bit "petite Europe," with the one exception: The administration were women.

Speaking of coffee and cake, Selfhelp tried to fill the need for the traditional European coffeehouse. In its outreach offices, it offered opportunities to get together, to feel less lonely, to share a cup of coffee, lots of past history, and future dreams! But the agency always had to strike a balance between keeping alive many traditions and at the same time encouraging adjustment to the new country.

As the clients grew older their needs changed, and slowly an employment agency became a geriatric agency. The older people's need for more secure housing became more obvious. And, again, it was the women who came to the rescue. Some families lived in large apartments and took in boarders, becoming "boarding mothers." And so another program was born. Again, both the boarding mother and her elderly, often sickly boarder were clients of the agency. They needed each other, and both needed the agency. This program died a natural death when more nursing home beds and more housing became available. Also, because of the distribution of restitution pensions, the economic need for boarding mothers grew less pressing.[8] Selfhelp and its sister agency, United Help, created housing, having by now built five apartment houses.[9] A closely related group created the Margaret Tietz Nursing Home, an initiative, once again, spearheaded by a woman.[10]

There are other programs, too many to describe. All grew organically; none was forced. Young families needed employment, so Selfhelp placed children in available summer children's camps and hired baby nurses. Older people needed secure housing, home care, support systems, summer vacations, and recreation. Counseling was and is needed by all groups. Counseling, being available, listening with a trained ear, and lending a helping hand – these are the *Begleitmusik* (background music) of Selfhelp's work today.

Today's client, much older and frailer, needs other services, including advocates in the fight for entitlements. The job is often made difficult by the clients' European attitude toward help: "That is charity. I never in my life needed that." Men, in particular, find government entitlements, such as Medicaid, difficult to digest. And there are those who, as a result of age and illness, are not able to make their own decisions. In these cases, the agency functions as a court-appointed conservator. As an agency designed to meet clients' changing needs in an ever-changing political climate, the organization has come a long way.

I am often asked, "Do survivors of the Holocaust age differently?" The answer is, yes and no. Basically, the problems of aging face all of us but more so the survivor. There is loneliness for the family that was lost, there are regrets for youth lost. Death is yet another separation to come. There is guilt about things done or left undone. But in most lives there is also a little garden of cherished memories to be called upon in moments of despair. I would say that the problems of aging are intensified in the survivor. Even today, Selfhelp is in contact with 1,500 survivors. When survivors age, they experience a "second immigration" of sorts. Suddenly, words come more easily in the mother tongue. As in the beginning, there are apt to be economic hardships, and, most important of all, there is the loss of friends and family members. Once more the survivor has to search for the support of a substitute family. In one form or another, all older people have to deal with these problems, but they are intensified for the survivor.

---

8   Under the terms of a law of September 18, 1953, the Federal Republic of Germany provided indemnification for victims of National Socialist persecution.

9   United Help, Inc. was founded by the American Federation of Jews from Central Europe, to foster both Jewish culture and acculturation to life in the United States.

10   The Margaret Tietz Center for Nursing Care, Jamaica, Queens, specializes in care for aged Holocaust survivors.

In its counseling services, Selfhelp has also learned that despite the immigrants' successful adjustment as a group, problems do not stop with the first generation. Most of Selfhelp's clients join at age sixty-two, and many children become clients out of a desire to help parents who are in their nineties! I call this group "survivors without an accent." A case in which a client of sixty-five asks for help finding a nursing home for his ninety-five-year-old mother is unusual, but it has happened. It is no surprise that the vast majority of Selfhelp's clients are women. In that respect our population does not differ from the rest of the world.

Today, Selfhelp is one of the largest home care agencies, and its program for Hitler's victims still exists. The agency's original mandate has never been forgotten, but the organization is proud to share experiences acquired in the field of geriatrics. It is significant that the top administration is American-born, but the board of directors is predominantly European, though as time passes it is increasingly made up of second-generation Americans. It is sometimes reassuring to see past and present meet. Let me share with you a personal anecdote: Last month, as I traveled back from Europe, I began to talk with my neighbor on the plane. He had no accent whatsoever and told me he was raised in Argentina and now lived in New Jersey. He was returning from – of all places – Mecklenburg–Schwerin, where his grandparents had run a hat store. He was bringing a hat from the still existing establishment to his father. When I said I worked with Selfhelp, he told me his father always says, "I'll never forget the wonderful ladies of Selfhelp. Where would we all be without them?" So, the early volunteers of Selfhelp are not forgotten. This illustrates part of my philosophy, shared by our organization: "The hands change, but the work must go on." As long as there is a Selfhelp, the former refugee from Hitler has a helper and an advocate because this agency considers itself to be: "Its client's last surviving relative."

14

"My only hope":
The National Council of Jewish Women's
Rescue and Aid
for German–Jewish Refugees

LINDA GORDON KUZMACK

The National Council of Jewish Women (NCJW) was "my only hope" recalled a German–Jewish refugee in 1940.[1] "Walter" was one of a few thousand German–Jewish refugees from Nazism who emigrated to the United States between 1933 and 1941. Council intervention even helped a few Jews escape Europe in the years before the United States entered the war. The NCJW located refugees' relatives trapped in Europe and attempted to secure their release. In some cases, they succeeded.

Most of the NCJW's war work, however, was devoted to protecting thousands of refugees as soon as they put foot on American docks. When German–Jewish refugees first arrived in the United States, a National Council of Jewish Women social worker or volunteer was often the first person to greet them upon arrival. The NCJW helped these émigrés find a home, employment, and social services; educated them in American customs and citizenship requirements; and lobbied tirelessly for legislation to lift immigrant quotas, ease naturalization requirements, and protect aliens' legal rights.

Despite these accomplishments, this chapter suggests that NCJW members were severely hampered by their status as women, Jews, and of German origin. United States government agencies and male Jewish leadership severely restricted the Council's activities, and the NCJW nearly tore itself apart through its own internal disagreements and conflicts with other agencies.

---

1 *Council Woman* 1, no. 1 (March/April 1940): 3–4.

THE NCJW AND AMERICAN JEWRY

On the eve of World War II, the NCJW, led primarily by German–Jewish women, was particularly conscious of the precarious position felt by Americans of German–Jewish origin.[2] All Jews felt vulnerable. At best, they were surrounded by the Protestant majority's belief in a Christian United States. At worst, Jews were engulfed by an anti-Semitism that escalated with the Depression, political isolationism, and the rise of fascist sympathies. Profascist vehicles, such as Father Coughlin's radio program and Henry Ford's newspaper, the *Dearborn Independent,* heightened anti-Jewish sentiment.[3]

Jewish women's organizations were further restricted by American and Jewish attitudes toward women. American culture glorified women as wives and mothers and encouraged volunteer activities that were perceived as extensions of the home. World War I had briefly opened new avenues for working women, but these became more restricted during the interwar period. When men joined the military during World War II, women were needed to fill their places at home. Although this opened more employment and volunteer service possibilities, these remained tenuous advances. American women still lacked political power, for they rarely participated in policy and leadership decisions, either in government, private employment, or religious life.[4]

Jewish tradition reinforced these attitudes and prohibitions, confining women to home and family.[5] At the turn of the twentieth century, a burgeoning Jewish women's movement led by American German–Jewish

2 Richard Wiebe, *The Search for Order* (New York, 1967), 2–4, 58; Naomi W. Cohen, *Encounter with Emancipation: The German Jews in the United States, 1830–1914* (Philadelphia, 1984), 39–43; Robert N. Bellah, *The Broken Covenant: American Civil Religion in Time of Trial* (New York, 1975), 45; Jonathan S. Woocher, " 'Civil Judaism' in the United States," 2, American Jewish Archives.

3 Leo P. Ribuffo, "Henry Ford and *The International Jew,*" *American Jewish History* 69 (June 1980): 437–77; Cohen, *Encounter with Emancipation,* 109.

4 Carroll Smith-Rosenberg, "The Female World of Love and Ritual: Relations between Women in Nineteenth-Century America," *Signs* 1 (Spring 1975): 1–25; Gerda Lerner, "Placing Women in History: Definitions and Challenges," *Feminist Studies* 3 (Fall 1975): 5–14; Lois W. Banner, "A Reply to 'Culture et Pouvoir' from the Perspective of United States Women's History," *Journal of Women's History* 1, no. 1 (1989): 101–7; Joan W. Scott, "Gender: A Useful Category of Historical Analysis," *The American Historical Review* 91, no. 5 (Dec. 1986): 1067; William H. Chafe, *The American Woman: Her Changing Social, Economic, and Political Role, 1920–1970* (New York, 1970), 151–60.

5 Paula Hyman, "The Other Half: Women in the Jewish Tradition," in Elizabeth Koltun, ed., *The Jewish Woman: New Perspectives* (New York, 1976), 106; Myra Shoub, "Jewish Women's History: Development of a Critical Methodology," *Conservative Judaism* (Winter 1982): 39; Linda Gordon Kuzmack, "Aggadic Approaches to Biblical Women," in Koltun, ed., *Jewish Woman,* 252; Steven M. Cohen and Paula Hyman, eds., *The Jewish Family: Myths and Reality* (New York and London, 1986), passim; Rachel Adler "The Jew Who Wasn't There: Halacha and the Jewish Woman," *Response* 7 (Summer 1973): 77.

women encouraged growing numbers of Jewish women to move out of the home. An increasing number of Jewish women volunteered in charitable (*tzedakah*) organizations and became more active in communal and national life. German–Jewish women even created their own independent women's organizations, enabling them to undertake their own social, religious, and communal causes. Despite women's growing involvement in Jewish life, men continued to control Jewish religious and communal political power.[6]

THE NATIONAL COUNCIL OF JEWISH WOMEN

Hannah Greenbaum Solomon, an upper-middle-class German–Jewish matron, organized America's first Jewish Women's Congress as part of the 1893 Chicago World's Fair. At the Congress, Solomon and her primarily German–Jewish Reform coterie of friends created the National Council of Jewish Women, which was patterned after the Federation of Women's Clubs. Being *German* as well as American Jewish women, they believed not only in their dedication to home and family but also in their mission to elevate morally and otherwise assist their poorer sisters. Most of these early Council members were Reform Jews, inheriting religious liberalism from mid–nineteenth-century German–Jewish pioneer reformers.[7]

The NCJW was committed to Judaism, American ideals, and the strengthening of an American Jewish womanhood that was moving toward independence under the impact of early twentieth-century feminism.[8] The Council formed Jewish study groups for members' religious and cultural self-improvement. Concluding that as a "religious body" it should be involved in charitable ventures, the NCJW engaged in social service projects to help immigrants and "less fortunate" girls and women. Yet, similar to non-Jewish and male-run German–Jewish philanthropic organizations, middle-class Council volunteers preferred to help German Jews and looked down upon the poorer immigrants from Eastern Europe who needed

6 Linda Gordon Kuzmack, *Woman's Cause: The Jewish Woman's Movement in England and the United States, 1881–1933* (Columbus, Ohio, 1990).
7 Hannah Greenbaum Solomon, *Fabric of My Life: The Story of a Social Pioneer* (1946; reprint: New York, 1974), 109; H. G. Solomon, *A Sheaf of Leaves* (privately printed, 1911), 127; *Papers of the Jewish Women's Congress* (Philadelphia, 1894), 61–2, 190, and 218–62; Ellen Sue Levi Elwell, "The Founding and Early Programs of the National Council of Jewish Women: Study and Practice as Jewish Women's Religious Expression," Ph.D. diss., Indiana University, 1982, 9 and 100–1; National Council of Jewish Women, *The First Fifty Years*, 22; Cohen, *Encounter with Emancipation*, 325–6.
8 Faith Rogow, " 'Gone to Another Meeting': A History of the National Council of Jewish Women," Ph.D. diss., State University of New York at Binghamton, 1988, 241–2.

greater assistance. The NCJW's bias, of course, was similar to that of American and Jewish society as a whole.

Although dominated by German–Jewish Reform Jews, the Council prided itself on including members from Reform, Conservative, and Orthodox Judaism. These women were drawn together by similar interests but divided by different religious and cultural perspectives.[9] To build a united organization, therefore, NCJW determined to avoid "controversial" political issues that threatened the organization's fragile unity.

However, determining which controversial issues were acceptable and which were to be avoided became a complex issue almost immediately. The NCJW's devotion to women's causes quickly led it into radical ventures. In 1908 the Council launched an international campaign against "white slavery," the heavily Jewish-run traffic in women, often Jewish women, who were tricked and forced into prostitution.[10] During the same era, the NCJW also campaigned for Jewish women's religious and communal equality, gaining greater participation for women in Jewish life. Many NCJW leaders joined the national suffrage movement, helping to win the vote for American women.[11] Yet, the NCJW officially avoided a formal statement supporting women's right to vote until nearly 1940.[12] The problem of whether or not to avoid controversy would haunt the NCJW throughout its efforts to assist victims of the Holocaust.

RESCUE AND REFUGEE AID

During the late 1930s through 1940, the Council attempted modest rescue efforts. They tried to help individual German–Jewish refugees save family members like "Walter's" mother, who was trapped in the Gurs internment camp in southern France. In this case, they failed.[13] The Council also financed the German–Jewish Children's Project, bringing children to the United States via England, as well as supported fifty scholarships for refugee students.[14]

The Council's early rescue ventures, however, were halted by 1940, partly because of the difficulties of providing overseas aid in war-torn Eu-

9   NCJW, *President's Report*, Mrs. Maurice L. Goldman, 17th Triennial, 1943. NCJW Papers, Manuscript Division, Library of Congress, 6.
10   On this issue, see Kuzmack, *Women's Cause*, chap. 3.
11   Kuzmack, *Woman's Cause*, chaps. 2 and 6.
12   NCJW, *Report*, Committee on Social Legislation, 18th Triennial Convention, 1946, 2. National Council of Jewish Women Collection, Manuscript Division, Library of Congress.
13   NCJW, *Council Woman* 3, no. 4 (Nov. 1942): 2.
14   NCJW, *Report* of the National Committee on Ways and Means, 17th Triennial, 1943, 1; *Council Woman* 1, no. 4 (Dec. 1940/Jan. 1941): 6.

rope. As we shall see, far more serious pressures were exerted by the United States government on the Council and other volunteer organizations to avoid any foreign rescue missions. The Jewish communal leadership also strongly encouraged the Council to concentrate its efforts on supporting the American war effort and to help refugees once they landed in the United States.

As a result, the NCJW focused exclusively on aiding refugees after they had arrived in the United States. This enabled the Council to aid Jewish victims while conforming to the state department's near-fiat that restricted help to immigrants. In this way, they exerted a powerful national presence as a loyal American organization.

By the end of 1938, when nearly the entire quota for immigration from Germany and Austria had been filled, the Council developed a formal program to help the newcomers.[15] The NCJW concentrated almost exclusively upon social service, legislative lobbying, and assisting refugees when they arrived on American shores. The traditional NCJW Jewish study circles continued but remained muted in the background.[16]

The Council's immigrant aid program had begun in 1903 when the NCJW assigned agents to greet unaccompanied women and girls at the docks. Council volunteers[17] and professional staff steered these newcomers to temporary shelters, then to permanent lodgings, education, jobs, health services, and training in becoming "good Americans."[18] As noted earlier, the NCJW become an international leader in the fight against the "white slavery" of Eastern European Jewish women forced into prostitution.

Drawing upon its extensive background in serving the foreign born, the NCJW created comprehensive social welfare projects ranging from health care to housing to job training to assisting refugees newly arrived from Nazi Germany.[19] The Council publicized this task as one particularly suited to women's modern role, combining activist leadership with wartime service.

The Council worked according to "rulings from Washington" that "multiply and change with 'blitzkrieg' speed."[20] Once immigrants arrived

15 NCJW, *President's Report*, 16th Triennial, 1940, C–3. NCJW Papers, Manuscript Division, Library of Congress.
16 NCJW, *Report of the Committee on Contemporary Jewish Affairs* and "Our Future Plans," Social Welfare Committee Chairman's Report, 18th Triennial Convention, 1946. National Council of Jewish Women Collection, Manuscript Division, Library of Congress.
17 NCJW, *Social Adjustment Report*, 16th Triennial (1940): 2–3.
18 NCJW, *Council Woman* 3, no. 4 (Nov. 1942): 2.
19 *Statistical Tabulation of Social Welfare Activities of Council Sections*, Oct. 1940; *Report*, Social Welfare Committee, 16th Triennial, 1940; *Report*, Committee on Social Welfare and War Activities, 17th Triennial, 1943. NCJW Papers, Manuscript Division, Library of Congress.
20 *International Service Report*, 16th Triennial (Nov. 1940): 1–3. NCJW Papers, Manuscript Division, Library of Congress.

in the United States, the NCJW helped them with getting passports and visas and establishing their legal status. This was especially critical for refugees who overstayed their visa permits or who had transit visas to countries that would no longer accept them.

At the same time, the Council waged intensive legislative campaigns against discrimination and demanded the lifting of immigrant quotas. Council publications kept members abreast of legislative changes.

The Council's Service to the Foreign Born, directed by Cecilia Razovsky, undertook a four-point program[21] of direct assistance to primarily German–Jewish immigrants:

1. *International Service.* From 1938 to 1939, the national office handled 18,191 cases, and mail totaled 48,000 letters from clients abroad and in the United States. In 1940 the Council's national office received 34,638 letters requesting assistance and registered 6,891 appeals for help in person. People asked for and received help in filling out affidavit forms, locating relatives, finding transportation, and the like. The national office receptionist handled 9,571 personal and telephone interviews.

   The Council's Service to the Foreign Born handled 3,000 immigration cases, 32,000 Central Location Index Registrations, and 15,000 search cases. Each NCJW social worker normally handled 200 cases per month, ranging from tracing a relative to arranging for migration of a family. In wartime, this case load increased to an average of 600 cases per month. The national professional staff made approximately seventy field visits across the United States during 1940.

2. *Port and Dock Work.* In 1933 and 1934 the National Council assisted more than 2,000 immigrants annually at the ports; 2,300 in 1935; more than 5,000 in 1936; 8,100 in 1937; and 16,000 in 1938 and 1939. In 1940, Council dock workers greeted 558 boats in thirteen ports and helped 14,656 arriving immigrants find emergency housing and employment. In only the first two months of the war, Council workers helped more than 1,000 passengers. The Council also represented interned and detained aliens at immigration hearings.

   Council sections aided refugees from around the world. The Boston Council Section reorganized its dock service to help arrivals from the Kitchener refugee camp in England. In 1940 they aided 710 newcomers. The Miami Section assisted 294 refugees from Cuba and elsewhere in December 1939 alone.

3. *Social Adjustment.* Council volunteers and professionals provided English classes, social clubs, and complimentary Council memberships. The entire program was designed to Americanize the newcomers, so they would "not be a peculiar

---

21 NCJW, *Port and Dock Service Report* (Nov. 1940): 1; *Report,* Service to Foreign Born Committee, 16th Triennial, 1940; NCJW, *Report,* Mrs. Irving (Katherine) Engel, Chairman of National Service to Foreign Born Committee, 18th Triennial, 1946, 3; *Social Adjustment Report,* 16th Triennial (Nov. 1940): 1; *Naturalization and Citizenship Report,* 16th Triennial, 1940, 1; NCJW Papers,' Manuscript Division, Library of Congress.

animal to the American non-Jew, so that relationships in the community will
be created without prejudice or bias."[22]

4. *Naturalization.* NCJW sections encouraged refugees to apply for citizenship,
guided them through the process, and organized Americanization classes. To
assist Sections in performing these tasks, the Council issued *Shop Talk* and other
publications that listed and interpreted all new immigrant legislation. By 1940
the Council had helped to naturalize approximately half a million immigrants.
A series of Council resolutions urged the U.S. government to ease immigration
quotas and end discrimination, particularly in immigration and naturalization of
aliens.[23]

The NCJW's programs proved so effective that in 1940, the Council was
asked to help the President's Advisory Committee for the Aid of European
Refugees (War Refugee Committee) to settle German and German–Jewish
political, literary, artistic, and academic leaders rescued from southern
France.

Campaigns for social legislation remained a part of every phase of this
Council program, including strategy and lobbying efforts for such key legislation as fair employment practices, price control, federal aid to education,
and immigration.

Several problems cropped up in developing such a massive project. Fi-
nancing a national program in wartime caused major internal difficulties.
Council members worried that they might not be able to manage the task
alone. At the same time, they feared that by accepting outside government
or nonsectarian organization funds they risked being taken over by outside
agencies. Concerned about a loss of independence, the Council voted to
finance its entire national program of service to the foreign born itself,
rejecting outside assistance.[24] Their crusade succeeded despite arguments,
disaffections, severe budget limitations, and conflicts with other agencies.

The Council, for example, worked closely with the Jewish community's
National Refugee Service (NRS), the umbrella social service agency created
by American Jewry's National Coordinating Committee. In 1939 the
Council reached an agreement with the NRS. The agreement provided
that NCJW would continue its port and dock work at Ellis Island and other

22 NCJW, *Resolutions,* National Committee on Foreign Born, 16th Triennial Convention, 1940, 2–5.
23 NCJW, *Resolutions,* National Committee on Foreign Born, 16th Triennial Convention, 1940;
    Report of Committee on Resolutions to 17th Triennial Convention, 1943; *Report* of Committee
    on Social Legislation, 18th Triennial Convention, 1946, 2; *Resolutions,* National Committee on
    Foreign Born, 18th Triennial Convention, 1946. National Council of Jewish Women Collection,
    Manuscript Division, Library of Congress.
24 NCJW, *Council Woman* 2, no. 1 (March/April 1941): 6. NCJW Papers, Manuscript Division,
    Library of Congress.

ports, as well as its Americanization and Naturalization, International Service, and Social Adjustment projects. The NRS would handle relief cases, case work treatment, transportation, employment, and resettlement. However, the NRS did not stick to the terms of this agreement, causing confusion, overlapping, and duplication of effort. The NCJW's demands for clear-cut division of responsibility and function were not implemented until after the war.[25]

THE ISSUE OF PATRIOTISM

Ever aware of the requirement to portray its mission in patriotic terms, the Council justified its projects by citing then–Attorney General Francis Biddle's post–Pearl Harbor speech calling upon citizens to help aliens feel welcome and to "foster loyalty" among them. In line with Biddle's directive, the Council defined its wartime social welfare activities as "service encompassing every phase of community life striving to win the war."

In this vein, the Council created an Alien Volunteer Project in December 1941. Sections of the NCJW interviewed immigrants, tabulated their skills, and directed them to local NCJW civilian defense and education projects. The project also published materials and trained volunteers to work within their communities to combat the antialien hysteria sweeping the nation. It represented aliens who had to defend their loyalty before the justice department's Alien Enemy Hearing Boards.[26]

The need to assert its patriotism dictated the Council's wartime efforts, just as it affected American Jewish leadership as a whole. American Jewry felt squeezed between the plight of European Jews and the not-so-subtle threat of being labeled unpatriotic and un-American should they provide assistance to their European co-religionists in a manner not sanctioned by the government.

Feeling vulnerable to charges of being unpatriotic, American Jews leaned over backward to demonstrate their patriotism as Americans. Historically cautious about the effects of large-scale Jewish immigration upon their own position as Americans, Jewish community leaders were reluctant to fight publicly a state department unwilling to ease quota restrictions in order to admit large numbers of Jewish refugees. Despite an outpouring of sympathy

---

25 NCJW, *President's Report,* 16th Triennial, 1940; NCJW, *Report,* Service to Foreign Born Committee, 16th Triennial, 1940. NCJW Papers, Manuscript Division, Library of Congress.

26 NCJW, *Report,* Mrs. Esther B. Kaunitz, Director, Department of Service to Foreign Born, 16th Triennial Convention, 1943. NCJW Papers, Manuscript Division, Library of Congress.

from many American citizens, Jewish leaders argued over whether and how it might be possible to rescue large numbers of European Jews and the possibilities of a campaign to persuade the American government to act.

Most Jewish leadership, typified by the American Jewish Congress (AJC) and the leaders of the American Jewish Joint Distribution Committee (JDC), not only remained profoundly cautious about recommending European rescue or relief plans but also avoided suggesting immigration and naturalization proposals that ran counter to state department wishes.

Intracommunal battles among Jewish organizations further hobbled efforts to help European Jews.[27] Jews of German ancestry, once the aristocrats of American Jewry, fought with the Eastern European Jews who now dominated them in numbers and were rapidly assuming leadership in certain American Jewish organizations. Pro-Zionist and anti-Zionist, religious and secular factions constantly fought over communal policies.

German–Jewish leaders also feared that spending too much money on Jewish causes overseas might harm American Jewry as a whole. As a result, contributions for overseas rescue were drastically reduced, forcing severe budget cuts and policy changes by all Jewish groups engaged in such work.[28] This led to the NCJW's exclusive concentration on aiding immigrants only upon their arrival in the United States.

Cooperation became one key to asserting Jewish patriotism. American Jewish Congress leaders in particular urged Jewish organizations to stress nonsectarian aid efforts. They hoped that by minimizing segregation from other groups, they might prevent an anti-Jewish backlash.[29]

Following this dictum, the Council cooperated with government and community service projects whenever possible.[30] The NCJW sent volunteers, funds, or both to nearly every major public and private welfare organization and to leading government agencies as well: the USO, the Red Cross, the U.S. Treasury Department, and the War Food Administration. Council members spent hours serving meals, visiting sick soldiers, running bond sales. Council members also joined the WACS, WAVES, the Red Cross, the USO, Travelers Aid, Jewish Welfare Boards, and similar organ-

---

27 David S. Wyman, *The Abandonment of the Jews* (New York, 1985), 311–40; Yehuda Bauer, *American Jewry and the Holocaust: The American Jewish Joint Distribution Committee, 1939–1945* (Detroit, 1981), 35–7; Judith Tydor Baumel, *Unfulfilled Promise: Rescue and Resettlement of Jewish Refugee Children in the United States, 1934–1945* (Juneau, Alaska, 1990), 12–22.

28 Yehuda Bauer, *American Jewry and the Holocaust: The American Jewish Joint Distribution Committee, 1939–45* (Detroit, 1982), 40–1.

29 Bauer, *American Jewry and the Holocaust,* 36.

30 NCJW, *Council Woman* 2, no. 1 (March/April 1941): 6–7; *Council Woman* 3, no. 1 (March 1942): 1. NCJW Papers, Manuscript Division, Library of Congress.

izations. Simultaneously, the NCJW worked closely with national consumer groups.[31]

Moreover, the Council joined the government's defense council, and later created its own chairmen on defense activities, who became NCJW's war activities representatives to government organizations. The NCJW even maintained a program for selling war bonds.[32] In the legislative arena, the NCJW was particularly proud of its delegation to the Women's Joint Congressional Committee.[33]

Recognized as one of America's preeminent women's organizations,[34] the NCJW was invited to become an integral part of a host of war-time government, private, and international agencies and committees, including the 1943 United Nations Relief and Rehabilitation Conference.[35] The Council disseminated information about these joint projects to its members. Internal publications kept members current on new legislation and government projects with which the Council cooperated, as well as independent Council projects and classes.

In 1944 the Council assisted the War Refugee Board on two projects: (1) preparing names of those last known to be in occupied Europe who were eligible for U.S. immigration visas; and (2) assisting the Emergency Refugee Shelter at Fort Ontario in Oswego, New York. For its part, the Council supplied social workers, clothing, supplies, and a service for locating relatives.[36]

31 NCJW, *Report* of Mrs. Gerson B. Levi, Chairman, Social Welfare Committee, 18th Triennial Convention, 1946; "Our Future Plans," NCJW Social Welfare Committee Chairman's speech, 18th Triennial, 1946, 2.
32 NCJW, *President's Report,* Mrs. Maurice L. Goldman, 17th Triennial, 1943, 4–6. NCJW Papers, Manuscript Division, Library of Congress.
33 Council worked on legislation pertaining to price control, the Lanham Act allotting funds for child care centers, the Mental Hygiene Act, grade labeling, continuation of UNRRA, the Patman Housing Bill, and so on. NCJW, *Report* of Mrs. Gerson B. Levi, Chairman, National Committee on Social Welfare, 18th Triennial Convention, 1946; *Report,* Committee on Social Legislation, 18th Triennial Convention, 1946; *Council on the Washington Scene,* Report of Mrs. Louis Ottenberg, NCJW Delegate to the Women's Joint Congressional Committee, 18th Triennial, 1946. National Council of Jewish Women Collection, Manuscript Division, Library of Congress.
34 NCJW, *President's Report,* Mrs. Maurice L. Goldman, 17th Triennial, 1943, 6. NCJW Papers, Manuscript Division, Library of Congress.
35 Council memberships in national committees included the Civilian Defense program to improve morale and strengthen welfare programs; the 1943 Advisory Committee on the Food for Freedom Conference; Standards Advisory Committee of the OPA; National Salvage Committee of the War Production Board; Executive Committee of the Social Protection Committee of the Federal Security Administration. Council also cooperated with private organizations, including the Advisory Committee on Volunteer Service of Community Chests and Councils. See NCJW, *Report,* Committee on Social Welfare & War Activities, 17th Triennial, 1943; *Report* of Mrs. Gerson B. Levi, Chairman, National committee on Social Welfare, 18th Triennial Convention, 1946. NCJW Papers, Manuscript Division, Library of Congress.
36 *Council Woman* 5, no. 4 (1944): 4–5; *Council Woman* 5, no. 5 (Sept. 1944): 5; *Eighteenth Triennial*

RESCUE VERSUS PALESTINE

Despite the Council's caution and strategy of cooperation, by 1943 over-whelming information about the death camps and angry demonstrations by rank-and-file American Jews caused Jewish leaders to press the U.S. government to mount rescue attempts.

Still, the American Jewish male leadership, aware of its limited resources, remained divided over whether to emphasize rescue or the creation of an independent Jewish state in Palestine that could welcome Jewish refugees who might survive the war. Zionists organized an American Jewish Conference that placed resolutions supporting both Palestine and rescue on the agenda. The NCJW sent voting representatives to the conference.

American Jewish Conference delegates, predominantly pro-Zionist, felt that creation of a Jewish state in Palestine was more important and more practicable than immediate attempts to rescue European Jews. Members of the NCJW were politically divided over the question of rescue versus creation of a Jewish state. Still, Council leaders had long been haunted by the knowledge that the United States government and the Jewish community could have done more to rescue Europe's Jews from the gas chambers.[37] At the conference, the NCJW became one of only two organizations that voted to support both rescue efforts for European Jews and unlimited immigration to Palestine. To keep internal peace within the Council itself, NCJW delegates abstained from the overwhelming vote demanding creation of a Jewish state.

The NCJW placed itself squarely in the forefront of Jewish attempts to rescue Jews. At its 1943 Triennial, the NCJW voted to support rescue efforts through cooperation with the American Jewish Joint Distribution Committee. To fulfill this goal, the Triennial emphasized its support of the "Joint," ORT, the American Jewish Conference, and other Jewish organizations.[38]

In 1943 the Council's Seventeenth Triennial created a Department for Overseas Service dedicated to serving Jewish Holocaust survivors. Immediately upon the latter's liberation in 1945, the Council initiated its program of overseas reconstruction. This effort originally began in 1920, when the

Report of Service to Foreign Born Committee, 18th Triennial (1946). NCJW Papers, Manuscript Division, Library of Congress.

37 *Council Woman* 5, no. 4 (1944): 4–5; *Council Woman* 5, no. 5 (Sept. 1944): 5; *Eighteenth Triennial Report* of Service to Foreign Born Committee, 18th Triennial (1946). NCJW Papers, Manuscript Division, Library of Congress.

38 NCJW, *Report on the American Jewish Conference,* 17th Triennial (1943): 6–7; *Report* of Mrs. Albert A. May, Chairman, National Committee on Contemporary Jewish Affairs, 17th Triennial (1943): 4–5. NCJW Papers, Manuscript Division, Library of Congress.

NCJW founding executive committee member Rebecca Kohut traveled to Europe to determine refugee needs following World War I. The Council subsequently funded reconstruction units of professional social service experts who were sent to Europe to aid refugees. The Council revived the Congress of Jewish Women in Vienna in May 1923 and organized a follow-up congress in Hamburg in 1926, held in part to discuss these problems. Suspended at the outbreak of war in 1939, these congresses were revived by the Council after World War II.[39]

In 1945 the Council's overseas program started in earnest. Social workers from the NCJW were assigned to displaced persons camps in Germany and to reconstruction programs in Belgium and Holland. Others were assigned to represent Jewish displaced persons (DPs) as liaison with the U.S. Army and United Nations Relief and Rehabilitation Administration (UNRRA). They organized food, transportation, shelter, clothing, and jobs, and helped to locate relatives, facilitated immigration to the United States, and established homes for unattached girls in Europe.

RIVALRY

For these efforts, the Council earned high praise from the Jewish community. Dr. Joseph Schwart, European director of the American Jewish Joint Distribution Committee, was enthusiastic in praise of these ventures.[40] The U.S. government, the Red Cross, and other national organizations were equally enthusiastic.[41] Nevertheless, organizations jealous of the Council's achievements charged that they were duplicating other agencies' work.

In response, many NCJW members felt that the Council was not receiving its proper credit. Council leadership tried to soothe bitter feelings, responding that the Council's goal was to "interpret and further" government projects.[42]

Part of the problem was a result of duplication and conflict with organizations with which the Council attempted to cooperate. Noncooperation

---

39 NCJW, *Council's Work in Europe Immediately Following World War I,* 17th Triennial (1943): 1–3; *Report* on Overseas Service, 18th Triennial, 1946.
40 NCJW, *Report* of Overseas Committee, 18th Triennial, 1946; *Council Woman* 5, no. 6 (Oct. 1944); *Council Woman* 5, no. 7 (Nov. 1944): 5; *Report,* National Committee for Overseas Service, 18th Triennial, 1946; *President's Report,* Mrs. Joseph M. Welt, 18th Triennial, 1946; *Minutes,* Pre-Triennial Board Meeting, 18th Triennial, 1946; *Eighteenth Triennial Report* of Service to Foreign Born Committee, 18th Triennial, 1946; *Message from Our Staff Overseas,* Hortense U. Goldstone, 18th Triennial, 1946. NCJW Papers, Manuscript Division, Library of Congress.
41 *Council Woman* 4, no. 4 (Sept./Oct. 1943): 5. NCJW Papers, Manuscript Division, Library of Congress.
42 NCJW, *Panel Report,* Social Welfare and War Activities Session, 16th Triennial Convention, 1943. NCJW Papers, Manuscript Division, Library of Congress.

was so severe that "some of the social agencies . . . compete in a fashion one would expect of rival railroads or two peddlers hawking their wares," commented the chairman of the Council's Service to the Foreign Born committee. The Council "signed agreements and [has] conscientiously fulfilled them, only to find that these agreements have been treated as the proverbial scraps of paper by the other parties." There was a desperate need to end "this jockeying for power and this desire for self-perpetuation."

The Jewish Welfare Board, for example, rejected one Council plan for cooperation and instead established the Women's Division of the National Jewish Welfare Board. Although the NCJW was an affiliate of the Women's Division, it regarded the division as duplicating Council Army and Navy services.

In one cooperative agreement, the NCJW was supposed to help only women newcomers, and members of the Hebrew Sheltering and Immigrant Aid Society (HIAS) were supposed to meet men and families. When immigrants needed relief, the Council was to transfer them to the National Refugee Service. This process never fully worked, particularly because of opposition from HIAS, which had tried to take over the NCJW's assignments at the docks, similar to attempts that had failed before World War I.

In March 1945 it became clear that the National Refugee Service was duplicating some of the work of the Council's Service to the Foreign Born program. Bitter arguments were intensified by awareness that the first quota of immigrants approved by President Truman had almost arrived. Finally, in 1946, the groups successfully negotiated a merger of the Council's national Service for the Foreign Born with the National Refugee Service, creating the United Service for New Americans, Inc. (USNA).

The USNA combined the national services of both organizations, providing "the largest and most comprehensive program ever provided for the foreign born in the United States." The Council provided 50 percent of the governing board and membership, plus sixty-three staff members; the National Refugee Service was dissolved. Because the NRS was a constituent service of the United Jewish Appeal, the UJA provided funds for the merged program in its first year. The Council's Overseas Service Program continued as an NCJW program that was funded by local welfare funds.[43] The Council lost its national Service to the Foreign Born in this new merger but retained its local SFB programs and expanded its overseas projects.

43 NCJW, *Report* of Mrs. Irving (Katherine) A. Engel, Chairman of National Service to Foreign Born Committee, 18th Triennial, 1946; *Report* of Executive Director, 18th Triennial, 1946; Katherine A. Engel, "United Service for New Americans," *Council Woman* 8, no. 1 (Fall 1946): 6. NCJW Papers, Manuscript Division, Library of Congress.

Although there were initial problems in the first few months, duplication between the Council and NRS did cease. Attempts to blend into this merger failed. Still, on the whole, SFB Chairman Katherine Engel judged the merger a practical and public relations success for the Council, which won praise for its cooperation.

CONCLUSION

The National Council of Jewish Women provided invaluable social welfare assistance to German–Jewish refugees, many of whom would never have survived financially or emotionally without their help. The Council's social and legislative programs also marked a major step in Jewish women's visibility and influence in national civic and Jewish social welfare causes. Council members learned to wield the political process well and continued to use it with skill in the postwar world.

The cost, however, was high. By war's end, although sixteen new sections were created, the Council lost seventeen old sections and was struggling to attract new members.[44] Some members resented the constant fund raising; others turned to more glamorous war-time agencies. The NCJW was nearly torn apart by the vicious infighting and competition among Jewish and non-Jewish organizations.

Furthermore, despite its early attempts to rescue German Jews in the mid-1930s, the Council, quashed by the same government pressure that limited male-run American Jewish organizations, had remained nearly totally silent on the need to rescue European Jews from 1940 until the American Jewish Conference in 1943.

The Council's secondary position to male-run Jewish organizations continued into the postwar world. Despite sitting on nearly every major public social welfare board and committee, the Council failed to achieve major political leadership in either Jewish or non-Jewish society.

Still, by war's end, this group led primarily by German–Jewish women had provided critical assistance to thousands of German–Jewish refugees and had facilitated a modest growth of Jewish women's influence in the Jewish community and wider American society.

---

44 NCJW, *Report on Extension*, by Mrs. Benjamin Spitzer, 18th Triennial, 1946, 1. NCJW Papers, Manuscript Division, Library of Congress.

15

The Genossinnen and the Khaverim: Socialist Women from the German-Speaking Lands and the American Jewish Labor Movement, 1933–1945

JACK JACOBS

Much has been written in both popular literature and more scholarly works on the strained encounters between Yiddish-speaking and German-speaking Jews.[1] Whatever their relations may have been in the world at large or in earlier periods, there is no evidence of any such strains between the socialist exiles from the German-speaking lands (many of whom were of Jewish origin) and the American Jewish labor movement in the years of the Third Reich. To the Jews of Central Europe, Yiddish-speaking Jews living in Germany and Austria before the Nazi era may well have been, to use Jack Wertheimer's phrase, "unwelcome strangers."[2] The socialist exiles from Germany and Austria, both those who were Jewish and those who were not, were perceived by the Jewish labor movement in America, however, not as strangers but as comrades in struggle. The women exiles from German-speaking Europe who were in contact with the American Jewish labor movement during the war, moreover, seem to have formed even deeper and longer-lasting bonds with that movement than did their male counterparts.

The organization most instrumental in creating ties between Jewish socialists in America and socialist exiles from the German-speaking lands was the Jewish Labor Committee (JLC). There were no women in the national

---

1 Research for this chapter was made possible by a grant from the Friedrich Ebert Stiftung. My thanks as well to Dr. Susanne Miller, who commented on an earlier draft and who also helped me to obtain relevant materials.
2 Jack Wertheimer, *Unwelcome Strangers: East European Jews in Imperial Germany* (New York and Oxford, 1987).

leadership of the JLC either before or during World War II. The JLC, moreover, did not specifically orient its rescue and relief activities toward women. There were, however, a number of women who were aided by the JLC during the war years, including a significant number of women from German-speaking Europe.

By the time the JLC was founded, on February 25, 1934, both the German and the Austrian Social Democratic and labor movements had suffered dramatic and disheartening defeats on their home territories. The JLC, which was created in New York at a meeting attended by representatives of a number of trade unions, the Workmen's Circle (a Jewish fraternal and insurance order), the Forward Association (publisher of a Social Democratic–oriented Yiddish-language daily), the Left Poale-Zion (a labor Zionist grouping), and the Jewish Socialist Verband, expressed support for the anti-Nazi and antifascist forces of Central Europe from the time of its founding.[3] Indeed, support for progressive and democratic antifascist and anti-Nazi forces was among the chief aims of the JLC in the years immediately following its establishment and a matter to which it devoted sustained attention. When, for example, Borukh Charney Vladeck, the guiding spirit of the JLC in its early years, visited Europe in 1935, he had a series of meetings with the German and Austrian Social Democrats living in exile in Prague and elsewhere and discussed with these leaders the ways in which the JLC could support their work.[4] In the late 1930s, following Vladeck's death, both right-wing Social Democrats affiliated with the SOPADE (the Social Democratic Party of Germany in exile) and left-wing Socialists affiliated with New Beginning (Neu Beginnen) received substantial financial support from the JLC.[5] It should, therefore, come as no surprise that the JLC acted with all the means at its disposal to aid German and Austrian socialists who were trapped in France by the Nazi invasion of May 1940. Its decision to do so was a result of ideological commitments, that is, a belief in internationalism, antifascism, and socialism, and the warm personal ties that had been fostered over a period of years.

Mobilizing its contacts in the American labor movement, the JLC succeeded in convincing the American government to allow a select group of

---

3   George L. Berlin, "The Jewish Labor Committee and American Immigration Policy in the 1930s," *Studies in Jewish Bibliography, History and Literature in Honor of I. Edward Kiev* (New York, 1971), 46.
4   Ephim Jeshurin, ed., *B. vladek in leben un shafen* (New York, 1935), 237.
5   Minutes of the Office Sub-Committee of the JLC, May 11, 1939, Jewish Labor Committee Collection, Wagner Archives, Tamiment Institute (New York). Meeting of the Office Committee Together with the Officers of the Jewish Labor Committee and the Representatives of the Labor Committee in the Joint Boycott Council, July 21, 1939, Jewish Labor Committee Collection, Wagner Archives, Tamiment Institute.

political refugees to enter the United States on visitors' visas. Having obtained assurances that emergency visitors' visas would be provided, the JLC turned to its contacts among exiles already in the United States for aid in preparing the lists of individuals for whom visas would be requested. Karl Frank, Rudolf Katz, and Joseph Buttinger were among those who provided the JLC with relevant names. But Hedwig Wachenheim, a former member of the Prussian Diet, who played an active role in the affairs of the SOPADE-oriented German Labor delegation, may have played an even more decisive role in this process. In fact, the only extant document describing the criteria by which individuals were chosen for inclusion in the list of Germans for whom visas would be requested by the JLC was written by Wachenheim. Wachenheim notes in this document that the first names submitted by Rudolf Katz were those of the leading lights of the SOPADE – Vogel, Breitscheid, Ollenhauer, among others. It was, significantly, Wachenheim who added the names of the wives of these individuals to the visa list, as well as the names of several other women. Marie Juchacz, who had been a member of the Reichstag and of the executive committee of the SPD throughout the Weimar years, for example, was placed on the list at the suggestion of Hedwig Wachenheim, and so was Marie Arning, who, like Wachenheim, had been a member of the Prussian Diet. In the same memo in which Wachenheim lists the women she believed ought to be put on the visa list, she also reported on the criteria that she used when endorsing or rejecting proposed names. She declined, for example, to endorse individuals who were proposed by the left-wing Socialist Hagen but whom she did not know or those who, she believed, had been Communists. Wachenheim, keeping in mind the relevant provisions of American immigration law and herself a veteran of the bitter battles between Social Democrats and Communists that had taken place in the Weimar Republic, also declined to endorse "Fifth Columnists" and attempted to reserve places on the visa list for only those political figures who were in immediate danger of being turned over to the Gestapo. All nonpolitical friends and relatives, Wachenheim insisted, must be excluded from the list. "I declined to put Mrs. [Karl] Kautsky [who was at that time in Amsterdam] on the list," Wachenheim notes:

This is a list of those people who are to be saved from the Gestapo, and not of those people who are already in its hands. Mrs. Kautsky's sons must attempt to bring her out.[6]

6 Memo by Wachenheim, n.d., Rudolf Katz Collection, Box 2, File: Frank Bohn Reise, Hoover Institution on War, Revolution and Peace (Stanford, Calif.).

The first list compiled by the exiles from Germany already in the United States and submitted to the JLC contained eighty-eight family names. A second list, made up of individuals from Austria, contained twenty-four family names. Supplementary lists were created as additional names were brought to the attention of those in the United States.

The women from Germany and Austria for whom the JLC requested visas fell into three categories. Several of the women on the list were themselves relatively prominent political activists or well-known anti-Nazi cultural figures. The writers Adrienne Thomas, Hertha Pauli, Toni Kesten, and Hilde Walter were all on the original list of individuals for whom visas were requested. Other women for whom visas were requested – Margarethe Haber (the daughter-in-law of the Nobel Prize winner Max Haber) and Antonie Wels (the widow of one-time SPD chairman Otto Wels) – were relatives of prominent individuals but not particularly prominent in the wider world in their own right. A third category of women who received visas with the aid of the JLC is made up of rank-and-filers who were neither prominent nor related to prominent figures but who had worked for prominent anti-Nazis or on the office staffs of one or another of the German Socialist groups.

Having aided these women in their escape from Europe, the JLC took pains to ensure that they would survive in the United States. Some were met by representatives of the JLC upon arrival. Material aid was provided to those who could not support themselves. Though the JLC was not eager to entangle itself in the political disputes among the several exile groups, it also provided political support to various organizations by providing speakers for events sponsored by the exiles,[7] and by publicizing activities undertaken by exile organizations.[8] Eva Lewinski, who was born into a Jewish family in Goldap, East Prussia, in 1910, attended university in France and became active in the *Internationaler Sozialistischer Kampfbund* (ISK) (International Socialist Fighting Alliance) after returning to Germany. She went into exile in France in 1933 and arrived in New York in October 1940 with a JLC-sponsored visa. Lewinski reported on her relations with the JLC in a letter to Willi Eichler dated January 1, 1941, that is well worth quoting at length:

The actual SOPADE circles here are not interesting. . . . I have good relations with them as well, but these aren't very close. In contrast, a much more intense rela-

---

7   Otto Leichter to Adolf Held, Oct. 1, 1945, Jewish Labor Committee Collection, Wagner Archives, Tamiment Institute.

8   Leichter to Samuel Estrin, Nov. 8, 1945, Jewish Labor Committee Collection, Wagner Archives, Tamiment Institute.

tionship has developed between us (I say "us," though I am alone here, because I am considered the group's representative) and the Jewish Labor Committee, which not only has great influence but also has very helpful, warm, and open people within its leadership ranks (mostly former Mensheviks). When anything very difficult arises and I no longer know where to turn . . . I can go to these people, present the problem to real comrades, and ask for their advice. To date, their willingness [to help] has always been there and their advice good, thoughtful, and effective. Apart from this form of immediate aid for our friends who need to be saved, however, is that these people are also very receptive to ideas, interested in our thoughts, and willing to promote some of them. It is possible that I will be called upon to give lectures to their English-speaking section. I have been asked when we will publish the *Warte* again. Before we definitely decide to do this, they would like to give us concrete proposals in connection with fund-raising and other, related matters. – All this as a way of saying that the interests of these people extend beyond mere assistance. That is all the more important since this Jewish Labor Committee is the only socialist organization here in which old thoughts, tied to a receptivity for new ideas, continue to exist. To date I have met only the older generation, mostly men over 40 or 50. What the next generation looks like, those born here for the most part, I don't yet know. I will discover that in my first lecture to the English-speaking section.[9]

One of the major attempts undertaken by the JLC to provide political support for exiles revolved around a group created in early 1943 through the efforts of the JLC: the Council for the Underground Labor Movement in the Axis Dominated Countries of Europe. The Council was designed to include the accredited representatives in the United States of all socialist and democratic labor groups that had been forced into exile by the rise of the Nazis and Fascists. Groups from Czechoslovakia, France, Hungary, Italy, Norway, and Poland, as well as the Austrian Labor Committee and German groups, participated in this Council. In fact, at least four different German groups were represented within the Council – the German Labor Delegation, the ISK, New Beginning, and, after sustained and heated objections by the German Labor Delegation, the German Socialist Workers' Party (SAPD). Eva Lewinski served as the representative of the ISK to this Council, and in this capacity had regular contact with leading figures in the JLC, the American Representation of the General Jewish Workers' Bund in Poland, and in other Jewish socialist and labor organizations. She supported the efforts of the SAPD to obtain a seat on the council, participated actively in Council meetings, and is known to have submitted a detailed

9 The *Sozialistische Warte* was a journal published by the ISK in Paris. Eva Lewinski to Willi Eichler, Jan. 1, 1941, Bestand IJB/ISK, Mappe 39, Archiv der Sozialen Demokratie, Friedrich-Ebert-Stiftung (Bonn). For additional information on Lewinski, see her curriculum vitae in the Jewish Labor Committee Collection, Wagner Archives, Tamiment Institute.

memorandum to the council on the reconstruction of the German labor movement.

Of course, not all contact between the socialist exiles from the German-speaking lands and the Jewish labor movement was mediated by the JLC. The Workmen's Circle, for example, encouraged the formation of a German-speaking branch during the war years that was made up of both Jewish and non-Jewish socialist exiles. Though Marie Juchacz, who was already in her sixties when the branch was formed, was technically too old to become a member of the Workmen's Circle at that point in her life and was not of Jewish origin, she was allowed to become a member of the branch without becoming a member of the Workmen's Circle itself, and was selected as the branch's chair.[10] Eva Lewinski, Erna Lang, and Frieda Albrecht also played leading roles in the work of this branch, which became known as the Solidarity Branch 424E. In 1944 and 1945, this group sponsored a regular series of lectures by prominent exiles and others dealing with political issues. Juchacz, for example, gave a talk entitled *"Unsere Aufgaben angesichts der grossen Europäischen Entscheidungen"* (Our Tasks in View of the Great European Decisions). At this meeting – and, we can safely assume, at others as well – the evening's program also had an artistic component, that is, duets by well-known concert singers, recitations, and so on.[11] According to Erna and Joseph Lang, the members of the Solidarity Branch took their work quite seriously. "Do you still remember our debates," the Langs once wrote,

our plans and resolutions . . . as though the world only had to wait for our findings? We wracked our brains thinking about what Germany would look like after the so-called Thousand-Year Reich, what we should do to completely eliminate National Socialism and intolerance in order to ensure the foundations of a different Germany.[12]

The branch, it would appear, was a small group of like-minded, German-speaking socialist exiles and was designed to provide a congenial atmosphere, a nest in an unfamiliar world. It was a group in which women played notably prominent roles.

Female exiles from the German-speaking lands were on good terms not only with the JLC and with the Workmen's Circle but also with the representatives in New York of the Jewish Workers' Bund. When, in the

---

10 Fritzmichael Roehl, "Marie Juchacz. Leben und Arbeit," (typescript, 1958), 303, Marie Juchacz Nachlass, Mappe 5, Archiv der Sozialen Demokratie, Friedrich-Ebert-Stiftung.
11 Meeting notice, Oct. 27, 1944, Friedrich Adler Collection, Mappe 12, International Instituut voor Sociale Geschiedenis (Amsterdam).
12 Roehl, "Marie Juchacz. Leben und Arbeit," 299–300.

spring of 1943, Shmuel (Artur) Zygelboym, the Bundist representative to the London-based Polish parliament in exile, committed suicide as a way of drawing attention to the mass murder of European Jewry, and the Bund chose Emanuel Sherer to be Zygelboym's replacement, Erna Blencke of the ISK (who was not of Jewish origin) informed Willi Eichler that Sherer

knows all of us, has received your writings, has spoken with us – in a working group and after he had made some prefatory remarks – about the Polish workers' movement.[13]

Although the contact that socialist women from the German-speaking lands had with the Jewish labor movement mitigated their isolation to some extent, their first years in the United States were, nevertheless, difficult, often brutally difficult. Lewinski, referring to both the male and the female exiles and refugees, describes this period as follows:

It can be said, in general, that for most of us, especially for the older ones, these emigration and war years in New York were a lonely, heavy period of waiting. We had little desire to adapt to the totally new circumstances more than was absolutely necessary. And so we remained like an island of shipwrecked people in the big ocean of New York, that generously made it possible for us to go on living, but that did not become a home; our essential ties lay in Europe, and insofar as one was able to maintain some hope for a future, that was also oriented towards Europe.[14]

Marie Juchacz, who had already lived through the death of a younger sister with whom she had been particularly close, the separation from her children, and the specific problems caused by her relatively advanced age, seems to have had a particularly hard time. Yet, despite her personal travails, Juchacz provided an essential role model for younger socialist women. As Lewinski expressed it,

In these years Marie was for me not the great figure out of the past, not the first woman deputy to speak in the Reichstag. . . . For me she was the symbol of a woman and a mother who could not be satisfied with a fulfilled life of her own, but who . . . worked for a place in society for all who suffered injustice. . . . As had been Käthe Kollwitz, she was in her heart above all woman and mother. But it was not enough for [Juchacz and Kollwitz] to be that exclusively – both women saw too much misery around them.[15]

13 Erna Blencke to Willi Eichler, July 2, 1943, Bestand IJB/ISK, Mappe 48, Archiv der Sozialen Demokratie, Friedrich-Ebert-Stiftung.
14 Article by Eva [Lewinski] Pfister in *Marie Juchacz. Gründerin der Arbeiterwohlfahrt. Leben und Werk* (Bonn, 1979), 143–4.
15 Ibid., 145.

As Lewinski points out, she and a number of her friends had earlier believed that it "was ethically impossible to combine a fulfilled private life with a full commitment to work in public life" and had therefore decided not to have any children. Once the United States, however,

with tasks so totally different from those in former years, with contact with people who somehow had managed in their own lives to belong to both worlds, the private and the public, it became clear to us that a complete life for us, and in particular for me, would not be possible without children. Thus, in the beginning of my friendship with Marie, I was expecting my first child, and Marie – herself a mother and an active comrade – became for me an encouraging symbol that one could be both.[16]

The fact that Lewinski's decision to marry at this time was part of a larger trend has been noted by Karl-Heinz Klär. Not only Lewinski but also her fellow ISK members Gisela Peiper, Erna Mros, and Frieda Timmermann, all of whom had arrived in the States after the Nazi invasion of France, married during 1940 or 1941.[17]

Eventually, these socialist women – like all those who had fled from Hitler – came face to face with the question of whether they ought to continue to live out their lives in the United States or ought instead to return to Europe. By and large, it would appear, the non-Jewish women were more willing to return to Germany and Austria than were those of Jewish origin. Lewinski, for example, who had experienced anti-Semitism in Germany long before the Nazi period, decided to remain in the States. Juchacz, Erna Blencke, and Frieda Albrecht, on the other hand, all of whom were non-Jews, eventually went back to Germany.

In the postwar era, Samuel Estrin of the JLC corresponded with several of the German-speaking socialist women who had lived in New York in the 1940s, and he nurtured both political and personal relationships with them. Estrin's correspondence with Lewinski, and other sources, suggests both the extent to which Lewinski was able to acculturate and her continuing gratitude to the JLC. When Lewinski and her family moved to California several years after the war had ended, she wrote Estrin that "our friends here [are], as we expected, very nice and willing to help, but no Estrin,"[18] and that her husband had found work with the aid of the JLC office in Los Angeles. In the period directly after their arrival in California,

---

16 Ibid., 146.
17 Karl-Heinz Klär, "Zwei Nelson-Bünde: Internationaler Jugend-Bund (IJB) und Internationaler Sozialistischer Kampf-Bund (ISK) im Licht neuer Quellen," *IWK Internationale wissenschaftliche Korrespondenz zur Geschichte der deutschen Arbeiterbewegung* 18 (1982): 343.
18 Eva Lewinski Pfister to Samuel Estrin, June 25, 1950, Jewish Labor Committee Collection, Wagner Archives, Tamiment Institute.

Lewinski and her husband still found time to attend (at the invitation of the JLC representative in Los Angeles) at least one event sponsored by the Workmen's Circle.[19] Despite the fact that the people with whom they came into contact at this meeting made a good impression on Lewinski, activities of this kind, which tended to take place in the city of Los Angeles rather than in the surrounding suburbs, were simply too far from her home for her to attend regularly. Eventually, Lewinski and her family made American-born friends, and Lewinski became a teacher of French in a junior high school. The demands placed on her time by her family and career, it would appear, left little time or energy for political activity. In 1961 Lewinski wrote to Estrin that

We are all working hard, and try to keep the head above water. Not much contact with our friends in Europe – there just is not time to keep up an active correspondence. . . . Best regards to all old friends who still remember us. Keep well, and don't forget that we are and will remain friends in spite of the long stretches of silence.[20]

Those of Lewinski's old friends who had returned to Europe, on the other hand, by and large remained politically engaged and kept political connections to the American Jewish labor movement. In 1951, to take one significant example, Estrin attempted to convince Erna Blencke, who had returned to Germany, to become involved in a campaign against German anti-Semitism. He suggested to Blencke that a first step in such a campaign would be the printing of a pamphlet expressing the perspective of the SPD on relevant issues, and he also suggested that it might be possible for Blencke to be paid for work done in conjunction with this campaign.[21] Estrin's letter is written in a style that suggests he considered Blencke to be someone who could be trusted with sensitive and confidential information. Although Blencke's response to Estrin is apparently no longer extant, it is clear that Blencke – like other Socialists who had survived the war by living in the United States – had developed warm feelings about the JLC as a result of her contacts with that organization during the Nazi era.[22]

The attitudes and activities of the American Jewish labor movement facilitated the survival of key female Social Democratic and labor activists from Germany and Austria, and thereby contributed to the rebuilding of Central European Social Democracy in the postwar era. Moreover, fe-

19 Ibid., Aug. 14, 1950.
20 Ibid., July 20, 1961.
21 Samuel Estrin to Erna Blencke, Nov. 20, 1951.
22 Erna Blencke to Samuel Estrin, June 22, 1950, Samuel E. Estrin Collection, File 11, Internationaal Instituut voor Sociale Geschiedenis.

male exiles from German-speaking Europe who first established contact with the Jewish labor movement during the war years remained in contact with it for decades thereafter. They seem in general to have maintained such contacts longer than did their male counterparts. In time of crisis, the similarities in cultural background and in political orientation between the socialist exile women from Germany and Austria (the *Genossinnen*) and the leadership of the American Jewish labor movement (the *khaverim*) generally outweighed and overpowered their differences. The *Genossinnen* and the *khaverim,* it would appear, were kindred spirits, and as such had considerable rapport with one another.

16

New Women in Exile:
German Women Doctors and the Emigration

ATINA GROSSMANN

It was terribly hard the first year. I was tied down with a young child. I was tied down with fatigue. I was tied down with trying . . . professionally I haven't lost anything. All right, I lost something but I got back here.

Alice Nauen, pediatrician, Hamburg/Boston, 1971[1]

I

For both male and female doctors the story of exile from Nazi Germany is one of loss of status and identity and painful, arduous reconstruction. The story of women's experiences, however, is highly complicated by gender. Like men, they confronted professional dis- and requalification. But they also faced intense gender discrimination in addition to prejudices against Jews and foreigners in the medical professions of their host countries. Furthermore, like all women émigrés, they were expected to provide material and emotional support for uprooted family and friends. A remarkable if minority group of refugee women did eventually return to the practice of medicine. However, the unique niche that female physicians had carved out for themselves in the Weimar medical profession proved virtually impossible to replace or re-create.

The focus on exile in this chapter structures a story that is necessarily partial and fragmented. The sources consist to a great extent of records of refugee aid organizations, memoirs, and oral histories. They capture only certain women at very particular moments in their lives. Memoirs were often written by women who assimilated least successfully and felt compelled to tell their bitter story. Many accounts were composed in the immediate aftermath of emigration and are powerfully colored by the shock of expulsion,

---

1 Dr. Alice Nauen, interview conducted by Herbert A. Strauss, Boston, Mass., June 12, 1971, 20. By permission of Research Foundation for Jewish Immigration, Inc.

the hardships of daily survival and adjustment, as well as the relief of having reached safety.[2] They do not necessarily reflect the authors' future roles in the host country. This is, of course, also true of the émigré organizational sources. Oral histories, on the other hand, are often collected toward the end of women's lives when the immediacy of the exile experience has passed. Exile therefore must be conceived as both a kind of permanent status that marks someone's biography and as a particular moment in which one is perceived and perceives oneself as an exile. For some, often the younger women, this identity shifted and changed; sometimes it was almost fully replaced by a new life. For others, probably the majority, who continued to live in a mostly refugee world, it remained prominent and determinate. A question that continually weaves through this story is whether and how women shift identities and re-invent themselves differently from men.

It is also important to remember that the terms "woman" and "women" are never stable categories. The example of women doctors, who became in many cases both displaced professionals and supporters of their families, highlights the importance of attending to differences among women refugees that are determined by marital status, age, number of children, place of origin, religious and political identification, class, and occupational status. Although most female refugee professionals were single, doctors had been the most married group of academically educated women in Germany; many of them had not only husbands but also children who urgently needed financial and emotional support.[3] For doctors as with other women, being single had advantages and disadvantages. Speaking of her own ability to decide quickly on emigration, the Berlin Social Democrat and physician Käte Frankenthal noted, "that one can only do truly sensible things in life if you are alone."[4] Single women had in some cases more mobility and less pressure to do menial labor to provide for children and retraining husbands but also less support and apparently more loneliness.[5]

---

2 See the remarkable collection of life stories composed for the essay contest on "My Life in Germany Before and After 1933" sponsored by Harvard University in 1940. Preserved in Houghton Library archive collection, Harvard University, Cambridge, Mass.

3 For discussion of German women doctors' negotiation of work and motherhood, see Atina Grossmann, "German Women Doctors from Berlin to New York: Maternity and Modernity in Weimar and in Exile," *Feminist Studies* 19, no. 1 (Spring 1993): 65–88. For discussion of refugee women in the United States, see Christine Backhaus-Lautenschläger, . . . *Und standen ihre Frau* (Pfaffenweiler, 1991).

4 Käte Frankenthal, *Der dreifache Fluch: Jüdin, Intellecktuelle, Sozialistin. Lebenserinnerungen einer Ärztin in Deutschland und im Exil* (Frankfurt/Main, 1981), 260.

5 Examples of single professional women who had been well established in Germany and then died impoverished, underrecognized, and lonely in the early years of exile include Alice Salomon and Helene Stöcker. See also Backhaus-Lautenschläger (1991), 275–84. For a more upbeat perspective, see Erna Barschak, *My American Adventure* (New York, 1945).

Age and stage of professional development were clearly significant in determining further development in host countries. Precisely the generation of Weimar "new women" who had come of age before the Depression hit and had so hopefully established themselves after the war and during the innovative stabilization years, were most disabled. The young were able to adapt more easily, learning the language, getting schooling and training in their new homelands or, in certain cases, in temporary exile countries such as Italy or Switzerland. On the other hand, a surprising number of fiercely determined refugee women doctors were able to revive their medical careers in middle age, usually after years of hardship and struggle.

To understand what exile meant for women doctors, we have to locate them in several comparative contexts. We need to consider where they were coming from and what their lives had been like before they were forced to leave Germany. We also would do well to compare their fate with that of their "Aryan" and politically acceptable colleagues who remained in Germany throughout the Nazi period and World War II. Finally, we need to keep in mind comparisons with male physicians and with women refugees who were not professionals.

This chapter presents two different but overlapping groups of women. The first group includes women, mostly those who were born before or around the turn of the century, who had been well established and known in Germany before 1933. Often affiliated with the Social Democratic or Communist parties, they had been activists in the social welfare and sex reform initiatives of the Weimar Republic. They had worked in campaigns for legal abortion, staffed birth control and sex counseling clinics, and served as welfare and health insurance clinic doctors. The second broader category encompasses refugee women doctors as a whole, a group whose numbers, in the words of one observer, were "remarkably high," have so far been neither precisely determined nor deemed worthy of separate study. Indeed, it has been estimated that 12 percent of the approximately 6,000 physicians who emigrated from Germany were women, a percentage that topped both their representation among German doctors as a whole and among German physicians identified as Jews.[6]

More perhaps than any other group of refugees (certainly more than

6 Hans Peter Kröner, "Die Emigration deutschsprachiger Mediziner 1933–1945. Versuch einer Befunderhebung," *Exilforschung. Ein internationales Jahrbuch* 6 (1988): 83–97, claims that women constituted 10.5 percent of all Jewish physicians in Germany and 8.5 percent of all physicians in 1933 (my own figures are closer to 6.5 percent), 86. Kröner also notes (p. 95) that the story of women physicians in exile remains to be told. My own incomplete and continually growing name list, compiled from the Biographical Archives of the Research Foundation for Jewish Emigration, the Medical Directories of New York State for 1951 and 1959, as well as numerous other written and

women taken as a whole), women doctors expressed (and not only in nostalgic retrospect) a deep sense of satisfaction and pleasure in their professional and personal lives before 1933. As Charlotte Wolff wrote in her
memoirs about life as a young clinic physician in Weimar Berlin, "Heaven
was not somewhere above us, but on earth, in the German metropolis."[7]
Rachel Straus reflected in Palestinian exile in 1940 that her hectic years in
Munich as Jewish and feminist activist, mother of five, and physician were
the happiest and most satisfying of her life.[8]

The sense of loss experienced by exiled women doctors helps to rela-
tivize the focus on women's supposedly superior coping skills that has
characterized much discussion of women and emigration from Nazi Europe. It is frequently assumed that women's familial priorities and the relative weakness of their attachment to public status, as well as their generally
greater social flexibility, meant that they adjusted to exile better than men.
Women carried with them more practical training in modern languages
and household skills as well as a greater willingness to accept employment
beneath their (bourgeois) status. The fact that, as one refugee woman doctor put it, "It isn't as hard for a woman to cook, as it is for a man to scrub
floors," made them more adaptable to foreign lands, indeed turned them
into primary and lifesaving breadwinners in the early years of emigration.[9]
Women's mediating contacts with social service agencies and their children's schoolteachers often made them into the primary translators of the
new world for their families. Attention to women doctors can both confirm and undermine that comforting maternal story. Starting the story in
Germany highlights how much this is a story of loss and the very high
costs of exile for women, as well as, in some cases, of successful adjustment
and retooling.

oral sources, currently includes 213 names, of whom 68, barely a third, can be confirmed as having
reestablished some form of medical practice. Most but not all of these names represent women who
came to the United States. According to Kröner (p. 90), 84 percent of all exiled German physicians
eventually landed in the United States, Great Britain, or Palestine/Israel. The biggest gaps in my
own research are the fate of women doctors who went to Great Britain and Palestine. Kathleen
Pearle's pioneering work on the United States, done in conjunction with Stephan Leibfried and
Florian Tennstedt, takes note of several women but pays no specific attention to gender. Marion
Berghahn, *German–Jewish Refugees in England* (London, 1984); Paul Weindling, "The Contribution
of Central European Jews to Medical Science and Practice in Britain, 1930s–1950s," in Werner E.
Mosse and Julius Carlebach, eds., *Second Chance: Two Centuries of German-speaking Jews in the United
Kingdom* (Tübingen, 1991), 243–54; and Doron Niederland, "Deutsche Ärzte-Emigration und ge-
sundheitspolitische Entwicklungen in 'Eretz Israel' (1933–1948)," *Medizinhistorisches Journal* 20, nos.
1–2 (1985): 149–84. None discusses women doctors.
7 Charlotte Wolff, *Hindsight. An Autobiography* (London, 1980), 66.
8 Rachel Straus, *Wir lebten in Deutschland. Erinnerungen einer deutschen Jüdin 1880–1933* (Stuttgart,
1981), 141, 143, 259.
9 Alice Nauen, interview transcript, 33.

II

By 1933 women doctors constituted an important and visible, although numerically small, force within the German medical profession, especially in the burgeoning arena of social medicine. In 1909, two years after the German census had estimated that 30 percent of the German labor force was female, there were only 82 women physicians in the entire German Reich.[10] In 1925 the census counted 2,572 women physicians, 5.4 percent of the total and over a thirtyfold increase from the pre-1914 figures.[11] Concentrated in urban areas, many had been trained and licensed during World War I and were employed by the municipal health services and insurance systems that constituted such an important part of the Weimar social welfare network. In 1924 they had established their own professional organization, the League of German Women Doctors (*Bund deutscher Ärztinnen*), which about 900 women had joined by the end of the Weimar Republic. By 1933, 3,376 of the 51,527 physicians in Germany were women, and medicine had become the major course of university study for women.[12]

Almost half of all Weimar women physicians were married, usually to other physicians, and producing a respectable average of 1.65 children each.[13] Excluded from the higher ranks of the profession, women physicians were willing to negotiate their multiple commitments by accepting compromises in their careers, which in turn often led to lower status, lower paid but personally and politically rewarding positions as public health employees. About 70 percent of women doctors were general practitioners (*praktische Ärzte*). Specialists were concentrated in fields such as pediatrics, dermatology, sexually transmitted diseases, psychiatry, and obstetrics and gynecology (the latter usually as general practitioners), which served women and the poor.[14] Unlike elite male doctors in universities and private specialty practices, and despite their overwhelmingly bourgeois origins, women came into daily contact with the working class and working-class politics. This led to an unusually high degree of left-wing activism in a profession noted for its conservative, indeed reactionary politics.[15]

10 *Monatsschrift Deutscher Ärztinnen* 4, no. 1 (1928): 2. See James Albisetti, "Women and the Professions in Imperial Germany," in Ruth-Ellen B. Joeres and Mary Jo Maynes, eds., *German Women in the Eighteenth and Nineteenth Centuries: A Social and Literary History* (Bloomington, Ind., 1986), 94–109.

11 *Statistik des Deutschen Reichs*, vol. 408 (1925): *Volks- und Berufszählung*, 301.

12 *Die Ärztin* 9, no. 12 (1933): 260–1. According to the census for 1925, almost a quarter of women doctors were under thirty and 45 percent were between thirty and forty. *Berufszählung*, 302.

13 This birth rate topped that of any other civil servant group. *Die Ärztin* 9, no. 12 (1933): 260–1.

14 See *Die Ärztin* 7, no. 4 (1931): 100.

15 See among many sources, Michael H. Kater, "Hitler's Early Doctors: Nazi Physicians in Pre-

Women doctors were particularly visible in Berlin; in 1932 the city boasted 722 women physicians, by far the largest concentration in the Reich.[16] Jewish women were also particularly prominent among female medical students and urban women doctors; in Berlin at least 270 were Jews.[17] Women, most of them Jewish, on the political left, or both, directed five of the sixteen municipal Marriage Counseling Centers (*Eheberatungsstellen*) and were well represented among the ranks of school physicians (*Schulärzte*) operating out of district health offices that were dominated by Social Democrats and Communists. All five physicians staffing the prenatal care service of the Berlin Health Insurance Association (*Verband der Krankenkassen Berlins*) were women who handled a total of about 25,000 consultations annually as part of a network of polyclinics (*Ambulatorien*) committed to innovative concepts of social and preventive medicine. Dr. Alice Vollnhals-Goldmann and her all-woman team of doctors and social workers used the new prenatal and family advice clinics to pioneer a comprehensive health service for women that offered counseling on contraception as well as on healthy pregnancy, childbirth, and breastfeeding. Women doctors also played a leading role in the association's marriage and sex counseling centers, as well as the birth control counseling centers run by Helene Stöcker's League for the Protection of Mothers (*Bund für Mutterschutz*) and other women's groups.[18]

Women doctors were especially prominent among the vanguard ranks of Weimar "new women" who were juggling career, marriage, and motherhood. The attempt to reconcile maternity with paid work and to produce new women capable of rationally and lovingly managing both was central to the Weimar social project and to the "modern" identity of the Republic. As

depression Germany," *The Journal of Modern History* 59 (1987): 25–52; Michael H. Kater, "Professionalization and Socialization of Physicians in Wilhelmine and Weimar Germany," *Journal of Contemporary History* 20 (1985): 677–701; Michael H. Kater, "Physicians in Crisis at the End of the Weimar Republic," in Peter D. Stachura, ed., *Unemployment and the Great Depression in Weimar Germany* (Basingstoke and London, 1986), 49–77; Claudia Huerkamp, "The Making of the Modern Medical Profession, 1800–1914: Prussian Doctors in the Nineteenth Century," in Geoffrey Cocks and Konrad H. Jarausch, eds., *German Professions, 1800–1950* (New York, 1990), 66–84.

16   *Die Frau* 11, no. 9 (1935): 148.

17   This figure is based on the names collected and estimates made by the *Gruppe Berufstätiger Frauen medizinischen Fachgruppe* of the *Jüdischer Frauenbund* in Berlin, January 1934. Material in Gesamtarchiv der Deutschen Juden, Bundesarchiv Potsdam, Aussenstelle Coswig. I am grateful to Sharon Gillerman, History Department, UCLA for sending me these documents.

18   *Jahrbuch der Ambulatorien des Verbandes der Krankenkassen Berlins 1930–31*, 13. In 1931, the Berlin municipal marriage counseling centers in Friedrichshain, Neukölln, Reinickendorf, Wedding, and Charlottenburg as well as the Confidential Center for Married and Engaged Couples in Charlottenburg, were all directed by women doctors. See Max Hodann, *Geschlecht und Liebe in biologischer und gesellschaftlicher Beziehung* (Berlin, 1932), 245–57; *Jahrbuch der Krankenversicherung* (Berlin, 1926–27, 1928–29, 1930–31); also Charlotte Wolff, *Hindsight. An Autobiography*, 95–111; and government reports in the Bundesarchiv Koblenz, Reichsgesundheitsamt 86/2379 (5).

middle-class professionals, women doctors enjoyed for a brief and precarious period a peculiar conjunction of traditional bourgeois privilege (especially household help) and radically expanded, albeit subordinate, employment opportunities. This liminal moment provided an extraordinary opportunity for integrating family and career without overwhelming guilt or exhaustion, and it was later often remembered with bittersweet nostalgia as a kind of special "best of times" before the coming of the "worst of times."

III

With the triumph of National Socialism, the fate of this extraordinary group of professional women came to a dramatic divide. When the Nazis purged and reorganized the German health system in 1933 and 1934, many women doctors fell victim to *Gleichschaltung* (coordination) as Socialists or Communists, as "double earners," and as Jews or spouses of Jews; frequently, some were in all those categories. The April 1933 law for the restoration of the Civil Service (*Wiederherstellung des Berufsbeamtentums*) and a broad range of other restrictive regulations promulgated in the spring of 1933 fundamentally transformed the landscape of medical practice in Germany. Politically suspect non-Aryan, and "double-earning" employees were dismissed from the municipal and communal health systems in which they had been so active. They were also denied access to health insurance eligibility and other money-making work such as Sunday and night-time housecalls, thus cutting off a major source of their livelihood.

An extremely high proportion of the physicians working in urban social health services were Jews and on the political Left. Well over 50 percent of all Berlin municipal hospital doctors and even more in the public clinics were Jewish. In the not atypical "Red Wedding," a district in Berlin known for having a high concentration of left-wing voters, 80 percent of the doctors in the children's hospital were Jewish, as were 80 percent of the public welfare doctors, five of the six school physicians, three of the six school dentists, and the directors of the infant and children's, prenatal care, and marriage counseling services.[19] The Nazi regime denounced the bold Weimar social welfare experiments, such as the health insurance and municipal polyclinics, as profligate purveyors of fiscal waste, sexual immorality, and eugenic irresponsibility that disproportionately benefited the "unfit" and

---

19 *Verwaltungsbericht der Bezirksverwaltung Wedding für die Zeit vom 1. April 1932 bis 31. März 1936*, no. 11 (Berlin, 1936), 29. See in general the *Verwaltungsberichte* of the Berlin *Bezirke*, which detail the dismissal of welfare, public clinic, and hospital personnel.

"asocial" at the expense of "worthy" healthy citizens. Clinics for birth control and sexual advice were closed and retooled as Counseling Centers for Gene and Race Care (*Erb- und Rassenpflege*). Physicians associated with birth control and the sex reform movement, many of them women and Jewish, were denounced and arrested as abortionists.

The removal of Jews and the politically unreliable was an eminently economic as well as ideological act. The process of "liquidating useless and politically unreliable employees and replacing them with staff above suspicion" (*einwandfrei*)[20] offered the new Nazi authorities a means to restore political order, trim a supposedly bloated welfare budget, cut back by attrition the total number of employees (*Sanierung*), and finally fulfill the Depression campaign promise to purge from public jobs women who could be classified as double earners. A disproportionate number of these purged doctors were women who had found congenial employment opportunities in the municipal and health insurance system. Indeed, women were particularly affected because unlike Jewish men they were unable to claim "Hindenburg exemptions" as frontline World War I veterans (although the *Reichsbund jüdischer Frontsoldaten* did try to gain exemptions for non-Aryan women doctors who were widows of veterans).[21] They were also much less likely to have large practices with private patients who would continue to use their services outside of public clinics and without insurance reimbursement. Even when some Jewish physicians managed to have their insurance eligibility temporarily restored, women benefited less because they tended to work in clinics and hospitals rather than in independent private practices.[22] Dismissed women physicians tried to continue working, often by assisting in the practices of their husbands (until they were restricted to the position of *Krankenbehandler*, or clinical assistants, in 1938), went on staff at "Jewish hospitals" or in Jewish organizations, and of course desperately tried to emigrate, sometimes "selling" flourishing practices to eager Aryan colleagues. A whole generation of established and highly qualified physicians was expelled, and the careers of a significant number of young women doctors who had just begun to establish themselves were suddenly cut off.

20 Landesarchiv Berlin (Aussenstelle, former Stadtarchiv), Rep. 47–09, Sign. 109, Lichtenberg. In Berlin's Lichtenberg district, for example, 129 employees were fired in 1933 and replaced by only 89 new staff members.
21 Bundesarchiv Potsdam, Reichsministerium des Innern (RMI) 26401, Nichtarische Ärzte, April 1933–April 1934.
22 Despite the fact that 2,000 "Aryan" physicians were brought in to replace them, a significant number of non-Aryan physicians were readmitted to panel practice after having been banned by Decree of the Reich Ministry of Labor on April 22, 1933. By September 30, 1938, when licensing was denied to all of them, there were still 3,152 "non–Aryan" physicians in Germany, of whom 709 were allowed to continue as *Judenbehandler*. See Kröner (1988), 85.

After 1933, therefore, one group of German women doctors faced discrimination, disqualification, exile, and incomplete reconstruction in foreign lands; the other experienced continued if altered professional existence in the Third Reich and then in the two postwar Germanies. In large cities like Berlin, the purges decimated hospital and clinic staffs at the same time that Nazi population policy generated an enormous demand for doctors able and willing to handle the daunting new racial hygiene tasks. In fact, the selective pro- and antinatalism of Nazi eugenic and population policy as prescribed in the July 1933 law, which mandated sterilization for the physically and mentally "unfit" and the provision of marriage loans and other benefits for the "fit," did offer new spheres of activity and influence for women physicians. A 1934 report noted that it fell especially to the female doctor to handle the human trauma of the eugenics program. Women were best suited, for example, to explain to other women that they were "unfit" to bear children, no matter how deeply they wished to have them:

For this one needs extraordinary tact and often it is only the psychological sensitivity and warm heart of a motherly woman who can alleviate these apparent heartships and even extract some understanding for the absolute necessity of such measures.[23]

Many "Aryan" women doctors, especially younger ones who did not remember the years of struggle for professional recognition, saw in Hitler's Third Reich, with its stress on sex-segregated social welfare and the selective encouragement of motherhood, the promise of new professional opportunities. Not the least of these were the job openings indicated by the list of Jewish names appearing under the rubric "Resignations" in *Die Ärztin,* the journal of the League of German Women Doctors.

The new Nazi state claimed a commitment to improving mothers' status and health, even as that same regime was destroying health insurance clinics, shutting down birth control counseling centers, and dismissing precisely those colleagues who had pioneered the institutions concerned with maternal and child welfare. The League of German Women Doctors justified its willingness in 1933 to purge its ranks of the racially and politically "unfit" in terms of its long-standing commitment to the interests of women:

The League was always completely apolitical in its goals and ideas, quite purposefully only promoting the interests of women, children and the family.[24]

23 "Die Frau als Ärztin," in *Deutsche Frauen an der Arbeit* in Bundesarchiv Potsdam, DAF (Deutsche Arbeitsfront) 62–03/7089.
24 *Die Ärztin* 9, no. 6 (June 1933): 118.

"Aryan" women doctors, having acquiesced in the *Gleichschaltung* of their professional association, fought hard and not without success to protect their professional status under the changed political circumstances. They assailed the "double-earner" regulations, insisting that two incomes were necessary for the maintenance of an adequate standard of living for their families and that only married women could truly understand the personal health needs of German women. Precisely because their "superwoman" tasks required discipline and robust health as well as maternal instinct, they were the kind of *Übermenschen* required by the National Socialist state. The League of German Women Doctors defended its members as being "not just overly refined, purely intellectual, unfeminine creatures . . . but competent practical women who can cope with all demands."[25]

When both male and female Jewish and politically suspect physicians were excluded from insurance and civil service positions in the spring of 1933, there had been no such pleading. On the contrary, the women doctors' league argued (correctly) that married women doctors were now more necessary than ever, as a result of the particularly severe loss of non-Aryan physicians in specialties serving female patients.[26] Hertha Nathorff, general practitioner and director of a Berlin marriage counseling center, clearly remembered the banishment that contrasted so sharply with what she had felt was the progressive stance of her professional organization. One evening in the spring of 1933 at a regular League meeting, she was confronted by unfamiliar women, some of them already wearing swastikas on their collars, who suddenly informed her and about twenty-five of her colleagues that the Jewish doctors should "leave the premises, we are now coordinating with the Nazi state." Non-Jewish Communist and Social Democratic colleagues from whom she had expected support no longer dared appear at the meetings.[27]

As with so many organizations that capitulated to Nazi *Gleichschaltung* in hopes of preserving their autonomy, the League's expectations were eventually disappointed and it was dissolved by the Reich Medical *Führer* in 1936. Collaboration and professional survival had come at a price. Despite continuing increases in the total number of women physicians, the proportion of nonpracticing female doctors, most of them presumably married and pressured by the double-earner campaign, climbed from 4.8 percent to

25 *Die Ärztin* 9, no. 12 (Dec. 1933): 262.
26 *Die Ärztin* 11, no. 9 (Sept. 1935): 147.
27 This is a composite of two very slightly different versions of the same event related by Hertha Nathorff, once in an interview in New York on June 16, 1980, and earlier in her essay on "My Life Before and After 1933" submitted to Harvard University researchers in 1940. Essay in Houghton Library, Harvard University, no. 162.

17 percent between 1930 and 1937. The coming of the war and the final exclusion of all non-Aryan practitioners, however, once again reversed that trend, cementing women's presence in the postwar medical profession in both Germanies.[28]

Unlike their colleagues in exile, whose biographies and careers were so profoundly, often permanently disrupted, "Aryan" women doctors who remained in Germany continued to work in relatively seamless fashion. Women found employment as doctors in the Counseling Centers for Gene and Race Care, in the League of German Girls, and in other National Socialist women's institutions. A very few "Aryan" champions of abortion reform and birth control in the Weimar years were able to retreat safely into "apolitical" private practice. Anne-Marie Durand-Wever, a sex reform activist in the League of German Women Doctors, worked quietly in Berlin's West End and apparently continued to provide birth control for her patients. She reemerged into public life after the collapse of National Socialism, first as an officer of the Communist-inspired *Demokratischer Frauenbund Deutschlands* and finally, after her estrangement from the East, as a co-founder of the postwar West German planned parenthood organization *Pro Familia*.[29] Another Weimar sex reform activist, the Saxon general practitioner Barbara von Renthe-Fink, briefly fled to Switzerland at the beginning of the Third Reich when threatened with arrest for communist activities and the loss of her health insurance eligibility. She shed the doctor husband who had bestowed her with unwanted double-earner status, discontinued all political activities, and moved to the larger town of Chemnitz, where she fortuitously took over the well-outfitted practice of an emigrating Jewish internist. Renthe-Fink also returned to public life after 1945, first as a health officer for the Soviet occupation and then as a Social Democratic health functionary in West Berlin, her commitments to birth control and women's emancipation revived.[30]

In another bizarre twist of fate, Alice Vollnhals-Goldmann, the dynamic abortion rights advocate and former director of the infant and prenatal clinics of the Berlin Health Insurance League, fled Germany to Shanghai with

28 Michael H. Kater, *Doctors Under Hitler* (Chapel Hill, N.C., 1989), 92–3, 108.
29 Interview with Dr. Durand Wever's daughter, Annemarie Florath, Berlin-Johannistal, Dec. 1991. See Reingard Jäkl, "1945 – Eine politische Chance für Frauen?" in *"Ich bin meine eigene Frauenbewegung": Frauen-Ansichten aus der Geschichte der Grossstadt* (Berlin–Schöneberg, 1991), 268–97. See also the archives of the Demokratischer Frauenbund Deutschlands (DFD) [formerly located in East Berlin, GDR, current location of archive unfortunately unclear] and International Planned Parenthood Federation Archives (IPPF) archives at the David Owen Centre for Population Studies at the University of Wales in Cardiff.
30 Barbara von Renthe-Fink, *So alt wie das Jahrhundert. Lebensbericht einer Berliner Ärztin* (Frankfurt/Main, 1982).

her husband, the social hygienist Dr. Franz Goldmann, only to return to Nazi Germany in 1936 after her divorce. Unlike her husband, who had languished depressed, she used her many languages and social skills to quickly build up a busy pediatric and gynecological practice among both the native Chinese and the foreign colony in Shanghai. When her marriage collapsed, Vollnhals-Goldmann reverted to being Alexa von Klossowski from an aristocratic anti-Semitic Russian family. Freed of her Jewish mate and once again acceptable for health insurance privileges, the reinvented Alice/Alexa practiced in working-class Kreuzberg with great energy and pleasure until three days before her death in 1969. Her doctor's sign announced in the language of her Weimar commitments, "Counseling Center for Women and Girls, Birth Control."[31]

At the end of the war, the miserable conditions in bombed-out cities, the mass flight of women and children from the East, and the rape of German women by occupation, especially Red Army, soldiers disrupted women doctors' lives in a fundamentally new way but also broadened yet again their public health responsibilities. Some women doctors who had been active National Socialist party members were briefly denied private practice privileges as part of denazification proceedings in the Western zones. Ironically some of them were then assigned to work in the public health offices and hospitals that certified and provided abortions for the large numbers of women who were pregnant as a result of rape.[32] Reasonably uncompromised women professionals on the other hand, especially doctors, lawyers, and journalists, played an important role in the women's councils and organizations that were set up immediately after the end of the war in East and West. Women doctors as professionals carried on and indeed expanded their ranks during and after World War II. But the progressive social health experiments in which some of them had played such a leading role were forever destroyed. With rare exceptions, the doctors who had nurtured those projects were forced out of the profession and out of Germany.

IV

Keep in mind that exile did not begin the moment the Nazis came to power, even if circumstances of medical practice did drastically change after

31 I am indebted to Itta Vollnhals, Berlin, for generously sharing memories and memorabilia of her mother-in-law as well as to Christine Antoni, Medizin-Historisches Institut, Freie Universität Berlin, for information on Franz Goldmann.

32 Doctors in the Soviet occupation zone, unlike in the Western zones, were exempted from denazification. See, for example, the files of the district Ministry of Health offices in Landesarchiv Berlin, esp. Neukölln, Rep. 214.

the April 1933 laws. Some politically active women doctors such as Lilly Ehrenfried and Käte Frankenthal did leave by the spring of 1933, but most remained in Germany practicing their professions long after the Nazis had taken over. They assisted in husbands' practices, supported a Jewish clientele and often worked for Jewish institutions. The *Jüdischer Frauenbund* in Berlin almost immediately set up groups for professional women who had been purged from their own professional organizations. The medical group (*Medizinische Fachgruppe*) listed about seventy members in Berlin at the beginning of 1934 and was planning meetings that combined social support and continuing professional exchange.[33]

Women physicians with their large numbers of women patients were particular targets of the regime's tougher enforcement of antiabortion laws. Especially Jewish and politically outspoken women doctors who had worked in birth control and sex counseling centers were repeatedly subjected to attempted entrapment. A woman and three men arrived in young Dr. Lilly Ehrenfried's Berlin office in the winter of 1933; they claimed that she had ordered them to appear for a scheduled abortion. Ehrenfried vehemently denied ever doing such procedures and hastily fled to Basel and then to Paris.[34] Hertha Nathorff was arrested in 1936 on charges of having referred a sickly seventeen-year-old for an abortion in 1928. Having cleared herself of that charge, she was then visited several months later by an elegantly dressed woman offering money for "help."[35] The stories have a common pattern. The Hamburg general practitioner Henriette Magnus Necheles wrote in 1940:

That people could be punished for acts committed many years before represented a grave danger. . . . Once a physician was arrested, he could wait for months without a hearing. Then, perhaps, the proceedings would begin. First insurance practice reports going back to 1924 would be scrutinized. If the records revealed too many miscarriages, then the patients would be summoned and questioned about anything and everything. They frequently were told that the physicians had confessed and their testimony was only a formality. Not every woman could withstand such torment, many said yes in order to avoid further interrogation. If, in spite of all this, the accused was released as innocent, his practice had, in the meantime, long since vanished.[36]

---

33   See material on *Gruppe berufstätiger Frauen, Medizinische Fachgruppe* (doctors, dentists, pharmacists, nurses) of the *Jüdischer Frauenbund* in Berlin; for February 1934 they planned a meeting in the hall of the *Reichsbund jüdischer Frontsoldaten* with a lecture on stomach and intestinal diseases. Gesamtarchiv der deutschen Juden, Bundesarchiv Potsdam, Aussenstelle Coswig.

34   Dr. Lydia (Lilly) Ehrenfried, memoirs, Kfar Saba and Paris, 1968, in Leo Baeck Institute, New York. I am grateful to Christian Pross, M.D., for donating a copy of this unpublished manuscript.

35   Wolfgang Benz, ed., *Das Tagebuch der Hertha Nathorff: Berlin–New York, Aufzeichnungen 1933–1945* (Frankfurt/Main, 1988), 88. See also pages 28 and 31 of the original essay, Houghton Library, Harvard.

36   Henriette D. Magnus Necheles, "Reminiscences of a German–Jewish Woman Physician," Chi-

Memoirs suggest that many women doctors remained in Germany for as long as they could practice and fulfill their vocation of helping others and making themselves useful. Some wrote eloquently about how their role as mothers as well as the impossibility of continuing their professional work pushed the final decision to emigrate. Alice Nauen, who worked as medical director of a Jewish girls orphanage, remembered:

I had a very full life, as long as one could practice. We left when we had a child and when my license was taken away. We realized now it's time.[37]

Henriette Necheles, who described giving up her medical practice in Hamburg as being akin to "burying a beloved relative," wrote about the arduous process of emigration:

Old tax returns, new tax returns, leaving things behind in escrow (so that we could smuggle valuables across the border), birth certificates, drivers' licenses, declarations of non-belief. I don't think there was any kind of document that did not have to be submitted and investigated. Time flew, most of our money was deposited so that we could not back out, the time for my confinement drew near and our courage began to erode.

But, "thoughts of my second child woke me up. Never again a German–Jewish child; no new second class citizen."[38] Women also recorded the pain of watching their practice vanish, patients no longer daring to come or sliding in through the back door. Hertha Nathorff described her shock at seeing a boy whose difficult birth had interrupted her engagement party fourteen years earlier suddenly stand in her consultation room in October 1935 wearing a Hitler Youth uniform.[39]

Dr. Edith Kramer on the other hand did not get out in time, having been distracted by her husband's fatal illness. She remained in Berlin as a *Krankenbehandler* until 1942. Frequently harassed by Gestapo agents who tried to induce her into performing illegal abortions, she carried on a curious medical practice. She cared for the sick but also provided certificates of exemptions from forced labor on account of contagious disease, and wrote prescriptions for sleeping pills with precise instructions on the amount required for a lethal dose. In June 1942 she was transported east to a girls' labor camp. Wearing her Jewish star and riding a bicycle adorned with a swastika, she tried to treat everything from pneumonia to scarlet fever and

cago, 1940, original deposited in Houghton Library, Harvard University; reworked and translated by Ruth F. Necheles, New York, 1980, 49. I am grateful to Eleanor Riemer for giving me this manuscript.

37 Alice Nauen, interview transcript, 7.
38 Henriette D. Magnus Necheles, 1980, 56–57.
39 Hertha Nathorff, 1940 essay, 26.

dysentery without benefit of instruments, medications, or disinfectants, cheered only by gifts of bread, cigarettes, and chocolate smuggled in from a nearby British prisoner of war camp. Her valiant efforts to try to improve conditions earned her incarceration in a Gestapo prison back in Berlin on charges of sabotage. While she sat in jail, "her girls" were all deported to Auschwitz: "Thus because of my sabotage I am the only survivor of Antoninek." Kramer was then sent to Theresienstadt, where she worked in the camp infirmary. In February 1945 she was among the lucky 1,200 inmates taken by train to Switzerland, where she worked in a sanitorium for tubercular orphan boy survivors whom she finally accompanied to a new home in Australia. At age forty-eight she resumed her medical studies at the University of Sydney, aided by young women students who took English notes for her. With a little boost from the corner grocer, who referred skeptical patients to the German–Jewish lady doctor after she had expertly patched him up after an accident, she reestablished a modest practice.[40] In yet another example of the fates of German–Jewish women doctors, the ear, nose and throat specialist Else Levy continued to direct her department in the Berlin *Jüdisches Krankenhaus* until she was forced underground, denounced, and deported.[41]

V

Women doctors who could fled to all corners of the world, to Shanghai and the Soviet Union, to Palestine, England, Australia, and in most cases to the United States. In these countries they found a social and family system and a medical establishment that were much less hospitable to the combination of personal, professional, and political commitments that they had managed in the Weimar Republic. Indeed, for most of the predominantly

---

40 Edith Kramer (Freund), "Hell and Rebirth: My Experiences during the Time of the Persecution," Leo Baeck Institute, memoir 283. Personal interview.

41 Berliner Geschichtswerkstatt, *Der Wedding. Hart an der Grenze. Weiterleben in Berlin nach dem Krieg* (Berlin, 1987), 82. It would be interesting to determine whether women doctors were less likely and able to emigrate than were men, and how that varied by age and marital status. According to a Letter to the Editor of *The New York Times* printed on March 14, 1937, from Jonah B. Wise, Co-Chairman Joint Distribution Committee Campaign, 1,500 to 1,600 Jewish doctors remained in Berlin. Seventy percent of Jewish doctors left in Germany were 45 years of age or older and 45.4 percent were 55 or over. Reprinted in Dr. Kathleen M. Pearle, *Preventive Medicine: The Refugee Physician and the New York Medical Community 1933–1945* (Bremen, 1981), 221. Marion Kaplan has suggested that despite their manifest willingness, women, especially older women, enmeshed in extended family obligations, were the least able to emigrate from Germany. See her article, "Jewish Women in Nazi Germany: Daily Life, Daily Struggles 1933–1939," *Feminist Studies* 16 (1990): 579–606. The later the emigration, the more difficult it was to be relicensed. New York State, for example, which had been the most liberal, imposed formidable reexamination requirements in October 1936.

Jewish, Social Democratic, and Communist (but very bourgeois) women physicians, the harsh days of emigration were the first time that they actually faced an unwillingness to accept women as physicians or had to concern themselves with domestic drudgery.

Hertha Nathorff was bitterly articulate in her emigration diary about the loss of her identity as a Weimar "new woman." She grieved not only for her comfortable home and social position but most especially for her ability to combine work in the profession that was most meaningful to her with the life of a wife and mother. Filled with resentment, Nathorff worked as her husband's office assistant (even for a while as a singer in a jazz nightclub) and as a volunteer in the New York refugee community. In Berlin, with adequate money and servants, in a milieu where doctor couples (albeit with the husband in the superior position) were not uncommon, self-assured, successful husbands had not objected to their wives' work. Indeed, they often expressed pride and pleasure in their companionate marriages. Now, in the uncertainty of exile, men reverted to traditional notions of women's place and gender hierarchy. Nathorff lamented about her displaced husband, "He can't escape from his civil servant milieu, his pride, his stupid pride, that he has to be and will be the family breadwinner, it torments him, but he also torments me."[42]

Nathorff shared her fate with many refugee women doctors. Husbands and colleagues slowly reestablished their practices and their professional circles, their bourgeois identities. The wives, no matter what their original occupation, worked initially as cooks, housekeepers, and nursemaids to support themselves and their family while the men studied for the dreaded foreign language and medical licensing exams. There was little support for women doctors to do the same, not from the medical profession or from the refugee aid societies who always repeated the discouraging message, "They don't need more doctors here, and certainly not women doctors."[43] There was also no support from husbands who now, bereft of status and household help, needed wives to be wives, to help *them*.

Hertha Riese, the former director of a *Bund für Mutterschutz* Marriage and Birth Control Counseling Center in Frankfurt[44] and a distinguished figure in the sex reform movement, escaped Germany with her husband, the neurologist Walter Riese. Whereas her husband was (barely) able to

---

42 Wolfgang Benz, ed., *Tagebuch* (1988), 189–90.
43 Quoted in Miriam Koerner, "Das Exil der Hertha Nathorff," *Dachauer Hefte* 3, no. 3 (Nov. 1987): 239.
44 Riese's co-director Lotte Fink emigrated to Australia and became active in International Planned Parenthood.

support himself with grants for displaced scholars from the Rockefeller Foundation, the internationally known Hertha Riese learned that adjustment to the United States meant not only domesticization as a woman but also political deradicalization. Penniless and depressed in New York in 1942, she wrote a poignant letter seeking help from her old comrade in the birth control movement, Margaret Sanger:

I do not mean to interfere with the ways Mrs. S. feels she can recommend me and I certainly do not either intend to renegade my convictions or my past endeavor. The question under the very difficult situation of getting a start within a very complicated set-up . . . is not to put an emphasis on Birth Control.[45]

Walter Riese, having landed a lonely position at the Virginia College of Medicine in Richmond, pleaded to no avail with the Rockefeller Foundation on his wife's behalf:

Mrs. Riese made innumerable efforts to make use of her capacities. She failed everywhere. For the last months she has been doing a very hard and very primitive physical work, just like any unskilled woman.[46]

Hertha Riese finally found a position as an educational therapist working with delinquent black children in Richmond. When she asked for aid to support her volunteer mental hygiene work in the juvenile courts, both the Rockefeller Foundation and the National Committee for Resettlement of Foreign Physicians turned her down because her situation did not constitute an "emergency."[47] Exasperated with Riese's unwillingness to accept her fate as wife of a medical school professor in Richmond, Virginia, the Rockefeller Foundation concluded that "Mrs. R. is rather difficult."[48]

In a similar case, another sex reform doctor, Sidonie Fürst, supported the family while her husband studied for his exams and renewed professional contacts. She worked as an assistant at Margaret Sanger's Birth Control Bureau in New York for $5.00 a week while practicing night nursing and still trying to keep up with her own studies. The National Committee for Resettlement of Foreign Physicians judged her to be ". . . very well-

---

45 Hertha Riese to Miss Rose, Feb. 10, 1942, Box 69/Folder 664, Margaret Sanger Papers, Sophia Smith Collection, Smith College. Sanger did her level best to rescue colleagues from Nazi Europe, persevering in the face of heartbreaking pleas and maddening stonewalling from American authorities. Her efforts and those of her assistant, Florence Rose, which led co-workers to refer to their "Refugee Department," are documented in her papers but have not received sufficient attention. See also Box 659 in the Sanger papers at Smith College and *Margaret Sanger Papers Project Newsletter* 5 (Spring 1993): 2.

46 Walter Riese to Robert A. Lambert, M.D., Dec. 3, 1942. Rockefeller Foundation Center Archives (hereafter: R.F.), R.G. 1.1. Series 200, Box 97, Folder 1180.

47 Robert A. Lambert, memo, April 29, 1943. R.F., R.G. 1.1. Series 200, Box 97, Folder 1180.

48 Robert A. Lambert, memo, Dec. 1, 1944. R.F., R.G. 1.1. Series 200, Box 97, Folder 1180.

educated in dermatology" with ". . . excellent experience in sexual science and birth control methods . . . and [a] modest, sincere, and attractive personality." The committee complained, however, that such eminently qualified women doctors were reluctant to accept the usual émigré jobs of governess or domestic servant and persisted in harboring illusions about rejoining their professions. When Dr. Fürst not surprisingly failed her licensing exams, the committee and her husband were confirmed in their judgment that in the United States, "Women are extremely difficult to place in the medical profession."[49]

The setup, as Hertha Riese had put it, was difficult and complicated indeed. An organization such as the Rockefeller Foundation, which was explicitly committed to rescuing the flower of European science, was not interested in ordinary medical practitioners, which of course is what women doctors were. But the general committees set up to help refugee physicians were also unsympathetic to the substantial number of women who hoped to reestablish their medical careers. By 1940 the Rockefeller Foundation Special Research Aid Fund for Deposed Scholars in Medicine had aided forty-six refugees. None of them were women. Of the few female scholars aided by the Rockefeller Foundation, none was in medicine.[50]

Women doctors had to confront the double American prejudice against female physicians and foreign professionals, which was exacerbated by the further double jeopardy of bias against both Jews and Germans. Additionally, the many women who had been active in the campaigns for legalization of abortion and access to birth control services suffered from the American (not entirely unjustified) identification of sex reform with "immorality" and communism.[51] For professional women, exile was not only a shift from country to country, from National Socialist persecution to safety, but also expulsion from the avant-garde cultural milieu of large German cities. In

---

49 Vocational Summary from Physicians Committee, Nov. 1940, included with letter to Sanger from Community Service Society of New York, April 14, 1941. Margaret Sanger papers, Box 659, Sophia Smith Collection. On the general fate of refugee physicians specializing in sexually transmitted diseases, see Alfred Hollander, "The Tribulations of Jewish Dermatologists under the Nazi Regime," *The American Journal of Dermatology* 5, no. 1 (1983): 19–26.

50 A list of displaced (not yet funded) medical scholars compiled in London in 1936 included eight women, mostly at the assistant or researcher level. See material on the Emergency Committee in Aid of Displaced Foreign Physicians in R.F., R.G. 2, Series 717, as well as that on the Rockefeller Foundation Special Research Aid Fund for Deposed Scholars in R.F., R.G. 1.1, Series 200. These papers as well as the Margaret Sanger papers also provide ample evidence for the intense (although often genteel) anti–Semitic prejudice directed against refugee scholars and professionals.

51 American physicians represented in the American Medical Association also feared that refugee doctors, accustomed to a national health insurance system, would subvert the privatized American medical model with notions of (supposedly inferior) "socialized medicine." See Kathleen M. Pearle, "Ärzteemigration nach 1933 in die USA: Der Fall New York," *Medizinhistorisches Journal* 19 (1984): 127–8.

the United States, Weimar new women were likely to be politically and sexually suspect, adding to the burden of readjustment for women professionals. Ironically, the America that had often appeared in Weimar as the epitome of all that was "modern," the America that had sent Margaret Sanger to Berlin with funds to help establish birth control clinics and had provoked extensive debate about the "modern woman" and the new forms of companionate heterosexuality, proved in reality to be perhaps efficient but sexually philistine and politically conservative. Käte Frankenthal's "brusque, funny" manner, mannish attire, and conviction that "I've never been married, I've never had children, I've never had a dog and that's how I like it"[52] must have fit uneasily into her position as marriage counselor for Jewish Family Services in Manhattan. Charlotte Wolff's candid and erotic definitions of lesbianism also clashed with the genteel world of intense female friendship in postwar London. Even respectably married women like Riese or the Boston pediatrician Alice Nauen went against the current of 1950s and 1960s American ideologies of female maternalism and domesticity. As Nauen noted in a 1971 interview:

Our group has never really needed a Women's lib because professionally in the past, we had an easier life. I mean we were liberated, the German–Jewish woman in many ways. . . . But we were much more liberated than our contemporaries here. Our sex liberation came earlier. I mean in the academic world, the sex liberation of my generation was just as limitless if not more so than it is here.[53]

Probably the most amazing (and ironic) example of deradicalization and adaptation to the "American way of life" was the fate of Dr. Else Kienle. A fiery defender of women's rights against the male medical establishment, she had became a heroine for the Communist-led movement to abolish Paragraph 218 – the section of the Criminal Code dealing with abortion. When imprisoned in 1931 as an abortionist, she secured her release through a well-publicized hunger strike.[54] Rescued from Germany by the charming alcoholic American she expeditiously married, Kienle became a successful cosmetic surgeon of somewhat dubious respectability in New York. She quickly transferred her passionate commitment to the betterment of women from the struggle for birth control and the right to control one's own body

---

52   Personal communication from Dr. Erika Fromm to Kathleen Pearle, May 16, 1950. I am grateful to Professor Stephan Leibfried for providing this material on Frankenthal.
53   Alice Nauen, interview transcript, 42.
54   See Else Kienle, *Frauen. Aus dem Tagebuch einer Ärztin* (Berlin, 1932); and Atina Grossman, "Abortion and Economic Crisis: The 1931 Campaign Against Paragraph 218," in Renate Bridenthal, Atina Grossmann, and Marion Kaplan, eds., *When Biology Became Destiny: Women in Weimar and Nazi Germany* (New York, 1984), 66–86.

to women's right to bodily self-improvement. In 1940, she published a book called *The Breast Beautiful* dedicated:

To the medical profession – the specialist as well as the family physician – which is daily confronted with one of mankind's foremost problems – and – to women who love beauty and have longed for that heritage which is particularly their own – Beautiful Breasts.[55]

Another noted Communist campaigner for abortion rights, Martha Ruben-Wolf, committed suicide in 1939 in the Soviet Union she had so zealously propagandized, after having unsuccessfully protested Stalin's 1936 recriminalization of abortion.[56] Other former activists laboriously reestablished medical practices in the United States. Minna Flake, a veteran of the Association of Socialist Physicians (*Verein sozialistischer Ärzte*), drew her patient pool on Manhattan's upper West Side from old comrades she had counseled while running a refugee aid group in Paris before the war.[57]

Many women doctors, probably about two-thirds, simply never practiced again, becoming doctors' wives or at best their office assistants. A significant number turned to nonmedicalized forms of psycho- or physiotherapy for which licensing and financial requirements were not so stringent. They were eventually able to fulfill in different form their original notion of medicine as a holistic social vocation. Lilly Ehrenfried, a young Berlin doctor who had traveled in Communist circles, returned happily in French exile to her first love, gymnastics.[58] Charlotte Wolff became a psychoanalyst in London. Käte Frankenthal, former Berlin city councilwoman, doctor, and abortion rights campaigner, established a psychotherapy practice in New York after she had initially supplemented her earnings by selling Good Humor ice creams in the summer between seeing patients and using her psychological insights to tell fortunes in nightclubs.[59]

The lesser known, and luckier among them, who were not so closely identified with sex reform and weighed down by the baggage of highly politicized careers in Germany, sometimes became the feisty tough-

55 Else K. La Roe, M.D., *The Breast Beautiful* (New York, 1940), dedication page. See also her incredibly expurgated memoir, *Woman Surgeon* (New York, 1957).
56 Ruben-Wolf's husband and comrade in arms Dr. Lothar Wolf had been sentenced as a spy; he died in despair on September 9, 1940. *Internationales Ärztliches Bulletin Zentralorgan der Internationalen Vereinigung Sozialistischer Ärzte,* vols. 1–5 (1934–9). Reprinted with a Foreword from Florian Tennstedt, Christian Pross, and Stephan Leibfried (Berlin, 1989), xi. On Martha Ruben-Wolf, see also Susanne Leonhard, *Gestohlenes Leben. Schicksal einer Politischen Emigrantin in der Sowjetunion* (Frankfurt/Main, 1956), 48–9.
57 Interview, Renee Barth, daughter of Minna Flake, Chester, Conn., July 18, 1990.
58 Lydia Ehrenfried, unpublished memoirs.
59 Käte Frankenthal (1981, Afterword by Kathleen Pearle and Stephan Leibfried), 242–5 and 249–67.

minded German–Jewish pediatricians we might remember from our own childhoods. Alice Nauen, who struggled hard and finally successfully to reestablish herself as a pediatrician in Boston, reported the prejudices she faced:

It was not only towards the refugee physician . . . but towards the woman. You know, at that time women in American medicine were not accepted. I was at that time at the meetings always the only woman. They didn't like it. It was the German and the woman. I had two against me.[60]

VI

Given the enormous obstacles, it is remarkable how many women already in middle age overcame the prejudices against women doctors, older women, foreigners, and Jews. If approximately two-thirds of exiled German women doctors were never able to practice medicine again, at least one-third, and not only the younger ones, did. Female physicians were of course located, as they had been already in Germany, in subordinate positions within the profession. In my sample of about fifty women who were in 1959 practicing medicine again in New York State, predominantly New York City, only eight were specialists and even then in less desirable and less prestigious specialties such as pathology, psychiatry, venereal disease, tuberculosis treatment, and pediatrics. None of them had a prestigious teaching hospital affiliation. Ilka Dickmann, an internist from Prague who eventually became a public health official in the United States, worked as a charwoman in London before embarking on an adventurous tour of duty as a district nurse in village outposts on the impoverished remote southern coast of Newfoundland. With a touch of irony she reported:

Officially I was the district nurse, but I was also the doctor, dentist, veterinarian, social worker, first aid teacher, librarian and even undertaker. Of all my duties, I was obviously best qualified as a doctor because I had practiced internal medicine for 12 years in Czechoslovakia.[61]

In a certain sense, then, women doctors returned to the social service fields in which they had long been so involved. But now they did so in a new context, in the absence of the large working-class movement and comprehensive national health insurance system that had lent their work

---

60 Alice Nauen, interview transcript, 23. For discussion of the barriers against women, especially married women and mothers, in the American medical profession in the 1930s and 1940s, see Regina Markell Morantz-Sanchez, *Sympathy and Science: Women Physicians in American Medicine* (New York, 1985), 232–350.
61 Ilka D. and William J. Dickmann, *The Long, Long Trail with You* (Manhattan, Kan., 1984), 18–19.

financial security and political significance. In Germany women had been prominent in precisely those fields such as birth control and social medicine that were most underdeveloped in the United States.[62] In the framework of an American private practice, women lost the arenas in which they had been trained to function. They left professional work entirely, resettled into related fields, took low-level clinic and hospital jobs, or adjusted to the demands of private practice. Their medical practice, although still primarily in the social caregiver mode, changed meaning and status in an American context where medicine was organized and practiced so differently.

Women found niches for themselves in newer and marginal areas such as psychiatry, psychoanalysis (especially for children and families), sexually transmitted diseases, pathology, and pediatrics.[63] Sponsored by female colleagues, some women became active in the German Medical Society of New York (renamed the Rudolf Virchow Society in 1939), which had become a professional home for refugee doctors after the Jewish newcomers had defeated the old guard German–Americans in a struggle over whether to condemn the discrimination against non-Aryan physicians in Hitler's Germany.[64]

The poignant biographies contained in the curriculum vitae submitted to the Virchow Society reveal the determination of middle-aged women compelled to reenter their chosen profession, often after long years of forced hiatus. After having been well established in Germany, they worked in American welfare institutions, in venereal disease and tuberculosis clinics, in Veterans Administration hospitals, in outpatient clinics in poor neighborhoods (in New York, especially Harlem Hospital, Montefiere Hospital, and New York Infirmary), and in state psychiatric hospitals and penitentiaries while waiting to be relicensed for private practice. For example Dr.

---

62 The United States's experiment with federally funded maternal and child welfare clinics, in which many women doctors had found a professional home, had ended a good decade earlier with the repeal of the Sheppard-Towner Act in 1929. See Morantz-Sanchez (1985), 266–311.

63 Among male doctors also, psychiatry/neurology and pediatrics followed right after internal medicine as the dominant specialties of the émigrés. The distribution among émigré doctors was disproportionate to the percentages among German doctors as a whole (10 percent were psychiatrists and neurologists compared to 2 percent of all German doctors; 5.8 percent were pediatricians compared to 2 percent), reflecting the tendency of Jews as well as women to cluster in new or marginal specialties. Refugee psychiatrists had a significant impact on the development of mental health programs in the state hospitals and institutions for the criminally insane, where many of them found employment. See Kröner, *Exilforschung* (1988), 90.

64 The German Medical Society had been founded in 1860; it was renamed the Rudolf Virchow Medical Society in 1939 and merged with Pirquet Society of Clinical Medicine in 1976. The highly contested 1933 vote is documented and membership material collected in the Society Papers on deposit in New York Academy of Medicine Library, Rare Book Room.

Valerie Handsell, born in Erfurt in 1899 had practiced child psychiatry and pediatrics in Dresden; from 1940 till 1949 she worked as a staff psychiatrist at Rockland State Hospital. When she finally received her New York State license after the war in 1948 (at age forty-nine), she began work at the Harlem Hospital Mental Health Clinic. Dr. Sophie Hirsch, born in 1899 in Breslau, managed to secure a New York license in 1938 and to open a practice for women and children on Central Park West. Dr. Alice Naegle, born in 1890 in Stuttgart, had worked as a specialist in dermatology and sexually transmitted diseases for twenty years from 1919 to 1938. In 1949 when she was finally licensed in New York State, she opened a practice in the Bronx and served as house physician for the United States Committee for Care of European Children. Dr. Lotte Strauss, born later in 1913, completed her medical training in exile in Sienna in 1937 and eventually became the head of pediatric pathology at Mount Sinai Hospital. A letter to the Virchow Society from Dr. Augusta Flakenstein on November 22, 1947, expressed the particular hardships confronting women doctors:

I regret very much to be forced to withdraw my membership application for personal as for financial reasons. I am completely overburdened with my practice (still much too small besides) and all housework without help that I am never able to go out for a meeting.

The Society agreed to suspend her membership dues for a year so that she and her physician husband could both retain their memberships.[65] We do not know how Dr. Flakenstein managed after that, whether, like about a third of her colleagues, she managed to persevere in medicine or whether, like about two-thirds, she relinquished her cherished identity as physician, perhaps working as office help for her husband.

Men and women both confronted anti-Semitism, anti-Communism, economic crisis, and professional jealousies in their new homelands. But, revealing again the ways in which gender constrains women more powerfully than men, their identities as wives, mothers, sisters, or daughters were clearly more salient than men's were as equivalent family members. Women professionals were more overburdened with housework and childcare; they also seemed to suffer more from the disruption of childbearing and child-raising patterns. They often would forgo children, having only one when they might have intended to have more, making the decision to send children away to boarding schools or foster homes during the difficult period of adjustment. As suggested at the beginning of this chapter, women's de-

---

65 Material collected in Papers of Rudolf Virchow Society, Rare Book Room, New York Academy of Medicine.

termination to carry on may have masked the enormous price paid for that coping.

The ability to find niches, whether in medicine or in related social service occupations, was absolutely critical. For Alice Nauen, the ability to find a sympathetic female mentor and a hospitable women's institution in which to work was absolutely critical to her ability to reestablish herself. She was lucky enough to find an "angel" in the only successful woman pediatrician in Boston, a patrician "Mayflower American" who was willing to let a refugee colleague share her office and relieve her on night calls, thereby providing an entrée into private practice. She also found a protective and supportive temporary niche as the Radcliffe College physician, a job she relished because the women's college tolerated her bringing her young son with her to work and allowed her to make the necessary transition from refugee physician to "European-trained physician."[66]

A significant number of those women doctors who managed to continue their professional careers after emigration turned to related nonmedical fields, particularly social work, psychotherapy, and psychoanalysis. In the United States, these occupations were considered "womanly" and "caring" in much the same way that general medical practice was viewed in Germany. Women doctors therefore had to readjust their sights, find the appropriate niches in the new country as they already had in Germany, and become social workers, therapists, public health doctors, pediatricians, and child psychiatrists. A striking number of women refugees seem to have carried their social convictions into a concern for minorities in the United States, working in black neighborhoods and with black children.[67]

Thus, refugee women doctors renegotiated the balance of work, personal life, and politics that they had achieved in pre-Nazi Germany. They reinvented themselves, sometimes several times, as they moved through several countries and several occupations. Some managed to regain a foothold in the medical profession, but for virtually all of them, reconstruction came at the cost of the rich social and political identities that had been particular to new women in Weimar Germany.

---

66 Alice Nauen, interview transcript, 24.
67 Alice Nauen prided herself on having a practice that was 15 percent "Negro"; Hertha Riese did educational therapy work in the Richmond black community; and Harlem Hospital employed several refugee physicians. Hilde Lachmann-Mosse, daughter of the publisher of the *Berliner Tageblatt* and a pediatrician, co-founded the Lafargue Clinic in Harlem, the first free mental health clinic in the eastern United States. See her papers in the Leo Baeck Institute, New York. See also Hertha Riese, *Heal the Hurt Child: An Approach through Education Therapy, with Special Reference to the Extremely Deprived Negro Child* (Chicago, 1962).

17

Women Emigré Psychologists and Psychoanalysts in the United States

MITCHELL G. ASH

One might expect precisely those women who had already taken up the systematic study of the conscious or unconscious mind to be especially sensitive to the gendered dimensions of their own experiences.[1] Nancy Chodorow has argued, however, that this is not the case. In an essay entitled "Seventies Questions for Thirties Women," she reports that in her interviews with émigré women psychoanalysts, her subjects repeatedly denied the significance of their gender for their professional work. Chodorow distances herself from this phenomenon by giving it an abstract sociological name – low gender salience. But she acknowledges that her interviewees forced her to see that ideas are rooted in varying social and cultural conditions and that "differences in women's interpretations of a situation may be understood not only in terms of structural categories like class or race, but also historically, culturally and generationally."[2]

Implicitly, at least, Chodorow's work also raises questions that are more specific to the lives of these particular women. The following remarks are intended as a preliminary exploration of these issues, focusing mainly on the careers and memoirs of selected émigré women psychologists and psychoanalysts. What did these women émigrés share? How did their multiple identities – as upper-middle-class educated professional women in the patriarchal culture of German-speaking Europe, as Central European Jews, and as members of emerging professions that have become central to twentieth-century culture and society – relate to one another? How did their experiences of forced migration from Nazi-

---

1 Thanks are due to the participants at the conference "Women in the Emigration after 1933," and also to the members of the Berlin Forum for History of Psychoanalysis for useful comments on earlier versions of this chapter.
2 Nancy J. Chodorow, *Feminism and Psychoanalytic Theory* (New Haven, Conn., 1989), 200.

occupied Germany and Austria affect their careers, thinking, and practice as psychologists or psychoanalysts?

The data, memoirs, and interviews I examine come from two groups that, contrary to widespread misconceptions, were quite distinct, although they began to interact more intensely during the period under discussion. *Psychologists* were trained in experimental laboratories in German-speaking universities, although many worked in clinical settings before or after their emigration; most *psychoanalysts* or *psychotherapists,* though not all, were medically trained. Each group confronted different challenges, although these were linked in significant ways by societal demands on the psychological professions and by the exigencies of American academic and professional cultures in the 1930s, 1940s, and 1950s.

Insofar as they remained academics after they came to the United States, both male and female émigré psychologists encountered then-dominant neo-behaviorism's insistence in the 1940s and 1950s on objective or scientific methodological conventions, a style that clashed with their own, equally strictly schooled mixture of experimental and phenomenological or hermeneutic orientations. Women émigrés also confronted an emerging gender-based status hierarchy within both academic and applied psychology. Full professorships were likely to be available to them before 1940 only in women's colleges or in the field of child development. In the applied sector, women were concentrated mainly in the less prestigious and less well-paid areas of educational psychology and youth work, which were more person-oriented than was industrial psychology.[3] In the 1940s and 1950s, new opportunities emerged with the rapid growth of clinical psychology.[4] Problematic in this expansion, however, were unclear roles within psychiatric institutions and the uncertain scientific standing of clinical research. At the same time, academic psychologists reworked their relationship with psychoanalysis by attempting to subject psychoanalytic concepts to experimental tests.[5] In the process, psychologists benefited from and helped to shape an altered cultural climate marked by changes in the discourse on sexuality (e.g., the Kinsey report) and a widespread tendency to analyze societal problems in terms of individual psychopathology.

3 Laurel Furumoto, "On the Margins: Women and the Professionalization of American Psychology," in Mitchell G. Ash and William R. Woodward, eds., *Psychology in Twentieth-Century Thought and Society* (Cambridge, 1987), 93–114.

4 For initial overviews, see A. R. Gilgen, *American Psychology Since World War II: A Profile of the Discipline* (Westport, Conn., 1982), chap. 9; David Shakow, *Clinical Psychology as Science and Profession: A Forty-Year Odyssey* (Chicago, 1969). For a more critical perspective, see Nikolas Rose, *Governing the Soul: The Shaping of the Private Self* (London, 1990).

5 Gail A. Hornstein, "The Return of the Repressed: Psychology's Problematic Relations with Psychoanalysis, 1909–1960," *American Psychologist* 47 (1992): 254–63.

Emigré psychoanalysts and psychotherapists confronted different but in some respects parallel challenges. These included intense debates over admission of nonphysicians to training, conflicts over technique that centered around the emergence of institutionalized training programs developed in part by German-speaking analysts in the early 1930s, and theoretical splits in which gender issues were involved to some extent (for example, the debate between Karen Horney and Sandor Rado in the 1930s and 1940s over the roles of culture and instinct in neurosis).[6] According to recent critical accounts, the result was the conversion of psychoanalysis from a mixed group of physicians and avant-garde intellectuals into a medical specialty, and the reorientation of psychoanalysis and psychotherapy's aims from self-discovery to social adaptation.[7] Emigré women were involved in all aspects of this complex transformation and on all sides of every debate. The psychoanalysis of children and women posed central issues in psychoanalytic theory and practice; thus, in contrast to the situation in psychology, emphasizing these subjects did not necessarily mean reduced prestige for women analysts.

This study of women émigrés in two professions combines quantitative data about their career patterns and more detailed analysis of women émigrés' accounts of their own experiences. Memoirs and oral histories, usually considered firsthand accounts, are documents constructed according to expressed or implied narrative conventions and are often directed to particular audiences. In male scientists' memoirs, authors may reflect on or discuss themselves as persons, but they tend to subordinate that side of the tale to stories of profession choice, the trajectory of scientific careers, and accounts of what they see as their contributions. Emigré women psychologists and psychoanalysts tried to adopt the conventional form of the scientists' memoir, including its self-aggrandizing aspects. However, as I will try to show, the life histories of émigré psychologists and psychoanalysts, male and female, are not linear, but broken narratives. In the course of recalling these lives for publication, it often became necessary to break in some way, con-

6 For a broad historical overview, see, for example, Edith Kurzweil, *The Freudians: A Comparative Perspective* (New Haven, Conn., 1989).

7 On the professionalization of psychoanalysis in America, see Nathan G. Hale Jr., "From Berggasse 19 to Central Park West: The Americanization of Psychoanalysis, 1919–1940," *Journal of the History of the Behavioral Sciences* 14 (1978): 299–315; John C. Burnham, "From Avant-Garde to Specialism: Psychoanalysis in America," *Journal of the History of the Behavioral Sciences* 15 (1979): 128–34. The most trenchant political critique of the outcome is Russell Jacoby, *The Repression of Psychoanalysis* (New York, 1983). In *Governing the Soul,* Nikolas Rose goes still further, arguing that the very idea of self-discovery itself was recast in functionalizing terms during the psychotherapy boom of the 1950s and 1960s. For critical discussions of Jacoby, see Kurzweil, *The Freudians,* and Ben Harris and Adrian Brock, "Otto Fenichel and the Left Opposition in Psychoanalysis," *Journal of the History of the Behavioral Sciences* 27 (1991): 157–65.

sciously or not, with the narrative conventions of scientific success stories. Moreover, in apparent contradiction to the findings of Nancy Chodorow mentioned earlier, in the published memoirs of the émigré women psychologists and psychoanalysts discussed here gender was a central concern, more important even than the wrenching cultural changes brought by forced migration. In this respect, the personal and the professional dimensions of their life histories are tightly interwoven.

PSYCHOLOGISTS

The Emigrés as a Group

Until recently, it was widely believed that the Nazis destroyed psychology in Germany. Perhaps this belief stemmed from the widespread conflation of psychology with psychoanalysis – though as recent scholarship has shown, psychoanalysis, too, survived and prospered under Nazism. In fact, the proportion of German-speaking psychologists who emigrated is far lower than that of psychoanalysts. Of the 308 members of the German Society for Psychology who lived in German-speaking countries or taught in German-speaking universities in 1932, a total of 45, or 14.6 percent, had emigrated by 1940.[8] Adding the considerable number of émigré psychologists who worked outside the university system or who had recently completed their training and had not yet joined the Society when they emigrated yields a total of 120 émigré German-speaking psychologists discovered thus far. Of these, eighty-four went to the United States, twenty to Great Britain, and eleven to Palestine; the others scattered to Turkey and various Latin American countries.

An overview of the émigrés' careers reveals three trends that are important for this study:

1. Most interesting is the relatively *high percentage of women* – 31.7 percent of German-speaking émigré psychologists in general, 44 percent of Austrians, who in turn made up 44.2 percent (50 of 111) of all émigré psychologists for whom data were available. The field appears to have attracted women in increasing numbers during the interwar period. Liberal Jewish and socialist backgrounds were liberating factors for women entering the professions in Austria. But the presence of the highest-ranking German-speaking woman psychologist, Associate Professor Charlotte Bühler, as dissertation advisor in Vienna, was surely responsible for the high number of Austrian women émigré psychologists.

---

8   Mitchell G. Ash, "Disziplinentwicklung und Wissenschaftstransfer – deutschsprachige Psychologen in der Emigration," *Berichte zur Wissenschaftsgeschichte* 7 (1984), 209.

2. Especially important for an analysis of émigrés' later careers are their *ages at emigration*. Sixty-four percent of the émigrés were forty or younger; for the Austrians, and for all émigré women as well, the figure is 75 percent. This factor alone may be a predictor of subsequent professional success, relatively independent of gender; younger émigrés had more time to become acclimated to a new milieu or to struggle through difficult times until the situation of psychology changed after 1945.

3. Also significant are the *career patterns* of all émigrés. Of the 103 émigrés for whom occupational data were available, 48 (41.7 percent) took up clinical or other applied work, rather than academic careers, after emigrating. For the Austrians this figure is significantly higher – 24 of 44 (60.6 percent). The same is true specifically of women; 22 of 38 (57.9 percent) for whom data are available entered applied rather than academic careers. For women who emigrated at age thirty or younger, the percentage is higher still; twelve of sixteen (75 percent).[9]

As explanations for these data, two hypotheses can be suggested: Clinical or other applied work was necessary for the émigrés' survival, especially during the Depression and World War II, when academic posts were difficult even for nonimmigrants to obtain: Clinical and other applied positions were opportunities presented by the growth of psychology both as an academic discipline and as a profession in the United States, beginning in the 1930s and accelerating in the late 1940s and 1950s. Both hypotheses are correct, only for succeeding periods. In psychology, as in other disciplines, émigrés often struggled at first, often receiving only one-year stipends or other short-term employment. Significant professional opportunities arose mainly in the postwar period, with rising demand for psychological expertise in clinical and other psychological fields financed by a rapidly growing economy and legitimated by an emerging therapeutic culture. In the end, for many German-speaking psychologists, especially for the Austrians among them, enforced migration had an unexpected, highly ironic result – involuntary but nonetheless successful career change and upward mobility.

To explain the high percentage of Austrians and of women in this group, it is necessary to examine briefly the situation of psychology in German-

9   The following data come from information on émigré psychologists published in preliminary form in Ulfried Geuter et al., *Daten zur Geschichte der deutschen Psychologie*, vol. 1 (Göttingen, 1986). Updated information on émigrés who went to Britain is presented in my essay, "Central European Emigré Psychologists and Psychoanalysts in the United Kingdom," in Werner E. Mosse et al., eds., *Second Chance: Two Centuries of German-Speaking Jews in the United Kingdom* (Tübingen, 1991), 101–20. Counted as psychologists were individuals who received a doctoral degree from a German university for work on a psychological topic, or those who were active either professionally or academically in psychological fields before they emigrated. People who interrupted their studies or who could be considered members of several disciplines have generally been included; those who were primarily active as Freudian psychoanalysts before their emigration are excluded. These are considered further subsequently.

speaking Europe before considering the careers of three émigré women, two from Austria and one from Germany.

In the interwar years, psychology in German-speaking Europe was in transition from a largely academic discipline recruiting its members from the educated elite to a science-based profession. The field remained a sub-specialty of philosophy in German and Austrian universities until 1941. Demand for psychological expertise rose, however, and many university institutes added applied departments. Important debates among psychologists revolved around competing responses to pressing practical concerns.[10] The Vienna Psychological Institute, headed by Karl and Charlotte Bühler, was on the leading edge of this trend. The institute was founded in 1922 in part because the leaders of the Social Democratic Party's school reform program hoped for scientific support for their child-centered approach to education.[11] During the 1920s and early 1930s, women worked primarily in the department of child and youth psychology under Charlotte Bühler and in the Research Center for Economic Psychology headed by Paul Lazarsfeld. The child and youth psychologists created tools for assessing children's development in rooms located at the city's adoption center. The Research Center for Economic Psychology did market research and studied the sociopsychological effects of unemployment during the Depression in the famous study called "The Unemployed of Marienthal."

After the fall of the Social Democratic government in Vienna and the installation of an authoritarian regime in 1934, the situation in psychology remained surprisingly stable at first. In 1936, police raided the Research Center for Economic Psychology and arrested Marie Jahoda (then Marie Jahoda-Lazarsfeld), because they suspected her of using the Center as a mail drop for the Social Revolutionary underground organization. After intervention by foreign colleagues, she was released on condition that she leave the country, and she went to Britain. The Center itself, however, continued operating. The women in the department of child and youth psychology tried to continue as before, apparently with some success. Despite nostalgic accounts to the contrary, many émigré psychologists from Austria were products more of this 1930s milieu than of "Red Vienna." Particularly the

10 See Mitchell G. Ash, "Psychology in Twentieth-Century Germany: Science and Profession," in Geoffrey Cocks and Konrad H. Jarausch, eds., *German Professions, 1800–1950* (New York, 1990), 289–307.
11 For more detailed accounts, see Mitchell G. Ash, "Psychology and Politics in Interwar Vienna: The Vienna Psychological Institute, 1922–1942," in Mitchell G. Ash and William R. Woodward, eds., *Psychology in Twentieth-Century Thought and Society* (New York, 1987); Christian Fleck, *Rund um "Marienthal." Von den Anfängen der Soziologie in Österreich bis zu ihrer Vertreibung* (Vienna, 1990), esp. 135ff.

younger ones among them were willing and able to engage in applications-oriented basic or in straightforward applied research – an ability that proved useful after their emigration. Some, like Else Frenkel (later Else Frenkel-Brunswik), acquired additional training in psychoanalysis while keeping the fact a secret from the Bühlers.[12] All of this, as well as the complicating role of generational differences and the centrality of the personal dimension for at least some émigré women's careers, is evident in the first two cases considered here – Charlotte Bühler herself and her student, Hedda Bolgar.

Charlotte Bühler

Charlotte Malachowski was born in 1893 into a privileged upper-middle-class home as the daughter of a prominent architect and a frustrated opera singer.[13] From her talented mother she evidently received support, if not pressure, for an independent career. After beginning studies in biology and psychology in Berlin, Charlotte turned to work on the psychology of thought at the University of Munich. If there was any discrimination against her on gender grounds, she does not mention it. In Munich, she met and married her teacher, Karl Bühler, an authority on her research topic. They did research together on children, including their son and daughter, but she also worked independently on the psychology of adolescents, using a diary method of her own devising. They moved to Dresden in 1918 and then to Vienna in 1922 when her husband was appointed professor there. After a year in the United States as a Rockefeller Fellow in 1924–25, she added more objective observational methods and statistics to her armamentarium. Precisely these methods were employed in the measures of early childhood development (*Kleinkindertests*) that she developed with her associate Hildegard Hetzer. These methods were intended to be research instruments, but they were created in a diagnostic setting and had an implicit applied purpose. By the early 1930s, Charlotte Bühler had expanded her theoretical and research program to the course of human life as a whole, thus helping to lay the foundations for what is now called life-span development psychology. She adapted rather quickly to the new regime by creating a new department for family psychology. In the mid-1930s, however, she ex-

---

12 On Else Frenkel-Brunswik, see the biographical introduction by Nanette Heiman and Joan Grant in *Else Frenkel-Brunswik: Selected Papers, Psychological Issues*, vol. 8, monograph 31 (1974); Brewster Smith, "Else Frenkel-Brunswik," in Barabara Sicherman et al., eds., *Notable American Women: The Modern Period* (Cambridge, Mass., 1984), 250–2.

13 For the following, see Charlotte Bühler, "Charlotte Bühler," in Ludwig Pongratz et al., eds., *Psychologie in Selbstdarstellungen*, vol. 1 (Bern, 1972), and Melanie Allen, "Charlotte Bertha Bühler," in *Notable American Women: The Modern Period*, 119–21.

plored options abroad, moving to Britain for a year to teach and begin a
practice in 1935 at the Parents' Association of London. Then she returned
to Vienna.

Charlotte Bühler's memoir takes a complicating turn after her emigration
first to Norway in 1938 and then to the United States in 1939. Here the
linearity and depersonalization prescribed by the master narrative of scientific progress end, and the tone turns bitter:

> The situation in America was extraordinarily unfortunate, partly due to our earlier
> rejections of offers, partly because many available positions had been given to em-
> igrants from Germany. Karl accepted a professorship in [St.] Scholastica College in
> Duluth, Minnesota, from where he was appointed at St. Thomas College in St.
> Paul, Minnesota in 1940. . . .
>
> As many other hopes departed, I accepted an appointment at the – by the way
> quite excellent – St. Catherine College in St. Paul, Minnesota, the sister institution
> of Karl's St. Thomas College. . . .
>
> The years 1940 to 1945 were difficult for us both. Despite our very enjoyable
> teaching at the two colleges we both missed the possibility of doing research with
> doctoral students. The description of different attempts to get to the East Coast
> would fill pages.[14]

The cryptic words about "attempts to get to the East Coast" refer to
Bühler's attempts to establish herself as a therapist in New York, while at
the same time teaching in a temporary appointment at Clark University in
Worcester, Massachusetts. At this point the gendered and personal dimension that had never been absent from this story takes it over completely:

> Finally I concluded that without Karl . . . this was no life at all and I decided to
> give up the East Coast and return to him. Even now I see myself in my Chevrolet
> driving the more than 1,000 miles from Worcester to Minneapolis alone; I re-
> member the pouring rain on the Pittsburgh (sic!) Turnpike and my fear during
> overnight stays in motels, especially in southern Ohio.
>
> Karl was happy to have me back. I took a job as a clinical psychologist at Min-
> neapolis General Hospital and immersed myself with increasing interest in diagnosis
> and psychotherapy in the Freudian system. . . . In spite of all this activity I was
> incapable of writing for about ten years after our emigration. . . . I had had a sort
> of inner collapse, just like Karl, whose way of battling his depression I cannot
> describe here.[15]

Karl and Charlotte Bühler were well known in the United States and
Britain before 1938 through translations of their work on developmental
psychology. But this basically positive reception was of little help after their
emigration. In part this resulted from the lateness of their decision to leave,

14   Bühler, "Carlotte Bühler," 32ff.
15   Ibid., 34.

as Charlotte Bühler writes, but other aspects were involved as well. For a woman who had been used to considerable independence and control of her students' work in Vienna, it was exceedingly difficult to become accustomed to the nominally egalitarian mores of a small college in the American Midwest. As University of Minnesota department head Richard Elliot wrote to his Harvard University colleague Gordon Allport in 1942, Charlotte Bühler's female colleagues in nearby St. Paul were very satisfied with her teaching but found her "too imposing and aggressive for their quiet environment."[16] Often enough Americans thought the émigrés arrogant; such behavior was clearly even less tolerable in women.

Family and professional motives combined in Charlotte Bühler's decision to move to California and begin clinical practice there. Her son had begun engineering studies at Caltech in Pasadena, a grandchild was about to be born there, and she had a feeling of not belonging in the Midwest. From this point on, the Bühlers' career paths diverged completely: "While my own development took a new upward path," she writes, "Karl's began to descend."[17] After she accepted a position at Los Angeles County Hospital in 1945, she rapidly found a niche in the milieu of therapists and psychiatrists in the Los Angeles area, eventually becoming one of the founders of the so-called humanistic psychology movement, which brought together academic psychologists and nonpsychoanalytic therapists critical of both behaviorism and psychoanalysis. Her prewar work on development and the human life cycle was republished in Germany and Austria, and her later writings were also published in Europe. In contrast, Karl Bühler gradually lost contact with organized science.

Charlotte Bühler's shift to clinical work, her confession of ambivalence about that step, and her recognition of its consequences for the career of her considerably older, originally higher-status husband offer an example of the significance of age for émigré women's career options and of the role of clinical practice as a vehicle of adaptation. The case of Hedda Bolgar supports and enriches this interpretation.

Hedda Bolgar

Born in 1909 in Zurich as the daughter of a Marxist political theorist and a journalist, Hedda Bolgar identified more with her father's profession and

---

16   Richard M. Elliot to Gordon W. Allport, Dec. 4, 1942, Gordon Allport papers, Harvard University Archives.
17   Charlotte Bühler, "Carlotte Bühler," 37.

began by studying social sciences in Vienna.[18] After being rejected there on account of her gender, she then changed to philosophy and psychology. She quickly joined the group around Charlotte Bühler and Hildegard Hetzer and completed her doctorate in 1934 with a study of youth experiences as reported in diaries, using the method Bühler had developed. The Vienna institute in those years was, she recalls, "a very intense place" with a formal atmosphere; "Charlotte [Bühler]'s lectures were public events – I once counted sixteen black dresses she wore in one semester." Many women students were married, but when one had a baby "nobody assumed she would stay home [since] Charlotte had done both." Like her teacher, Bolgar recounts that she saw no need to emigrate after the Dollfuss regime took power.

Even before the German invasion, however, she had written to various clinics in the United States to inquire about improving her mastery of diagnostics. She received an offer from the Michael Reese Clinic in Chicago shortly before the invasion. Thanks to this and her Swiss birth she obtained a visa in Zurich. At the Michael Reese Clinic she encountered an unusually effective constellation of psychiatrists and psychologists cooperating under the leadership of Samuel Beck. As she recalled, connections with the Chicago Psychoanalytic Institute were good, and her Vienna training was fully accepted and recognized: "They did not know that my doctorate was in philosophy and had nothing to do with psychoanalysis." After a year she found a position in a Yale University research project studying alcoholism at New York's Bellevue Hospital, but she returned to Chicago, as Charlotte Bühler did to Minnesota, for personal reasons – her husband did not like New York. She survived the war in office work, a part-time job with a Jewish vocational service, and private practice. The contrast to the glamour of the Vienna institute meant that at first the experience of emigration entailed a significant loss of status.

A certain irony and a source of lingering resentment is that Bolgar's route to successful acculturation was blocked at first by her own teacher, Charlotte Bühler. After a year of study with Jean Piaget and August Forel in Geneva, Bolgar recalls, she had developed with Liselotte Fischer, also a student of Bühler's, a diagnostic instrument for use in child development studies. The instrument was later called the "World Test," because it is based on observing children at play in an object-filled environment, rather than on paper-and-pencil tests or play with single toys.[19] Charlotte Bühler had already

18   The following account is based on an interview by Hedda Bolger with the author in Los Angeles, Jan. 14, 1984.
19   Hedda Bolgar and Liselotte K. Fischer, "Personality Projection in the World Test," *American Journal*

published a version of the test through the Psychological Corporation in 1941, and Bolgar recalls that when she and Fischer attempted to market their test in the late 1940s, Bühler threatened to sue. Bühler later regretted this, telling Bolgar that she had been driven to it by anxiety for her own professional security.

The career breakthrough came, as it did for many other émigrés, after the war, when Bolgar became chief psychologist at the Chicago Mental Hygiene Clinic, which had received contracts to extend the clinical training provided in three university programs. It was then that she became more intensively involved with psychoanalysis. Her many-sided experience brought her the directorship of the clinical training program at the University of Chicago in 1950. Perhaps she exaggerates slightly when she says, "The people supposed that I did psychoanalysis, so that's what I did." Here she struggled to open up possibilities for clinical training to nonphysicians until 1956. After a brief interlude in a research project on aging in Kansas City, Franz Alexander brought her to Mount Sinai Hospital in Los Angeles to head the department of clinical psychology. At the same time she helped organize the California School for Professional Psychology, an independent training institute. In 1974 she became the director of the Wright Institute, an important psychotherapeutic training center in Los Angeles.

Erika Fromm

The career of Erika Oppenheimer (later Erika Fromm) shows that career patterns such as that of Bolgar were not limited to émigré Viennese women, nor were they due entirely to acculturation pressure in the United States.[20] Born in 1910 and trained in experimental psychology under Gestalt theorist Max Wertheimer in Frankfurt, Fromm moved quickly into practical work upon emigrating to the Netherlands in 1934, working as a clinical diagnostician at an asylum in Apeldoorn. She was able to make this move in part because she was familiar with the work of Adhemar Gelb, a close colleague of Wertheimer's in Frankfurt, who had adapted experimental methods for use in clinical studies of perception in brain-injured patients. Upon coming to Chicago in 1936, she crossed paths briefly with Hedda Bolgar at the Michael Reese Hospital. Eventually she combined academic and clinical research in experimental studies of hypnosis as professor of

---

of Orthopsychiatry, 17 (1947): 117–28; cf. Charlotte Bühler and George Kelley, *The World Test. A Measure of Emotional Disturbance* (New York, 1941).

20 The following account is based on an interview by Erika Fromm with the author in Chicago, Nov. 15, 1983.

psychology at the University of Chicago. Her career pattern thus differed somewhat from Bolgar's, proceeding from basic research to practice and then to more practice-oriented basic research. Like Bolgar, however, the preference of her husband, a businessman, decided her location.

Such examples show how the intersection of European preadaptation and contemporary societal trends in the United States made possible a significant career in science-based professional practice, especially for younger émigrés. Of particular importance is the way in which Bühler, Bolgar, and Fromm entered clinical work – by reconstructing diagnostic instruments originally developed for basic research for use in practical diagnostics. Such adaptations did not occur without complications. Some were more strictly professional in nature, such as Bolgar's struggle to legitimate clinical research and training in academic settings. Others combined the personal and the professional, such as the "mother–daughter" competition between Bolgar and Bühler that resulted from their parallel shift to clinical work. Both the interweaving of the personal and the professional as well as the tension between generations are also visible in the stories of émigré women psychoanalysts.

PSYCHOANALYSTS

The Emigrés as a Group

There is as yet no complete count of the number of psychoanalysts in Germany up to 1933 or of émigré analysts thereafter.[21] Thanks to recent research by Johannes Reichmayr and Elke Mühlleitner, the situation is better for Austria.[22] There is surely no need to revise the well-known fact that the Nazi conquest of Austria decimated psychoanalysis there. Important for this chapter is the high number of women among the émigrés. According to Reichmayr, of the sixty-eight full and associate members of the Vienna Psychoanalytical Society in the years 1930 to 1938 who were actually practicing

---

21 The discussion here is limited to Freudian psychoanalysts. For an initial survey of Emigré Adlerian therapists, see Bernhard Handlbauer, " 'Lernt fleissig Englisch!' Die Emigration Alfred Adlers und der Wiener Individualpsychologen," in Friedrich Stadler, ed., *Vertriebene Vernunft*, vol. 2: *Emigration und Exil österreichischer Wissenschaft* (Munich and Vienna, 1988), 268–87.

22 For the following, see Johannes Reichmayr, "Die Vertreibung der Psychoanalytiker," in M. Stadler, ed., *Vertriebene Vernunft*, vol. 1: *Vertreibung und Emigration österreichischer Wissenschaft* (Vienna, 1986), esp. 142ff; Elke Mülleitner, *Biographisches Lexikon der Psychoanalyse. Die Mitglieder der Psychologischen Mittwoch-Gesellschaft und der Wiener Psychoanalytischen Vereinigung 1902–1938,* unter Mitarbeit von Johannes Reichmayr (Tübingen, 1992). This book, though highly informative, has limitations as a source for quantitative research on émigrés' careers. For example, the survey excludes candidates and analysts in training.

psychoanalysts, sixty-three emigrated. Of these, more than half (thirty-two) were women, including six Americans. Of the remaining fifty-seven, thirty-one were men and twenty-six women. Of the thirty-five émigrés who went to the United States, sixteen were women, of whom eight were married to other analysts.

Obviously, the psychoanalytic profession, at least in Vienna, was remarkably open to women. Equally notable is the acknowledged stature of many of the women within the movement, from Helene Deutsch, Grete Bibring, and Marianne Kris to Anna Freud herself. It is more difficult to assess the effects of emigration on these women's careers or on the development of their thought and practice.[23] As an initial approach to this issue, I will consider three careers: Helene Deutsch and her erstwhile trainee, Margaret Schönberger Mahler, both of whom emigrated from Vienna; and Clara Happel, who came to the United States from Hamburg and Berlin. Gender issues and generational rivalry are central to the first two narratives. For Helene Deutsch, the struggle to succeed as a woman and the personal dimensions of life and career were even more important than the experience of cultural change.

Helene Deutsch

Helene Rosenbach was born in 1884 in Przemysl, a middle-sized town in Galicia; her father, Wilhelm, was a widely known and respected lawyer.[24] Thus, like other members of Freud's inner circle, she came from an upper-middle-class background. She was also a member of a provincial elite striving to make a way into the metropolis through innovation. The psychological core of her childhood, in her account, was a classical reverse Oedipal constellation. Identification with her father, she suggests, helped compensate for her sense of social inferiority as a Jew. She hated her mother, who, she claims, beat her and burdened her with vain expectations of a son. Her "liberation from the tyranny" of her mother (p. 131) and from small-town bourgeois norms for women came with help from local socialist leader Herman Lieberman, who became her lover. In 1907, she moved to Vienna when Lieberman was elected to parliament and she passed the university en-

---

23 For initial attempts at the biographical level, see, for example, Elizabeth Young-Bruhl, *Anna Freud* (New York, 1986) and Paul Roazen, *Helene Deutsch: A Psychoanalysts's Life* (New York, 1985). On émigré psychoanalysts in Britain, see Ash, "Central European Emigré Psychologists and Psychoanalysts in the United Kingdom."

24 Unless otherwise noted, the source for this account is Helene Deutsch, *Confrontations with Myself: An Epilogue* (New York, 1973). Further citations from this source are given in parentheses in the text.

trance exam. One of only seven women to study medicine in her year, she soon encountered discrimination from a professor of internal medicine. She forced him to examine her, and "Out of spite I made an excellent showing in the exam. He spat out the questions without looking at me, and addressed me as 'Mr. Rosenbach' " (p. 95).

When the relationship with Lieberman, who was married, ended because Helene wanted to become a mother, she fled Vienna to Munich for a year, where she met Felix Deutsch, a psychiatrist who was successful in his own right in the field of psychosomatic disorders and who later supported her allegiance to Freud's ideas. They were married in 1912, the year she received her medical degree. By this time she had already been introduced to Freud's writings, and during World War II she met and entered training analysis with the master himself. The entry into discipleship was sealed with two sacrificial gestures. As a condition of entering didactic analysis, Freud required her to give up her position at the psychiatric clinic of Werner Wagner von Jauregg. Then he ended the didactic analysis after about a year, because he needed her hour for the "Wolf Man." When she reacted with "the first depression of my life" (p. 133), Freud encouraged her by making her his assistant.

Deutsch's loyalty to Freud and her organizational skills were quickly rewarded, and she became a pioneer in the professionalization of psychoanalytic training, helping to found the Vienna Ambulatorium, becoming head of the Vienna Psychoanalytic Society's Training Committee, and taking charge of its Training Institute in 1925. In the same year she published two monographs that soon became standard sources for psychoanalytic views on women. At the height of her career, the transfer to the United States began. In 1930, she was one of nine prominent psychiatrists invited to attend the first International Congress of Mental Hygiene in Washington, D.C., organized by Clifford Beers. Journalists called her a "Lady in waiting at the Freudian Court" (p. 173). Contemporary evidence indicates that she had already put out feelers for a U.S. post at that time.

Her second trip to the United States in 1934 was permanent, yet personal rather than career motives decided the timing: "Nobody knew how terribly I grieved at having to leave not only Freud but also everything I held dear in psychoanalysis. Why did I do it? I was seeking security – but not primarily for myself and my husband. For a long time I had been in a state of extreme anxiety about our beloved son," Martin, who had been active in students' resistance to the Dollfuss regime (p. 174). When Stanley Cobb invited Felix Deutsch to establish a psychosomatic research center in the psychiatric department of Massachusetts General Hospital, for one year only, it was she who seized the opportunity. Not the political situation in Austria but their son's decision to study physics at MIT led to mother and son's rushed departure in September 1934, leaving Felix behind at first.

A letter to Felix from this period clearly shows that from the beginning Deutsch had the attitude needed for success in the United States:

One thing is clear: *anyone,* whoever he may be – you, I, famous or obscure – must make his way here from the very beginning. The most glorious past is only a visiting card, which is more likely to cause difficulties, because it raises expectations and makes one more critical. One must close the curtains on one's European past and build only on what one *is,* what one is *capable of.*[25]

On her arrival Deutsch's calendar was already filled with patients, most referred by Americans who had been in training with her in Vienna. She eventually informed Freud, who in fact had not approved of her departure from Vienna, that it would be impossible to return.[26] He replied the day the Nazis invaded, ending his letter with an injunction to "remain true to analysis," which she interpreted "as a mission given to me by Freud, which I automatically tried to fulfill" (p. 179). Teaching and training were the chief activity of émigré psychologists, and one can imagine the tension that arose within the Boston Psychoanalytic Society between her and Hanns Sachs, who had been sent by Freud himself to organize training there. Nonetheless, she soon became firmly established as a leading teaching analyst.

Deutsch acknowledges that there was controversy in Boston about lay analysis as well as the implications of the GI Bill, which granted analytic training to war veteran psychiatrists at government expense and thus appeared to reduce autonomy in candidate selection. However, she writes, "As time went on, the older and younger newcomers reached emotional agreement among themselves, as well as with those whose land they had invaded; we became their pupils and they became ours" (p. 182). Though she acknowledges that "of course the European procedures had to be adjusted to American conditions and needs" (p. 181), she does not indicate how this worked in detail. Her biographer, Paul Roazen, writes that Deutsch was skeptical of schematized procedures in psychoanalytic training and retained that view in America. However, he adds that in Boston she was obliged to keep detailed written records of her work as a training and

25 Quoted in Roazen, *Helene Deutsch: A Psychoanalyst's Life* (New York, 1985), paperback ed., 284f.
26 Deutsch does not mention Freud's disapproval of her emigration; see Roazen, *Helene Deutsch,* 278, 287.

control analyst and thus became involved, willingly or not, in more elaborate, bureaucratized certification procedures.[27]

This could be read as support for the argument that émigrés helped convert psychoanalysis in the United States into an instrument of adjustment, but Helene Deutsch had already participated in that development before her emigration.

Margaret Mahler

Born in 1897, Margaret Schönberger was brought up in a German- and Hungarian-speaking Jewish family in Sopron, in the Hungarian part of the Austro-Hungarian Empire.[28] As the daughter of a provincial elite Jewish family – her father was president of the town's Jewish community – her background is comparable with that of Helene Deutsch, but the potential conflict between Hungarian and Jewish ethnicity plays a surprisingly small role in Mahler's memoir. Class, gender, and a reverse Oedipal constellation are central. Mahler writes that she was rejected by her young and beautiful mother, who regarded her as an intruder. Again like Deutsch in some respects, compensation came from her father, who eagerly adopted her as a "son." In response, she turned to her father's realm of intellect, science and medicine: "Never having learned how to compete with other women as a woman, I learned instead how to avoid defeat as a woman in a world of men" by developing a strong drive for independence at an early age (p. 9). This émigré narrative exhibits rather high gender salience, but, like Deutsch's memoir, it is also shaped by a relatively orthodox psychoanalytic view of gender roles.

Mahler writes that she experienced both gender discrimination and anti-Semitism during her medical training at the universities of Munich, Jena, and Heidelberg. Whether her gender was a factor in her choice of pediatrics as a specialty, as it was and remains for many other women physicians, she does not say. Instead, she devotes considerable space to her tortured, competitive relationships with the dominating mother figures Anna Freud and Helene Deutsch at the Vienna Psychoanalytic Institute. She was refused admission to training analysis with Anna Freud and referred by her to Deutsch in 1926. Deutsch decided after a little more than a year that Mar-

---

27   Ibid., 244ff, 247, 312.
28   For the following, see Margaret S. Mahler, *The Memoirs of Margaret S. Mahler*, ed. Paul Stepansky (New York, 1987). Further citations to this source are given in parentheses in the text. This account is not strictly a memoir but a document constructed by Stepansky on the basis of a long autobiographical fragment and other sources, including Mahler's interview with Nancy Chodorow. The authorial voice is nonetheless convincingly that of Mahler herself.

garet was "unanalyzable" (p. 60) and recommended a therapeutic analysis before further training. She writes that she was saved from this personality conflict by a friendly father figure. August Aichhorn accepted her secretly as a training analysand, gave her access to patients through his extensive network of city-funded youth centers, and encouraged her to start a practice for children in 1934. Soon afterward, at the age of thirty-nine, she married Paul Mahler, a "highly cultured and gentle" but "far from successful" chemist "who very much needed, in his adult life, both a mother and a father" (pp. 78–9). During this entire period of conflict, she published little.

This changed soon after her emigration in 1938. Mahler describes the decision to emigrate and the following visa formalities as relatively easy, though she acknowledges that separation from her family was painful. After five months in Britain, she arrived in New York, and soon confronted the issue of medical licensing, as well as the splits and bitter competition within the New York Psychoanalytic Society. She passed the medical examination on the first attempt. However, although she gratefully acknowledges efforts by Lawrence Kubie and others to help bring analysts to the United States, she notes that they were less than welcome in New York. The pressure to "go 'pioneering' to Buffalo, Utica, Syracuse or some other upstate location" (p. 102) was considerable – a situation quite comparable with efforts by Ernest Jones to channel émigrés in Britain away from London and into provincial cities like Birmingham.[29] For Mahler, this pressure was compounded by gender discrimination. When her husband found a job in Elizabeth, New Jersey, Kubie encouraged her to go there and start a private practice: "I naturally declined this invitation" (p. 103).

Mahler quickly became a member of the New York Psychoanalytic Society, but her pragmatic and effective response to its endemic conflicts was to seek professional and institutional support outside the group. The initial entrée came at Caroline Zachary's Institute for Human Development, where she met Benjamin Spock. She was accepted there because she had practiced Rorschach diagnostics as well as child psychoanalysis in Vienna. She then worked at the New York State Psychiatric Institute and at Einstein College of Medicine, where she did the research with schizophrenic children that made her early reputation. A second breakthrough came in the 1950s, when she became head of the training program in child analysis at the Philadelphia Psychoanalytic Institute and then took a position at the Master's School, a private, independent institution that gave her access to "normal" children and freedom to work with them as she wished. There

29 See Ash, "Emigré Jewish Psychologists and Psychoanalysts."

she carried out the comprehensive psychoanalytic study of child development for which she is best known.[30]

At all of these positions, collaboration with Americans was important.
Indeed, Mahler testifies that emigration itself had a stimulating impact on
her life and work:

It was only the stressful situation of emigration and relocation in America that
mobilized my creativity, prompting me to bring out of hibernation ideas that had
long been slumbering, to communicate them orally, to write them down. . . . It
signified the falling away of the stamp of eternal student status that the awesome
Vienna Psychoanalytic Institute, however unwittingly, bestowed on young analysts
[p. 113].

In this respect, at least, Mahler views her emigration as a liberation: "With
the stress came new vistas, new curiosity, new opportunities and vital new
sources of collegial support."

Clara Happel

Not all these lives were success stories. Before she decided to emigrate in
1934, Clara Happel had lost six near relatives in six months, including her
sisters, mother, and father, and had been divorced by her non-Jewish husband, a prominent physician.[31] A state department official in Berlin made
her situation still worse by writing on her immigration papers: "Woman
with two children will become a burden to the U.S." (p. 195). After arriving
with her son and daughter and being rescued from Ellis Island by her colleague and friend Hanns Sachs, Happel rejected an offer from the Men-
ninger Foundation in Kansas and tried to start a private practice in Detroit,
while sending her children to school in New York and Los Angeles. Her
inevitable loneliness was accentuated by the lack of an émigré community
and the political atmosphere of the city from which the notorious Father
Coughlin broadcast his blatantly racist and anti-Semitic radio programs. She
was even interned briefly as an enemy alien after being denounced by a
psychotic former patient. The coming of war did not help. As she wrote
to one of her children in 1942: "It is impossible at the moment to find
anything with all the defense workers and engineers. But especially so for

---

30 Margaret S. Mahler, *On Human Symbiosis and the Vicissitudes of Individuation* (New York, 1968);
Margaret S. Mahler, F. Pine, and A. Bergman, *The Psychological Birth of the Human Infant: Symbiosis
and Individuation* (New York and London, 1975).
31 For the following, see Volker Friedrich, "Briefe einer Emigrantin. Die Psychoanalytikerin Clara
Happel an ihren Sohn Peter (1936–1945)," *Psyche* 42 (1988): 193–215. Further citations to this
source are given in parentheses in the text.

someone who is *jüdisch,* non-citizen, *Psychoanalytiker* and non-licensed physician" (p. 202). She went into deep depression, recovering only briefly in 1944 and moving to New York, resolved to prepare for the medical license and start again. Richard Sterba, a Vienna émigré who was then the leading analyst in Detroit, later called her "an unhappy person, in essence joyless (*unfroh*), suffering from her loneliness" (p. 196). Rejected both by Germany and its personification, her husband, she made gestures toward returning to reality but never fully left the status of mourner and did not make the emotional break with the past that would have been necessary for acculturation. She committed suicide in September 1945.

NONMEDICAL PSYCHOTHERAPISTS

The Case of Ruth Cohn

As the career of Ruth Cohn shows, the struggles of women émigré psychoanalysts and psychotherapists without medical training were different in certain respects from those of women with medical degrees, although the difficulties they encountered as women were similar.[32]

Cohn, who was born in 1913, left Berlin in 1933 in the middle of her university studies but writes that she had already decided to become a psychoanalyst. Between 1933 and 1939, she studied various subjects in Zurich, changing fields in part to retain student status and the concomitant residence permit, coped with a difficult relationship with a man whom she married in order to help get his family out of Germany, and also underwent a training analysis with Medard Boss, who was then still a Freudian but already beginning to distance himself from orthodox views. In her account of the analysis, she portrays herself as a *braves Kind* (good kid) who obeyed the sometimes destructive commands of her father substitute (p. 218).

Cohn arrived in New York in 1941; her mother had already come in 1938, but it took three years to coordinate the necessary affidavits and transit visas. An official of the New York Psychoanalytic Society praised her "outstanding training" but informed her incorrectly that a law against analytic practice by nonphysicians would soon be in effect. He suggested that she take up child therapy (p. 225). Fellow émigré Bruno Klopfer, who helped establish Rohrschach Diagnostics in America, offered her an assistantship at

---

32 For the following, see Ruth C. Cohn and Alfred Farau, *Gelebte Geschichte der Psychotherapie: Zwei Perspektiven,* 2nd. rev. ed. (Stuttgart, 1984), Book 2. Further citations to this source are given in parentheses in the text.

Columbia University, but she declined because she did not want to "test and teach academically my whole life" (ibid.). Although it was not her preference, Cohn followed the suggestion that she work with children and was accepted as a trainee at the Bank Street School for Early Childhood Education, a private progressive institution. Then she worked as an assistant psychologist, for the salary of an untrained practical nurse, at an asylum in upstate New York where her psychiatrist husband was a resident. She had no supervision, could not participate in staff consultations, and lacked the status to prevent children from being released too soon or transferred to chronic wards against her recommendation. She had seen America "at it's best" [sic] and as a "snake pit" [sic] in a few short years (p. 227).

Cohn soon left this position – and also her husband – and went into private practice. In the struggle for referrals, she was aided by Paul Federn but not by other analysts. "My offices? The first: a room in a shabby pension rented by the hour; the second: the office of a kindergarten (evenings only); the third: two rooms in a basement apartment next to the hot water heater" (p. 229). Nonetheless, she writes that within three years she was able to buy an automobile and hire help for her children. No clearer evidence is needed of the growing demand for help with "problem children" in post-war America. Cohn moved quickly from child to adult therapy, because it seemed more effective to her to work with parents and children together (p. 231). In 1948, she heard that Theodore Reik was organizing a group of nonmedical psychoanalysts, and she joined the National Psychological Association for Psychoanalysis. She soon became head of the group's train-ing committee, thus acquiring a key position analogous to that of Helene Deutsch in Boston and Anna Freud in London. This is an example of professionalization via alternative institutions.

In the 1950s Cohn went on to adult group therapy and workshops and worked for a time with Fritz Perls, the émigré founder of Gestalt therapy. She eventually developed her own innovative, holistic approach in group therapy with adults that was called Theme-Centered Interaction and inte-grated elements of Gestalt therapy, encounter groups, transactional analysis, and bioenergetics. She then re-imported this approach to Germany in the 1960s at the height of the "psychoboom" and a time of momentous change in West German society. She now lives in Zurich. Unlike Charlotte Bühler and Hedda Bolgar, and in part because she emigrated so young, her achieve-ment came less by adapting instruments from previous training than eclec-tically borrowing and recombining tools and concepts encountered in the new culture: "I was Americanized, pragmaticized. Practical (therapeutic) success was the important thing to me" (p. 208).

CONFRONTING THE HOLOCAUST

Judith Kestenberg

A fundamental issue that nearly all male or female émigrés faced, whether they were psychological professionals or not, was that of working through survivor guilt in connection with the loss of close relatives. All the memoirs discussed confront this problem in one way or another. When Helene Deutsch remembers the ghettoization of her home town in German-occupied Poland, she writes, "I often ask myself: did I do all I could to help?"[33] Margaret Mahler reports that she was deeply depressed on learning in 1945 of her mother's death in Auschwitz.[34] However, only one of the younger émigré women, Judith Kestenberg, made this perceived guilt a central research and clinical issue.[35]

Judith Silberpfennig, born in 1910, grew up in Tarnow, Poland, and Vienna before and during World War I. Like other female psychoanalysts, she had a privileged background. Her father was a factory owner and, like Margaret Mahler's father, president of the local Jewish community. She describes herself as "a nice Jewish girl from an orthodox household" (p. 160) who exhibited romantic socialist inclinations in her youth similar to those reported by Deutsch and Mahler. She experienced World War I as a trauma, because her family left her home city and went to Vienna while her father remained in Poland: "It is no accident that I began many years later to research the trauma of children who have suffered under the Nazi yoke" (p. 159). A second, more powerful layer of traumatic experience came with the deaths of her father at Auschwitz and her mother at the hands of Russian soldiers. She writes that at first she tried to sublimate this trauma in her work on the psychoanalysis of expressive movement in children and other topics. The issue became more conscious to her at first through her husband, a lawyer who also lost family members in the Holocaust and who dealt increasingly in the 1950s with restitution applications. Even then, she writes, she did not "wake up" until 1968, when she had a girl in analysis of the same generation as her daughter. The girl was the

---

33 Deutsch, *Confrontations*, 47.
34 Mahler, *Memoirs*, 119.
35 For the following, see Judith S. Kestenberg, "Kindheit und Wissenschaft. Eine biographische Skizze," in Ludger M. Hermanns, ed., *Psychoanalyse in Selbstdarstellungen*, vol. 1 (Tübingen, 1992), 147–202. Further citations to this source are given in parentheses in the text. See also Judith Kestenberg, "Natürlich möchte man das ungeschehen machen," in Hajo Funke, ed., *Die andere Erinnerung. Gespräche mit jüdischen Wissenschaftlern im Exil* (Frankfurt/Main, 1989), 246–63.

child of survivors and "looked like a concentration camp prisoner herself" (p. 188f.).

Eventually Kestenberg and her husband helped to establish the Group for the Psychoanalytic Study of the Effect of the Holocaust on the Second Generation.[36] She thus combined the personal and the professional in a way that aided (or rather completed) her own acculturation by working productively with American and European analysts, while at the same time helping other émigrés or their offspring. If she detects any differences in women's and men's situations in confronting memories of the Holocaust, they do not appear in her autobiography. And, sadly, her work with the problems of the second generation have not helped her to sublimate her own survivor guilt. Kestenberg remains in mourning: "Nothing is left of my father but a little mound of ashes. I do not know whether or where my mother is buried. Neither of my parents could enjoy their grown-up children and grandchildren. My children have no grandparents on my side" (p. 174). As she put it in a recent interview: "The work of mourning is not finished. We cannot end this work in our generation. We actually expect our children to continue it."[37]

CONCLUSIONS

Emigré women psychologists and psychoanalysts faced many of the same problems and difficulties as did male émigrés in these professions. In addition, however, they also contended with more specifically gender-related problems, from outright discrimination during medical training to more or less subtle status hierarchies within psychology and psychoanalysis (such as the pressure to go into child studies) to family demands. In their family-related motives for changing location, gender roles and professional issues intertwined. It is probably not necessary to decide which of the many identities – gender, professional, ethnic, or cultural – was more important to these women's lives. Each had an impact on all the others. Nonetheless, it seems clear that professional issues and institutions were or became central. They functioned as selective agencies deciding who would have a role at all and who would not, as filters and formulators of societal demands for particular forms of psychological expertise, and also as sources of identity, hence of emotion-laden conflicts with colleagues. Precisely because their situation was so complex and difficult, it is all the more remarkable that so

---

36 Judith S. Kestenberg and Milton Kestenberg, "The Background of the Study," in M. S. Bergmann and M. E. Jucovy, eds., *Generations of the Holocaust* (New York, 1982).
37 Quoted in Funke, *Die andere Erinnerung,* 259.

many of these women had memorable impacts on their professions and through them on American culture.

From the perspective of a social history of professions, one can isolate a number of career-determining factors, each of which has a gender component.

All the women considered here came from privileged upper-middle-class homes, some from provincial elite Jewish families. Many exhibit a similar psychosocial foundation for their drive to become professionals: identification with their fathers and difficult relationships with their mothers, driving them from the nest and away from easy acceptance of traditional bourgeois female roles.

Among psychologists, the early involvement of many women in child development work and especially in diagnostics gave them an important resource for career shifts after emigration. This is true as well for women psychoanalysts who worked with children, such as Margaret Mahler. But it would be false to overgeneralize this point or jump to stereotypical conclusions. Women émigrés were active in various fields of psychology and psychoanalysis, both before and after their emigration, and many, like Ruth Cohn, resisted pressures to specialize in child development.

Although émigré women often cite family reasons for their decisions either to emigrate or to change location after emigration – something male psychologists or psychoanalysts seldom do – it would be unwise to generalize prematurely here, too. For Mahler, for example, personal dimensions are clearly central to her comprehension of herself as a psychoanalyst but seem to have played no role in her decision to emigrate.

Career-complicating rather than career-determining were the problems of two-career marriages and of reconciling motherhood with a high level of professional commitment. Deutsch devotes considerable space to these issues in her memoir. She admits, for example, that there were problems involving her husband's refusal to become a domestic helper, but she insists that such issues "don't even exist as long as the more complicated human relationship is not confused with a sociological one." The same priority of emotional over cultural categories is evident in her views on motherhood and career: "It was seldom the household that threatened to come between me and my career. It was my motherhood, not the actual time it required, but in its libidinous demands." Regret for her own decision to engage a nurse for her son was an important reason she later argued that motherhood is a full-time emotional occupation, especially during the first two years of a child's life. Contemporary professional women will surely resonate with her rueful conclusion that such conflicts "can be worked out only on an individual basis, and with many compromises."[38] Ironically, she expresses surprise elsewhere in her memoir that so many of her students in America were men, without making any connection to her own dilemmas or to the medicalization of the profession and the low number of women in American medicine at the time.

Perhaps one reason for the professional success of these women was not that they were "relatively gender-blind," as Nancy Chodorow writes, but rather, as she acknowledges later in the same essay, that they had "a concept of femininity and the female life cycle" that "implicitly or explicitly included work and career." As a result, "their firm sense of gender difference did not feel like a life restriction, requiring 24-hour mothering or women's dependence on men."[39] They had a complex, integrated life stance of the kind that the current younger generation of successful professional women in the United States – and many men in the same generation – are beginning to take for granted.

In other respects, however, these narratives have much in common with those of male émigrés. These women reflect surprisingly little on the psychological or psychoanalytic aspects of the émigré experience itself and exhibit rather more of a tendency to rewrite their lives post hoc in terms of the innovations for which they are best known, as successful male scientists and professionals also do. Here Mahler's case is quite typical. Much of her life history can be read as a self-conscious re-creation on the basis of her own model of psychological development. Symbiosis, separation, and individuation are key concepts in her developmental theory; thus, it is only fitting that her account of her own life describes a long adolescence, with only gradual separation from her parents, as well as equally conflict-filled "symbiotic" or ambivalent dependency relations with and difficult separations from parent figures during her medical and especially her psychoanalytic training. Despite the obvious centrality of gender in Mahler's narrative, however, it would be unwise to claim any specifically female dimension in this history unless one assumes that dependency is a female characteristic. Edith Kurzweil had recently shown how male émigrés converted biography into theory, abstracting from their own experience of adaptation to make that concept central to psychoanalytic thinking.[40] In their narratives Mahler and her colleagues do the opposite, converting theory into autobiography.

Nonetheless, these remain broken narratives. Undercutting the émigrés'

38   Deutsch, *Confrontations*, 118–19, 122–24.
39   Chodorow, "Seventies Questions for Thirties Women," 199, 210, 213.
40   Edith Kurzweil, "Psychoanalytic Science: From Oedipus to Culture," *Psychoanalytic Review* 79 (1992): 341–60.

tendency to create success stories are their ironic reflections on their own innovations. Particularly stark is the contrast between psychologist Erika Fromm's statement that "America was very good to us" and that immigrants had no disadvantages compared with Americans, with her admission else-where in the same interview that "we starved at first."[41] In response to a question about the reception in the United States of the Gestalt psychology she had learned in Germany, she dwelled on the rejection of any talk of imagery or phenomenology in the age of neo-behaviorism. Deutsch reflects with similar irony on the fate of her greatest single contribution to psycho-analytic technique: "I regret the great dependence of future analysts on control analyses. . . . More and more, I feel like someone who has been working in an artist's studio and suddenly finds himself (sic) in a factory."[42] Similar regrets, some of them quite bitter, have also been expressed by émigré men, such as Bruno Bettelheim and Frederick Wyatt.[43]

A final dimension of irony emerges when one considers the role these émigré women played in the history of thought about women in modern society. A rather blatant example is the claim in 1970 by Therese Benedek, an émigré from Budapest who became a prominent training analyst at the Chicago Psychoanalytic Institute, that women's "mothering behavior is regulated by a pituitary hormone" that is absent in men, so that nurturing behavior in females and providing food and security in males is "not a culturally imposed . . . but 'nature's order.' "[44] Also problematic, though in a different way, was Frieda Fromm-Reichmann's concept of the "schizo-phrenogenic mother." In a 1940 paper she attributed "the child's fear of his domineering mother" to the social structure of American families, which in her view was the opposite of patriarchal family structures in Europe.[45] By 1948 her emphasis shifted to the biological aspect. Adopting Harry Stack Sullivan's and Clara Thompson's tendency to see the roots of psychosis in disturbed interpersonal relations, Fromm wrote:

The schizophrenic is painfully distrustful and resentful of other people, because of the severe early attraction and rejection that he (sic!) has encountered in important

---

41 Erika Fromm interview.
42 Deutsch, *Confrontations*, 208.
43 Bruno Bettelheim, "Kulturtransfer von Österreich nach Amerika, illustriert am Beispiel der Psy-choanalyse," in *Vertriebene Vernunft*, vol. 2: 216–20; Frederick Wyatt, "The Severance of Psycho-analysis from its Cultural Matrix," in Edward Timms and Naomi Segal, eds., *Freud in Exile: Psychoanalysis and its Vicissitudes* (New Haven, Conn., 1988), 145–55.
44 Therese Benedek, "Fatherhood and Providing," in E. James Anthony and Therese Benedek, eds., *Parenthood: Its Psychology and Psychopathology* (Boston, 1970), 167.
45 Frieda Fromm-Reichmann, "Notes on the Mother Role in the Family Group" (1940), reprinted in Dexter Bullard, ed., *Psychoanalysis and Psychotherapy: Selected Papers of Frieda Fromm-Reichmann* (Chicago, 1959), 291–2.

people of his infancy and childhood, as a rule mainly in a schizophrenogenic mother. (As a result he withdraws) into an autistic private world motivated by fear of rejection, distrust and his own hostility which he abhors as well as anxiety resulting from this hatred.[46]

In the early 1950s such thinking meshed only too well with the then-current trend to blame mothers for autism and other disturbances occurring in the earliest stages of development.

Such examples raise uncomfortable questions about émigré women psychologists' and psychoanalysts' roles in the history of psychology and psychotherapy from the 1940s onward. In the 1940s and 1950s, Sander Gilman argues, the status of Jewish psychoanalysts "in the closed world of American medicine" was tied to the prestige of European science, but the scientific status of American medicine was tied to a biological-functional model of medical practice. Indeed, psychoanalysis seemed attractive because it helped psychiatry reenter the biological mainstream of medicine.[47] On this interpretation, émigré women, like their male colleagues, perceived what counted as science at the time and responded accordingly. Perhaps that is also the case for those émigré psychologists, male and female, who rode the wave of psychoanalysis' popular appeal to make careers in clinical psychology. If this is so, then the view often expressed that women are socialized to be more adaptable and flexible than men could have ironic results in this case. A full account of women émigrés' psychological thinking must acknowledge that this was and is likely to remain highly contested intellectual terrain.

---

46   Fromm-Reichmann, "Notes on the Development of Treatment of Schizophrenics by Psychoanalytic Psychotherapy" (1948), repr. in *Psychoanalysis and Psychotherapy,* 163f.
47   Sander L. Gilman, "Constructing the Image of the Appropriate Therapist: The Struggle of Psychiatry with Psychoanalysis," in *Freud in Exile,* 31.

18

Destination Social Work:
Emigrés in a Women's Profession

JOACHIM WIELER

Social work, a profession concerned with the most disadvantaged and marginal populations in society, is often considered to be itself marginal, much like its clientele. And when it comes to professionals in exile in the United States as a typical destination for refugees, much has been written. Many names of various groups and individuals come to mind very easily, but who knows of any social workers? In contrast to other professions, social work has led a sort of shadow existence in the realm of exile research, and there are some rather plausible reasons for that. It is my hope that this shadow can be lifted and that some light can be shed on the contributions of women from Germany, Austria, and other Nazi-occupied territories. These women – and not only in my opinion – had a remarkable impact on the development of social work as a profession in North America and elsewhere. It is impossible to pay tribute to all of them and to cover all the important issues, but the following pages will, I hope, open more avenues for further research and deeper memories.[1]

Research on social workers in exile has been patchwork so far, and the reasons can easily be traced: The profession is notoriously concerned with "fire fighting," that is, with taking care of immediate needs that cannot be postponed. Social work colleagues who had come to this country as refugees told me in interviews that they did not have time to record their stories for future generations. They were surprised at such a question and told me that they were fully occupied with their own adjustment, usually not in the field of social work, and were overwhelmed by the business of helping others. The pressure of immediate needs – obvious as it may seem – appears to be

---

1   See my "Emigrierte Sozialarbeit nach 1933. Berufskolleginnen und -kollegen als politische Flücht-
    linge," in H.-U. Otto and H. Sünker, eds., *Sozialarbeit und Faschismus* (Frankfurt/Main, 1989), 306–
    27.

a major reason for the lack of historical awareness in our profession and absence of recorded life-stories in our profession, and not only in the realm of exile research.

For a long time, social workers did not appear on the lists of refugees under a special professional or occupational category. If they were mentioned at all, they were usually subsumed under categories such as sociologists, educators, and psychologists. Making the distinction was indeed difficult because many of the pioneer social workers, particularly social work educators, were trained in the traditional social science disciplines before they entered the young profession and taught in schools of social work. Dr. Alice Salomon (1872–1948), the most prominent pioneer and honored as the founder of social work as a women's profession in Germany, was the first to suggest that social workers should not be trained in the highly academic universities, where the concern was primarily abstraction, that is, *die reine Lehre* (pure learning). She also believed that teachers of social work should have a university education as well as practical experience in the various social science disciplines that contribute to social work's holistic orientation.[2] This conglomeration of backgrounds can be found in the catalogue of professions at the Leo Baeck Institute under the rubric *Sozialarbeit und Sozialpädagogik* (social work and social education). The first listing of émigrés under the heading "social work" in one of the major research sources appeared in 1983.[3] In all, 113 social workers are listed, fifty-five women and fifty-eight men. Yet this list is still incomplete. Cross-references with archival sources in the Social Welfare History Archives in Minneapolis, Minnesota, in the Sophia Smith Collection in Northampton, Massachusetts, and personal knowledge of refugee social workers in several countries suggest that to the list could be added the names of probably more than 200 social workers. Moreover, this list contains those who were social workers before they left Germany and other Nazi-occupied territories and those who became social workers in exile. The biographical descriptions show a variety of academic backgrounds, which was typical in the early development of social work as a growing profession.

The years immediately following the war were not times of critical reflection on the darkest period in Germany's history. My parents and my parents' generation did not tell us much about that time. It seemed too

---

2 Alice Salomon, "Die deutsche Akademie für soziale und pädagogische Frauenarbeit im Gesamtaufbau des deutschen Bildungswesens," *Deutsche Zeitschrift für Wohlfahrtspflege* 5, no. 3 (1929): 137.
3 *International Biographical Dictionary of Central European Emigrés 1933–1945*, vol. 3 (Munich, 1983), 204.

embarrassing or painful. The major focus was on survival and reconstruction (*Wiederaufbau*). At the end of the 1970s, I found that many of the social work pioneers, most of them women and many of them refugees, had been forgotten. Critical questions from students concerning social work during the Nazi period, my half-digested childhood experiences as a refugee within war-torn Europe (I was born in 1938 in Poland, and in 1945 my mother took us five children to the West), and my own undernourished sense of history challenged me to fill that vacuum. A few other colleagues joined me in this search. Slowly, biographical sketches or more comprehensive accounts of refugee social workers emerged. At first these concerned older and more prominent exiled social workers, but as the search went on, many surprising (re)discoveries were made.

Traditionally, social work has been considered to be a women's domain, and the roots are easily traced to the women's movement. It is less well known that Jewish women particularly were extremely influential pioneers in the profession's development and expansion. To substantiate this claim, I will recall a few figures.

Although many gaps concerning the complex refugee movement of the period after 1933 remain, we have relatively accurate figures about the decrease in Germany's Jewish population. The number of German Jews diminished from January 1933 until May 1939 from approximately 525,000 (estimated) to 213,390 (that is, by nearly 60 percent). At the end of the war, 25,000 Jews still lived in Germany.[4] Figures of the pre-Nazi period indicate that in Prussia − and most likely in other regions as well − proportionately more Jews than Gentiles had entered and worked in the helping professions. At least 90 percent of the refugee social workers whom I have personally met and who were included in my research came from Jewish backgrounds. That so many were Jewish is not widely known and indicates the great loss of potential in the area of social work in Germany and Austria and elsewhere. When one considers that social work as a profession has grown out of the women's movement(s), largely enhanced by Jewish emancipation, it becomes increasingly clear that Jewish women in Germany were the driving force in the development of professional social work.[5] The loss through enforced emigration indicates the serious setback that still haunts the pro-

4   Herbert A. Strauss, ed., "Jewish Emigration from Germany. Nazi Policies and Jewish Responses," *Leo Baeck Institute Yearbook* 25 (1980): 317.

5   Joachim Wieler, "The Impact of Alice Salomon on Social Work Education," in *60 Jahre International Association of Schools of Social Work. Eine Festschrift* (Berlin, 1989), 16.

fession. In the following pages are the names and brief biographies of at least some of the women who contributed to the helping professions and thus to more fairness in human relations.

Alice Salomon (1872–1948) was one of the founding mothers of social work and particularly of social work education.[6] She published twenty-eight books and approximately 250 articles, mostly on policy analysis, education, women's issues, and international and intercultural social welfare.[7] She knew personally virtually every major figure involved in international social work education between 1910 and 1948. But when she died in her New York City apartment, she was almost immediately forgotten. My own research centered on her life under Nazi rule (1933–1937) and in exile (1937–1948).[8] Because she was such a key person in the development of social work, I begin by giving an overview of her life and contribution.

At the turn of the century, when social work training courses sprang up all over Europe and in the United States, Salomon established the first full one-year course in Berlin (1899). She pursued her own academic studies and wrote her doctoral dissertation on the controversial theme of "The Causes of Unequal Payment for Men's and Women's Work," a topic still vigorously debated. In 1914, at a time when she was well known in Germany, she converted to Christianity but maintained a prominent place in Jewish circles.

In 1917 Salomon established the German Conference of Schools of Social Work, a precursor of similar confederations in other countries. In 1925 she initiated and headed the Women's Academy of Germany (*Deutsche Akademie für soziale und pädogogische Frauenarbeit*), an institution for the promotion of social work research, continuing education, training for institutional leadership, and recruitment of social work educators. Four years later, she was elected the first president of the International Committee of Schools of Social Work (now the International Association of Schools of Social Work, or IASSW).

While providing leadership in the area of social work, she was also an

6 On Salomon's life and career, see Marlis Dürkop, "Alice Salomon und die feministische Sozialarbeit," in R. Baron, ed., *Sozialarbeit und soziale Reform. Zur Geschichte eines Berufs zwischen Frauenbewegung und öffentlicher Verwaltung* (Weinheim and Basel, 1983), 52–80; Hans Muthesius, ed., *Alice Salomon, die Begründerin des sozialen Frauenberufs in Deutschland. Ihr Leben und ihr Werk* (Cologne, 1958); Renate Orywa and Annette Dröge, eds., *Alice Salomon in ihren Schriften. Eine Bibliographie* (Berlin, 1989).

7 Among them: Alice Salomon, Siddy Wronsky, and Eberhard Giese, *Soziale Therapie* (Berlin, 1926); and Alice Salomon, "Jugend- und Arbeitserinnerungen," in E. Kern, ed., *Führende Frauen Europas* (Munich, 1928), vol. 1: 3–34.

8 Joachim Wieler, "Alice Salomon," *Journal of Teaching in Social Work* 2, no. 2 (1988): 165–71; Joachim Wieler, "A Life Dedicated to Humanity: Alice Salomon under Nazi Rule (1933–37) and in Exile (1937–48)," *International Social Work* 31 (1988): 69–74.

activist in the women's and peace movements. Her close association with
Jane Addams led people to characterize her as the "Jane Addams of Germany." She never entered the arena of partisan politics, but her reputation
for reconciliation and consensus building were such that the Ministry of
Foreign Affairs gave her the privilege of traveling on a diplomat's passport
during the Weimar Republic.

Upon her sixtieth birthday in 1932, Salomon received high honors,
among them a honorary doctor of medicine degree for her accomplishments
in social hygiene. The school that she had founded in Berlin was renamed
the Alice Salomon School of Social Work. One year later, however, everything that Alice Salomon had stood for came under attack. She lost all her
public positions and was pressured by the Nazis to give up all other positions. For example, she was forced to resign from the presidency of the
International Committee of Schools of Social Work. Repeatedly, she complied with the government's demand but was immediately reinstated by
unanimous action of the organization's board of directors.

Salomon decided to stay in Germany to aid the departure of younger
colleagues. With the help of the Russell Sage Foundation and a social workers' relief organization called "Hospites," she was urged to leave Germany
– if only temporarily – to compile the first international study on social
work education.[9] When she returned from a speaking tour of the United
States, however, she was summoned by the Gestapo, interrogated for hours,
and confronted with an ultimatum: Leave Germany within three weeks or
be sent to a concentration camp. The real reasons are obvious: her Jewish
heritage (her ancestors had settled as so-called *Schutzjuden* under a special
dispensation from Frederick the Great), her close connections with the
confessing church (*Bekennende Kirche*), her humanistic views and practices
(she was a critic of social Darwinism as well as extreme collectivism), her
intellectual and feminist activities, and her adherence to pacifism and internationalism. As a result, she was forced to emigrate via England to the
United States.

In spite of helpful connections and promises of assistance, Salomon –
now sixty-five years old – was unable to find employment and became
dependent on the support of friends from Europe and within the United
States. She made herself available to speak on various topics and tried to
publish articles through a literary agent. She completed her autobiography
in 1944 but could not find a publisher.[10] She was invited to the White

---

9 Alice Salomon, *Education for Social Work. A Sociological Interpretation Based on an International Survey*
   (Zurich, 1937).
10 Her autobiography was finally published in Germany in 1983: *Charakter ist Schicksal. Lebenserin-*

House, honored by international groups and women's organizations, and mentioned from time to time in the press. Her letters during these years speak of much despair, the loss of relatives, the deprivation of her German citizenship, the annulment of her doctor's degree by the Nazis, and health problems. In addition, for financial reasons, she had to share her small apartment with another tenant.

Alice Salomon died alone in her apartment on August 29 or 30, 1948, at the very time when the Cold War divided her birthplace, Berlin, into two parts. The date, time, and exact cause of her death are unknown. The door to her apartment had to be forced open, and she was found on the floor next to her bed. Relatives identified the body and the press was notified. A witness recalls that he had hoped to find many friends and colleagues from Berlin at her funeral, but only four or five people accompanied her casket to the burial ground in Evergreens Cemetery in Brooklyn. There was no ceremony. A gravestone with a simple and clear inscription bears witness to this day: Alice Salomon, 1872–1948.

The research on Salomon widened my circle of contacts with other émigrés, and heightened my awareness of pioneer social workers in exile who are no longer living. Let me mention just a few of the latter.

Marie Juchacz (1879–1956), who founded the German Workers Welfare organization (*Arbeiterwohlfahrt*) in 1919, was the first woman to address the National Assembly (*Nationalversammlung*) meeting in Weimar.[11] The Nazis liquidated Workers Welfare soon after they came to power. Some of the workers were murdered, and many had to run for their lives. Marie Juchacz was among the latter. In 1941, after several detours, she arrived in New York City at the age of sixty-two and "was faced with the painful reality that, without adequate knowledge of the English language and without special training, America did not have much use for her."[12] In 1945 she founded – together with others – a Workers Welfare organization in New York in order to start a care package project. She returned to Germany in 1949. In contrast to the older generation, younger women refugees seemed to have fewer difficulties, particularly when they entered the United States at an earlier date.

Hedwig Wachenheim (1891–1969) was a graduate of the Alice Salomon School of Social Work and a member of the central board of the Workers Welfare from the beginning to 1933. She was editor of the journal *Arbei-*

nerungen, ed. R. Baron and R. Landwehr, with an epilogue by Joachim Wieler (Weinheim and Basel, 1983). The original version, written in English, still awaits publication.

11 *Marie Juchacz, Gründerin der Arbeiterwohlfahrt. Leben und Werk* (Bonn, 1979).
12 Lotte Lemke, *50 Jahre Arbeiterwohlfahrt* (Bonn, 1969), 14.

terwohlfahrt and founded their school of social work (*Wohfahrtsschule der AW*) in 1928 in Berlin. She lost her positions in 1933 and arrived in the United States in 1936 via Switzerland and France. After the war she was engaged in welfare programs sponsored by the U.S. military government in Stuttgart and Frankfurt, and she maintained professional relationships in both countries.[13]

Hertha Kraus (1897–1968), who became director of the social welfare department in Cologne at the age of twenty-six, described in a letter to an American friend the situation at work shortly after the Nazis came to power:

... everything has blown up – laws, contracts, the whole government. So has my job, probably. Just now "on leave" as hundreds of others who served the republic with all their heart and mind. We are all "on leave," the whole Cologne crowd you met and many others. Most of them are not socialists, but a good many are women. This is the time for full-sized men. No female foolery.[14]

Eventually, Hertha Kraus found refuge at Bryn Mawr. She became a well-known social work teacher, spoke at large professional gatherings, was influential in the bureaucracy of the federal government, published comprehensively, and was one of the first exile women who returned to Germany. She was closely associated with the Quakers and was instrumental in the foundation of neighborhood centers throughout Germany.

Juchacz, Wachenheim, and Kraus particularly demonstrate an understanding of social work that is closely aligned with policy issues and critical social politics, and thus with political awareness and active intervention in that arena.

Other women emigrated to Palestine and England. Siddy Wronsky (1883–1947) came from an assimilated Jewish family in Berlin. She was director of the welfare archives (*Archiv für Wohlfahrtspflege,* now *Deutsches Zentralinstitut für soziale Fragen*) in Berlin and edited the *Deutsche Zeitschrift für Wohlfahrtspflege.* She also taught at the Alice Salomon School of Social Work. With Salomon, she expanded on the development and differentiation of the American casework methodology. She was a member of the board of the Central Jewish Welfare Organization in Germany (*Zentralwohlfahrtsstelle der Juden in Deutschland*). At the end of 1934, now in Jerusalem, she continued her teaching:

13 Hedwig Wachenheim, *Vom Grossbürgertum zur Sozialdemokratie. Memoiren einer Reformistin* (Berlin, 1973).
14 Kraus cited in Joachim Wieler, *Erinnerung eines zerstörten Lebensabends. Alice Salomon während der NS-Zeit (1933–1937) und im Exil (1937–1948)* (Darmstadt, 1987), 107.

She began with one student in the corner of her room among books that she had brought along from Berlin. . . . Five female students graduated at the end of the one-year course. Within a few years, these beginnings had turned into a real training program with a substantial faculty and became the School of Social Work in Jerusalem of the Vaad Leumi.[15]

Just like others of the older generation, Wronsky had difficulty with the new language, but her impact on the development of professional social work cannot be overestimated. "Siddy Wronsky and her life's work stand for many Jewish educators and social workers who carried the ideas of the educational reform movement to Palestine and planted the seeds for the growth of Jewish education and welfare."[16]

Other women who were closely associated with the pedagogical reform movement emigrated with their pupils and developed alternative schools for refugee children in exile.[17] Edith Cassirer-Geheeb (1885–1982) was a student of Alice Salomon's and, together with Paul Geheeb, emigrated with the famous *Odenwaldschule* to Switzerland. Under difficult circumstances, this school continued as Ecole d'Humanité.

Hildegard Gudilla Lion (1893–1970) and Emmy Wolf (1890–1969) were experienced social workers and teachers at the German Women's Academy (*Deutsche Akademie für soziale und pädagogische Frauenarbeit*) in Berlin. Hilde Gudilla Lion was director of the academy when Salomon, then its president, resisted pressure to dismiss her on account of her Jewish heritage. The German Women's Academy was subsequently dissolved. Lion left for England and founded the Stoatley Rough School in Haslemere, Surrey, in 1934. She operated this international and interdenominational school for refugee children with Emmy Wolff, Eleonore Astfalck, Luise Leven, and Johanna Nacken. Several of the social workers whom I interviewed in the fall and winter of 1990–1 had been at the Stoatley Rough School as young boys and spoke enthusiastically about their formative years in the care of these women.

During a recent sabbatical semester, I conducted thirty-five taped interviews with colleagues who had been forced to leave Germany, Austria, and other Nazi-occupied territories after 1933 – some of them as children – and who later became social workers in the United States.[18] I established these

15 Franz-Michael Konrad, "Paradigmen sozialpädagogischer Reform in Deutschland und Palästina. Erinnerung an Siddy Wronsky (1883–1947)," *Soziale Arbeit* 36 (Dec. 1987): 465.
16 Ibid., 466.
17 Hildegard Feidel-Mertz, ed., *Schulen im Exil. Die verdrängte Pädagogik nach 1933* (Reinbek, 1983).
18 This oral history project on the mutual influences between German/European and Anglo-American social work and social welfare was supported by the German Marshall Fund of the United States. Most of the interviews were conducted in German, but the interviews with a few younger social workers were done in English. The interview material, in the form of tapes and transcripts,

contacts through my earlier work on exiled social workers. I began with fifteen interviews, mostly with men teaching at schools of social work throughout the United States. The predominance of men was surprising because it does not correlate with the male–female ratio in the entire profession. As time went on and I met personally with my interview partners, I received names and addresses of other former refugees, some of them in the area of teaching but most were women practicing in various fields, with several in "active retirement." At the end of my tour, I had interviewed twenty women and fifteen men. Thirty-four are of Jewish descent. Many described themselves as coming from assimilated families and from Social Democratic backgrounds. The same is true for social workers of the pioneer generation mentioned earlier.

To let the interview partners know my interests and also as a sort of warm-up for the interview, whenever possible I sent them in advance a list with questions and issues (see the appendix to this chapter). Not all the questions applied in all cases and not all partners responded to all questions and the stories differ considerably. But there are also areas in which there are astonishing similarities.

Most of the interview partners who began their social work careers in the United States trace the motivation for this choice largely to their refugee experience. For some, there were clear links or significant episodes. One individual, for example, still feels so grateful about his rescue as a child and the care he was given at Stoatley Rough School in England that this became a decisive factor in his choice. For others, the connections are more covert but still identifiable on closer inspection. One woman talked about her responsibilities as a child within the family regarding the aftermath of the Holocaust.

We were so much involved in our parents' struggles and in a sense helped them survive. As for myself, I was not in touch with my own struggle to survive. . . . So for my mother . . . she relied on me a lot. Actually, my mother could have used therapy. She was, as were others, very wounded by what had happened and I think I really served to some extent as her therapist – as young as I was. . . . When I went to social work school, one of my courses was on family therapy and I had to research my own family, and do a genogram. . . . Here I was part of the family script. . . . In my own therapy, which I have had, my own therapist said to me that I probably kept my mother out of the hospital or a mental institution just by being there for her. And so I think I got practice and experience over the years, and I think also

has been deposited at the Deutsches Zentralinstitut für soziale Fragen (DZI), Bernadottesstrasse 94, D–14195 Berlin, Germany.

the desire to understand what makes people do what they do, and probably just having a little more empathy for victims.[19]

Some colleagues even attributed their later specializations regarding the "classical methods" in social work – as, for instance, in social group work – to their innovations under tremendous pressure. One example was related by Louis Lowy, professor emeritus at Boston University. As the oldest individual in the youth barrack in Theresienstadt, he was not allowed to teach younger children in the traditional way. So he invented methods and techniques of group interaction that later led to differentiated social group work.[20]

Gisela Konopka (b. 1910), professor emerita at the University of Minnesota and considered to be the "mother of social group work," had been arrested twice as a member of the German and Austrian resistance movement. The memories of her long and painful struggles before entering the United States in 1941 are impressively recorded in her book, *Courage and Love*.[21] She sees a clear continuum, stretching from the beginning of her teaching career in Germany, through her odyssey in various countries, and in her continued teaching of social work in the United States.

The never-ending discussion, if not the most controversial debate among social workers, focused on the question of individual assistance (for instance, through direct and often clinical services) versus structural change (for instance, through the improvement of social policy or perhaps large systems intervention in terms of community organization).

Although all interview partners felt that they had learned invaluable lessons during their American social work training with regard to direct social services and sophisticated methods of providing individual help, they almost all stressed that they wished and are still hoping for a stronger network of policy provisions in public social welfare, medical and financial security, and thus more emphasis in teaching social policy. Most references were made to the early development of the insurance provisions introduced during the Bismarck era and public welfare developments during the Weimar Republic. The emphasis on these universal provisions was clearly traced to their European experiences and heritage. This influence was most pronounced in the German interviews with older colleagues, but it can also easily be identified in the interviews with younger social workers. This is the voice of a colleague who was born to Polish refugees in a displaced

---

19 Taped interview with Sylvia Kaminski-Zeldnis, 1990.
20 Saul Bernstein and Louis Lowry, *Neue Untersuchungen zur sozialen Gruppenarbeit* (Freiburg, 1975).
21 Gisela Konopka, *Courage and Love* (Edina, Minn., 1988).

persons camp and who is now working in the health care field in Connecticut:

It's not that I'm against collectivism. As I look at what's happening in our health care system, because that's what I'm involved in . . . and see . . . insurance companies in terms of how much power they really have: in the health care system and ultimately in the quality of people's lives. You know that I think that socialized medicine would be wonderful so that people would get their medical and emotional and health care needs met across the board.[22]

Another colleague, born in Poland and now working at the Institute on Aging in Los Angeles, comments on her understanding of the historical differences underlying the development of social policy:

I think that Europeans have a much longer history of social responsibility to each other. America was a frontier . . . with rugged individualism still prevailing in much of our thinking. We had a frontier up to such a long time that if you couldn't make it you just moved out to that frontier with much wider opportunities. . . . Europeans had a much longer history of being boxed in and realizing that they had to take care of each other. . . . And so there is a whole ethos that takes generations to develop: in the people, in the institutions, and then in the response systems.[23]

One colleague, a child of refugees from Frankfurt am Main and now engaged at the University of Washington, questions the still-prevailing emphasis on British welfare traditions:

The emphasis on social welfare history here in the United States is on Elizabethan Poor Laws, English social services, and how those systems got transferred to the United States. And yet the United States has many immigrants from many European countries who also brought with them their traditions. And then we had this big influx of immigrants during the Nazi period . . . including lots of professionals who influenced social work whether it be in teaching social work or in public welfare jobs and in government, . . . and they didn't come from the English tradition. , , , And now we have more Asian cultures coming that bring more Eastern traditions.[24]

The German emphasis, just before the Hitler period, was clearly – and not without its own controversy – on public social responsibility. Therefore, the question of engagement in public or private social services was not only an issue for social workers in Germany but also became a challenge and problem for those who reached the United States.

22   Taped interview with Sylvia Kaminski-Zeldnis, 1990.
23   Taped interview with Natalie Gold, 1991.
24   Taped interview with Margaret West, 1991.

Actually, refugee social workers with experiences in public welfare and who had been dismissed from public welfare institutions, in particular, would have been very welcome in the United States during the New Deal era when public social services became more popular. These hopes diminished as the enthusiasm for the New Deal dwindled away. A special issue of *Social Work Today* addressed issues of the new immigration to the United States. And one article, written by Joanna Colcord, focused especially on refugee social workers.

The vast majority of immigrant social workers come from the public service, and could doubtless make their best and speediest adjustment here in public social work. They are unable to secure public employment, however, until they have completed naturalization, which involves a delay of at least five years. Their opportunity must be found in the meantime in the private field, to the experimental nature of which they are not conditioned. The German social worker is likely to find here a lack of fixed and formal procedures which distress[es] his orderly mind. The fluidity of our social work concepts leave him "all at sea." . . . When they learn their way around the house, and are no longer always bumping themselves on the furniture, they will bring reinforcements to the struggle of American social workers for higher standards of work and a better-defined professional status.[25]

The article speaks of much tension regarding the transfer of social work knowledge and practice from Europe to the United States. Colcord describes German training that took place in "vocational schools, usually having no relation to institutions of higher learning." A little later she adds:

A canvass, by no means complete, of refugees currently registered in schools of social work, shows forty-six in twenty schools. At least twenty of them hold doctor's degrees from Germany and Austria, while seven or more were trained in schools of social work. Fifteen have had no previous experience in social work proper, but seven of these have worked in allied fields.[26]

Her estimations stand in contrast to Alice Salomon's observations and complaints that she wrote to a European friend at about the same time:

The social workers here act as if everything that was learned and done in Europe is totally inferior. They do not even admit our graduated social workers with years of practical experience to the schools: "Have no academic standards." Well, we have to bear that. It is very difficult for the young colleagues.[27]

Obviously, a good number of social workers did find work in their field or were admitted to schools of social work, some with generous scholarships.

25 Joanna Colcord, "Refugee Social Workers," *Social Work Today* (Sept. 1939): 38.
26 Ibid., 37.
27 Salomon in Wieler, *Erinnerung eines zerstörten Lebensabends,* 299.

But it may be difficult to reconstruct completely what really happened. Many of them did domestic or factory work, one part-time student sold liquor for a living, others took care of their parents, and some started with semivolunteer work in social institutions as a preparation for professional training. Most of them spoke of great difficulties before they (re)entered the field of social work.

There is much, and partly fascinating literature about how social workers assisted various groups of refugees.[28] But since an assumption exists that social workers have difficulty accepting help when they themselves need it, I began to wonder if they helped each other, if they were able to ask for and accept help when they needed it. With regard to social workers that I encountered in my research, I found the assumption to be wrong. There were those who were supported by relatives and did not need help from any agency. The ones who came as children (for instance, those who left Germany on children's transports to England) mentioned various Jewish agencies. Others, perhaps half of them, sought and accepted help from other support groups – for example, the Hospites, who were closely related to the Russell Sage Foundation, and the Committee on Displaced Social Workers. As pointed out, Alice Salomon was assisted by the Hospites. In the early years of the Nazi period, the decided goal of the Hospites group was to assist colleagues in Europe. Only when the situation became more desperate did they urge social workers throughout the United States to provide affidavits to colleagues who wished to emigrate. There is no clear evidence of how many affidavits were given, but there are numerous accounts of financial and material assistance from 1934 until after the war.[29]

Initially, it was surprising how little contact there seemed to be among social workers who had come from Europe. In some cases, interview partners were amazed by my list of names. I had assumed that they formed a circle of mutual trust and support within their own professional group. I soon learned, however, that in their struggles to survive and adjust to their new life, they wanted to associate more with their American neighbors. Amazingly few had moved to the areas of refugee concentrations in the large cities – for example, the Washington Heights area of New York City. Perhaps this speaks for their adaptability to new situations and life circum-

28 Herbert A. Strauss, ed., *Jewish Immigrants of the Nazi Period in the USA*, vol. 2: *Classified and Annotated Bibliography of Books and Articles on the Immigration and Acculturation of Jews from Central Europe to the USA since 1933* (New York, 1981).
29 Archival holdings of Hospites in the Sophia Smith Collection at Smith Collection, Northampton, Mass. I found this interesting source more or less accidentally through an ad in the *New York Times*.

stances. In any case, the common assumption – part of the so-called "help-ers" syndrome – that social workers are unable to accept assistance was not confirmed.

More needs to be said about the process of acculturation of social workers as immigrants. Their experiences have probably influenced the way in which they work professionally with their clients. There is a vivid and controversial discussion on the ready acceptance of social work methods that the United States exported and that social workers in other countries rather uncritically imported. The focus of these discussions has been on the time following World War II. But it would probably be interesting to take the first step before the second and draw more attention to the time before the era of National Socialism and evaluate the developments in a larger context. Family-centered social work is a case in point.

Experts on family issues in Germany claim that the development of family-focused work is a genuine contribution by social work to the helping pro-fessions and that it has been so almost from the beginning. "Friendly visitors" and later social workers visited families and found that there were often financial, medical, educational, psychological, legal, and other prob-lems in a given family. In their holistic view and in their attempt to avoid the overlap of various services, they developed a comprehensive family approach (*Familienfürsorge*). After World War I this program was integrated into the existing structure of public services but not without controversy.

The German Women's Academy, founded in 1925, conducted exten-sive research on various aspects of family life, partly to respond to the crit-icism and partly to undergird family work with a wide and solid research base. By 1933 thirteen volumes of studies had been conducted and more were planned. The end of the Women's Academy also brought an end to these promising developments. Many teachers and students of the academy were from Jewish backgrounds, and there is reason to believe that they may have had some influence on Jewish as well as other family services wherever they went. Years later, in the 1950s and 1960s, more sophisti-cated concepts of family treatment – but this time with a much narrower and more clinical focus – were (re)introduced to Germany and embraced as family therapy. Could this have possibly been a fruitful exchange of col-lective thinking for more individualized ideas?

These questions on the mutual influence across the Atlantic will keep us occupied, and the discussion will be continued by coming generations of social workers, maybe especially by those who are following in the footsteps of their parents.

Two of my interview partners were children of émigrés, one whose mother was a social worker. There are a good many more who could and probably should be interviewed in the future. It is assumed that members of the second generation can tell a lot about the impact of the refugee experience of their parents on their own lives and perhaps on their career choices. The gender question, also rather closely tied to the roots of the European culture, is part of the heritage that still seems to have a lot of weight. I want to finish with a passage from an interview with a colleague who is a third-generation social worker in the health field in Boston and the granddaughter of a well-known economist who taught at the New School for Social Research:

> I felt for myself that getting an MSW was perfectly acceptable in my family and it was somewhat expected. A master's degree, that's good, that's fine. In my own mind [I] thought what it would be like if I got a Ph.D. But I didn't grow up assuming that I would get a doctorate, assuming that I would teach. I grew up assuming that I would do something to help people and that I would work real hard at it, and I think that's exactly what's happened. . . . To a certain degree she (my mother) combined both. She's done some teaching but she's never got a doctorate. That's something that's not been so acceptable for women in my family.[30]

With this open end, it seems almost impossible to come to a proper conclusion. Too many details have been left out and the many facets are difficult to bring together into a coherent whole. So instead of trying to provide that comfortable or perhaps painful sense of closure, I want to return to one question in my encounters that puzzled both the interviewer and the interviewed colleagues. As short as the question was, it seemed to be one of the most moving: "Do you still feel like a refugee?" Answers differed, but most responded that this experience has not ended and it probably never will.

APPENDIX

Questions and Issues for an Oral History Project Supported by the German Marshall Fund of the United States

1. What can you share about your own and perhaps your family situation before coming to the United States?
    Before 1933:
    • Was there any connection with social work or any similar activities?

---

30 Taped interview with Janet Rustow, 1990.

- Would you comment on your religious background, political or other affiliations, educational experiences, and so on?

  From the time Hitler came to power to your departure:
- Can you comment on the increasing pressures?
- How did you cope with them?
- Was there any support by social work or other agencies?

  About the reasons for your escape, the route, and circumstances of the jour-
  ney:
- What led to the final decision to escape the Nazi terror?
- Who was most helpful in your efforts to leave Germany or any other occupied
  country?
- Did you seek refuge in any country other than the United States first?

2. What can you share about your adjustment and settlement in the United States?

   Upon your arrival:
- How did you cope with languages and cultural differences?
- Who was most helpful after your arrival, and what was most helpful?
- Did you benefit from the collegial support group or the support group for
  the rescue of displaced social workers?

  Longer-term adjustment:
- How did you enter the field of social work?
- Is there any connection between your refugee experience and your motivation
  for social work?
- If you had studied social work or anything else before coming to the United
  States, were you given credit for your previous studies?
- Which aspects of your previous studies and work experiences were helpful in
  your adjustment?
- Where did you study and how did you manage financially?
- How difficult or easy was it to find a social work position?
- Did you have contact with other refugees, perhaps social workers, at that
  time?

  Retrospectively considering the refugee experience:
- Besides concrete support, are/were there any authors or special personalities
  who particularly helped you to understand and master your life as a refugee
  or a child of a refugee?
- How soon did you consider United States citizenship?
- Do you still feel like a refugee? Have you ever considered returning to Europe
  for extended periods?

3. Contributions of social workers from Germany and other European countries
   to the growing profession of social work and the field of social welfare in the
   United States.
- What can you say about the ideas on social welfare that you retained from
  your German/European background?
- Were you able to apply some of these ideas to your studies, your work, and
  perhaps your teaching in the United States?
- Do you have any records of your work experiences, copies of degrees,

publications, awards, and so on that you might want to share and add to this oral history collection?

- What can you say about other refugee social workers and their contributions to the United States?
- This question is probably difficult to answer, but in your opinion: In which area (s) did they have their strongest impact?

4. Contributions of (former) refugee social workers to the reconstruction of Germany and perhaps other European countries after 1945.

If you went back to Germany or other European countries (and it would be good to have dates and places):

- What were your motivations and goals?
- Did you encounter problems with your acceptance as a former citizen of Germany or another European country?
- Did you encounter problems, however subtle, with regard to the introduction of new – or old – ideas in social work? (Examples would be very helpful.)
- What were the responses of German and other European students and colleagues to the (re) introduction of the classical social work methods (social casework, social group work, community organization) until about 1965?
- What were the responses to the introduction of supervision in social work and to other innovative approaches?
- Regarding family therapy: was there any reference by German colleagues to the voluminous family research that paralleled the development of *Familienfürsorge* during the Weimar Republic and was broken off in 1933?
- With the emergence of the generic approach to social work methods: how receptive did you find German and other European colleagues and students?
- How was your experience with these colleagues and students with regard to other areas, such as curriculum development, the development of (practice) theories, or even a science of social work, professional development, and the like?
- Were there any joint projects with German and other European colleagues that were particularly interesting?
- Do you or did you know of any social work teachers and practitioners who had escaped the Nazi terror and went back to Europe after 1945? How would you evaluate their contributions and their impact on the German and other European social welfare systems? Again, any records and copies of documents would be helpful.

5. On the mutual influences of social work and social welfare in North America and in Europe.

- On the whole: What was the impact of German and other European refugees on the United States scene during different periods (e.g., the New Deal, the war period, and the postwar period)?
- On the other hand: Which role did former refugees play in influencing social work and social welfare in Germany and other European countries (e.g., shortly after World War II, during the Adenauer era, the student movement, and beyond)?

- How would you describe the most important mutual learning process of the past?

6. Future cooperation
   - Would you please share any observations on the similarities and differences of the welfare systems? What and how can we learn from each other?
   - Considering the ongoing processes of German unification and European consolidation, where would you see the most promising potential or future cooperation between social workers on both sides of the Atlantic?

19

Chicken Farming:
Not a Dream but a Nightmare

An Eyewitness Report

EVA NEISSER

Eva Berwin Neisser was born in Breslau in 1920, the daughter and granddaughter of business owners. After the Nazis confiscated her father's business, the family fled Germany, arriving in New York in October 1938. Under the auspices of the Jewish Agricultural Society, they moved to a chicken farm in Vineland, New Jersey, in 1941. In 1944 Eva obtained American citizenship and was able to join her fiancé of seven years, who had escaped to Peru. She worked in the main accounting office of Pan American–Grace Airways for three years. In 1948 she returned with her husband to New Jersey, where they started a chicken farm but gave up and opened a travel agency in 1956. After her younger of two children left for college, she returned to school, earning a B.S. in accounting and an M.A. in communications/public relations. She taught at Glassboro State College (now Rowan College of New Jersey) as a member of the adjunct faculty until her husband's terminal illness, when she took over full-time management of the travel agency. She continues to work six days a week, writes a weekly newspaper travel column, and spends time with her three grandchildren. This report was written in 1991.

The German–Jewish refugees who managed to reach New York or other large American cities in the 1930s arrived in the midst of the Great Depression, with unemployment rampant. Men found hardly any work, and the women were lucky if they obtained housecleaning jobs where, for a dollar a day, they did what back at home, their cooks, maids, and washerwomen had done for them.

Strange as it may seem to today's generation, no organizations existed to help our people financially. There was the Hebrew Sheltering and Immigrant Aid Society (HIAS),[1] which put newcomers off the ships into dor-

---

1 Founded in 1909, HIAS was an international refugee service that offered legal advice and financial aid to immigrants from eastern Europe. During the World War II, HIAS cooperated with other organizations to aid refugees from Nazism.

mitory halls where beds were separated by curtains; we hardly ever allowed a friend to spend more than a night that way. There was just one organization that did have money for immigrants, and that was the Jewish Agricultural Society (JAS), part of the Baron de Hirsch Fund.[2] The JAS had started in 1900 to help the victims of Russian pogroms.[3] Because Jews were not permitted to own land in Russia, the JAS felt that the greatest good they could do was to give these immigrants their own land. Apparently, without any research into soil or economic conditions or training, they parceled out haphazard tracts of mosquito-ridden, arid acreage. When their clients managed to survive, that was considered a success. The JAS still had considerable funds when it was confronted with a new wave of penniless refugees forty years later. Bless them, they offered help again.

So, here were our parents, in their early forties, the men with Latin or Greek as a second language, the women mostly conversant in French. They had no money, no jobs, and word went out that the JAS would lend them a second mortgage to buy a chicken farm. "Chicken farming" became the buzz word (in the way that "health insurance" is now the word to cure all aspiring politicians' ills).

The JAS had learned from past mistakes and established a training farm. They sent the *Herren Doktor* (Ph.D.s) and lawyers and dentists and pharmacists and *Gross-Kaufmänner* (businessmen or manufacturers) to Bound Brook, New Jersey, and showed them what the front and rear of a cow and chicken and sheep looked like. The gentlemen were amazed; they had only seen these creatures roasted on a plate before. But they had no choice, and neither had the women.

Hubby came back from the six-week session and told Muttchen, "We'll have a nice, big house, we'll be together all the time, and nobody can fire us. The chickens will understand German or French or Latin just as well as English. Our families will come for summer vacations. And the chickens will lay eggs after six months, and we'll pay off all our debts."

What the JAS did not explain was that they were able to buy up farms cheaply because the previous owners, Americans born on the land, had gone bankrupt. The feed mill, from which some of us bought our land,

---

2 The Jewish Agricultural (and Industrial Aid) Society was founded in New York in 1900 to help eastern European immigrants set up farms in the United States. It was a subsidiary of the Baron de Hirsch Fund, established in 1889 by Baron Maurice de Hirsch to fund agricultural colonies and trade schools for Jewish immigrants.

3 These violent attacks on Jews swept Russia and Russian-occupied territories in 1881 after the assassination of Czar Alexander II. Such attacks, as well as renewed violence in 1903, 1905, and 1920–1 spurred Russian–Jewish emigration to the United States.

owned thirty-seven farms. They sure were glad to see those suckers come and pay!

Well, there was no choice. Dad went out from New York, spent one day, looked at some places, and came back and said, "Muttchen, we have a farm. The house is nice, you'll like it." Questions remained: At what level do you hit ground water? Is there any fencing? What do the coops look like? But these were negligible items not worth quibbling over: "Let's pack up and get out of the city!"

And so we came. One hundred degree heat in the summer (at the same latitude as Gibraltar or Sicily), no air conditioning until twenty years later, mosquitoes, weeds shoulder high, and not a light bulb, a fence pole, or a nail left anywhere. The neighbors had stripped every portable item while the place was empty.

And so we started. The women bravely went out and raked litter over cement floors. They changed the straw in the laying nests, emptied out 100-pound bags of feed into pails and pushed wheelbarrows to the coop doors. They collected eggs from under the sitting hens and were pecked until they got the knack. They schlepped the egg pails back to the cellar – careful, careful, don't crack them! In the afternoon, the birds needed to be fed again. Four times a day, you went with a small dishpan brush and cleaned out the water fountains, and every spare moment, you sat with a sandpaper brush and cleaned eggs. Soap and water were taboo, and detergent certainly was not used – it took the protective coating off the shell. (Today, nobody cares!)

After supper, eggs were candled, weighed, and packed. To leave a dirty basket for another day was unthinkable! Sometimes eight hours were spent in the cellar. Add to that the running of a household that had no washing machines or dishwashers, cooking for a family of four or more, and attempting to keep a vegetable garden – all this done by women whose cooks took menu decisions in the morning, whose maids cleaned, whose mending women came after the washerwomen had done the laundry.

Who says chickens lay eggs after being raised for six months? It's a pious fantasy. Baby chicks die, they crowd and peck each other, and you must go out at night to set them apart while they are sleeping. They had to get vaccinated, but still they got sick: laryngo-tracheitis, worms, colds, diarrhea, mites, and, God forbid, cholera or Newcastle.[4] The range of sicknesses was

---

4 Laryngo-tracheitis and Newcastle could both be fatal. Laryngo-tracheitis, a constriction of the trachea, causes suffocation; Newcastle, a virus for which there was no vaccine, could kill entire flocks.

so extensive that the local veterinarian ran out of names and called anything
he couldn't diagnose "x-disease." "Name ist Schall und Rauch" (a name
is meaningless). No matter what the name, the result was the same: no eggs,
fewer eggs, eggs after nine months instead of six. And every day, the beasts
ate and the feed man wanted his money.

No money for anything: The women became experts at blending
chicken into ground meat and *Klopse* (fried or boiled meat or fishballs),
breaded schnitzel, chicken stroganoff, soup, fricassee, salad. And cracked
eggs complemented the balanced diet: omelets, pancakes, scrambled, fried,
hard-boiled, *Haeckerle* (chopped eggs). You name it, we ate it.

No money to buy clothes: So what use were the good dresses they used
to wear for the weekly theater and opera subscriptions? The silk gown got
shortened and was worn in the chicken coop; Dad's dinner jacket was worn
there, too. Luckily, the chickens didn't know it was funny. Luckily, feed
was delivered in printed cotton bags. These got emptied carefully, shaken
out, washed, and sewn into curtains, aprons, skirts, blouses, bedspreads. The
only problem was that Mrs. Fischer across the road and Mrs. Berliner around
the corner wore the same pattern.

Once a year the lilacs bloomed. A great chance to make some real money:
Mum got up real early, around 4:00 A.M., and started cutting twigs. At
5:30 a neighbor pulled up with a truck to go to the city and sell lilacs.
"Hooray, Mum has some dollars!" Dad's source of income was chicken
manure: He shoveled, dinner jacket or not, and the manure man picked
up the heaps. That was another great source of cash.

Repairs were needed: The pump broke down, and there was no water.
Dad needed a bit of resilient wire and took it off his violin. He managed
to fix the pump. "I took the G-string, and *jetzt geht sie wieder,*" he says.[5]
Other repairs were not so easy: The chicken coops needed the roofs tarred
or it would rain in, so Mum and Pop sat on the roof and nailed on new tar
paper. The fence poles broke down and rotted. We creosoted the new
poles at the bottom, then dug new holes with a post hole digger, unrolled
new wire, and nailed up new fences.

I am not talking about my generation, born as babyboomers after World
War I. We were young, we had not been exposed to a life of comfort as
adults, we could adapt quite easily. True, my generation lost a chance for
the expected university education and, instead, slogged it out on the farm,
in factories, at typewriters, until much later we could catch up with our

---

5   "And now it goes again."

losses. But I am talking about our parents, our mothers, who had gone through a war, through inflation, through a period of settled years that they thought would last, making up for their own bad times. Instead, they did what they would not have asked their own staff to do. They used to paint, embroider, play the piano, and supervise their households. But they pushed up their sleeves and set to work. And when the farms did not bring in a living, they went into the local clothing factories and worked at piecework rates to make the extra dollars to send their younger kids to college.

Vineland, in southern New Jersey, thirty-five miles southwest of Atlantic City, thirty-five miles south of Philadelphia, had between 450 and 500 German–Jewish refugee families (and one Italian–Jewish family). They all followed the same dream of independence and survival, no matter what the cost. They managed and considered themselves lucky to be alive.

There was a dire need to give all these families something beyond the chicken manure, some vestige of their former lives. My father, Martin Berwin, a businessman from Breslau, and some of his friends organized the Poultrymen's Club of Vineland, later branching out into the Cumberland County Egg Cooperative.[6] They rented a club hall and for more than twenty years our farming couples had a place to go on Saturday night: Philosophers from the University of Jerusalem, comedians from the Vienna stage, singers from the former *Kulturbund,*[7] and lecturers from all over came, as did local attorneys and agricultural agents to teach necessary facts. Coffee and cake or *Wuerstel* (small sausages) and potato salad made "The Club" the place to go. Group health insurance and cooperative marketing of eggs brought economic advantages. On holidays, religious services were conducted in the hall.

My mother's generation never ceased being ladies. It wasn't only the one evening a week that they relapsed into their former selves; they never changed. When they went across the street for a quart of milk, they put stockings and heels on and took their overalls off. That was the way one behaved to show self-respect and respect to others. Even widowed and living alone, in their eighties and nineties, they remained the same, unaffected by chicken or other manure: The table was always set nicely, the good porcelain was in use, and the vase had fresh flowers. One didn't eat

---

6   The Poultrymen's Club of Vineland was a support group set up by and for the immigrants. Jewish farmers also set up purchasing or marketing cooperatives, such as the Cumberland County Egg Cooperative, to limit individual costs.

7   The *Kulturbund deutscher Juden* was established in Germany in 1933 by a group of Jewish actors, musicians, and performers who had lost their jobs when Hitler came to power. They arranged cultural events for the Jewish community.

in the kitchen or take one's girdle off. (One woman I know once said, "A German–Jewish woman is a woman who uses a knife and fork and a crystal glass even when she is alone in a room." She may have been right.)

In every emigration, the age of transplanting is the crucial factor: Children of school age adapt naturally and, through school and scholarships, have an open road before them. Young people barely out of school but without higher education, forced to go into the job market unprepared, have a harder time and lose chances open to their younger sisters. Women in their late thirties and forties and older were the true heroines of the emigration. They were thrown into strange and demanding circumstances and had to sink or swim. They not only "swam" and worked like peasants but also retained their culture and civilization. To their children and grandchildren, they were and still are the admired role models. Like the Indian *fakir,* who walks through fire and comes out unscathed, they went through hardships one can't even begin to detail in a few short pages and still came out as great ladies.

20

The Occupation of Women Emigrés:
Women Lawyers in the United States

FRANK MECKLENBURG

The immigration of professionals from Nazi Germany has become a major field of research in the past ten years.[1] It is perplexing, however, to see that the legal profession, until recently, remained by and large ignored.[2] This is all the more astonishing given the role lawyers played in public life in Germany as well as in the United States. The majority of higher civil service positions in Germany were then, and still are, occupied by people with legal training. The role of lawyers in American public life has attained almost mystical dimensions. Between 2,000 and 4,000 lawyers from Central Europe took refuge in the Unites States, of whom approximately 10 percent managed to return to their original profession. There is a number of examples of jurists who had started promising careers in their home country and who achieved considerable fame in their country of exile, among them Otto Kahn-Freund in England and Chaim Cohn in Israel. Unmatched in numbers and achievement were refugee lawyers in the United States with names like Albert Ehrenzweig Jr., Rudolf Schlesinger, Max Rheinstein, Arthur Nussbaum, and Stefan Riesenfeld to name only a few of so many who left a lasting impact on the American legal sphere.[3] Nevertheless, the

---

1   Although older studies recognized lawyers in the roster of the professional immigration, for instance, the classic study by Maurice R. Davie, *Refugees in America. Report of the Committee for the Study of Recent Immigration from Europa* (New York and London, 1947); or Donald Peterson Kent, *The Refugee Intellectual. The Americanization of the Immigrants of 1933–1941* (New York, 1953); and in the 1960s for instance by Laura Fermi, *Illustrious Immigrants. The Intellectual Migration from Europe 1930–1941* (Chicago and London, 1968); the truly ground-breaking study was published in 1983 by Herbert Strauss and Werner Röder, eds., *International Biographical Dictionary of Central European Emigrés, 1933–1945,* 3 vols. (Munich, 1983).

2   Ernst C. Stiefel and Frank Mecklenburg, *Deutsche Juristen im amerikanischen Exil (1933–1950)* (Tübingen, 1991).

3   In September 1991, a symposium was held in Bonn, Germany, with the title "Der Einfluss deutschsprachiger juristischer Emigranten auf die Rechtsentwicklung in den USA und in Deutschland." Some forty contributions covered larger parts of the impact of refugee legal scholars and their disciples, all of which needs further exploration. The proceedings will be published by Mohr-Siebeck Publishing, Tübingen.

adjustment problems were grave, more than in any other profession, (1) because of the fundamental differences between European continental law, which is based on Roman law, and American law, which developed from English common law, and (2) because German academic training had provided lawyers with ample knowledge of Greek and Latin but barely anybody knew English. Given the importance that language plays in the legal sphere, this posed a severe obstacle.

We therefore find a large number of refugee lawyers who moved into other fields, mostly, however, those whose knowledge could be applied in other ways. Most prominent was college teaching in history, political science, and international relations, fields to which men such as Eugen Rosenstock-Huessy, Hans Kelsen, Karl Loewenstein, and Hans Morgenthau turned. Others went into real estate, finance and banking, public accounting, or insurance; still others became legal librarians or worked in management positions. The number of women in all these areas was small.

In Germany, women were able to enter the legal profession at a late point compared with other nations in Europe. Only the politicians of the Weimar Republic opened the path to women in the legal area of the civil service. Through the universities and the examination process, the state controlled all access points into the legal profession. In July 1922 legislation was passed that gave women equal rights in filling civil service positions. The first woman lawyer was admitted in 1922; the first woman judge in Germany was appointed in 1924. The male monopoly, however, remained basically unchallenged. By the early 1930s, among the total number of attorneys in Berlin, for instance, women made up only one-quarter of 1 percent, in Munich one-half of 1 percent. Of seventy-four women who worked as judges in 1930, sixty-six were temporary because they were still in residency.[4]

The number of women lawyers whom we find in exile is therefore small. Most of those who did not complete their training in Germany did not attempt to go back into law. However, some found their experience with continental law to be a useful background for other careers. Elisabeth Lunau, daughter of the socialist politician Ludwig Marum, had started her legal training in 1929 in Heidelberg and managed to pass her first state exam on March 6, 1933, in Berlin. However, she could not start her practical training, the *Referendariat,* and so she learned *Heilgymnastik,* something she

---

4 See *Juristinnen in Deutschland. Eine Dokumentation (1900–1984),* published by the German League of Women Lawyers [*Deutscher Juristinnenbund*] (Munich, 1984), 14. The numbers for Berlin were eight women among 3,000; for Munich, four among 700.

could use in exile as well. After her escape from the abyss, she eventually became a hotel manager and was active in the national organization of hotel housekeepers. She was elected to the organization's board and took on the revision of its bylaws and even drafted a manual of policy and procedures. She was one of the few people in the profession who at the time had a college degree. Her legal training came in very handy for the work in the professional organization.[5]

Robert M. W. Kempner, a refugee lawyer from Berlin and American prosecutor at the Nuremberg trials, reported that he employed a number of former *Referendarinnen* as translators and document analysts in the trials against German war criminals.

An unusual example of making use of her former legal training is Lilli Kretzmer, retired immigration lawyer from Worcester, Massachusetts. Although she had studied law at the University of Bonn, marriage, children, and emigration in 1939 prevented the completion of her training. She settled in Worcester and worked with the Jewish Family Service, helping Jewish refugees who came to the United States after World War II. The U.S. government regarded her work so highly that in 1949 she received her license as an immigration lawyer from the Department of Justice's Board of Immigration Appeals. Her work within the United Restitution Organization in the early 1950s enabled many refugees to file their claims for restitution against Germany. In 1966 she was awarded the German Order of Merit. In 1964 she became director of the Immigration and Naturalization Office of the Worcester Section of the National Council of Jewish Women and remained in that function for many years until she finally retired in the 1980s.[6]

Several female lawyers who earned degrees in the United States found entry into the profession via the route of more traditional women's occupations by becoming legal librarians. Kate Wallach, who had passed her second state exam in November 1933 in Berlin, was admitted to the bar of Wisconsin in 1942. She became a law librarian in 1949 at Louisiana State University, and since 1964 she has been professor of law at the same institution.[7] Lilly C. Melchior was a judge in Hamburg in 1931 and an attorney in Berlin between 1932 and 1936. After having been an assistant to Ernst Rabel in Ann Arbor, she became a law librarian at the University of Mich-

5   Interview with Elisabeth Lunau, New York, Fall 1991.
6   Interview Lilli Kretzmer, Worcester, Mass., 1989; Introduction to the Collection of Lilli (Cohn) Kretzmer, 1–2, in The Arthur and Elisabeth Schlesinger Library of the History of Women in America, Radcliffe College. See also Kretzmer's memoirs: "The Years which the Locust Hath Eaten."
7   The State of Louisiana is the only one in the union that has a state legal system based on civil law.

igan in 1944. Clementine Zernik, an attorney in Vienna until 1938, became a librarian at the United Nations in New York.

Almost all those women lawyers who came with law degrees and who had already practiced law in Germany returned to the profession after retraining. Only a relatively few of their male colleagues did so. For women to study law in Germany in the 1920s was no excuse for not knowing what else to study, as was true for many male law students. For a woman to become a lawyer or even a judge in a completely male-dominated environment meant extraordinary dedication to the field. This may also be the reason a large number of female lawyers came from families with strong ties to the legal professions. We find some women who achieved high levels of professional experience. The most prominent field they worked in is family law. Brigitte Bodenheimer, daughter of legal history scholar Ernst Levy, taught family law at the University of Utah and later in Davis, California. She became one of America's leading experts in that field, drafting much new law and also representing the United States at international conferences. Marie Munk, first woman judge in Germany, practiced as an attorney and as a jurist, mainly in family law and divorce law. Gertrud Mainzer, daughter of the leading labor law expert during the Weimar Republic, Hugo Sinzheimer, finally found the time in the 1960s to study law and eventually became a family court judge in New York. Others became attorneys. Margarete Berent, who had already finished her law studies in 1915 but was unable to begin working as an attorney in Berlin until 1925, became an attorney in New York in 1949. Ilse Coe had been an attorney in 1935 in Königsberg and practiced again in New York. One of the outstanding legal practitioners in the United States was Magdalene Schoch, the first woman law professor in Germany. She had worked at Albrecht Mendelssohn-Bartholdy's Institute of Foreign Affairs in Hamburg, had wide experience with British common law, and published several contributions to legal encyclopedias on that topic. In the United States she worked as a foreign law expert for the Department of Justice. Helen Silving-Ryu, born Silberpfennig, with degrees in political science and law from the University of Vienna, was admitted to the New York bar in 1944. After the war, she worked in the office of the Alien Property Custodian in the Justice Department, which employed Magdalena Schoch, Ernst Fraenkel, Heinrich Kronstein, and other refugees. Silving-Ryu later was a professor of law at the University of Puerto Rico and specialized in penal law.

Several women lawyers, who already in Germany had started promising careers, resumed their work in the United States and gained considerable positions. Among the most prominent figures by way of her achievements and, at the same time, because these went widely unrecognized is Maria Magdalena Schoch. She earned her doctor of laws in 1920 from the University of Würzburg with a thesis on "English War Legislation Against Enemy Corporations" and subsequently became a research assistant to Albert Mendelssohn-Bartholdy. The latter had moved from the University of Würzburg to the newly founded University of Hamburg. "This opened an entirely new world to me," Schoch wrote, ". . . it did not take long before Hamburg became my second home."[8] She helped build the library of foreign law and lectured on conflict of laws and comparative law. In 1932 she was promoted to assistant professor in comparative and private international law at the University of Hamburg, the first woman with a regular faculty position in a German law department. When in the late 1920s Mendelssohn-Bartholdy established the Institute of Foreign Policy at the University of Hamburg, "which played an important role in the international relations of Hamburg," Schoch became the librarian as well as the editor of the journals *Europäische Gespräche* and *Amerika-Post*. During that period, she received a fellowship to go to England and study the judicial system. Her training in the Anglo-American system culminated in the receipt of a Rockefeller Foundation fellowship, which in 1934–5 took her for a year to the United States, where she visited a number of law schools. When she returned to Hamburg, Mendelssohn-Bartholdy had emigrated to England and she too felt that the time had come for her to leave. Schoch was not Jewish.

When I left Germany in the fall of 1934, there seemed to be still a reasonable chance, in the light of conditions as they then existed, that the Nazi regime would not last. I still do not feel that I was unduly optimistic in hoping at that time that the regime would break down under internal and external pressure, and that persons like myself, brought up in liberal and democratic beliefs, would have an opportunity to help rebuild a new and decent Germany. When I returned in November 1935, however, my impression was entirely different.[9]

In 1936 she traveled to England to attend the funeral of Mendelssohn-Bartholdy, despite warnings of serious consequences by the Nazis. She finally left for the United States in 1937.[10] In retrospect, however, she remarked that the stay in Germany until 1937 had allowed her to gain

---

8 Magdalene Schoch, "A Bit About My Career," 1–2, fragment, SUNY Albany, University Libraries, Special Collections, German Intellectual Emigré Collection.

9 "Curriculum Vitae," 1942, 4, in SUNY Albany, University Libraries, Special Collections, German Intellectual Emigré Collection.

10 Although Schoch came after the war to Germany for occasional visits, she never thought of returning. She responded to a call from the University of Hamburg after the war by saying that she would "never set foot into that institution."

insight into the mechanisms of the Nazi regime that proved to be very
useful for her engagement in the American war effort. Beginning in September 1938 she worked as a research assistant at the Harvard University
Law School in her areas of expertise: comparative law and private international law. In August 1943 she took a leave of absence to join the Office
of Economic Warfare in the Reoccupation Division of the Laws Section,
where she worked in research and analysis in the areas of "legal implemen-
tation of economic controls in enemy countries and methods of economic
administration." Later in the war she went into the Foreign Economic
Administration (FEA), where she participated in the "formulation of recommendations for Military Government."[11] She worked in the research
and drafting process of the civil affairs guides for the U.S. military government in Germany, where she collaborated with other refugees, notably with
Ernst Fraenkel of FEA as well as with Otto Kirscheimer, John Herz, and
Franz Neumann from the Office of Strategic Services (OSS) on issues of
legal reform and the abrogation of Nazi laws in Germany.[12] Toward the
end of her tenure at FEA, in the second half of 1945, she was promoted to
section chief in the Property Control Division (Ex-Enemy and Neutral
Property Section) and finally served as acting division chief. Her duties were
to formulate proposals for military government action under the Potsdam
declaration regarding disarmament and reparations. With Ernst Fraenkel she
co-authored a legal study, "Extra-territorial Effect of Economic Measures
Taken by the Occupying Powers in Germany: Problems and Recognition
and Enforcement." Although this work went widely unnoticed in the aftermath, especially when only a short time later the conflicts of the Cold
War rendered many of the antifascist efforts moot, the intellectual potential
that unfolded in those wartime agencies, such as FEA, OSS, the Office of
War Information (OWI), the Office of Price Administration (OPA), the
Lend-Lease Administration, and so on, needs to be reevaluated. This is
particularly true for studies in those areas where no American experts were
available and where refugees became irreplaceable advisors. They were
more than willing to use their expertise – their inside knowledge of Germany and the rest of Europe – to help bring down the fascist menace. In
no other area was this more true than in the legal field where American
knowledge of common law was of no help in analyzing state and society
in continental Europe. German lawyers such as Magdalena Schoch, Max

11   "Curriculum Vitae," [1946], 3, in SUNY Albany, University Libraries, Special Collections,
     German Intellectual Emigré Collection.
12   Status of Reports, Entry 44, Box 2, The National Archives, RG 226, Records of the Office of
     Strategic Services.

Rheinstein, Karl Loewenstein, Franz Neumann, and others, who were familiar with both the German legal system as well as its Anglo-American counterpart, could function as translators between these worlds. They lent their expertise in the drafting of plans for the liberation and the subsequent rebuilding of Europe. Most refugee lawyers in these fields subsequently remained active in the areas of international and comparative law, either as teachers at an American law school or, as in the case of Schoch, the Department of Justice. There she worked as an expert on foreign law for more than twenty years.

Nevertheless, the field in which women legal experts gained the most recognition and influence is that of family law, which includes marital property law, divorce law and divorce procedure, child custody law, adoption law, juvenile courts, and the like. Here we find several women lawyers with outstanding careers and expertise. Brigitte Bodenheimer, who had had two legal educations and three children, and who was admitted to the bars of the states of Washington and Utah, worked in the mid-1950s with a citizen's committee on divorce to establish a state marriage-counseling service attached to the divorce courts. From 1960 until 1965 she served as chairperson of the Utah state bar committee on juvenile courts. The committee worked to revise juvenile court law, "including [establishing the] independence of these courts from the existing control and supervision of the State Welfare Department. In an all-out effort the committee saw this legislation through two stormy legislative sessions and constitutional litigation."[13] As a result of this work Bodenheimer was appointed commissioner on uniform state laws for the state of Utah. After 1962 she also taught law. It was only in 1964, after the nepotism rules were lifted (her husband, Edgar Bodenheimer, was already a law professor at the University of Utah), did she become an associate professor of law. She took the backseat again when her husband accepted a position at the law school of the University of California at Davis. At Davis she became an unsalaried research professor. Again, only in 1972, when the California nepotism rule began to be relaxed, was she appointed professor of law. She taught courses on family law, marital property law, and children and the law. From 1967 to 1968 she was a member of the National Conference of Commissioners on Uniform State Laws to draft the Uniform Child Custody Jurisdiction Act, which later became law in eleven states. "The Act seeks to prevent changes in the custody of children of divorce

---

13 Brigitte M. Bodenheimer, Curriculum Vitae, Sept. 1976, in Brigitte Bodenheimer file, Research Foundation for Jewish Immigration.

by the courts of other states and to deter parental child abduction and the retention of children after out-of-state visits. This project," Brigitte Bodenheimer wrote in 1976, "has required my attention, including consultation provided to many persons throughout the country, up to the present day."[14] In 1970 she was "employed by the California law revision commission to prepare a background study and recommendations for legislation in the area of child custody and guardianship law. This study was published by the *Stanford Law Review* in 1971." In 1973 she laid the legal groundwork for revision of the state's adoption law in a study published in the *Southern California Law Review*.

Although family law is an important legal field and many scholars and practitioners, both male and female, are active in it, it seems, however, that the women we find working in this field dedicated a special kind of involvement in their occupation. One person who deserves to be retrieved from obscurity is Marie Munk. Coming from a family of several generations of lawyers, she studied law before World War I and passed her juris doctor exam in 1911. Because females were barred from applying to take the bar exam, she worked in a legal aid clinic in Munich that provided advice to women: "Many of our cases dealt with quarrels between landlord and tenants, but the majority with family problems, and with the rights of the illegitimate mother." She also worked as an assistant in a law firm and was active in the German feminist movement. During World War I, Munk became the vice president of an association of women in the legal professions, later affiliated with the German Association of University Women and with the German National Council of Women. Within these forums she had already fought, with Margarete Berent, for the legal equality of women. In 1924 she was the first woman in Germany to pass the bar exam; she subsequently practiced law in Berlin. "Many of my cases dealt with family relations, particularly divorces, custody of children, adoption, support, and separation agreements."[15] She also published articles on divorce and other marital problems in newspapers and journals, among them Magnus Hirschfeld's *Zeitschrift für Sexualwissenschaft*.[16]

---

14 Ibid., 2.
15 All quotations from Marie Munk, [Autobiography], manuscript, Landesarchiv Berlin, Helene Lange Archiv, Nachlass Marie Munk.
16 *Vossische Zeitung,* June 29, 1924, supplement, "Ehescheidung und Eheläuterung. Denkschrift der Frauenvereine"; "Der Ehebruch als Ehescheidungsgrund. Von Rechsanwältin Dr. Marie Munk in Berlin," *Zeitschrift für Sexualwissenschaft* 14 (March 1927): 103–6; "Die Juristin von Rechtsanwältin Dr. . . . ," *Merkblätter für Berufserfahrung der Deutschen Zentralstelle für Berufsberatung der Akademiker e. V.,* new edition 1928.

In 1929 Munk achieved her long-sought dream by becoming a judge, the first woman judge in Berlin. She was said to have tried more than 2,000 divorce cases until she was expelled from her position by the Nazis. Aside from her work on the bench, she also taught at the School of Social Work of the *Innere Mission* in Berlin. She lectured on legal subjects related to social work, that is, laws on domestic relations, especially divorce laws and divorce procedures, criminal law, especially juvenile law and procedures, as well as government and administrative law.

In June 1933, Munk traveled as the president of the German Federation and of the Berlin Club of Business and Professional Women to Chicago to attend the International Congress of the International Federation of Business and Professional Women. Munk had been the founder of the German Federation in 1931. Following the conference, she went on a lecture tour, speaking about the role of women and the situation in Germany after the Nazi takeover. In April 1934 she emigrated to the United States, resuming the contacts she had made on her trip ten months earlier. She "at once took up the study of family law and of penal law in its relation to women. In this capacity she visited many penal and correctional institutions and was for five months a member of the staff of the New York State Training School for Girls at Hudson, New York."[17] She was forced to return to Germany when her mother died in 1936.

When Munk finally came back to the United States, she had to start the immigration procedures over again because of her absence from the country for more than a year. She moved to Philadelphia and began a prolific writing career that resulted in a number of articles on legal problems in contemporary Germany. She also worked on a longer research project on the "effect of the First World War upon the gainful employment of women."[18] The study was commissioned by the International Federation of Business and Professional Women and was sent in 1940 to the vice president of the organization, Mrs. Gunnar Myrdal in Stockholm.[19] Subsequently, her

---

17 From a report by Helen Havener, New York, no date.

18 Marie Munk, LLD, "Child Care in Germany," *Your Child in School and at Work. Quarterly Journal of the Public Education and Child Labor Association of Pennsylvania* 1, no. 3 (1937): 8–11; "The Philosophy of Criminal Justice in the United States and in Germany," *The Prison Journal. Devoted to the Science of Penology. Published Quarterly by The Pennsylvania Prison Society* 17, no. 3 (1937): 349–57; "Legal Training in Germany," *The Double Tau, Journal of the National Legal Sorority* 9, no. 1 (1938), 11ff; "Nazi Ideology and the Christian Church," *Religion in Life* (1939): 483–96.

19 Letter from Lena Madesin Phillips, president of the International Federation to the various officers all over the world, Sept. 24, 1940. The manuscript was Marie Munk, "The Position of Women during and after the War." Unpublished manuscript, 1940, Landesarchiv Berlin, Helene Lange Archiv, Nachlass Marie Munk.

highly praised work provided for further research projects. In 1940 she conducted a study on German laws and institutions affecting civil liberties for the United Press Association.[20]

Throughout this period, however, Munk continued to work on issues that had interested her during the years in Germany, publishing over the years a number of articles concerning marital relations.[21] In 1939 she was a visiting lecturer at Hood College, a women's college in Frederick, Maryland, where she taught courses in social sciences, religion, domestic sciences, history, and German. In the fall semester of the same year, she taught at the Smith College Summer School of Social Work, where she started a research project, "Family Law and Procedure."

When the United States declared war on Japan and Germany in December 1941, Munk became an enemy alien. Nevertheless, a series of lectures sponsored by the Carl Schurz Foundation took her to North Carolina, where she encountered southern segregation. As a result of her practical experience as an attorney and judge, she passed the Massachusetts bar exam in December 1943, without having gone to an American law school. Only after she became an American citizen in 1944, however, was she admitted to the bar in that state. Nevertheless, because of unspecified circumstances, she did not join a law firm in Massachusetts but became a marriage counselor in Toledo, Ohio, in association with the Court of Domestic Relations.[22] Her attempts to be admitted to the Ohio bar failed and after an eighteen-month stay, she returned to Massachusetts in 1945 and settled in Cambridge.

After several years of research, teaching, and writing, Munk's professional life took a final turn with the onset of claims for reparations for lost properties and opportunities in Germany in the 1950s. "In this work I was able to use my knowledge of German and English, and also my familiarity with German law. It seems to me that this work which I have been doing for

---

20 Letter of recommendation from C. Edmonds Allen of the United Press Association to Henry Allen Moe of the Guggenheim Foundation, Jan. 28, 1941.

21 "Husband and Wife and Their Property in the Laws of Domestic Relations. Proposals for Changes Toward Equal Rights," *Living. Quarterly Published by The National Conference of Family Relations* 2, no. 4 (1940): 93–9; "Putting the Brakes on Divorce," *Survey 1 Midmonthly. Journal of Social Work* 82, no. 3 (1946): 75–7; "Toward Success in Marriage," *The Women's Press. The National Magazine for Young Women's Christian Associations* (1947): 21–2; "Do We Need Better Enoch Arden Laws?" *The Bar Bulletin* 19, no. 9 (1948): 270–4; "Uniform Divorce Bill," *Women Lawyers Journal* 40, no. 1 (1954): 3–5.

22 Munk devotes a whole chapter of her memoirs to her time in Toledo with many sociological and psychological observations and conclusions rendered from approximately 2,000 cases dealt with during that period. See her autobiography, pt. 2, chap. 5.

more than seven years," she wrote in her memoirs, "has somehow completed the cycle of my life. For many refugees, whom I have been able to help, life has become more easy by the compensations which they have been and are getting from abroad."[23]

23 Marie Munk, [Autobiography], pt. 2, chap. 7.

21

Fashioning Fortuna's Whim:
German-Speaking Women Emigrant Historians
in the United States

CATHERINE EPSTEIN

Summing up her life as a historian, Helene Wieruszowski once wrote that although subject to "the whims of Fortuna," her life had been "rich in human experiences and filled to the brim with hardships and pleasures, promises and frustrations."[1] Wieruszowski's remarks capture much of the story of the sixteen women who were or became historians following their emigration from German-speaking Europe to the United States after 1933. All these women underwent the hardships of emigration as an adult or as a child. As historians, they experienced the pleasures of unanticipated intellectual discoveries, the promises of new or renewed careers, and the frustrations of being women in the male-dominated history profession. Yet, although they share the commonalties of being women, refugees, and historians, little else unites these women. They have had very different historical interests, varying degrees of success within American academia, and very different reactions to their situations as women and as refugees. Some have taught at large universities, others in small colleges, and still others have pursued their historical research largely independent of institutional affiliations. Some of these women emigrant historians have married, some divorced, and some remained single. Some of them became mothers; others remained childless.

Who are, or were, these women refugee historians? How did their lives and careers differ from those of male refugee historians? How did emigration influence their historical work? What contributions have they made to the study of history in the United States? Finally, did the emigration of

---

1 I wish to thank all those historians who answered my inquiries. In addition, my thanks to Emily Haddad, Jeremiah Riemer, and Sophia Rosenfeld for their help at various stages in the preparation of this chapter. Helene Wieruszowski, Preface to her *Politics and Culture in Medieval Spain and Italy* (Rome, 1971), ix–xvii, xv.

German, and especially German–Jewish, women have an impact on the historical profession in postwar Germany?

Of the sixteen women emigrant historians, five had completed their university studies in Germany before their emigration to the United States, four came to the United States as teenagers or young adults, and seven came as children. The five women historians who came to the United States with university degrees in hand are among the 88 "first-generation" refugee historians who came after Hitler's accession to power.[2] They include the Medievalists Emmy Heller[3] and Helene Wieruszowski[4]; the Jewish historian Selma Stern-Täubler[5]; Charlotte Sempell,[6] the only historian of modern Europe among this older group of women refugee historians; and Erika Spivakovsky,[7] a historian of the Renaissance. Among this group, Emmy

2   These five women are fully documented in Catherine Epstein, *A Past Renewed: A Catalog of German-Speaking Refugee Historians in the United States after 1933* (New York, 1993). Among the forty-six refugee historians who emigrated to the United Kingdom and stayed at least two years, two were women: Gertrude Bing (1892–1964), who studied the history of the classical tradition; and Eva Gabriele Reichmann (1897–), a historian of German–Jewish history. See Christhard Hoffmann, "The Contribution of German-speaking Jewish Immigrants to British Historiography," in Werner E. Mosse, ed., *Second Chance: Two Centuries of German-speaking Jews in the United Kingdom* (Tübingen, 1991), 153–75, here 174–5. There were no "first-generation" women historians from Austria. Among the 144 documented women refugee academics from Austria, only two studied history, and none, it seems, attained an academic position in the field of history either in Austria before 1938 or in their host countries thereafter. See Edith Prost, "Emigration und Exil österreichischer Wissenschaftlerinnen," in Friedrich Stadler, ed., *Vertriebene Vernunft*, vol. 1 (Vienna, 1987), 444–70, 451.

3   Emmy Heller, born in Frankfurt in 1886, received her Ph.D. degree in Heidelberg in 1926. Financed by the Notgemeinschaft der deutschen Wissenschaft from 1926–36, she pursued research on Thomas of Capua. From 1937–56 she taught at Brooklyn College. In addition, she taught at Barnard College from 1938–39, and held awards from the American Philosophical Society and the American Council of Learned Societies in 1948, and the Alice Freeman Palmer Fellowship in 1953–54. She died in Glen Cove, New York, in 1956.

4   Helene Wieruszowski, born in Elberfeld in 1893, completed her dissertation under the direction of Wilhelm Levison in 1918. She worked at several research institutes, trained as a librarian, and then worked in the university library in Bonn from 1928–33. She spent the years 1934–40 engaged in private research in Spain and Italy. After coming to the United States, Wieruszowski lectured at Johns Hopkins University from 1940–42, taught at Brooklyn College from 1944–49, and was professor of history at City College in New York until her retirement in 1961. She died in Sorengo, Switzerland, in 1978.

5   Selma Stern-Täubler, born in Kippenheim in 1890, received her Ph.D. degree in Munich in 1914. She was a research fellow at the Akademie für die Wissenschaft des Judentums in Berlin from 1918 until her dismissal in 1933. In the United States, she was the first archivist of the American Jewish Archives in Cincinnati, a position she held from 1947–57. Stern-Täubler died in Vienne, Switzerland, in 1981.

6   Charlotte Sempell, born in Osnabrück in 1909, received her Ph.D. degree in Munich in 1931. Sempell chose to leave Germany after 1933 because she found Hitler's regime repugnant; she is not of Jewish origin nor did she belong to left-wing political movements in Weimar Germany. Following her emigration, she married a Yiddish writer. She taught at Brooklyn College from 1947–74.

7   Erika Spivakovsky, born in Hamburg in 1909, received her Ph.D. degree in Berlin in 1933. From 1936–39 she was an instructor in Spanish at the University of Melbourne in Australia. She has never taught history in the United States, but she has published several long studies on the Spanish Renaissance. From 1962–64 Spivakovsky held a fellowship from the Radcliffe Institute for Independent Study at Harvard University.

Heller and Charlotte Sempell were not of Jewish origin, although both married Jewish men.

Among the younger group of women historians, several experienced delays in the start of their careers: Ann Beck taught modern English and African history;[8] Ursula Lamb specializes in Latin American history;[9] and Susan Groag Bell[10] and Gerda Lerner[11] pioneered courses in women's history in the United States. Among those who came to the United States as children, Renate Bridenthal teaches modern German and women's history;[12] Ruth Kleinman is professor of early modern European history;[13] Johanna Menzel Meskill is professor of Chinese history;[14] Sylvia Strauss teaches English and women's history;[15] Renée N. Watkins has taught Renaissance and Reformation history;[16] and Dora Bierer Weiner has specialized in the history of medicine.[17] In addition, Hanna Holborn Gray, the daughter of Hajo Hol-

8   Ann Beck, born in Braunschweig in 1905, received her Ph.D. at the University of Illinois in 1948. Her professional career has included stints as professor of history at Centenary College in Arkansas from 1948–50; as instructor at the University of Connecticut from 1950–52 and 1953–54; as research associate at Columbia University from 1952–53; as associate professor at the Detroit Institute of Technology from 1954–57; as associate professor at Dakota State College from 1957–60; and as associate and professor of history at the University of Hartford from 1960–73.

9   Ursula Lamb, born in Essen in 1914, chose to leave Germany as an exchange student in 1935. She received her Ph.D. from Berkeley in 1949. She taught at Barnard College and Columbia University from 1944–51 and lectured at Oxford University from 1958–60 and at Yale University from 1962–74. She has been professor of history at the University of Arizona in Tucson since 1974.

10 Susan Groag Bell, born in Troppau, Czechoslovakia, in 1926, received her M.A. from the University of Santa Clara in 1970. Bell taught at the University of Santa Clara from 1971–81 and has been teaching at Stanford University since 1982.

11 Gerda Lerner, born in Vienna in 1920, received her Ph.D. from Columbia University in 1966. She taught at the New School for Social Research from 1963–65 and at Long Island University from 1965–68. In 1968 she became professor of history at Sarah Lawrence College and since 1980 has been Robinson-Edwards Professor of History at the University of Wisconsin in Madison.

12 Renate Bridenthal, born in 1935, received her Ph.D. from Columbia University in 1970. Bridenthal taught at Borough of Manhattan Community College from 1966–7, and has taught at Brooklyn College since 1967.

13 Ruth Kleinman, born in Berlin in 1929, received her Ph.D. in 1959 from Columbia University. She taught at Bucknell University from 1957–58, Connecticut College from 1959–62, and at Brooklyn College from 1958–9, and since 1962. She has been professor of history at Brooklyn College since 1975.

14 Johanna Menzel Meskill, born in Frankfurt in 1930, received her Ph.D. degree from the University of Chicago in 1957. She taught at Vassar College from 1956–68, and has been at Lehman College in New York City since 1968. At Lehman College, Meskill has been professor of history since 1973, as well as acting dean from 1979–81 and dean of humanities since 1981.

15 Sylvia Strauss, born in Berlin in 1931, received her Ph.D. from Rutgers University in 1968. She has taught at Kean College in New Jersey since 1966.

16 Renée N. Watkins, born in Berlin in 1932, received her Ph.D. from Harvard University in 1959. She taught at Ithaca College from 1961–3, at Smith College from 1963–7, and has been at the University of Massachusetts in Boston since 1967.

17 Dora Bierer Weiner, born in Fürth in 1924, received her Ph.D. at Columbia University in 1951. She taught at Columbia University from 1949–51; at Barnard College from 1951–6; at Sarah Lawrence College from 1957–62; and at the Teacher's College, Columbia University, from 1962–3. From 1962–5 Weiner was research associate at the Albert Einstein College of Medicine. In

born, the refugee historian who taught for years at Yale University, received her Ph.D. in history from Harvard University in 1957. Gray, recent past president of the University of Chicago, has taught history at several universities and has published several important articles on the Italian Renaissance.[18] As far as I could determine, all but one of these younger women historians are of Jewish origins, although many came from assimilated families.[19] Finally, although not the subject of this essay, another group of women historians deserves mention: those women who are the daughters of refugees, historians such as Atina Grossmann and Marion Kaplan.

Information on women emigrant historians, although sparse, is found in biographical dictionaries of American academics as well as in biographical reference works on émigrés.[20] In addition, many of these women historians have published short remarks on their emigration and other experiences in the introductions to their historical works. One woman, Susan Groag Bell, has written her memoirs.[21] Finally, nine of the sixteen women emigrant historians wrote detailed letters in answer to my inquiries.

Like male refugee historians, women historians of the older generation were compelled to interrupt their research work by the Nazi takeover of power. Forced to emigrate, they often experienced years of flux before their arrival in the United States. Once in America, they had to teach and write in a new language, acculturate themselves to a different academic style and method, and make professional contacts in foreign academic surroundings. They began their American teaching careers unaware of how colleges functioned, unsure of how to advance their careers, and advised not to ask too many questions.

Helene Wieruszowski's circumstances following her emigration were typical of both male and female refugee historians. After her compulsory emigration in 1934, Wieruszowski spent the years until 1940 engaged in private research in Spain and Italy. These years were not, however, peaceful idylls of scholarly musings but, rather, years in which Wieruszowski was, she wrote, "subjected to drastic changes, frequent resettlements, and more

     1965, she began teaching at Manhattanville College, where she became professor of history in 1978. She is now professor of medical humanities at the University of California, Los Angeles.

18 Hanna Holborn Gray, born in Heidelberg in 1930, received her Ph.D. from Harvard University in 1957. She taught history at Harvard University from 1957–60, at the University of Chicago from 1961–72, and at Northwestern University from 1972–4. From 1974–8 she was provost and professor of history at Yale University; she served as acting president at Yale from 1977–8. From 1978–93 she was president of the University of Chicago, where she is now professor of history.

19 Ursula Lamb is not of Jewish origin.

20 Particularly useful have been the *Directory of American Scholars* (Lancaster, 1942–); and Herbert A. Strauss and Werner Röder, eds., *International Biographical Dictionary of Central European Emigrés,* vols. 1–3 (Munich, 1980–83).

21 Susan Groag Bell, *Between Worlds* (New York, 1991).

or less forcible readjustments." Writing about herself in the third person, she went on to describe how "she was not free to follow a self-elected path but had to grab materials for her research as they came her way, prepare them for publication as the occasion arose, and use the language which was called for."[22] After her initial adjustment to life in the United States, Wieruszowski attained a professorship at City College in New York. In her case, emigration created career opportunities unthinkable in Europe. Given both the structure of German academia and the poor position of women within that structure during the Weimar period, it is highly unlikely that Wieruszowski would ever have achieved the rank of professor had she remained in Germany.

Selma Stern-Täubler also experienced an abrupt, unwanted interruption in her historical research. During her years as a research fellow at the *Akademie für die Wissenschaft des Judentums* in Berlin, she had begun a massive study entitled *Der Preussische Staat und die Juden*.[23] Stern-Täubler accompanied her husband, Eugen Täubler, the noted historian of ancient and Jewish history, to Hebrew Union College in Cincinnati in 1941. There she broke off work on her project because, as she once wrote, "When I emigrated to America in 1941, I was unable both for technical, and more importantly, for psychological reasons to continue my task."[24] Instead, Stern-Täubler wrote a novel, *The Spirit Returneth,* published in 1946.[25] She returned to her study of the Prussian state and the Jews much later. Stern-Täubler never held a teaching position in Germany or in the United States, but she was the first archivist of the American Jewish Archives in Cincinnati.

The other older women refugee historians experienced similar career displacements. The oldest of the women refugee historians, Emmy Heller, had published some works on Thomas of Capua. Her emigration, however, seems to have very much slowed her research work. In the United States, she published only a long chapter entitled "Die Feudalzeit," in Fritz Karsen's *Geschichte unserer Welt* in 1947.[26] At the age of fifty-one, Heller held a university teaching position for the first time in her life; she taught at Brook-

---

22 Wieruszowski, *Politics and Culture in Medieval Spain and Italy,* ix.
23 Selma Stern-Täubler, *Der Preussische Staat und die Juden,* part 1: *Die Zeit des Grossen Kurfürsten und Friedrich I* (Berlin, 1925; reprint: Tübingen, 1962); part 2: *Die Zeit Friedrich Wilhelms I* (Berlin, 1938; reprint with new introduction: Tübingen, 1962); part 3: *Die Zeit Friedrichs der Grossen* (Tübingen, 1971); part 4: *Gesamtregister zu den sieben Bänden,* ed. Max Kreutzberger (Tübingen, 1975).
24 Ibid., pt. 3, xi. Translation by author.
25 Selma Stern-Täubler, *The Spirit Returneth . . . A Novel* (Philadelphia, 1946). Revised edition in German as *Ihr Seid meine Zeugen: ein Novellenkranz aus der Zeit des Schwarzen Todes 1348–49* (Munich, 1972).
26 Emmy Heller, "Die Feudalzeit," in Fritz Karsen, ed., *Geschichte unserer Welt,* 2 vols. (Berlin, 1947), 2:5–194.

lyn College from 1937 to 1956. Emigration also compelled Charlotte Sempell to interrupt a promising career as a historian. During her years of
emigration in Paris and Uruguay, Sempell did not pursue historical research
at all. In 1947, at the age of thirty-eight, she joined Helene Wieruszowski
and Emmy Heller on the faculty of Brooklyn College.

Altogether, Brooklyn College has employed almost one-third of all
women refugee historians at some point during their professional careers.
Helene Wieruszowski, Emmy Heller, and Charlotte Sempell all taught
there; Renate Bridenthal and Ruth Kleinman have now held positions there
for years. The college, founded only in 1930, often filled its part-time and
evening positions with poorly paid women academics in the 1940s and
1950s. Although it was the first coeducational liberal arts institution in the
New York City system, the college's decision to hire refugee women probably stemmed from its precarious financial situation. As Charlotte Sempell
recalls, "I was looking for a part-time position because I had two young
children";[27] at her evening instructorship, she earned the "fabulous pay of
$3.25 an hour."[28] Furthermore, with an overwhelmingly Jewish student
population in a largely Jewish section of New York City, Brooklyn College
not surprisingly hired a high proportion of Jewish faculty members. Although neither Sempell nor Heller was of Jewish origins, refugees from
Central Europe were, to many Americans, by definition Jewish. Finally,
given its location, Brooklyn College was attractive to refugee academics,
many of whom settled in metropolitan New York. Liberal in its traditions
– the college was the first white institution to hire an African-American
historian, John Hope Franklin, on a permanent basis in 1956.[29] And Brooklyn College was the one institution where a number of women refugee
historians were able to find long-term teaching positions.[30]

As Charlotte Sempell's remarks concerning why she accepted a part-time,
poorly paid position at Brooklyn College suggest, women refugee historians' careers were decisively shaped by the demands of marriage, raising
children, and running households. Clearly, their families presented a predicament for these women refugee historians. In an obituary of her close
friend, Helene Wieruszowski succinctly summed up Heller's career as follows: "As the wife of a Jewish doctor and the mother of three children she
could not devote herself entirely to her academic work and thus had to

27 Charlotte Sempell to author, letter dated July 30, 1991.
28 Charlotte Sempell to author, letter dated April 24, 1989.
29 Peter Novick, *That Noble Dream* (Cambridge, Mass., 1988), 472.
30 For a history of Brooklyn College, see Murray M. Horowitz, *Brooklyn College: The First Half-
    Century* (New York, 1981).

struggle for a career in her new, foreign surroundings."[31] Charlotte Sempell, who never received tenure at Brooklyn College, links her lack of promotion to her family: "As I am married and raised two children I never made it to tenure."[32] Family demands, of course, were not confined to the older generation of women refugee historians. Most of the women who emigrated as children chose not to comment on the impact their private lives have had on their professional careers. However, one wrote: "It was tightrope walking, teaching full-time, running a hospitable house, be[ing] supportive of my husband's very demanding career, and rais[ing] three boys."[33]

Among the older group of refugee academics who emigrated to the United States, there were a number of individuals who had received degrees in history at German universities but who did not become historians in the United States. It is, of course, impossible to know how many of these actively sought positions as historians after their emigrations. Because the number of refugee women with German doctoral degrees in history is low in proportion to the number of men with the same degree, women are especially over-represented among those who did not become historians here. Three of the four known individuals in this category are women.[34] Similarly, in a study of refugee historians in Britain, Christhard Hoffmann names seven individuals who had hoped to work as historians but who were forced to find work in other fields. Three of these seven were women.[35]

Edith Lenel's career was typical of those who had received a Ph.D. degree in history but who did not end up teaching history in the United States. Lenel, the last student of Hans Rothfels to receive a degree in Königsberg in 1935, worked for a year as an assistant to Hans Kohn at Smith College in 1936–7. Lenel did not even apply for teaching positions in history at this

31 Helene Wieruszowski, "Emmy Heller," *Deutsches Archiv für Erforschung des Mittelalters* 15 (1959): 612. Translation by author.
32 Charlotte Sempell to author, letter dated April 30, 1990.
33 Letter to author, dated Nov. 17, 1991.
34 Rosy Bodenheimer (1900–) received her degree in Giessen in 1930; the title of her dissertation was "Beitrag zur Geschichte der Juden in Oberhessen von ihrer frühesten Erwähnung bis zur Emanzipation." In the United States, Bodenheimer worked for many years in the library of the Baltimore Hebrew College (now University). Edith Lenel (1909–) received her degree in Königsberg in 1935; the title of her dissertation was "Friedrich Kapp, 1824–1884: ein Lebensbild." Finally, Charlotte Littauer-Blaschke (1897–) received her *Promotion* in Leipzig in 1922; she wrote on "Sebastian Francks Anschauungen vom politischen und sozialen Leben 1499–1542." In the United States, she taught German at various institutions from 1941–74.
35 These three women were Elsbeth Jaffé, Jenny Schwarz, and Ellen Littmann. See Hoffmann, 163. Elsbeth Jaffé received her doctorate in Freiburg in 1923; the title of her dissertation was "Die Ehepolitik Bonifazius' VIII." Ellen Littmann's dissertation was published in 1928. She received her degree in Cologne with a dissertation titled "Studien zur Wiederaufnahme der Juden durch die deutschen Städte nach dem schwarzen Tode." Information on Jenny Schwarz could not be found.

time. She considered her situation hopeless. Having just completed her dissertation, she had no publishing record, no teaching experience, and inadequate English language skills. She became a librarian at Montclair State College. Later, she became professor of German, and eventually chair of the German department at the college. In an interview with me, Lenel recounted how she had wished to pursue historical research, particularly on Francis Lieber, the German–American political scientist. On several occasions, she unsuccessfully sought scholarships from the college to study Lieber's papers. She was told that funds were available only for studies of teaching methodologies. In addition, Lenel's teaching load left her little time to pursue research interests.[36] Her career suggests one alternative career path taken by refugee women who, although historians by training, did not become professional historians in the United States.

Among the older generation of refugee women, Toni Oelsner's situation was unique. In an interview recorded in the late 1970s, Oelsner, with considerable bitterness, narrated the course of her career in Germany and the United States.[37] Oelsner never received either her *Abitur* (high school leaving exam) or her *Promotion* (doctorate) in Germany. After working for some years, Oelsner began her studies at the University of Frankfurt in 1931, where she also became involved in left-wing student politics. After her emigration, she received her M.A. degree from the New School for Social Research in 1942. Thereafter, Oelsner spent the next forty years writing on topics of Jewish social and economic history, with occasional support from various foundations and research institutions. Although Oelsner published a monograph, several articles, and many encyclopedia entries on topics of Jewish history during the Middle Ages, she never attained a teaching position. She did not, however, attribute her frustrated academic career to her sex. Instead, she believed that her lack of a doctoral degree and her interest in Jewish history, combined with the anti-Semitism and McCarthyism of the 1950s, kept her out of the American historical profession:

For years afterward I applied for positions at colleges, but I didn't have a Ph.D. I'm not even sure of the reasons. . . . All my work was on Jews, and maybe that played a role in not being accepted for college positions. Right upon my arrival Gerth had written: "You have no idea how much anti-Semitism exists here, es-

36 Interview with Edith Lenel in Newtown, Pa., on August 22, 1988. Lenel published an article based on Lieber's papers: "Barthold Georg Niebuhr und Wilhelm von Humboldt. Briefe im Nachlass von Franz Lieber," *Historische Zeitschrift* 200 (1965): 316–31.
37 "Dreams of a Better Life: Interview with Toni Oelsner," *New German Critique,* no. 20 (1980): 31–56.

pecially in the Midwest." Then the McCarthy era began, and anybody suspected for ever having been a leftist was mistrusted.[38]

At the same time, Oelsner was probably disadvantaged by her sex as well as by her age. Although other refugee women historians were able to begin their teaching careers relatively late in life, Oelsner was not so fortunate; she was already forty when she began her unsuccessful search for a college teaching position. As the small number of German-speaking women historians who successfully found teaching positions suggests, women refugees experienced much greater difficulty in their integration into American academia than did their male counterparts.

For women emigrant historians, the age at which they left German-speaking Central Europe had considerable impact on how their emigration influenced their careers as historians in the United States. As we have seen, for the older generation, emigration entailed an abrupt career rupture. These women had to interrupt their research projects and for the first time teach in college and university settings. Women refugees who arrived in the United States having either begun university studies or just completed secondary school in Europe often started their university careers relatively late in life. These women include Ann Beck, Susan Groag Bell, Ursula Lamb, and Gerda Lerner. They experienced delays in the start of their graduate education not only because of their emigration, but also because they married and had children. Writing about the period between completion of her secondary school education and the start of her college career in the United States, Lerner reflected: "I became a refugee and later made my way to America. Here I married, raised two children, and earned my living at every variety of women's jobs. . . . It was as good an education as any for becoming a specialist in the history of women."[39] Susan Groag Bell began her graduate education in her late thirties, a fact that very much influenced her future work in women's history. Bell's rejection from the Stanford University doctoral program because she was past the age of thirty-five led her to compile biographical information on women throughout history who had begun careers after turning thirty-five. In turn, this project led Bell to many other works in the field of women's history.[40]

Finally, for the seven women who emigrated as children, childhood emigration often played a role in their decisions to become historians. One woman wrote, "I have always felt deeply grateful to the United States for

38 Ibid., 49.
39 Gerda Lerner, *The Majority Finds Its Past* (New York, 1979), xvi.
40 Bell, *Between Worlds*, 214–15.

rescuing me and my family from an awful fate. I decided that the best way I could repay my debt was to interpret the European heritage I valued and teach this to young Americans. So that's why I became a historian."[41] Another stated:

My emigration as such influenced me to become a historian because I felt like the last survivor of an exterminated culture and wanted to do honor to the dead. I also felt a need to gain status through my intellectual heritage, a substitute for the material and social advantages which I would have had if there had been no emigration.[42]

Yet another historian felt:

The intellectual involvement with German history was also my way of transcending the emotional pain of the emigration, in particular the way in which it destroyed my family. My father committed suicide shortly after our arrival in New York City in 1941. My mother became increasingly paranoid in her later years. My brother tore himself away in his teens and was only a visitor in our home. For me, studying the past, "identifying with the aggressor," seemed like a way out of the turmoil.[43]

Whether out of gratitude to the United States, a need to compensate for losses incurred by emigration, or a reaction to a family situation brought on by emigration, women emigrant historians' decisions to study history often stemmed from their childhood emigration. Similarly, the only woman emigrant historian in France, Rita Thalmann, also chose to become a historian because of her experience of emigration from National Socialism and her father's murder at Auschwitz. Thalmann wanted to understand how a country such as Germany could descend into the barbarism of the Nazi period.[44] However, not all women emigrant historians believe that their emigration influenced their careers as historians. One historian wrote that because she left Germany at age eleven,

the emigration did not affect either my choice of career, or my choice of subject specialty, or my professional progress. . . . The most I can say is that my having been born and brought up in Europe made it easier for me to get along on my research trips, as well as to feel my way into the research materials.[45]

41   Letter to author, dated Nov. 17, 1991.
42   Letter to author, dated July 22, 1991.
43   Letter to author, dated Aug. 11, 1991.
44   Letter to author, dated Dec. 22, 1991. In personal conversation, Thalmann stated that she thought that she was the only woman emigrant historian in France. Rita Thalmann, born in Nuremberg in 1926, taught at the University of Tours from 1966–84. Since 1984 she has been professor of German history and civilization at the University of Paris (VII).
45   Letter to author, dated Aug. 4, 1991.

Women emigrant historians of all ages have written about how their emigration influenced the content of their historical work. Helene Wieruszowski's compulsory emigration and arrival in the United States gave her studies in medieval history new meaning during the initial, turbulent years of her emigration:

Since I had suffered and was still suffering personally from the tyranny of dictatorial governments my mind was more open than ever before to the prospect of living in a freer society and to the opportunity of participating in politics on equal terms with others. The medieval commune as a field of studies seemed to me an apt preparation to my future life in the New World.[46]

Wieruszowski, whose historical interests spanned many centuries of medieval history, attributed to her uprooting after 1933 the "hodge-podge character of historical themes, geographic areas, even epochs" that figured in her research.[47]

Emigration forced Selma Stern-Täubler to see her subject matter in new light. She broke off work on *Der Preussische Staat und die Juden* when she came to the United States, returning to the project only in 1958. The later volumes of this work were influenced not only by her emigration but also by the events of the intervening years. The last volumes of her work were, she wrote, "also formed by the experiences which America gave me, as I was compelled to come to terms with totally different social, political and societal circumstances, with totally different ideas, and with another mentality, and to sink myself into general American and American–Jewish history." Her encounter with the United States, she went on to explain, helped her to "understand the deeper meaning of the encounter between the Germans and Jews which occurred in Lessing's and Moses Mendelssohn's time."[48] At the same time, Stern-Täubler completed her work in the shadow of the Holocaust, when both the German–Jewish population and the Prussian state as entities had changed beyond all recognition.

For Charlotte Sempell, emigration exposed her to new approaches to history. Although her research on Bismarck continued after her emigration, it "show[ed] the growing influence of the new country's thinking."[49] Her initial work in Germany had focused on Bismarck and foreign relations, an approach typical of the historiography of Weimar Germany. In the United States, she turned her attention to Bismarck's domestic policies, Caprivi's experience with Bismarck's constitution, and Bismarck's financial situation

---

46 Wieruszowski, *Politics and Culture in Medieval Spain and Italy*, xiii.
47 Ibid., x.
48 Stern-Täubler, *Der Preussische Staat*, pt. 3, xi–xii. Translation by author.
49 Charlotte Sempell to author, dated July 30, 1991.

on the eve of his marriage. Later, Sempell concentrated on psychohistorical interpretations of Bismarck's conflicted youth.

Among the younger historians, Renate Bridenthal has made explicit connections between her refugee past and her professional interests. In the introduction to *When Biology Became Destiny,* a collection of essays examining the role of women in Weimar and Nazi Germany, Bridenthal and her coeditors, Atina Grossmann and Marion Kaplan, argue that they are posing the feminist version of the unavoidable questions of twentieth-century German history: "What went wrong? . . . How was Auschwitz possible?" The authors then add:

> We are particularly haunted by those questions because we also carry the baggage of German–Jewish families and identities. Our study of German history is always shadowed by our knowledge of the end of this particular story; it is a history that we or our families have experienced very directly. One of us was born in Germany and escaped as a young child; the other two are children of refugees. Our families have given us a sense of the extremes of German history in this period. . . . We carry with us a continuing obsession with that history, with the need to know why, and perhaps with a heightened sensitivity to the danger signals that our readers may recognize in this book.[50]

The refugee backgrounds of Bridenthal and her coeditors made their own study of German history more personal. At the same time, their background may have helped them to convey the horror of that history to their readers.

For other women historians who emigrated as children, the role of their emigration in their work in history is much less apparent. One woman felt that her family's experiences with fascism "probably also gave me the impetus to think more deeply about such ideas and events than others who were less affected by them." However, this historian quickly added, "Perhaps it makes sense to say that my emigration played a part in my historical thinking, but rather less so in my career as an historian."[51]

Finally, Gerda Lerner has explained how her emigration brought her insight into women's history. In the introduction to *The Majority Finds Its Past,* Lerner writes that "the culture shift I had made into a foreign language, a foreign history, and a new and different system of values, was in a sense an excellent preparation for the kind of work I would be doing." In Europe, she went on to explain, she had received an outstanding education. The United States and its history were, however, completely neglected in her

---

50 Renate Bridenthal, Atina Grossmann, and Marion Kaplan, eds., *When Biology Became Destiny: Women in Weimar and Nazi Germany* (New York, 1984), xii.
51 Letter to author, dated Sept. 12, 1991.

high school curriculum. This experience helped Lerner understand that in graduate school what "I was learning was based on unacknowledged bias and was in need of skeptical scrutiny and revision. What I was learning in graduate school did not so much leave out continents and their people as it left out half the human race, women."[52] In Lerner's case, then, emigration influenced the epistemological breakthrough essential for her studies in women's history. She also believes that her emigration gave her a heightened understanding of the nature of racial oppression. Lerner edited an important documentary history of black women in the United States, titled *Black Women in White America: A Documentary History,* a work informed by her own past as a refugee from Hitler's Third Reich.[53] In a recent comment, Lerner described herself "as a participant in World War II, a victim of Hitler, as a person whose life was deeply affected by World War II and by the Holocaust and who is also fully and painfully aware of the similar contradictions that exist in terms of racism."[54] Like Lerner, Rita Thalmann, the woman emigrant historian in France, links her understanding of oppression to her emigration and her experiences in Hitler's Germany. For Thalmann, "the oppression of women has been as unacceptable as other kinds of discrimination."[55]

Gender may well have been the most determining aspect of women emigrant historians' careers. All these women historians came up against the now familiar pattern of sexual discrimination in the academy. In this respect, women refugee historians' careers differed little, if at all, from those of women historians born in the United States. The sexual discrimination prevalent in American universities in the first decades of the postwar period doubtlessly prevented some women historians, particularly those of the older generation, from achieving their full academic potential. For those of the younger generation, sexual discrimination surely helped to slow their promotions within the field. In letters to me, almost every woman historian wrote that her sex had proved to be an obstacle in her professional career. Typical remarks included "I became a historian despite my sex,"[56] and "My status as a woman was quite simply a disability, a block."[57] One woman did write "I am not aware that gender affected any of my choices, nor can I say that it has affected my career." However, several lines later, she noted

---

52 Lerner, *The Majority Finds Its Past,* xvii.
53 Gerda Lerner, *Black Women in White America: A Documentary History* (New York, 1972).
54 Gerda Lerner, "Another View," *Journal of American History* 77 (1990): 588–9.
55 Rita Thalmann to author, letter dated Dec. 22, 1991.
56 Letter to author, dated Aug. 11, 1991.
57 Letter to author, dated July 22, 1991.

that during a job interview, a department chairman told her that he would honestly prefer to hire a man.[58] Almost every woman related at least one incident of sexual discrimination. One historian made the decision to specialize in the history of a particular geographical area because the professor who taught that area was more welcoming to women students than were other professors in the department.[59] Later, when this historian joined the faculty of another history department, she was asked simply to stay away from the department's large weekly lunches.[60] Another woman was told that she had received a job at a local college but was later sent a letter from the college saying that a younger individual, better able to identify with the college, had been hired in her place. The younger individual was male.[61] Several women historians complained of lower salaries, slower promotions, and fewer opportunities to advance their professional careers than those granted male historians in similar situations.

What, then, has been the contribution of these German women emigrant historians to the American profession? Among the small number of older refugee historians, several made important contributions in their fields of specialization. Helene Wieruszowski's work on medieval and Renaissance history is widely respected.[62] Perhaps her most important work was her collection of essays, *Politics and Culture in Medieval Spain and Italy,* published in 1971.[63] In addition, Selma Stern-Täubler's four-volume *Der Preussische Staat und die Juden,* in which she documented the process of Jewish emancipation in the Prussian state, is a classical work of Jewish history.[64]

Among the younger women emigrant historians, Gerda Lerner, Susan Groag Bell, and Renate Bridenthal played crucial roles in the development of the field of women's history. Their initial awareness of gender in history may have stemmed from their common experience of seeing the breakdown of traditional gender roles, which, as other essays in this volume attest, was so common in refugee families. In her memoirs, *Between Worlds,* Susan Groag Bell recounts how her mother, a traditional, dutiful wife with five servants in Troppau, emigrated with her daughter to England. Bell's father, who remained in Czechoslovakia, was later murdered in a concentration camp. Of her mother, Bell writes: "I don't think she missed her five servants for a moment. . . . During these years in London, several men had proposed

58   Letter to author, dated Aug. 4, 1991.
59   Letter to author, dated Aug. 23, 1991.
60   Letter to author, dated Dec. 7, 1989.
61   Letter to author, dated July 30, 1991.
62   See E. J. Polak, "Helene Wieruszowski," *AHA Newsletter* 20, no. 5 (1982): 15.
63   Wieruszowski, *Politics and Culture in Medieval Spain and Italy.*
64   Stern-Täubler, *Der Preussische Staat.*

marriage, but, as she said to me occasionally, 'Why should I take on an old man whom I will have to nurse, when my life is so good and pleasant and I can support myself?' ''[65] Although the other women historians' mothers may not have been so enterprising, these historians nonetheless experienced an émigré milieu in which traditional gender roles were frequently being questioned. Such an atmosphere may have led these historians to consider anew the role of women in history. In Bridenthal's case, progressive politics also played a role in causing her to question women's traditional roles. As she writes, "I was raised as a socialist, which made me at least a proto-feminist until the women's movement helped me to define myself as a feminist."[66]

Gerda Lerner had aggressively promoted the interests of women historians, as well as the study of women's history. After receiving her Ph.D. degree in 1966 at the age of forty-six, Lerner decided that she would spend her next twenty years bringing women's history into the mainstream of professional history. Lerner reasoned that she

would have to have impact on the academic world in a number of ways in order to make Women's History accepted: by actual research and writing; by proving the existence of sources; by upgrading the status of women in the profession; by proving that there existed student demand in this subject and moving from there to designing courses and graduate programs.[67]

In every one of these areas, Lerner has had a significant impact. She co-founded the Coordinating Committee on Women in the Historical Profession (CCWHP) at the 1969 meeting of the American Historical Association. An indefatigable organizer, Lerner has also organized many workshops, conference groups, and other meetings in order to foster a wide-ranging network of women historians.

At the same time, Lerner's prolific writings have contributed to the intellectual vitality of women's history. Besides her *Black Women in White America: A Documentary History,* Lerner published *The Female Experience: An American Documentary,* an anthology of documents on women's history that followed a periodization based on stages in female life, stages, rather than the traditional periodization of male history.[68] Finally, *The Majority Finds Its Past* is a collection of essays in which Lerner presents research findings to illustrate different aspects of women's history and historiography and reflects on her development as a historian of women. In her earlier work,

65 Bell, *Between Worlds,* 177–8.
66 Renate Bridenthal to author, letter dated Aug. 11, 1991.
67 Lerner, *The Majority Finds Its Past,* xxiv.
68 Gerda Lerner, *The Female Experience: An American Documentary* (Indianapolis, 1977).

Lerner had adhered to the "compensatory and contribution history" frame-work of women in history, which also viewed women as victims of op-pression.[69] In her later work, Lerner has stressed the autonomous activity of women, arguing that "[t]he true history of women is the history of their ongoing functioning in that male-defined world *on their own terms*."[70]

Like Gerda Lerner, Susan Groag Bell has devoted her career to women's history. In a charming memoir, *Between Worlds,* Bell has recounted her childhood in the Sudeten town of Troppau in Czechoslovakia, as well as her emigration to England. She came only much later to the United States. Bell edited the first collection of documents on the subject of women's history, a collection of great thinkers' attitudes toward women through the ages: *Women from the Greeks to the French Revolution.*[71] In 1983, she co-edited another anthology documenting the debate in Western countries over women: *Women, the Family, and Freedom: The Debate in Documents.*[72]

Finally, Renate Bridenthal has played an important role in advancing the now large and dynamic field of German women's history. Bridenthal is also a committed organizer; as co-president of the CCWHP, she oversaw the development of the Conference Group in Women's History as an associate body of the American Historical Association. With Atina Grossmann and Marion Kaplan, she helped establish the German Women's History Group, which still meets regularly, usually in New York City. She helped found the interdisciplinary Columbia seminar on women and society, as well as the women's studies program at Brooklyn College. Bridenthal has co-edited two important volumes on German and European women's history: with Claudia Koonz, *Becoming Visible: Women in European History,*[73] and with Atina Grossmann and Marion Kaplan, *When Biology Became Destiny: Women in Weimar and Nazi Germany.* She has also written several important articles on German women's history.

Apart from their striking contribution to the growth of women's history in the United States, women emigrant historians as a group have had little impact on the historical profession as a whole; their numbers have been too small and their interests too disparate. As noted earlier, these historians' historical interests span a wide range of chronological topics and geograph-ical areas. Unlike many male refugee historians who became prominent his-

69 Lerner, *The Majority Finds Its Past,* xxx.
70 Lerner, *The Majority Finds Its Past,* 148.
71 Susan Groag Bell, *Women From the Greeks to the French Revolution* (Belmont, 1973).
72 Susan Groag Bell and Karen Offen, eds., *Women, the Family, and Freedom: The Debate in Documents,* vols. 1–2. (Stanford, Calif., 1983).
73 Renate Bridenthal and Claudia Koonz, eds., *Becoming Visible: Women in European History* (Boston, 1977).

torians of modern Germany in the United States,[74] women historians who emigrated from German-speaking Central Europe chose to make their academic contributions in other areas of historical inquiry. Only two of the sixteen women emigrant historians concern themselves with modern German history: Charlotte Sempell and Renate Bridenthal. Many of the other women may have felt that modern German history was too closely linked with their own pasts to allow objective analysis. Alternatively, some of their American teachers may have steered them away from Central European history, suggesting that as emigrants from Germany their work might be better received in other fields of history. Male emigrant historians do not seem to have felt these same constraints.

Did the emigration of these women, most of whom were of Jewish origins, have an impact on the historical profession in Germany? As is well known, women historians have been and continue to be notoriously underrepresented in the German historical profession. Various explanations have been advanced to explain this phenomenon. One German historian, Hans-Jürgen Puhle, has argued that the German historical profession is structured in a way that is disadvantageous to women.[75] Puhle argues that the second book essential for a university career, the *Habilitationsschrift,* is generally written between the ages of twenty-five and thirty-five, child-bearing age for most professional women. In addition, socialization processes have left women historians at a disadvantage; they have a harder time "celebrating" and "selling" themselves on the academic market. Furthermore, Puhle believes that the traditional privileging of diplomatic, military, and financial history, with its absence of women as subjects, has also worked to women historians' disadvantage. German women have tended to write dissertations on church history, art history, the history of education, and intellectual history, topics perceived to be marginal to "real" history. Last, Puhle argues that until the 1960s, the German historical profession was unusually conservative and tradition minded in its interpretations of history, a conservatism also reflected in its personnel practices.

Although these arguments are surely important for an understanding of why there have been so few women historians in Germany, the compulsory emigration or murder of the Jewish population in the years following 1933 probably also significantly halted the progress of women in the German

---

74 For a catalog of first-generation refugee historians, many of whom were prominent historians of German history, see my catalogue, *A Past Renewed.* Male refugee historians who came as children or adolescents include, among many others, Werner T. Angress, Klaus Epstein, Hans Gatzke, Peter Gay, George G. Iggers, Klemens von Klemperer, George Mosse, and Fritz Stern.

75 Hans-Jürgen Puhle, "Warum gibt es so wenige Historikerinnen?" *Geschichte und Gesellschaft* 7 (1981): 364–93, 380–5.

historical profession. This argument can, of course, be only speculative, and the evidence is tentative. Nonetheless, a large percentage of the women who held academic positions in Weimar Germany were dismissed by the Nazis for racial reasons in 1933.

The high number of German–Jewish women among female academics during the Weimar period may be attributed to simple economics. Because German Jews were overrepresented among the German–upper-middle classes, more German–Jewish women had the financial security and leisure necessary to pursue university careers. Alternatively, the phenomenon of Jewish academic success may be linked to the long-standing Jewish tradition of Bible and Talmud study. Shulamit Volkov, however, has argued that Jewish academic achievement may perhaps best be explained by the social position of Jews in Germany. Although her essay concerns German–Jewish male scientists during the German Empire, her insights may help to explain the high numbers of German–Jewish women among the first generation of women in German academia. Because bourgeois Jews hoped to further their assimilation by extraordinary academic contributions to German culture, they felt a tremendous pressure from an early age to show academic brilliance.[76] Such sociopsychological motives may well have been more pronounced among men than among women, but well-educated bourgeois women may nonetheless have internalized this pressure to succeed. At any rate, the numbers of German–Jewish women among *Dozentinnen,* women who had completed their *Habilitationen,* suggests that German–Jewish women were unusually successful among female academics in Weimar Germany. Of the fifty-four *Dozentinnen* (lecturers) at German universities in 1933, fully half – twenty-seven – faced expulsion from their university positions after the Nazi accession to power. Although some of these women may have been dismissed for political rather than for racial reasons, most were nonetheless of Jewish origins.[77]

Only one historian, Hedwig Hintze-Guggenheimer, was among the fifty-four *Dozentinnen* employed in German academia in 1933, and because of her Jewish origins, she too was dismissed from her position. Hintze, the wife of Otto Hintze, published her *Habilitationsschrift,* titled *Staatseinheit und Föderalismus im alten Frankreich und in der Revolution* (State Unity and Federalism in the ancien régime and during the Revolution), in 1928.[78] She

---

76 Shulamit Volkov, "Soziale Ursachen des Erfolgs in der Wissenschaft: Juden im Kaiserreich," *Historische Zeitschrift* 245 (1987): 315–42, 332.

77 Elisabeth Boedeker and Maria Meyer-Plath, eds., *50 Jahre Habilitation von Frauen in Deutschland* (Göttingen, 1974), 369.

78 Hedwig Hintze, *Staatseinheit und Föderalismus im alten Frankreich und in der Revolution* (Stuttgart, 1928).

was *Privatdozentin* in Berlin between 1928 and 1933 and, after her dismissal, divided the years from 1933 to 1939 between research in Paris and caring for her husband in Berlin. In the aftermath of *Reichskristallnacht,* Hintze emigrated to Holland in 1939. Although she seems to have been offered an associate professorship at the New School for Social Research in 1941, Hintze could not follow up on the offer. Unable to sustain her precarious professional, financial, and physical existence, Hedwig Hintze committed suicide in Utrecht in 1942. With the emigration and death of perhaps the most prominent German woman historian, the German historical profession lost not only a brilliant and insightful historian but also a woman who might well have served as example, mentor, and supporter for other women historians.[79]

Although Hintze was the only historian among those women academics who lost university positions after 1933, the dismissal of so many other women academics surely halted the progress of all women, not only women historians, in German academia. Nazi policies meant that many fewer women professors and lecturers could serve as models and mentors for younger women interested in pursuing academic careers. In addition, Nazi race, gender, and educational policies prevented the somewhat more liberal hiring practices in fields such as chemistry, physics, or *Germanistik* (German language and literature) from spilling over into the field of history.

Although Hintze was the only woman historian with a university position, many women had completed doctoral dissertations in the field of history by 1933. By 1908, six women had achieved the *Promotion* (Ph.D.) in history; by 1933 another 414 women had attained this degree at German universities.[80] Unfortunately, it is extremely difficult to determine the percentage of women of Jewish origins among this group. However, bits and pieces of information known about many of these women either from their dissertations, which usually included curriculum vitae, or from other sources, indicate that at least thirty women who had completed their university studies in history at German universities were either forced to emigrate or suffered a worse fate.[81] Furthermore, it is likely that the Nazis, in

79 For more information on Hedwig Hintze, see Brigitta Oestreich, "Hedwig und Otto Hintze," *Geschichte und Gesellschaft* 11 (1985): 397–419.

80 Puhle, "Warum gibt es so wenige Historikerinnen?" 373. The number 414 is taken from a list of women who received the Ph.D. degree in history before 1933, compiled by Elisabeth Boedeker, *25 Jahre Frauenstudium in Deutschland,* no. 1 (Hanover, 1939). Boedeker omitted at least five women (see footnote 81).

81 These thirty women include seven women who stated their religion as Jewish in curriculum vitae in their dissertations. All seven had completed their dissertations by 1922; thereafter, it seems, German–Jewish women thought it best not to advertise their religion to a generally anti-Semitic profession. These seven women were Elisabeth Cohn, Margarete Henschel, Marie Helene Johanna

accordance with their Nuremberg Laws, would have classified as Jews some of those women who gave their religion as Protestant or Catholic. Although we do not know how many of these women would have pursued academic careers in Germany, the numbers of *Dozentinnen* forced to emigrate after 1933 suggest that German–Jewish women were particularly likely to achieve university careers.

Curiously, several German historians have argued that female students of working-class families were the group of female students most negatively effected by Nazi educational policies.[82] Such historians neglect to note, however, that the much larger number of German– and Eastern European–Jewish women university students were a more obvious target for Nazi harassment. Although Jews made up only slightly more than 1 percent of the German population, in the winter of 1913–14, 65.5 percent of female students in Prussia were Protestant, 21.5 percent were Catholic, and 12.9 percent were Jewish; in Berlin, 21.7 percent of the women students were Jewish, whereas only 8.9 percent were Catholic.[83] Although the percentage of Jewish women students had declined somewhat during the Weimar period, Jewish women were still highly overrepresented in the female student population of 1933. The loss of this Jewish women student body eliminated a group of women from German academia that may well have produced growing numbers of women academics.

Meyer-Cohn, Elise Schaefer, Adelheid Schiff, Zippora Schiffer, and Selma Stern. Another seven women, given the information offered in their curriculum vitae, are almost certainly of Jewish origins: Raissa Bloch, Lisa Eppenstein, Ina Friedlaender, Olga Herschel, Ljubow Jacobsohn, Golda Patz, and Sarah Schiffmann. Many of these women were born in Russia but emigrated to Germany in the aftermath of the Russian Revolution. Six women wrote that they were either "raised" or "baptized" as Protestants or Catholics, suggesting Jewish origins: Frieda Hoddick, Felicitas Kullen, Katharina Schäfer, Irmgard Schleker, Johanna Schultze, and Adelheid Karolina Elsa Wiehn. Four women who did not mention their religion are known to have emigrated from Hitler's Germany: Elsbeth Jaffé, who emigrated to England; and Charlotte Littauer-Blaschke and Charlotte Sempell, who both emigrated to the United States. Paula Masur, the sister of the refugee historian Gerhard Masur, followed her brother to South America in 1938.

Five women who had completed their dissertations on historical topics are not included among the 414 women Boedeker documented: Rosy Bodenheimer, Emmy Heller, Hedwig Hintze, Ellen Littmann, and Helene Wieruszowski. Finally, Erika Spivakovsky's dissertation was on a topic of literary history; she is therefore not included in Boedeker's list of women who completed dissertations in history.

82 Kristine von Soden, "Zur Geschichte des Frauenstudiums," in Kristine von Soden and Gaby Zipfel, eds., *70 Jahre Frauenstudium. Frauen in der Wissenschaft* (Cologne, 1979), 9–42, 29. According to Soden, the sons and daughters of working-class families made up 1.3 percent of the student population in 1932, but only 0.7 percent of the student population in 1941. In absolute numbers, approximately 1,150 students of working-class background were matriculated at German universities in 1932, a number reduced to roughly 330 in 1941. See also Irmgard Weyrather, "Numerus Clausus für Frauen – Studentinnen im Nationalsozialismus," in Frauengruppe Faschismusforschung, *Mutterkreuz und Arbeitsbuch* (Frankfurt/Main, 1981) 131–62, 145.

83 Gerta Stücklen, *Untersuchung über die soziale und wirtschaftliche Lage der Studentinnen* (Göttingen, 1916), 40.

The emigration of left-leaning, liberal, and/or Jewish male historians probably also helped retard the progress of women in the German historical profession after 1933.[84] In the last years of the Weimar Republic, such historians were beginning to make headway in the profession. Eager to renew and liberalize the substantive agenda of German history, refugee historians such as Eckart Kehr, George W. F. Hallgarten, Hans Rosenberg, and Alfred Vagts, had they remained in Germany, might well have come to advocate more democratic and meritocratic personnel policies within the historical profession; in several cases, these historians had themselves been victims of exclusionary professional practices. Unfortunately, to the best of my knowledge, no male refugee historian has left a statement on his views concerning women in the profession. A published list of students who completed their dissertations under Hajo Holborn's direction at Yale University between 1941 and 1968 suggests that Holborn neither actively promoted women students nor refused to direct their dissertations. Of his 55 students, seven were women, about what one might expect for an institution such as Yale between 1940 and 1970.[85] However, in a short, recently published memoir, Shulamit Volkov wrote the following sentences about her teacher, Hans Rosenberg:

[His] total concentration upon scholarship was further revealed in his full, unlimited acceptance of his women students. This was not the general rule in the Berkeley of the late 1960s, in that large history department in which not one woman had ever held a formal teaching position. Rosenberg had full confidence in his women students. In fact, the 1967–8 seminar included a number of outstanding women graduates, who were all treated by him with unwavering respect. He was, to be sure, always a European gentleman, but, while he often showed old-fashioned gallantry, there was absolutely no sign of condescension nor of any arrogance about him. This, I believe, was not a matter of feminism, but a result of his effort to support every talent and encourage every achievement; an egalitarian attitude based on his belief in the primacy of scholarship.[86]

Although Rosenberg may not be representative of male refugee historians, he was also surely not alone in his support of good scholarship by women.

84 Systematic studies on German-Jewish male professors' attitudes toward women in academia seem unavailable. However, in a study of male professors' opinions on allowing women university admission in 1897, Karin Hausen found that only one of 104 professors thought that women could positively contribute to academia. She notes that Professor Ottomar Rosenstrauch, a specialist for internal medicine, was almost certainly Jewish. See Karin Hausen, "Warum Männer Frauen zur Wissenschaft nicht zulassen wollten," in Karin Hausen and Helga Nowotny, eds., *Wie männlich ist die Wissenschaft* (Frankfurt/Main, 1986), 31–40, 38–9.
85 See "Hajo Holborn's Students," *Central European History* 3 (1970): 187–91.
86 Shulamit Volkov, "Hans Rosenberg as a Teacher: A Few Personal Notes," *Central European History* 24 (1992): 58–63, 61.

In the postwar period, on a per-annum comparison, fewer women achieved a *Promotion* in West Germany than in the last years of the Weimar Republic. In the years 1931–33, an average of thirty women per year completed a Ph.D. degree in history. Between 1946 and 1950, on average sixteen women a year received the Ph.D. for a dissertation written on a historical topic.[87] The low numbers of women who attained the Ph.D. degree in the immediate postwar period may be explained by the few available university spaces, as well as by the priority given to returning war veterans in the distribution of university places.[88] In addition, the Nazi idealization of women as mothers, housewives, and nurturers doubtlessly remained a powerful influence on gender relations well after 1945, keeping women from pursuing professional degrees. By the mid-1960s, twenty years after the end of the Nazi dictatorship, the numbers were still extremely low; only nine women attained the Ph.D. degree in history in 1964, twenty-one in 1965, and twenty in 1966.[89] By 1970, eighteen women historians had habilitated themselves at German, and after 1945, West German universities; another four had habilitated themselves in the German Democratic Republic.[90] By contrast, some fourteen women who had emigrated from German-speaking Europe as a result of Nazi policies had become professors of history at American colleges and universities, almost as many as *all* women historians in Germany.

Sixteen women who left Hitler's Germany were or became professors of history or independent historians in the United States. Although their lives and careers vary greatly, some generalizations are possible. Unlike their male refugee counterparts, women refugee historians were often compelled to compromise between career demands and family duties. They often interrupted their careers for many years, not only because of emigration but also because they had difficulty combining families with professional careers. Like women historians born in the United States, women emigrant historians suffered all the drawbacks associated with their gender in a male-dominated profession. At the same time, they enjoyed academic opportunities for which German women academics still struggle. Emigration often influenced the content of their historical research, their ways of thinking about history, and their decisions to become historians. As one woman historian has written, "My status as an emigrant and refugee from Hitler has infused all my scholarship and interpretations and made me more

---

87 Puhle, "Warum gibt es so wenige Historikerinnen?" 372, note 20.
88 Weyrather, "Numerus Clausus für Frauen—Studentinnen im Nationalsozialismus," 162.
89 Puhle, "Warum gibt es so wenige Historikerinnen?" 372, note 20.
90 Boedeker and Meyer-Plath, eds., *50 Jahre Habilitation,* 63–73, 289–90.

sensitive to questions of racial, ethnic, and sexual discrimination."[91] Other women emigrant historians would surely balk at such a sweeping characterization of themselves. Nonetheless, all the women refugee historians were subject to "the whims of Fortuna" after Hitler's rise to power, and each fashioned her own, highly individual response to that challenge.

91   Letter to author, dated July 31, 1991.

22

Exile or Emigration:
Social Democratic Women Members of
the Reichstag in the United States

CHRISTL WICKERT

I

Mit dem Gesicht nach Deutschland (My Face Turned toward Germany) was the title chosen by Erich Matthias for his 1968 report on emigration among Social Democrats.[1] This title reflects the feeling of many politicians, both men and women, who were forced to leave the German Reich in 1933. They took with them the ideals and political aims that had contributed to the creation of a republic structured along democratic lines. But their life's work was for the time being a failure. Nevertheless, they maintained an intense involvement in German political developments, and in the 1940s they took part in the elaboration of proposals for the restoration of political order after Hitler's defeat.

My research on Social Democratic women in the Reichstag and the Prussian *Landtag* has led me to conclude that the first generation of women members of parliament, who had broken into this male domain without role models to follow, had taken their political mandates much more seriously than did their male colleagues.[2] Female members of parliament had cultivated more intense contacts with their constituencies, thus gaining a deeper understanding of the worries and needs of their constituents, particularly those of women. They had put their findings and their knowledge to appropriate use in the course of discussion within their party groups or in speeches before parliament, thus contributing to an improvement in women's legal and social status. In 1933

---

1 Erich Matthias, ed., *Mit dem Gesicht nach Deutschland. Eine Dokumentation über die sozialdemokratische Emigration* (Düsseldorf, 1968).
2 Christl Wickert, *Unsere Erwählten. Sozialdemokratische Frauen im Deutschen Reichstag und im Preussischen Landtag 1919–1933,* 2 vols. (Göttingen, 1986).

325

most of the women who had gained prominence had been active as members of parliament or in other public institutions for more than ten years. But after 1930 at the latest, as increasing numbers of National Socialists came into state parliaments, these women were hindered in the exercise of the rights and obligations associated with their parliamentary work by the National Socialist members' disruptive and misogynistic behavior. Those among them who were Jewish, doubly stigmatized, were in particular danger after Adolf Hitler's seizure of power. This point is also raised by Käte Frankenthal in her memoirs, published in 1981 under the title *Der dreifache Fluch: Jüdin, Intellektuelle, Sozialistin*.[3]

National Socialists believed that women had no business in politics and that if they were nonetheless active in this sphere, they were to be opposed at every turn. As early as 1923, for instance, Toni Pfülf, the daughter of a Bavarian military officer, was described in the *Stürmer* as a "Jewess" with a "distorted grimace" because she had spoken out on the threat posed by the Hitler movement after the march on Munich's *Feldherrenhalle* on November 9. We also know that Communists and Social Democrats were the first to be harassed in 1933. Intellectuals and academics who refused their allegiance to this new movement also had to leave the country.

This chapter concentrates on four important Social Democratic women politicians: Käte Frankenthal, a member of the Prussian *Landtag* from 1930 to 1932; Marie Juchacz, leader of the Social Democratic women's movement from 1917 to 1933, chair of the Worker's Welfare organization (*Arbeiterwohlfahrt*), and a member of the Reichstag from 1919 to 1933; Toni Sender, a member of the Reichstag from 1919 to 1933; and Hedwig Wachenheim, co-founder and member of the central committee of Worker's Welfare from 1919 to 1933 as well as a member of the Prussian *Landtag* from 1928 to 1933.

First, allow me to return for a moment to the title of this chapter: "Exile or Emigration." The current academic discussion on the flight and expulsion of Germans during the Nazi period makes a clear distinction between exile and emigration.[4] The word "exile" is used to describe the situation of those for whom the country in which they had grown up and spent a

---

3 Käte Frankenthal, *Der dreifache Fluch: Jüdin, Intellektuelle, Sozialistin*, eds. Kathelyn M. Pearle and Stefan Leibfried (Frankfurt/Main, 1981).

4 On this topic, see in particular Hans-Albert Walter, " 'Öfter als die Schuhe die Länder wechselnd . . . ' Ein Überblick über die deutsche Emigration nach 1933," in Walter Zadek, ed., *Sie flohen vor dem Hakenkreuz* (Reinbeck, 1981), 10ff., esp. 12; Susanne Miller, "Rahmenbedingungen für das politische Wirken im Exil," in Friedrich-Ebert-Stiftung, ed., *Widerstand und Exil der deutschen Arbeiterbewegung 1933–1945* (Bonn, 1981), 454ff; Bertolt Brecht, "Über die Bezeichnung Emigranten" [1939], in Ernst Loewy, ed., *Literarische und politische Texte aus dem deutschen Exil 1933–1945* (Stuttgart, 1979), 484f.

major part of their professional life remained the focal point of their attentions, hindering at least in part integration in the country of refuge. As a rule, exiles returned to one of the two German states after the end of war. "Emigration," in contrast, describes a process leading to professional and social integration in the country of refuge, mostly culminating in a change of citizenship. Interest in the country of origin did not disappear completely, but it began to play a secondary role. It was often easier for younger people who had not yet developed a distinct professional identity to integrate in their new environment.

A particular problem for women in exile and emigration was the circumstance of their private lives. The examples I discuss here are all single women who had made their own lives in the Weimar Republic. Most of the men who left Germany in 1933 did so with their wives and female companions. These women provided significant help in making a new beginning, taking care of everyday life, and often willing to accept jobs below their qualifications in order to support their men. For them, the person, the body of their loved one, represented a piece of homeland, helping them find the courage to survive.[5] Käte Frankenthal, Marie Juchacz, Toni Sender, and Hedwig Wachenheim had no such person to lean on. Marie Juchacz, after an early divorce, had raised two children on her own; the others had decided against marriage and a family because they felt this was irreconcilable with their careers and politics, which were more important to them. Only Hedwig Wachenheim had the benefit of a close relationship with her love of many years, Hans Staudinger. He was married, however, and had emigrated to New York with his wife.[6]

The flood of memoirs on the book market bears witness to a need for coming to terms with lives often broken, situations often experienced by the generation born during the years of the *Kaiserreich*. Within this context, the memoirs of Jewish–Germans constitute a special case, evidence of their high degree of identification with German culture and thus the full extent of the tragedy of Jews in Germany.[7] Women did not begin writing autobiographies until the second half of the nineteenth century.[8] Their life sto-

---

5 Gabriele Kreis, *Frauen im Exil. Dichtung und Wirklichkeit* (Düsseldorf, 1984), 82ff.

6 A discussion of the problems of such a triangle can be read in Christl Wickert, "Politik vor Privatleben. Zum Selbstverständnis alleinstehender Parlamentarierinnen in der Weimarer Republik," in Elisabeth Flitner and Renate Valtin, eds., *Dritte im Bund: Die Geliebte* (Reinbek, 1987), 196ff.

7 Alfons Söllner, "Deutsch-jüdische Identitätsprobleme. Drei Lebensgeschichten intellektueller Emigranten," in Thomas Koebner et al., eds., *Gedanken an Deutschland im Exil und andere Themen, Exilforschung. Ein internationales Jahrbuch,* vol. 3 (Munich, 1985), 349ff., esp. 350.

8 Kay Goodman, "Die grosse Kunst nach innen zu weinen. Autobiographien deutscher Frauen im späten 19. und frühen 20. Jahrhundert," in Wolfgang Paulsen, ed., *Die Frau als Heldin und Autorin. Neue kritische Ansätze zur deutschen Literatur* (Bern and Munich, 1979), 125ff.

ries display the discontinuities experienced by their entire generation, as well as the special problems resulting from the fact that these women had to live a life different from what familial expectations had been. An autobiography is usually its author's attempt to put his or her life into a logically consistent perspective and give it appropriate meaning. Telling stories provides the writers with a particularly good medium in which to verbalize events, feelings, and expectations not visible in collections of statistical data and observations. Everything that is part of a story is essentially unique and resists generalization but should be compared to other sources as far as possible.

Käte Frankenthal and Toni Sender wrote their autobiographies in the late 1930s. These writings constitute a kind of reckoning with their political work in the Weimar Republic, their Jewish background, and their first years away from Germany.[9] The memoirs of Marie Juchacz and Hedwig Wachenheim, begun after 1945 at the instigation of political friends and family members, were never completed.[10] Both women died (in West Germany) while working on the manuscripts: Marie Juchacz, the returnee, in Bonn in 1956; the German-American Hedwig Wachenheim in 1969 during a stay in Hanover. These writings reflect the authors' realization that their efforts of the 1920s had not been completely in vain, for West Germany now had a democratic constitution and legal system.

Käte Frankenthal wrote her manuscript for a competition organized by the Widener Library at Harvard University among German emigrants "for the purpose of a purely academic collection of material to be used for a study of the social and psychological effects of National Socialism on German society and the German people." With this competition, psychologist Gordon Willard Allport, historian Sidney Bradshaw Fay, and sociologist Edward Yarnall Hartshorne were reacting to American interest in the academic discussion among sociologists regarding "life records," an interest that encouraged a more critical attitude toward the Nazi regime as well as aided the elaboration of proposals for the reconstruction of Germany after Hitler's defeat.[11] The manuscript was not published until 1981, five years after her death.

---

9 Toni Sender, *Autobiography of a German Rebel* (New York, 1939); German translation: *Autobiographie einer deutschen Rebellin*, ed. and with an intro. by Gisela Brinker-Gabler (Frankfurt/Main, 1981); Frankenthal, *Der dreifache Fluch.*

10 Marie Juchacz, "Kindheit, Jugend und erste politische Tätigkeit," in *Marie Juchacz. Gründerin der Arbeiterwohlfahrt. Leben und Werk,* ed. Bundesverband der Arbeiterwohlfahrt (Bonn, 1979), 7ff; Hedwig Wachenheim, "Vom Grossbürgertum zur Sozialdemokratie. Memoiren einer Reformistin," prepared by Susanne Miller (Berlin, 1973).

11 Inspired by the research done during the 1920s and the 1930s by William J. Thomas and Florian

As I describe the lives of these four women in the United States, the various times when they wrote their autobiographies should be kept in mind. Distance in time and differences in life experiences inevitably color every self-description.

II

Toni Sender, who had come to the United States in 1935, represented the Association of Free Germans in countless trips across the continent to speak on her experiences and to educate her listeners on the situation in Nazi Germany.[12] In 1939 she published her memoirs, *The Autobiography of a German Rebel.*[13] A British version appeared in 1945. These memoirs were not available to a broader readership until a German translation was published in 1981. With this book, Toni Sender wanted to document her new relationship with the United States. The final sentences are the words of an emigrant who was nonetheless trying to preserve her ideals from the 1920s:

Hitler has deprived me of my citizenship and property. It was the punishment for my love for liberty. I was a woman without a country until I went to the United States. . . . Liberty is to me not only an indispensable element of life, but also an obligation . . . towards the community that grants me the privilege of becoming one of its members. I thank America for accepting me and giving me an opportunity to start a new chapter of my life, a chapter that I will devote to the cultivation of the ideals for which the best of mankind has fought and died.[14]

At the time Käte Frankenthal wrote her autobiography, she was not yet able to make such a clear decision. The United States is not the topic of her reflections in the conclusion. Rather, she focuses on the possibilities for change to a more just and humane society:

When I think back on my life, I find that it was rich and that I owe myself nothing more. I have known many sides of life. The fact that in the end I have landed on the darker side confirms my theory that for the majority of people in our phase of development, there is no place on the sunny side. I am a socialist. I still believe in development, and in the idea that human society constructs the world to match its needs. The phase in which our individual fate has placed us does not correspond to the needs of society. This is why it is a phase of battle for what is to become of

Znaniecki. See, for example, Thomas and Znaniecki, *The Polish Peasant in Europe and America* (New York, 1958).

12 Christl Wickert, *Unsere Erwählten,* 1:272ff.
13 Presumably inspired by Angelika Balabanoff's *My Life as a Rebel* (New York, 1938), the German version of which had already appeared in Berlin in 1927 under the title *Erinnerungen und Erlebnisse.*
14 Sender, *Autobiography,* 304–5 (German version: 282).

it. I am not so sure that if I had had the choice, I would have chosen the phase that the next generation will live through.[15]

Marie Juchacz and Hedwig Wachenheim returned to Germany as soon as the war was over. The latter returned in the summer of 1945 as a member of the welfare commission of the American military government in Heidelberg. She remained an American citizen, however, but traveled to West Germany every year after 1951:

I did not go with the purpose of going over to the German side and staying in Germany; but I wanted to be able to establish friendly contacts with my old friends in the Social Democratic party on a political and personal level. . . . Homesickness is a special thing; it does not depend only on pleasant memories. From time to time, in the years of my emigration, I felt a sudden nostalgia for the smell of an overheated sleeping carriage, like those in which I so often traveled to electoral meetings.[16]

After her return in 1949, Marie Juchacz took a lively interest in the rebuilding of Workers' Welfare, in spite of the fact that she had not spent the last sixteen years in Germany. Her reunion with old political friends and her family (her brother Otto Gohlke, her daughter Lotte Juchacz, her nephew Fritzmichael Roehl) inspired her to start writing her memoirs. After his aunt's death, Roehl wrote a biography of her that was revised by Heidi Wachenheim and published in 1961.[17] Her memoirs, which stop in 1917, were not published until 1979, on the occasion of the fiftieth anniversary of the foundation of the *Arbeiterwohlfahrt*.

Initially, these four women all went into exile and not into emigration. For Käte Frankenthal and Toni Sender, exile ended in about 1940, after they had written their memoirs. Hedwig Wachenheim had also adapted to her new environment by then. Her manuscripts were an assessment of her life up to that point. All three had started to settle down in careers in the United States, Käte Frankenthal doing additional professional training.

III

Whereas Hedwig Wachenheim, Toni Sender, and Käte Frankenthal had gone to the United States relatively early – Wachenheim in the fall of 1935, Sender at the end of a lecture tour in early 1936, and Frankenthal in late 1936 on a visa obtained by her family – Marie Juchacz did not get to New

15 Frankenthal, *Der dreifache Fluch*, 245.
16 Hedwig Wachenheim, *Memoiren einer Reformistin*, 140–1.
17 Fritzmichael Roehl, *Marie Juchacz und die Arbeiterwohlfahrt*, rev. ed. by Hedwig Wachenheim (Hanover, 1961).

York until early summer 1941. All four, however, had left the German Reich by the spring of 1933 and had already gone through periods of exile in various European countries. At the time of their decision to flee to the United States, the three Jewish women were younger (Wachenheim was forty-four, Sender forty-seven, Frankenthal fifty-two) than Marie Juchacz, who was already sixty-two years old. Coming from middle-class families, the three younger women had the education and foreign-language skills needed to facilitate their orientation abroad. Whereas Hedwig Wachenheim, Toni Sender, and Käte Frankenthal sought and found the path to professional activity in public life, Marie Juchacz suffered from problems of orientation and limited knowledge of English:

> She had not gone to start a new life, but rather because . . . [she] had nothing else left. . . . She had achieved a high position in the past, because she had qualities that corresponded to the unique requirements of a particular time and place but were useless in another environment.[18]

I begin with Toni Sender and Hedwig Wachenheim, who had cultivated private contacts during their early years in New York and who were integrated into the circle of Social Democratic exiles. Marie Juchacz could not gain access to Social Democratic refugee circles, because she had become a member of the New Beginning (*Neu Beginnen*) group in 1933. Party leaders had opposed involvement in this opposition group.[19] Käte Frankenthal, a member of the Socialist Workers Party (SAPD) since 1931, discovered in Prague in 1933 that she could not count on the support of Social Democratic refugee aid. The SAPD had been founded in opposition to the Social Democratic Party (SPD) partly because of the latter's support for the rearmament of the Reichswehr.[20] SAPD sympathizers also criticized the lack of discussion on the dangers of National Socialism. After 1931 even older, private contacts between SPD and SAPD members were broken off. In New York, Käte Frankenthal kept out of discussions and disputes among political refugees.

Toni Sender's professional development bears witness to the successful life of an emigrant. She completed her study of economics, begun in Berlin, at the New York New School for Social Research.[21] She earned her living as an editor at the *Volkszeitung* (New York) and as foreign correspondent

18   Roehl, *Marie Juchacz*, 170.
19   For information on the Neu Beginnen group, see Kurt Kliem, "Der sozialistische Widerstand dargestellt an der Gruppe *Neu Beginnen*," Ph.D. diss., Universität Marburg, 1957.
20   For information on the SAPD, see Hanno Drechsler, *Die Sozialistische Arbeiterpartei Deutschlands* (Meisenheim/Glan, 1965).
21   Toni Sender's papers, box 1, *Lebensbeschreibung,* State Historical Society of Wisconsin, Madison.

for *Le Populaire* (Paris) and *Le Peuple* (Brussels). Between 1941 and 1944, she was the director of European labor research for the Office of Strategic Services (OSS). She became an American citizen in 1943. From 1944 to 1946, she worked as economic advisor for the U.N. Relief Administration and then as advisor for the U.N. Economic and Social Council as a deputy for AFL vice-presidents Mathew Woll and David Dubinsky.[22] In 1949 she became an advisor for the International Council of Free Trade Unions (ICFTU) in Geneva. Before going to the United States, Sender had spent some time in Czechoslovakia and Belgium. Turning her thoughts to Germany, she asked herself again and again:

Was Germany lost forever to the civilized world? . . . Maybe the nation had first to go through hell, but out of that terrible suffering, some day, a free nation would emerge – not the strife-torn republic of Weimar, but a free community, strongly rooted in a new social order.[23]

Through contacts dating from her work as editor of the workers' council newspaper of the metal workers' trade union (1919–33), she was able to establish herself in Belgium as editor of the Social Democratic *Volksgazet*. She thus continued to be involved in the workers' movement and in education. "However, in spite of all the friendship shown to me, I felt very lonely."[24]

In this situation, Sender accepted an invitation to make her first lecture tour of the United States in 1934. She hoped that new surroundings and challenges would bring her diversion from her ambivalent feelings (relief about her escape from the dangers of Hitler's Germany, isolation from German culture, loneliness). At the end of a later trip in late 1935, she had to decide where she wanted to settle: in Europe or North America. Returning to Europe would mean a secure job and good contacts with old friends. The lecture tours, however, had shown her to what extent people in the United States needed to learn more about National Socialism. She knew she would no longer return to Germany to live and work. As a result, she opted for a "full, interesting life" rather than "economic security," thus taking up a "rather difficult struggle for a livelihood," for "one chapter of my life was closed."[25]

Those who knew Sender have reported to me that she was "one of the

---

22 Anette Hild-Berg, "Toni Sender – aus Amerika ein 'Blick nach Deutschland,' " in Helga Grebing and Christl Wickert, eds., *Das 'andere Deutschland' im Widerstand gegen den Nationalsozialismus* (Essen, 1994).
23 Sender, *Autobiography*, 297 (German edition: 276–7).
24 Ibid., 299 (German edition: 278).
25 Ibid., 300 (German edition: 278–9).

unhappiest emigrants."[26] Although this is not obvious from her autobiography, her diary entries for the years 1937 to 1940 often reflect depressive moods that were partially a result of unhappy love affairs.[27] Uprooted as she felt, she longed for a companion to give her support. Even in her diary she remains discreet about people she cared for, referring to them only by initials.

Am frightfully torn and desperate. Better never to have loved than to despair so? Why can there be no love without conflicts? Why is everything always so difficult and in the end so alone?[28]

Loneliness and doubts about the meaning of life are the main themes of Sender's diary; she did not outwardly display these conflicts. Even when asked about the mood she projects, she seldom spoke about it. With Arthur Rosenberg, who spent several evenings helping her prepare her memoirs, she never spoke about her personal life. Hedwig Wachenheim, who is referred to as "H. W." in the diary, lived only a few blocks away and became her closest friend during those years. Wachenheim always managed to talk Sender into getting involved in activities in emigrant circles.

In 1933 Hedwig Wachenheim had not believed in "long-term Nazi domination." Even after she was dismissed from her position as an official of the Reich Ministry of the Interior, as a result of the Act for the Re-Establishment of the Civil Service, which effectively purged Jews from the civil service, she could not yet decide to leave the country. Not until she had to report to the Gestapo daily did she feel forced to make a decision:

This condemned me to complete inaction and isolation. I had always a very strong will to overcome the crises in my life and return to an active life – now too. For this reason I decided to emigrate, although I knew that this meant having to renounce everything which until then had made my life worth living.[29]

Wachenheim went first to Paris and studied one semester at the Sorbonne. In 1935 she spent a few months in Italy, went on to Great Britain, and from there managed to enter the United States. In New York she supported herself with assignments for the New School for Social Research (through Hans Staudinger) and occasional journalistic work; she became involved in the German Labor Delegation, where she was mostly concerned with newly arrived refugees. She is described as someone who quickly adapted to the

---

26 Interviews with: Hans Staudinger, New York, Oct. 11, 1979; Ernest Hamburger, New York, Oct. 9, 1979; Elsbeth Weichmann, Hamburg, June 25, 1979.
27 Toni Sender's papers, box 15, State Historical Society of Wisconsin, Madison.
28 Diary of Toni Sender, from Aug. 21, 1937.
29 Hedwig Wachenheim, *Memoiren einer Reformistin,* 141.

"American way of life."[30] Finally, she could once again join Hans Staudinger in their common passion, eating in good restaurants.[31] Her memoirs do not mention the time between 1933 and the summer of 1945. Nor does she describe the triangular relationship among herself, Staudinger, and his wife. Staudinger refused to talk to me about it. He merely stressed that Hedwig Wachenheim would have had no time for marriage in view of her strong commitment to politics. What fascinated him was the possibility of discussing politics and society with her, something he had not been able to do with his wife. Unfortunately, Hedwig Wachenheim's personal papers are no longer extant; Hans Staudinger had ordered that they be destroyed after his death (1980).

Käte Frankenthal, a member of the SAPD since 1931, had campaigned and made public appearances to raise awareness of the dangers of National Socialism.[32] Being Jewish, she was victimized by members of the NSDAP just as much as Toni Sender was in her constituency of Dresden–Bautzen. On March 18, 1933, she was fired without notice from her position as welfare physician for the municipality of Berlin–Neukölln: "I fit into every category that the Nazis abhorred: Jewish, socialist, seditious, and emancipated woman."[33] She enjoyed a certain amount of freedom of movement for a few weeks still and was even able to destroy office papers so that the Nazis could not get at them. After a final lecture tour, she avoided all contacts so as not to endanger anyone. She now understood:

I had nothing left to do in Germany and I knew that every passing hour meant unnecessary danger for me. . . . On March 31, 1933, I left the country. It was one day before the Jewish boycott officially ordered by the government.[34]

She was officially allowed to take 50 marks with her and hid a 1,000-mark bill in her powder box. But before she could leave, she was kept in custody for a day by the Gestapo in Dresden.

I was completely calm. I had been carrying cyanide in my pocket for weeks, as easy to reach as my hankie. I knew too much about the Nazis' methods to want to be submitted to them.[35]

---

30 Elsbeth Weichmann, *Zuflucht. Jahre des Exils* (Hamburg, 1983), 165.
31 Hans Staudinger, New York, Oct. 5 and 11, 1979.
32 Frankenthal, *Der dreifache Fluch*, 174ff.
33 Ibid., 190.
34 Ibid., 188–97.
35 Ibid., 197–8.

She managed to escape via Prague, Switzerland, Paris, back to Prague, where she worked for the Jewish Welfare Office refugee commission, which organized the emigration of Jews to Palestine and other countries. She had asked the Jewish committee for help because she had not wanted to get into arguments with the Social Democratic organization about the differences between persecution as an SPD or an SAPD member.[36] Frankenthal managed to get an American medical license when she arrived in New York in 1936, shortly before the legal prerequisites for such a license were changed. Because she did not have enough money to open a practice, however, she earned a living selling stockings and ice cream and as a fortune-teller. In spite of these initial difficulties, she no longer felt the sense of "bleak hopelessness" that had depressed her in Europe. Now she had more than merely the air to breathe; she had "the right to work and build up an existence." Every Saturday she spent a few hours in the New York Public Library:

I read with the old interest, but without purpose. I do not need to know. I do not hope for anything, and therefore there cannot be any frustration. I made my peace with reality and accepted it.[37]

These sentences show her attempt to fortify herself psychologically by reducing her expectations. Whereas in the 1920s she had seldom had the opportunity for private contacts, now she would have had time to make friendships. She made scant use of this possibility, however, as she herself writes. From 1943 to 1947 she studied at the newly founded New York branch of the School of Psychiatry; at the school, her closed attitude had a negative effect on her didactic analyses under Clara Thompson and Harry S. Sullivan. She refused to admit her feelings of loneliness, despair, fear, lack of self-esteem, and vulnerability. In spite of these difficulties, Sullivan became her teacher and her greatest role model. She later expanded his theories to include the effect of socioeconomic factors on behavioral disturbances in psychoanalysis.[38] Beginning in 1947, she worked as a family therapist and psychoanalyst for the Jewish Family Service in New York. After the Federal Republic was founded, she often traveled to Berlin; on January 30, 1973, she even celebrated her ninetieth birthday with old friends in Berlin.

The leadership of the SPD had fled to Prague in 1933. Because of her association with New Beginning, Marie Juchacz was the only member not

---

36   Ibid., 227, 236.
37   Ibid., 238–41; the quotation comes from Käte Frankenthal, *Ice Cream for Five Cents – Indigestion*, manuscript (New York, 1939), 3.
38   Ibid., 255–6. Epilogue by Kathelyn M. Pearle and Stefan Leibfried.

invited to go along. With her brother-in-law Emil Kirschmann, she went to Saarbrücken, where she opened a luncheon canteen for political refugees from Germany. After the referendum on the Saarland on January 13, 1935, Juchacz and Kirschmann crossed the Rhine into Alsace. Using Mulhouse as a base, they tried to contribute to political education in France via contacts in the German Reich. After German troops occupied Paris in the summer of 1940, the Jewish Labor Committee and the American Federation of Labor arranged for German emigrants in the United States, including Toni Sender and Hedwig Wachenheim, to meet with President Roosevelt. The purpose of the meeting was to prompt a rescue of refugees from the German labor movement who were still living in Vichy France. A list of 125 names was agreed upon, which included the names of Marie Juchacz and Emil Kirschmann. Meanwhile, Marie Juchacz had been interned in Gurs, from where she had fortunately managed to escape. On May 29, 1941, with her brother-in-law and other Marseilles friends, she arrived in New York City via Casablanca and Martinique. She spent several months until the fall of 1942 learning English at a foreign-language school run by the Quakers in Scattergood before she returned to the uncertainty of New York. There she met her old friend from the 1920s, Hedwig Wachenheim, who was "more energetic and active" than Juchacz had remembered.[39] Marie Juchacz did not feel quite at home in her new country: She found American life too full of meaningless phrases, too superficial, and too conventional.[40] She founded her own circle of exiles who for various reasons had not joined any of the existing groups. This little group joined the Workmen's Circle, a group of Jewish socialist workers associated with the Jewish Labor Committee. In this English- and Yiddish-speaking circle, she organized a German-speaking group that discussed the current political situation and the future of Germany.

IV

The four women discussed in this chapter remained true to the ideals of the labor movement and retained hopes for a new democracy in the wake of Hitler's defeat. Even the distance separating Käte Frankenthal and Marie Juchacz from the SPD did not stop them, each in her own way, from making their contributions to German politics after 1945. Toni Sender and Hedwig Wachenheim also continued their involvement with developments

---

39   Letter Emil Kirschmann, cited in Roehl, *Marie Juchacz*, 179.
40   Ibid., 176.

in Germany, which they had followed attentively over the years right from the beginning of their stay in the United States.

It was not until the end of the war that Marie Juchacz found her real vocation: Drawing on her experiences from the 1920s, she helped to establish material support for Social Democrats in Germany. At first, parcels to comrades could be sent only through the American military, which supported this initiative in view of postwar hardships. Parcels with foodstuffs still could not be sent by normal post. The Workmen's Circle supported the collection and purchase of goods, although public collections for such purposes were forbidden. Elsbeth Weichmann, who was also involved in this action, described her feelings in view of the situation at war's end: "We poor hunted dogs had, all of a sudden, become donors whose generosity was in loud demand. That was a new role. But in the last twelve years, we had learned to play a lot of roles."[41]

Social Democrats in the German quarter of New York started an initiative with similar intentions that was organized along the lines of the Workers' Welfare from the 1920s (helping people to help themselves); financially, they were able to send much richer parcels into the former German Reich. Marie Juchacz decided that collaborating with this action offered better possibilities, but to do so she had to break the ban of the German Labor Delegation. She thus wrote to Friedrich Stampfer in September 1945:

Political prominence is of absolutely no value to me. Aside from a certain personal bitterness, the reasons for which should not be totally unknown to you, personal reasons lead me to abandon active participation in politics. My feelings in this regard may be difficult to understand, but I believe that I can expect them to be respected. Help for Germany is another matter. This is what I have been saving the rest of my energy for, and this is what I want to use it for, in spite of all that has happened in the meantime.[42]

Marie Juchacz was rehabilitated and allowed to join in the work. This initiative led to the *Arbeiterwohlfahrt U.S.A Help* for the Victims of National Socialism, which was run in collaboration with the Labor League for Human Rights, the Red Cross, and other welfare organizations.

Toni Sender's diary entries give an idea of her reactions to and thoughts on events in Germany. She was particularly outraged after the conference held in Munich on September 29, 1938: "The result . . . is devastating. What should we deplore most – the cowardice of democratic leaders or the surrender of German ideals. This meeting shows clearly the beginning of

41 Elsbeth Weichmann, *Zuflucht*, 189.
42 Cited by Roehl in *Marie Juchacz*, 186–7.

the Nazification of Europe."[43] In her diary, she also comments on the events of the *Reichskristallnacht* in the context of a description of all anti-Jewish activities: "These days we are totally dismayed at the cruel barbarity against the Jews. Difficult to keep one's will to live. Reactions in the United States unbelievably strong."[44] By then she had abandoned hopes that fascism could be stopped, hopes she had still had after her last trip through Europe (Spain, France, Belgium) in the summer of 1937.[45]

In 1940–41, within the scope of her work for the OSS, Sender prepared a list of trade union activists from the 1920s, which also stated their party affiliation and relationship to National Socialism as well as their whereabouts after 1933. She also wrote a paper on the situation of trade unions in 1933, with possible perspectives for a refounding after victory over National Socialism. Her work was based on her critical attitude toward the work and the structure of the AFL.

Hedwig Wachenheim's discussion of her personal impressions are an attempt to understand the causes of the collapse of the Weimar Republic: "In Germany I had been a politician; I'm a politician by my very nature, even though in America my work was a kind of research, mostly about questions regarding German politics and administration."[46] In 1944, with Siegfried Aufhäuser, Ernst Fraenkel, Alfred Braunthal, and others, Wachenheim prepared a paper titled "Germany in the Transition Period," which discussed the restoration of democracy after the victory over Hitler: "This study is not a program for a German revolution"; its aim is rather "the complete elimination of Nazi influence in public life, legislation, and public administration."[47] For the restoration of public order, Hedwig Wachenheim recommended the involvement of Social Democrats and trade unionists, with their experience in the administration and parliaments of the Weimar era and as guarantors of democratic thought and action. The German workers' movement:

was the strongest democratic force in prewar Germany; if it is able to organize, it will become the pillar of democracy again. . . . The redemocratisation of Germany must be started with the re-organization of the labor movement. A revived German Social Democracy will be the best guarantee of German democracy in general. Although German Social Democracy has been outlawed, it persists as a community of thought, and in small underground discussion circles.[48]

43 Tony Sender's papers, box 15, Diary, Sept. 28, 1938.
44 Ibid., Nov. 13, 1938.
45 Ibid., June 26 to Aug. 2, 1937.
46 Hedwig Wachenheim, *Memoiren einer Reformisten*, 140.
47 Studies in Postwar Reconstruction, no. 3, ed. American Labor Conference on International Affairs, New York, 1944, 1. Hoover Library, Stanford, California.
48 Ibid., 11.

The welfare system, she predicted, would be faced with massive tasks as a result of the war, the expulsion and return of Germans, foreign workers, and concentration camp inmates. These tasks could be coped with only in collaboration with the *Arbeiterwohlfahrt* (Workers' Welfare), the trade unions, and other welfare organizations.[49] Within the framework of the Research Project of Germany's Position in European Postwar Reconstruction, Hedwig Wachenheim was commissioned by the Institute of World Affairs, New School for Social Research, to draft a study on the administration of public health in Germany between 1919 and 1945. This assignment gave her the opportunity to travel to the American zone of occupation in 1945 as a member of the military government.[50]

At the time of the Popular Front debates and while she was still in Prague, Käte Frankenthal spoke as a "free socialist" in favor of a greater participation of women, in particular in the labor movement.

If it is true that women can express feelings better than men, then it is surely a pity that the influence of women in the German labor movement is not more greatly felt. . . . The movement has not been given the emotional content that alone can spark the enthusiasm and fighting spirit of the masses. . . . The emotional quality contained in the awareness that a single movement, with clear goals, once again exists; that an individual group, as lost as it may be floating in the tidal wave of fascism, is still part of a greater fighting unit; that is the quality needed to revive the illegal movement. Is that a women's view? In any case it is more useful than the hard feelings of certain men, who cannot move away from old grudges and mistrust, just like the famous aunt who sits on the sofa and takes offense.[51]

Although Käte Frankenthal did not take part in discussions in emigrant circles, she worked in 1944–45 for the Council for a Democratic Germany. She is said to have been the main force responsible for the preparation of the section of a memorandum dealing with health policy, together with Felix Boenheim and Kurt Glaser. They knew one another from the *Verein sozialistischer Ärzte*, a physicians' organization in the 1920s with a Social Democratic leaning.[52]

Exile and emigration meant the loss of the emigrants' accustomed lifestyle, the tasks they had set for themselves, their life plans, their social and professional position. When they left Germany, these women could no longer relate to the milieu that they had known. To a certain extent, they lost contact with one another, partly as a result of political dissent among

---

49 Ibid., 29ff.
50 Cf. Wachenheim, *Memoiren einer Reformistin,* 139.
51 Frankenthal, "Frauen zur Einheitsfront," *Die neue Weltbühne* [Prague] 32, no. 5 (1936): 137.
52 "A Democratic System of Public Health for Germany, including Emergency Measures," New York, May 1945; cf. Pearle and Leibfried's epilogue in Frankenthal, *Der dreifache Fluch,* 259.

the various factions within the SPD or between the SPD and left-wing groups (such as the SAPD and New Beginning), even though in some cases they lived in the same areas or even in the same towns.

Outside Germany, all four women were to some extent involved in activities against National Socialism. They spoke about their work in the Weimar Republic and about what they had learned about the Third Reich since 1933, remaining true to broad socialist ideals. They hoped – after realizing that Hitler's rule was no short-term phenomenon – for the downfall of the regime, and once the war had started they prayed for its defeat. The three Jewish women did not consider returning to Germany in the future. Before National Socialism, their Jewish origins had not played a decisive role in their lives. As a result of Nazi ideology and the National Socialists' anti-Semitic policies, they fell back on their Jewish roots and this meant that a life in Germany was no longer possible. Nevertheless, they did visit the country regularly after 1945. In contrast, Marie Juchacz waited anxiously for the opportunity to return. In the end, only Marie Juchacz had remained an exile. The three Jewish women had more or less (with all their difficulties) integrated into American society; they had come as emigrants and became German-born Americans. This path would have been unthinkable without their previous education and their origins, which gave them a greater measure of flexibility. German language, culture, and politics had marked all of them and were to remain their frame of reference for their life in American society.

23

Women's Voices in American Exile

GUY STERN AND BRIGITTE V. SUMANN

Defining our subject during the course of our research meant proceeding in concentric circles. From a broad definition of women writers in exile, which would have included philosophers, historians, art historians, journalists, and literary critics, we were compelled to retreat to the narrower topic of abstraction about female contributors to the world of belles lettres. Our dilemma, an embarrassment of riches, may highlight once again – as the conference in Washington accomplished – the need and desirability of investigating the intellectual migration from Nazi Germany, particularly under the aspect of gender.[1]

A few examples marking our narrowing circles illustrate (in conjunction with our later observations on autobiographers) the scholarly pathway lying ahead. For two reasons we were tempted to include, stowaway-fashion, the philosopher Hannah Arendt. Although she is an author of nonfiction only some of her prose, as in her biographical volume *Men in Dark Times,* straddles the invisible line between flawless expository writing and *Kunstprosa,* or poetic prose.[2] Also, her undiminished influence was demonstrated anew when the prominent news analyst Charles Osgood, commenting on the controversy surrounding Clarence Thomas's confirmation as Supreme Court justice, quoted from her *The Origins of Totalitarianism.*[3]

In addition, Selma Stern-Täubler, leading historian and historiographer on Judaism, and Hanna Holborn Gray, one of the leading authorities on the Renaissance, spring to mind as historians.[4] Fran (Franziska) Hosken,

---

1 Gabriele Kreis, *Frauen im Exil. Dichtung und Wirklichkeit* (Düsseldorf, 1984). Kreis's book is one of the very few studies on women in exile. In addition, see Renate Wall's excellent, if brief, reference work: *Verbrannt, Verboten, Vergessen. Kleines Lexikon deutschsprachiger Schriftstellerinnen* (Cologne, 1986), with an informative introduction by the author.
2 Hannah Arendt, *Men in Dark Times* (New York, 1968).
3 Hannah Arendt, *The Origins of Totalitarianism* (New York, 1951).
4 To cite one example of her works, see Selma Stern-Täubler, *The Court Jew: A Contribution to the History of Absolutism,* trans. Ralph Weiman (New Brunswick, N.J., 1985). For a representative publication by Hanna Holborn Gray, see her *Renaissance Humanism: The Pursuit of Eloquence* (Indianapolis, 1963).

best known as an architect and designer, wrote on the history of architecture and city planning as well as in such seminal books as *The Language of Cities* and *The Functions of Cities*.[5] As far as journalism is concerned, émigré women did not work only in the newsrooms and editorial offices of German-language newspapers. Alice Oppenheimer was editor of the *Jewish Way;* Bella Fromm contributed to *Harper's Magazine* and worked for the *New York Post;* Adrienne Thomas contributed to the *Free World Magazine* of New York.[6] And as far as women as literary historians are concerned, we need mention only Melissa Gerhard, Helen Adolf, and Hilde Spiel. Spiel was briefly a resident of New York and the author of a history of modern Austrian literature.[7]

But to concentrate now on the women who wrote fiction or poetry: Only of late has the distinctive status of German women writers during the exile period been registered and tentatively assessed.[8] As a first result, it may not be an exaggeration to classify them as double exiles. As refugees from their homeland and mother tongue, they (especially the married ones among them) were often relegated as well to traditional women's roles, with the role of chief breadwinner not infrequently added to the three Ks (*Kinder, Küche, Kirche*). As Shelley Frisch, one of the few scholars to write on exiled women as a group, put it (before also naming some positive results of this reversal of fortunes):

An additional dialectical dilemma pertains principally to women. Exile implied a collapse not only of a political order but also of a social structure. This collapse often meant new fetters for the woman, who typically had to take on menial tasks in richer households as housecleaner, nursemaid, and cook to keep her own family fed and clothed while the man sought footing in a linguistically and culturally alien society.[9]

Renate Wall comes to an identical conclusion:

The ability of women to adjust to changed situations, to accept work "below their station," far exceeded that displayed by men. Lola Landau worked initially in Israel as a dishwasher and nanny. Elisabeth Hauptmann earned a modest living in St.

5   Franziska Hosken, *The Language of Cities* (New York, 1968) and *The Functions of Cities* (Cambridge, Mass., 1973).

6   For information on women in journalism, see Robert E. Casden, *German Exile Literature in America, 1933–1950. A History of the Free German Press and Book Trade* (Chicago, 1970), see index.

7   As an example of her excellent studies, see Melissa Gerhard, *Auf dem Weg zu neuer Weltsicht. Aufsätze zum deutschen Schrifttum vom 18.–20. Jahrhundert* (Bern, 1976). For Helen Adolf, see her *Visio pacis. Holy City and Grail: An Attempt at an Inner History of the Grail Legend* (State College, Penn., 1960). See also Hilde Spiel, ed., *Die zeitgenössiche Literatur Oesterreichs* (Zurich, 1976).

8   Kreis, *Frauen im Exil,* note 1; and *The Germanic Review. Special Issue: Women in Exile* 62, no. 3 (Summer 1987).

9   Shelley Frisch, "Introduction," *The Germanic Review* 62, no. 3 (Summer 1987): 108.

Louis as a maid, Hilde Marx worked as a nanny and salesgirl. Frequently the women were the ones who singlehandedly supported a family.[10]

Given the relative newness of this feminist approach to exile studies, that is, viewing exiled women apart from their men, it should come as no surprise that a separate roster of refugee women writers in the United States does not as yet exist and that the distinctiveness of their lives and works has been analyzed as yet only cursorily. Obviously, this omission cannot be rectified within the confines of a brief chapter. It is possible, however, to illustrate that the number of women writers contributing to a large variety of belles lettres far exceeds preliminary assumptions. Still more to the point, it is also possible to suggest hypotheses that may serve as springboards for further research on the ways their careers and their texts run parallel to or diverge from those of male refugee writers.

Immersing ourselves in exile literature, we discern five distinct tendencies in the lives and writings of women authors exiled in America. These texts may not differ in theme, motif, or content from texts written by men, but they certainly differ in the frequency and intensity of such components.

1. The women who came to America as wives or companions of male authors frequently emerged as writers in their own right, though on a different continent and much later than the men. Alice Herdan-Zuckmayer, the wife of dramatist Carl Zuckmayer, was virtually confined to their secluded farm in Vermont. She devoted all her time and efforts to running the farm and encouraging her husband's writing. Only after the completion of his most important exile drama did she write her refreshing autobiography, *Das Haus in den grünen Bergen,* as well as such charming fictionalized mementos as *Das Scheusal.*[11] A footnote to the delayed resumption of her writing career: Only after her death was her biography translated into English by a small Vermont publisher and *Das Scheusal* reissued in the Fischer pocketbook series.[12]

The case of Gertrud Thieberger is not dissimilar. She did not publish her exile poetry until the death of her husband, Richard Thieberger. Klaus Weissenberger intuits her motivation: "It can be attributed to the tactfulness of Gertrud Urzidil, to remain in the background with her own poetic achievements while her husband was still alive."[13] Her poetry would have

10 Wall, *Verbrannt, Verboten, Vergessen,* 75.
11 Alice Herdan-Zuckmayer, *The Farm in the Green Mountains,* trans. Ida H. Washington and Carol E. Washington (Shelburne, Vt., 1987).
12 Alice Herdan-Zuckmayer, *Das Scheusal. Die Geschichte einer sonderbaren Erbschaft* (Frankfurt/Main, 1972).
13 Klaus Weissenberger, "Lyriker im Exil," in John M. Spalek and Joseph Strelka, eds., *Deutschsprachige Exilliteratur seit 1933,* vol. 2: *New York* (Bern, 1989), pt. 2: 1107.

merited attention much earlier; time permits only a sample from a previously unpublished poem, here rendered in translation:

> No grave-side epitaphs reveal
> who this dead person was.
> All those who knew him feel
> that he a prophet was.
>
> That he went forth at God's command
> to stand guard at the gate
> that he survey the land,
> deep burrows excavate.
> But at the stair's base
> his symbols proclaim
> from beneath the staircase:
> at lips sealed tightly in one's face
> no fly takes aim.
>
> Don't the mirror undo
> Don't inter me in depths very far
> God will be close to you
> redeem Himself in you
> His child you are.[14]

Thieberger's deference to her husband's prestige may have dimmed her
own light. The exile scholar Shelley Frisch, speaking of Erika Mann, rightly
spoke of the need "to extricate . . . [her] from the male constellation in
whose shadow she usually remains eclipsed." This observation applies
equally to Thieberger and to many other women writers. In an interview
with novelist Stella K. Hershan, for example, Gabriele Kreis heard similar
sentiments:

Only now was she able to live as she pleased . . . meaning the independence which
includes in her mind living in this neighborhood and writing novels. Only now,
after her husband's death, does she have them published.[15]

2. There is yet another reason women writers exiled in the United States
have so frequently been expunged from memory. To reassert their individ-
uality apart from that "male constellation," they chose the vehicle of autobiography, "often as a 'one-time-shot.'" It is a genre whose *locus standi*

---

14 Poem by Gertrud Thieberger "Au Kafka." Thieberger's unpublished manuscript was obtained
    from the archives of the Leo Baeck Institute, New York. The translation, as well as other renderings
    from the German, are ours.
15 Shelley Frisch, "Précis of Erika Mann Biography," unpublished, 6–7. For an interview with Stella
    K. Hershan, see Kreis, *Frauen im Exil,* 145.

in literature is still debated: Is it fact, fiction, or "faction?"[16] In the case of established writers, the need to classify is less pressing; after all, their artistic medium, the word, is no different from the rest of their creative works. But autobiographies of lesser-known personalities, if published at all, court the speedy path to obscurity because they fall between canonical cracks, unless, of course, they focus on great luminaries. Without the sun of Dylan Thomas to light up the pages, Caitlin Thomas's autobiography, *Leftover Life to Kill,* however agonizingly beautiful, might be forgotten today. And as far as the exile women are concerned, who will remember, apart from the husband-hero or father, the heroine of Marta Feuchtwanger's *Nur eine Frau,* of Eva Lips's *Rebirth in Liberty,* of Katja Mann's *Meine ungeschriebenen Memoiren,* of Friderike Zweig's *Spiegelungen des Lebens,* or even more pointedly, of Erika Mann's *Das letzte Jahr: Bericht über meinen Vater?*[17] We do know that all but a few specialists have by now forgotten Bella Fromm's lively autobiography.[18]

True, there are exceptions. To choose one example from among many, Alma Mahler-Werfel's *And the Bridge Is Love* was rescued from oblivion by her flirtation with sensationalism.[19] As for the rest of the women writers mentioned, they live, even in their own autobiographies, in the shadow of males.

For that reason but for others as well, it may be important to rank autobiographies with belles lettres. As Erna M. Moore points out, the autobiographies of exiles tend to interpret individual fates as contemporary history. And as Gabriele Kreis puts it, autobiographies of exile women have an additional function, namely, to provide rare, but historically important glimpses of the everyday struggle of life in exile.[20]

3. The difficulties of publishing lyric poetry, either in the original lan-

---

16   The term "faction" is borrowed from the foreword by Truman Capote to his *In Cold Blood: A True Account of a Multiple Murder and Its Consequences* (New York, 1965). He means a factual account ordered like a fictional text.

17   Caitlin Thomas, *Leftover Life to Kill* (Boston and Toronto, 1957); Marta Feuchtwanger, *Nur eine Frau. Jahre, Tage, Stunden* (Munich, 1983); Eva Lips, *Rebirth in Liberty* (New York, 1942); Katja Mann, *Meine ungeschriebenen Memoiren,* trans. Hunter and Hildegard Hannum (New York, 1975); Friderike Zweig, *Spiegelungen des Lebens* (Vienna, 1964); Erika Mann, *Autobiographisches. Das letzte Jahr; Bericht über meinen Vater* (Frankfurt/Main, 1968); Friedelind Wagner, *Heritage of Fire. The Story of Richard Wagner's Granddaughter* (New York and London, 1945).

18   Bella Fromm, *Blood and Banquets: A Berlin Social Diary* (New York and London, 1942). Fromm's autobiography has, however, recently been reissued in hardcover in 1990 and as a trade paperback in 1992.

19   Alma Mahler-Werfel, *And the Bridge Is Love,* in collaboration with E. B. Ashton (New York, 1958). The later German version was even more sensational: *Mein Leben* (Frankfurt/Main, 1960).

20   Erna M. Moore, "Exil in Hollywood: Leben und Haltung deutscher Exilautoren nach ihren autobiographischen Berichten," in *Deutschsprachige Exilliteratur seit 1933,* vol. 1: *Kalifornien* (Bern, 1976), no. 1: 21.

guage or in translation, had particularly egregious consequences for women, though it bedeviled male exile writers as well.[21] As recently as August 1991, the German-American poet Lisa Kahn deplored (in a letter to me) the difficulties of finding publishers for poetry. Women were particularly stymied by the low salability of lyric poetry. If one of our authors' circle of exile acquaintances is any indication – it certainly can lay no claim to statistical accuracy – more women than men considered lyric poetry their favorite mode of expression. A more scholarly investigation of twentieth-century women writers comes to a similar conclusion:

Solely in regard to the preference for certain literary genres should attention be called to the difference between male and female authors. Women appear to be less inclined towards the writing of dramas – Hrosvitha von Gandersheim is an exception – but often demonstrate in their lives a one-sided talent for lyric poetry. The numerous poetry anthologies of German and non-German women writers constitute a sort of proof of it.[22]

Certainly, Margot Jost's conclusion describes the oeuvre of such exile women as Gertrud Thieberger, Ilse Blumenthal-Weiss, Vera Lachmann, and Lisa Kahn. To all these writers likewise applies an observation that Victoria Hertling made about the lyricist Lili Körber: "Exile robbed them of the opportunity of employing the literary forms which in the past had formed the basis of their artistic creations."[23]

Some exiled women lyricists, however, labored under yet another restriction. Anticipating some of the feminist themes of the women's movement, they wrote protest poetry. As Susan Cocalis puts it:

They all [i.e., the nineteenth-century poets she anthologized], however, express dissatisfaction with the social status quo, indicate an awareness of the particular forms of oppression that women experience, and suggest ways in which that situation could be changed.

These tendencies can be regarded as representative parts of an evolving tradition of women's poetry that has also come to be acknowledged as such by later generations of women. Much of the poetry written by women in the twentieth century may be characterized in the same way.[24]

---

21 Victoria Hertling, "Abschied von Europa: Zu Lili Körbers Exil in Paris, Lyon und New York," *The Germanic Review* 62, no. 3 (Summer 1987): 123.

22 Margot Jost, *Deutsche Dichterinnen des zwanzigsten Jahrhunderts* (Munich, 1968), 10. Although we agree with Jost's observation on lyric poetry as a genre preferred by many women writers, we do not agree that this phenomenon is a sign of a one-sided talent.

23 Hertling, "Abschied von Europa," 123.

24 Susan L. Cocalis, ed., *The Defiant Muse. German Feminist Poems from the Middle Ages to the Present* (New York, 1986), xix.

For example, Vera Lachmann's explicit attachment to a woman's world as a counterpart to a male-dominated society is illustrated in the poem, *In Eressos,* which depicts a love feast at the birthplace of Sappho. Lines such as "Here, my darling, did you open your eyes," certainly did not ease the thorny path to publication;[25] male critics, the feminist scholar Gisela Brinker-Gabler speculates, may have reproached women for female self-confidence expressed in the *form* of the lyric.[26] Gert Niers would say of *In Eressos:*

The author celebrates in this alcaic ode, consisting of four strophes, the exemplary female model and praises the woman and poetess. The poem, sustained by a manifest pathos, introduces, however, into its rigid form an original metaphoric language devoid of any conservative formalism ("The glittering ocean poured a consistent tone/from brocaded folds upon grey sands"). Even more than the preceding text we may validate this text as the human and poetic creed of the poet [Vera Lachmann]. It must also be considered an example of women's literature beyond the male establishment, but likewise beyond the market place of feminist theory.[27]

In short, when Gisela Brinker-Gabler remarks that within Nazi Germany a germinating feminist self-confidence was interred – "the onset of a feminist consciousness in lyric poetry were buried by the Hitler dictatorship" – it is fair to add that several of the exiled women writers kept the germinating plant alive.[28]

4. Yet women discovered an access road to American literature that they, far more often than the men, found congenial. Perhaps because books for children and juveniles required a less sophisticated American English vocabulary, or because children had not been corrupted by the world of the adults, several women – often with remarkable success – started to write in that genre. The partially completed bio-bibliography of exile literature for children by Zlata Fuss Phillips, while also listing such male authors as Oskar Seidlin, shows a preponderance of titles by women.[29] As one of these authors, Adrienne Thomas, who spent her exile in Austria, France, and the United States, would put it, she started writing a children's book because

25 Vera Lachman, *Golden tanzt das Licht im Glas* (Amsterdam, 1969), 212.
26 Gisela Brinker-Gabler, ed., *Deutsche Dichterinnen vom 16. Jahrhundert bis zur Gegenwart. Gedichte und Lebensläufe* (Frankfurt/Main, 1978), 14.
27 Gert Niers, *Frauen schreiben im Exil. Zum Werk der nach Amerika emigrierten Lyrikerinnen Margarete Kollisch, Ilse Blumenthal-Weiss, Vera Lachman* (Frankfurt/Main, 1988), 158.
28 Brinker-Gabler, *Deutsche Dichterinnen,* 65.
29 Zlata Fuss Phillips, a librarian at SUNY at Albany, kindly supplied us with a partial list and with other helpful information during a telephone conversation on Oct. 21, 1991, and in a letter of Oct. 25, 1991.

she could still communicate with them: "Perhaps one could still talk to children. I no longer had a common language with adults."[30]

The Austrian writer Hertha Pauli, who had never written a juvenile book before her immigration, became against all odds the most renowned of the immigrant writers of children's books. Her *Silent Night, The Story of a Song: The Story of the Christmas Tree,* and *Lincoln's Littlest Correspondent* became American classics.[31] I talked to Pauli several times about this aspect of her work in exile. "There is really no division between adult and children's literature. I tell the same story and merely change my image of my imaginary readers."

Some of the children's books contain remarkable reflections on exile, well within the comprehension of the intended age group. Here is a passage from Sonia Levitin's *Silver Days:*

We were together again with Papa. While we were separated, I'd wished and prayed for this every day. People always think that when a wish comes true everything will be perfect; it never is.

Mother, Annie, Ruth, and I had waited a whole year in Switzerland for Papa to send for us. None of us realized it would take so long. In fact, when we finally did see Papa again, Annie didn't recognize him. She was only three when Papa left Germany in secret, escaping the Nazis.[32]

5. Exile women writers, beyond succeeding as authors of children's books, also found a niche for themselves as screenplay writers. Although many established male writers also worked for the major studios, their salaries were mostly sinecures rather than wages for work performed.[33] With few exceptions, such as the continuous success of Alfred Neumann or the single script by Bertolt Brecht,[34] the established German authors were eclipsed in the topsy-turvy world of Hollywood by lesser-known but more adaptable scribes. These bits of Hollywoodiana have long been known, but it has been largely ignored that the studios employed no women as token writers.[35] Those women who did toil at the studios and on location, however, actually produced numerous usable scripts. "Gina Kaus, under the

---

30 Adrienne Thomas, *Reisen Sie ab, Mademoiselle?* (Vienna, 1940), 6–7. Quoted in Erika E. Theobald "Adrienne Thomas," in *Deutschsprachige Exilliteratur,* vol. 2: *New York,* pt. 2: 907.

31 Hertha Pauli, *Silent Night: The Story of a Song* (New York, 1951); *The Story of the Christmas Tree* (Boston, 1944); *Lincoln's Littlest Correspondent* (Garden City, N.Y., 1952).

32 Sonia Levitin, *Silver Days* (New York, 1989).

33 Hans-Bernard Moeller, "Exilautoren als Drehbuchautoren," in *Deutschsprachige Exilliteratur,* vol. 1: *Kalifornien,* no. 1:676–714.

34 Guy Stern, "Success in Hollywood: The Exception Alfred Neumann," *Internationales Jahrbuch für Germanistik* 3 (1977): 36–45. For a fuller discussion of Brecht's and his collaborators' part in the script of *Hangmen Also Die,* see Moeller, "Exilautoren," 690–1.

35 Ibid.

pressure of the prevailing situation, became a prestigious writer of film scripts," Victoria Hertling concludes.[36] As much can also be said of Salka Viertel.[37] And Hertha Pauli was engaged by no less a personality than Oscar-recipient Paul Muni to write a film script about the life of Alfred Nobel, a project thwarted only by Muni's progressively worsening eyesight.[38] Victoria Wolff, writer of best-selling popular novels, was able to sell numerous screen plays until a legal dispute terminated her career at MGM.[39] In his pioneering article about exiled writers in Hollywood (including Wolff), Hans-Bernard Moeller listed no fewer than ten women who contributed to varying degrees to scripts made into films. They range from such relatively well-known writers as Vicki Baum and Erika Mann to virtual unknowns such as Lilo Dammert and Lilly Hatvany.[40] Although greatly outnumbered on the studio lots by their male counterparts, three of the women script writers belonged to a small group of authors who had mastered the craft of writing for films, even though they had never worked in that genre before.

From among the subgroups making up the professional exile film writers, one circle is undoubtedly the most interesting. That is a group of six authors, who only by virtue of being exiled took up this calling. These beginners were Robert Thoeren, Salka Viertel, Gina Kaus, Victoria Wolff (Wolf), John (Hans) Kafka, and George Froeschel.[41]

Finally, Salka Viertel reworked scripts intended as star vehicles for Greta Garbo, thereby contributing to some of Garbo's greatest triumphs:

But there she became for a time the personal script writer for Garbo. The legendary actress from Sweden had her adapt no less than five roles, all of them ultimately filmed. Among them were *Anna Karenina* (1935) and *Queen Christina*, based on a seminal idea of Salka Viertel herself. The emigrant woman even became, according to Norman Zierold's judgment, recorded in *Garbo*, one of the most important among the few persons in the life of Garbo during the thirties. In addition Salka was of great significance for the exiles in California in general, because she made of her house a central meeting place between the worlds of literature and of film.[42]

---

36 Hertling, "Abschied von Europa," 228 and note 53. Also, see Dagmar Malone, "Gina Kaus," in *Deutschsprachige Exilliteratur*, vol. 1: *Kalifornien*, no. 1: 751–6.

37 Salka Viertel, *The Kindness of Strangers* (New York, 1969).

38 Guy Stern, "Hertha Pauli," in *Literatur im Exil. Gesammelte Aufsätze 1959–1989* (Ismaning, 1989), 282–302.

39 Rudolf Hirschmann, "Victoria Wolff," in *Deutschsprachige Exilliteratur*, vol. 1: *Kalifornien*, no. 1: 668–75.

40 Moeller, "Exilautoren."

41 Ibid., 698.

42 Ibid., 699.

Once we have acknowledged the foregoing distinctions between male and female exile writers – others no doubt will surface – we need to ask how to rectify the shortchanging of exiled women writers in the past. The belated publication of texts by women, undertaken by such publishers as Persona Verlag (Mannheim), is obviously one remedy. Another, in which academics can take a hand, is inclusion of women writers exiled in America in histories of literature, on reading lists, and in anthologies. Poets such as Ilse Blumenthal-Weiss; novelists such as Lore Segal and Hilde Spiel, only briefly in America; accomplished film writers of a later generation, such as Ruth Prawer-Jhabwala, who collaborated on *A Room With a View, Mr. and Mrs. Bridge,* and many others deserve added recognition.[43] But how shall we commemorate the accomplishments of women whose contributions can be classified as ephemeral entertainments at best but whose success against all odds commands respect? When one of the authors of this chapter was finishing high school in St. Louis, following his immigration to the United States, he tried to perfect his English by reading such popular magazines as *Liberty* and the *Saturday Evening Post.* Among the stories the teenager particularly enjoyed were those by Martha Albrand, by all indications a native American author. Not until the research for this chapter was being done did we discover that "Albrand" was one of several pseudonyms for a young German writer whose idiomatic English never betrayed that she had arrived in the United States the same year as the teenager![44]

To do even fuller justice to these women writers, we must seize upon a suggestion implicit in an observation by Shelley Frisch: "Their influence on both the writing community and the reading public was far-reaching during the years of exile."[45] It is this indirect influence that we have scarcely begun to appreciate. Let us provide a few examples, some of which still reach into the present. The life and works of Hannah Arendt inspired a novel by an American fiction writer.[46] Vicki Baum's novel and film treatment of *Grand Hotel* gave birth to the prize-winning American musical of the same name.[47] During the 1930s and 1940s, Erika Mann was one of the

---

43　For further information on Ilse Blumenthal-Weiss, see Gert Niers; for Hilde Spiel, see Roeder-Strauss; for Lore Segal and Ruth Prawer-Jhabwala, see Guy Stern, "Das Exil und die amerikanische Gegenwartsliteratur," in *Literatur im Exil,* 393–402.

44　For a more complete bio–bibliography, see Anne Evory and Linda Metzger, eds., *Contemporary Authors: A Bio–Bibliographical Guide to Current Writers,* New Revision Series, vol. 2 (Detroit, 1961–).

45　Frisch, "Introduction," 107.

46　Arthur A. Cohen, *An Admirable Woman* (Boston, 1983).

47　Vicki Baum, *Grand Hotel,* trans. Basil Creighton (Garden City, N.Y., 1931). Vicki Baum's novel appeared, of course, before her exile. For a thorough study of Vicki Baum, see Linda J. King, *Bestsellers by Design: Vicki Baum and the House of Ullstein* (Detroit, 1988).

most sought-after speakers on fascism and dictatorship; with the appearance of the German translation of the essays she wrote with her brother Klaus, her words are once again heard.[48] When male writers in Hollywood were abandoned by the studios after a one-year subsidy, they were saved from indigence by the door-to-door collections of Liesl Frank and Charlotte Dieterle.[49] Even today the imprint "A Helen and Kurt Wolff Book"[50] signifies quality at the publishing house of Harcourt Brace and Co. The steady stream of children's books by Sonja Levitin are available in countless libraries across the United States.

In lieu of a summary one need only recall the life of Hertha Nathorff, as chronicled by Renate Wall.[51] Nathorff, an established German obstetrician, changed careers several times to support her husband and son, subordinated her own career to that of her husband, also a physician, worked for her husband, and then trained fellow exile women in child care and nursing. She also found time to write poetry for newspapers, periodicals, and anthologies as well as to keep an extensive diary, which later won several literary prizes. Finally, after the death of her husband, she launched her fourth or fifth career: She became a psychotherapist, employed by the prestigious Alfred Adler Mental Hygiene Clinic.

We have suggested some of the circumstances that gave rise to and shaped the texts of women writing in exile. This is only a tentative first step. What a fellow researcher on this subject, Barbara Drygulski-Wright, observed about German women lyricists in general applies equally to the works of these exiled women writers: "What we see . . . is that a more adequate canon must complement traditional male perspectives with female perspectives, and only include uniquely female items, images, and forms."[52] We can only speculate on what some of these themes might be, beyond the obvious preoccupation with the postmodern details of everyday living. As Gabriele Kreis puts it: "The domain of women was the workaday weekday in life in their texts."[53] But is it not also true that they transmuted routine observation into vision? In one of Rose Ausländer's lyrics, the "I" of the

48   Klaus and Erika Mann, *Escape to Life: Deutsche Kultur im Exil* (Munich, 1990).
49   Moeller, "Exilautoren," 678.
50   For additional information on the professional career of Helen Wolff, see entry "Kurt Wolff" in Werner Röder and Herbert Strauss, eds., *Biographisches Handbuch der deutschsprachigen Emigration nach 1933,* vol. 1 (Munich, 1980), 833: "Ab 1961 für Harcourt Brace and World, Inc., New York, tätig (späterer Verlag Harcourt Brace Jovanovich), dort Hg. der Helen and Kurt Wolff Books unter eigenem Impressum (eine Praxis, die im Verlagswesen eine Neuheit darstellte). Ab 1963 Fortführung der Serie durch Helen M. Wolff . . ."
51   Wall, *Verbrannt, Verboten, Vergessen,* 136–7.
52   Barbara Drygulski-Wright in her review of *The Defiant Muse. German Feminist Poems from the Middle Ages to the Present,* ed. Susan Cocalis (New York, 1986), in *The Germanic Review,* 157.
53   Kreis, *Frauen im Exil,* 221.

poem almost catalogues the objects in her room until the last few lines summarize the exile experience:

VERSCHWOMMEN	CLOUDED-OVER VISION
Hinter erblindetem Fenster	Through dust-covered windows
was sich abspielt im Zimmer	no neighbor perceives
sieht kein Nachbar	what's taking place in this room
Fadenscheinige Spiralen	Threadbare spirals
im Teppich führen	in the carpet
zu sich selbst zurück	turn on themselves
zeitentgrünt	green patterns withered by time
Verschwommen	As through a cloud
lächelt das Rokokomädchen	the rococo girl,
aus Porzellan	made of porcelain, smiles
In der Holztruhe	In the wooden chest
Gespenster	ghosts
mit Tuch bedeckt	covered with rags
Nein wir nagen nicht	No, we don't suffer
am Hungertuch	pangs of hunger
das Land ist fett	the fat of the land abounds
die Herzwand	the heartwalls are thin[54]
dünn	

54 Rose Ausländer, *Noch ist Raum: Gedichte* (Duisburg, 1976), 94.

EPILOGUE

The First Sex

PETER GAY

I

The remarks the organizers invited me to give at the final gathering of the
conference on "Women in the Emigration after 1933" – now published
here – require something of a prelude. It will be, I warn the reader, a rather
personal prelude. But, then, when refugees get together, they reminisce.
When Fred Grubel originally asked me to give the concluding talk at the
conference, I gladly complied. I have views on refugee women, views I did
not mind sharing. And one of these views was that such a conference was
long overdue. I had thought so at least since 1966. I submit this perhaps
falsely precise date because it was in 1966 that I published a book from a
set of lectures I had given at Berkeley that year, and I dedicated that book
to "the many thousands of pilgrims, Jewish and not Jewish, German and
Austrian and Polish, whom Hitler compelled to discover America." And
in listing some of these discoverers, I included what I called "the spoiled,
idle wives who supported their unemployable husbands by washing floors,
making candy, and selling underwear."

I should quickly confess that in hindsight the adjective "spoiled" was not
only gratuitous but really rather cheap – a remark that had not earned its
way in reality. I might have recognized it as unfair if I had simply thought
of my mother in this context. In 1936 when it became plain that we would
be emigrating from Nazi Germany, my mother, frail as she was, suffering
from intermittent bouts of tuberculosis, took up sewing in a serious way to
have a craft to fall back on in emigration. My mother, who had never
worked outside the home, was going to be a seamstress in exile. Nor is this
all. I should have remembered that German–Jewish women, especially those
living under Hitler, had little opportunity to be spoiled. From 1933 on,
more and more of them entered the labor force as their husbands were fired
from their jobs or were prevented by Nazi legislation from following their
trade. I should have remembered, too, that after *Kristallnacht,* thousands of

German–Jewish women became effectively the head of the house. While their husbands were languishing in concentration camps, the wives managed the household alone and, too busy with children and the horrendous details of emigration, could not permit themselves to give way to anxiety. They were the ones who tramped to the Gestapo to get news of their husbands, and to one consulate after another to pick up information and inquire into possibilities for refuge.

But, this confession over, to return to my dedication. I wrote that these women, and in their own way their men, were "heroes, who are in danger of being forgotten and who deserve to be remembered."[1] I suppose I could stop right here, for this dedication sums up what I have called my views. The rest is commentary – with a small "c." If I go on it is not to say anything new – I was after all only supposed to summarize what the participants told one another for three days – but to bring together some of the disparate strands that run through these chapters.

When I said in my dedication that the refugees were in danger of being forgotten, I meant men as well as women. I meant among others my father, an intelligent but not very well-educated small businessman who came to this country at the age of forty-eight. He spoke little English, though he bravely labored to improve it. And, taking whatever job was offered him, including physical labor, he tried to secure his independence from family support. With the best of will, he never succeeded and died, a relatively young man, at sixty-two, another belated victim of Hitler. He was one of those refugees in danger of being forgotten. But the women's situation was worse: Very few of them had ever really been remembered.

The question of why it has taken so long before we have taken the topic of this volume seriously is of considerable professional interest. By and large, it has been men who have written the history of emigrants from Nazi Europe, and they have done so mainly from their own perspective. By and large, too, the history has been of famous emigrants – film directors, architects, composers, physicists – and the overwhelming majority of these were men. And on the rare occasion that a women had the nerve to be the historian, she was likely to adopt the man's point of view. Laura Fermi's well-known and well-meaning book on the emigration was titled, significantly enough, *Illustrious Immigrants,* and she too, as her title reveals, concentrated on the headliners. No one, it seems, cared much about Mrs. Lion Feuchtwanger or Mrs. Herbert Marcuse or Mrs. Albert Einstein except, one imag-

---

1 Peter Gay, *A Loss of Mastery: Puritan Historians in Colonial America* (Berkeley, Calif., 1966).

ines and hopes, their husbands. In Fermi's book, women are allotted a few casual lines and a two-page section, "The Wives of Intellectuals." Fermi finds these women hard to evaluate. They "came to this country," she writes, "as wives of European intellectuals and have remained very much in their husbands' shadow."[2] It is telling that a photo insert shows thirty men and six women. And of the latter, these are two female Manns – Thomas Mann's wife Katya and daughter Erika, and one female Serkin – shown with her husband Rudolf. They are pictured because their men are pictured. And so, except for occasional memoirs and some very recent, very welcome scholarly publications, the contributions of refugee women to shaping life in emigration has long been passed over in silence.

However overdue, though, the conference came off triumphantly and I am most pleased to have been a part of it. But my participation was not without its problems. In August 1990, while I was in Berlin, I received a call from the German Historical Institute: What title did I plan to give my talk? It seemed a virtually impossible question to answer. The task assigned to me was to sum up the papers to be offered, and at that time I had not seen, and could not have been expected to have seen, any of them. But the conference program had to be printed, and I had to produce a title. That is the origin of "The First Sex." I need hardly say what this phrase is intended to convey; it condenses into three words whatever views about refugee women I have.

It was, then, without information about any of the chapters that I went ahead and wrote this epilogue. Whatever limited authority I may claim for this early version of my remarks is a personal one. My mother was, of course, a refugee from Germany; so were my aunts. I could watch them, first, from 1939 to 1941 in Havana, then from 1941 to 1946 in Denver, and after that in New York.

Refugee women, I wrote in that premature draft, were heroines. I am speaking, and shall be speaking here, not of the well-known women who fled Hitler: Hannah Arendt, Marie Jahoda, Anna Freud. Their lives and their accomplishments have been sufficiently documented. It is not that their lives have lost their interest for us. But great-woman history is as problematic as great-man history. I am not recommending that we, as historians, turn away altogether from the attention that outstanding personages deserve, even if they have been shaped more by their age than they shaped

---

2 Laura Fermi, *Illustrious Immigrants: The Intellectual Migration from Europe, 1930–41* (Chicago, 1968), 375.

their age in turn. But the social historians of the past few decades have been right to observe that the time of the mute, inglorious women has come, and it is these whom I shall write about, precisely as the authors did in these chapters.

I want to write of women who had never published a book, or even an article, and who came to Britain, or Argentina, or the United States, as the wives of doctors, lawyers, professors, journalists, businessmen. In the Germany and Austria they had left behind, they had been assigned one of two roles: that of housewife or that of minor actress on a stage crowded with, virtually monopolized by, men. Some of the most intransigent among these women fought for the right to occupy center stage, but as some of these chapters have once again suggested, it was an uphill battle. At all events, most of the women were housewives. In her prologue to this volume, Marion Kaplan has reminded us that although 27 percent of German–Jewish women were employed in 1933, this was a low percentage compared to that for the general population, in which the figure was 34 percent. And even when these Jewish women had managed to defy their environment and make themselves into physicians or university lecturers, they were plainly and clearly the second sex.

Their status changed rapidly and dramatically after they left Nazi soil. When they landed wherever they landed – and often their first place of refuge would not be their last – far more of them worked than had enjoyed working, or been compelled to work, during their German years. In emigration they began to support the men who had, back in Europe, supported them. Their husbands were often broken in spirit, but the women kept up morale on the domestic front, often a tiny, crowded apartment – if they were fortunate enough to be able to afford such a luxury at all. While their husbands struggled to acquire, or improve, their English, the women forged forward in mastering the linguistic tools needed for a new life. While their husbands went back to school – to law school or medical school or what they called in Denver the free night school, the Opportunity School – the women took whatever job was available. And quite apart from the difficulties with a new language, unexpected work situations, and often grating, unfamiliar cultural habits, the refugee women found the world still in the grip of a widespread Depression. Work, even for the most fortunate, was simply hard to come by. Yet they did not disdain becoming servants, or cleaning women, or clerks in department stores, or humble laboratory assistants.

I recall in this connection my shopping trips to Lord and Taylor's in the late 1950s and the 1960s in search of an appropriate present for my wife.

Once in the store, I would be taken in hand by an intelligent and very patient – I am tempted to say, motherly – sales clerk. She was an expert to whom I could confide my perplexities about sizes, colors, and styles, a genial counselor from whom I could expect kindly and sensible assistance. And they all had, these sales clerks, the telltale accent that made them citizens of the Fourth Reich, as we called it on New York City's Upper West Side.

I recall in this connection, too, my first few months in this country in the spring of 1941, in Atlanta. I was staying with my mother's oldest sister and her husband, and their two sons. We had been very close in Berlin and continued to be close now. And it was – not to my astonishment at all – my aunt, reenacting on a smaller scale her way of life in Germany, who had opened a small clothing store with a loan from the American branch of the family – my aunt, not my uncle. His health was poor and his morale was low. In November 1938, when the Nazis had ravaged their store on the Olivaerplatz in Berlin, it was my uncle who had wept at the devastation and my aunt who had remained dry-eyed.

My Aunt Hede, granted, was an exceptional woman in many respects: energetic, driving, domineering. Her favorite saying was, "Unfortunately, I am always right." Although this sort of sublime self-confidence did not make her particularly lovable, hers was a character made for survival. She was also exceptional for having shown herself – all her life, mostly in retail trade – to be a highly competent businesswoman. Most of the refugee women I have called heroines had had no careers outside the home and had had ample domestic help. When they found themselves *being* domestic help, they rallied. That is why I have called them the first sex.

I hasten to add that my attempt to elevate refugee women should not be taken as an attempt to denigrate refugee men. Traumatic as the experience of Nazi Germany proved to be for German and Austrian refugee women, it can be plausibly argued – and I would be prepared to argue – that the trauma of Hitler bore down even more heavily on the men. Refugee physicians were suddenly without patients, refugee lawyers suddenly without clients; refugee businessmen suddenly without customers; refugee writers suddenly without readers or even without their language. There were ways of starting a new life for all of them, but those ways proved to be long, capricious, and very difficult. I do not want to intimate that all, or most, refugee men lived in exile in a permanent state of collapse. Many landed on their feet. But the dislocations, the narcissistic injuries, were often overwhelming.

To intensify the malaise, at times the tragedy, of life in emigration, the very heroism and adaptability of refugee women, so essential to survival, could become – and often were – sources of strain within the household. Thrust into the more or less unwelcome role of first sex, the women were only too keenly aware that they might well arouse bitterness at home rather than gratitude. Psychoanalysts write technical papers about the harsh consequences of role reversals. Well they might; it is not a comfortable state of being. It is not clear just how many of the refugee women who brought their families through the long emergency of the husband's unemployment or study for license examinations retreated to their old domestic role once the emergency was over. There is anecdotal evidence that women forced to be the first sex for some years relinquished that role and retreated to being the second sex once again.

Students of immigration to the United States, such as Oscar Handlin, have argued for years that in immigrant families women assumed greater power than they had had in the old country. What Handlin observed among lower-class and peasant immigrants from Eastern Europe or Italy also held true for refugee women from Germany and Austria. But with a difference: Even though many of the latter started out in lower-class occupations, working German refugee women sought to rise to better positions as soon as they were ready for it and they could find one. Even if they remained working women, they strove for and usually managed to join the middle class.

It would obviously be absurd to suggest that these wives were in any way pampered or protected in their new environment. Quite the contrary. Exile was not an easy or hospitable place. There was exhausting work during the day, there was buttressing the husband's morale in the evening. And more often than not, refugee women did not trade work in the world for work at home; they worked at home after they had come back from their job. But I am persuaded that the refugee women's sense that they must keep their household from falling apart gave them the psychological boost they desperately needed. It allowed them to mobilize resources that only a few had even known they possessed.

This is something of what I would have told you, at greater length if I had never read these chapters. Now that I have read them, I can say pretty much the same thing, though I shall be elaborating my fundamental argument with welcome confirmation from your work.

II

The recurrent theme brought up in these chapters – that of adaptability – needs to be underscored from the very start. In her chapter on German–Jewish women who fled Nazi Germany and became exiles in Brazil, Katherine Morris writes: "The upheaval of exile and immigration forced women out of their domestic life to a transitional type of existence, and their memoirs reflect this."[3] But so, of course, were men forced into a transitional existence as a result of exile and emigration. My point remains that women rallied – astonishingly and magnificently – in their new homelands. Of course, life was hard for refugee women – I have insisted on it. Catherine Epstein's chapter on German-speaking emigrant historians in the United States well shows how hard. Refugee women historians faced the same barriers as did American-born women historians: Tenure was a precious possession largely reserved for men. In that sense, refugee professional women were worse off than their male counterparts; it must have been small consolation that the careers of refugee women historians were slow to reach the longed-for top because native-born women historians faced the same obstructions.

Ironically, as Epstein also documents – though this hardly makes the refugee women's lot in America much better – they would have been worse off professionally had they returned to Germany after the war, because in that country the woman as professor of history was and is a rare plant. By 1970, Epstein tells us, "fourteen women who had emigrated from German-speaking Europe as a result of Nazi policies had become professors of history at American colleges and universities, almost as many as *all* women historians in Germany."[4]

I should add that not all male refugee historians – I am speaking here of those who came to the United States or Great Britain as adults – managed to land professorships equaling the prestige they had enjoyed or could have expected in Germany. Many ended up as librarians or as academic nomads. But my point about relative deprivation stands, however. I agree with Susanne Miller, who says flatly in her reminiscence: "Emigration and exile were generally easier for women than for men."[5] Speaking of the social agency Selfhelp, Gabriele Schiff informally confirms this judgment:

There is an interesting phenomenon to be noted: on the whole – and of course with exceptions – it was the woman who "carried the family through" always reminding me of the grandmother in Steinbeck's *Grapes of Wrath* or characters in Sholem Aleichem's stories.[6]

No categorical answer can cover the whole of the female and male emigrants' experience. Comparisons are, we know, odious, and when it comes

---

3 See Katherine Morris's chapter in this volume, 158.
4 See Catherine Epstein's chapter in this volume, 322.
5 See Susanne Miller's chapter in this volume, 88.
6 See Gabriele Schiff's chapter in this volume, 186.

to such profoundly felt a matter as comparative suffering, no firm conclusion seems possible – or even appropriate. In any event, what is central to my case is that the testimonies in these chapters breathe adaptability. Story after story tells of women's capacity to survive, even though they had been deprived of their homes, their servants, their circle of friends, and, only too often, beloved relatives. Susanne Miller recalls how, when she landed in London in 1935, she took up a job in a restaurant, doing all the chores – "it was hard and strenuous work," she recalls – and although she had taken on the work to support socialist anti-Nazi organizations, "during the first years I had hardly any energy left to devote myself to political and intellectual matters."[7] She describes her family in Vienna as conservative and prosperous, and she had certainly not been brought up with all the advantages to slave in a restaurant. But she did slave – often cheerfully.

An equally striking instance of female adaptability emerges in Frank Mecklenburg's chapter on refugee women lawyers. Among those who came to the United States with a degree and some experience in a law practice, he writes, "Almost all those women laywers . . . returned to the profession after retraining. Only a relatively few of their male colleagues did so."[8] It would be interesting to pursue the reasons for this disparity in some detail, but meanwhile the facts are just another tribute to women's capacity to deal with adversity.

Rita Thalmann, writing about Paris, stresses the same quality. Refugees became typists or nannies, they did knitting and sewing for a pittance. "Privileged women," Thalmann writes, "who had connections and could to some extent adapt easily" – her German word is *Anpassungsfähigkeit* – "got by." One of the women she instances was later to reach considerable if controversial distinction in the United States: Hannah Arendt. Heidegger's student not long before, Arendt worked from 1933 to 1940 in an agency overseeing the emigration of Jewish children to Palestine. Others who had fled to Paris, like the Communist Gerta Pohorylles, sold newspapers and worked as a model, and the painter Doris Kahane took employment as a cleaning woman. The point is not that these often highly educated refugees did not refuse these humble ways of surviving. What else, one might ask, could they have done? The point is that they never permitted their unpromising and disheartening situations to destroy their aspirations to become what their talents and their training had fitted them to be: Arendt, a philosopher, Pohorylles, a professional photographer, and Ka-

---

7   See Susanne Miller's chapter in this volume, 83.
8   See Frank Mecklenburg's chapter in this volume, 292.

hane, a painter.[9] We find the same courageous sense of self in other auto-biographical reports, such as Rachel Cohn's dealing with emigrant women in Palestine after 1933.

To be sure, not all these stories are inspiring. How could they be? Atina Grossmann, in her chapter on refugee women doctors, points out that some of this marvelous adaptability could bring in its wake what she calls "der-adicalization." Her example is the physician Else Kienle, who had been imprisoned in Germany before 1933 for performing illegal abortions. Upon her move to the United States, she commercialized her professional training in ways she would have detested in her political days in Weimar Germany. She became, Grossmann reports, "a successful cosmetic surgeon of somewhat dubious respectability in New York," turning her earlier impassioned pleas for women's sexual freedom into cash. The most conspicuous instance of this "deradicalization" came in 1940 when she published *The Breast Beautiful,* a wholly mercantile, self-serving venture. I must offer two glosses in passing on this example: I think it rather unfair to call Kienle's transformation an "adaptation to the 'American way of life.'" The American way of life, as numberless refugees can attest, was not simply the chase for the dollar or the selling out of ideals. And second, I suggest that it might be interesting to pursue the psychological pressures under which Dr. Else Kienle translated political convictions into monetary rewards. Freud has called attention to a character type he calls the exception: someone who has suffered so much that she finds it possible to set aside the usual moral restraints to get revenge on the world by living as unscrupulously and as self-indulgently as possible. But these comments apart, I have no quarrel with the central argument of Grossmann's chapter, which supplies further evidence for the capacity of refugee women to rise above trauma – at least outwardly.[10]

Among the most vivid of such reports is David Kranzler's on German refugees in Shanghai: "Typical of their incongruous situation," he writes, "is the picture of a long queue of refugees, still dressed in their good clothes, women in the latest fashions, even in fur coats, waiting with tin cups and plates in hand for their ration of food at the *Heime*." But not all was pathos: "One former resident remembered," Kranzler continues, "how her mother and her friends would gather together around a single light bulb, knitting sweaters and dresses for sale in some shops – earning a little money in order to buy margarine for their bread." And then the conclusion to which, as you know sufficiently by now, I remain committed:

9   See Rita Thalmann's chapter in this volume, 55.
10   See Atina Grossmann's chapter in this volume, 233.

It also buoyed their spirits, and whereas their husbands wandered about aimlessly, it helped the women make most of the family decisions. Such a situation crushed many a man's spirit. No wonder that some thirty-six refugees, mostly men, committed suicide; it was the women who withstood the traumatic events far better than the men.[11]

Almost no one knowing the average German–Jewish housewife in the 1920s would have predicted such an outcome.

III

Thanks to the chapters in this volume and a handful of recent scholarly investigations, we now have a more solid basis for expanding our knowledge of refugee women than we have ever had. We – I should say, more accurately: the contributors to this book – are collaborators in putting together a sizable and complex mosaic, with more and more pieces in place, enough to glimpse the outlines of the portrait we are working toward: the portrait of the refugee woman.

On the basis of the material we now have available to us, let me suggest briefly some of the directions this work might take, as new pieces belonging to that mosaic are discovered and put where they belong. None of these directions will come as a tremendous surprise; they are comments on what many refugee historians are already doing. It seems to me inescapable that we must keep up the strenuous labor of interviews and – even more important, as the ranks of the survivors thin out, keep up the thoroughgoing evaluation of whatever we can muster from the archives: from letters, from diaries, from unpublished autobiographies. Every so often, we all know, prominent historians declare themselves impatient with this sort of grubbing work. A few years ago, in the pages of *The New York Times Magazine,* my friend Simon Schama attacked the monographic efforts that nearly all of us depend on as narrow scholarship for its own sake; he even resorted to the shopworn commonplace that specialists are people who know more and more about less and less.

This strikes me not only as ungrateful but also as self-damaging – the most imaginative of synthetic historians need to rest their conclusions on the solid basis of fact. My former colleague at Columbia University, the Byzantinist Ihor Sevcenko, used to distinguish between two kinds of historians: butterflies floating above the landscape of the past, and caterpillars burrowing underground, digging away blindly from pebble to pebble. Rec-

---

11   See David Kranzler's chapter in this volume, 132–3.

ognizing that a world without butterfly historians would be a dull place, without apology he classed himself among the caterpillars. As we move toward making that portrait of the refugee woman ever more legible, we dare not discourage the caterpillars and hope they can make the butterflies' imaginative flights realistic and tough-minded.

What should the caterpillars dig for and the butterflies think about? Let me suggest three areas. I know there are more. Take, first, the vexed question of how German–Jewish women dealt with life under the Nazi regime. It has been argued that it was probably the women who took the initiative in pressing for emigration from Hitler's Germany. The evidence, Sibylle Quack admits, is fragmentary and murky. On the one hand, women were supposed to stay put to take care of aged relatives or to keep the family, often deprived of its breadwinner, intact. At the same time, because women were less patriotic than their men, less impressed by the Iron Cross in which their husbands took such misplaced pride, and more concerned about their children's future, they were more eager to leave the country than their husbands were.[12]

In her impressive contribution on Jewish women in Nazi Germany, Marion Kaplan offers some corroborating material. One bit of testimony she quotes from a housewife struck me as particularly telling. "A woman sometimes has a sixth sense," Kaplan quotes this informant as saying. "I said to my husband, 'You know, I think we will have to leave.' He said, 'No, you won't have a six-room apartment and two servants if we do that.' But I said, 'Okay, then I'll have a one-room flat with you. But I want to be safe.' "[13] This captures a marvelous moment: the adaptability that refugee women showed abroad appears almost full-blown in this commonsensical reminiscence about a comment before emigration.

More work is needed in this area. When it is done, it will have to take into account anecdotal evidence such as the vignette I shall now offer from my own family. My mother was far more reluctant to emigrate than my father. This was true even though her situation in the United States, which was our ultimate goal, promised to be quite comfortable. She had a brother here, who had, upon marrying a young American woman in the early 1920s, left Germany to join a prosperous family that owned half a dozen hardware stores in northern Florida and southern Georgia. What is more,

12 See her "Changing Gender Roles and Emigration: The Example of German Jewish Women after 1933 and their Emigration to the United States, 1933–1945," presented at Bremerhaven, 1991; this paper will be published in Dirk Hoerder and Jörg Nagler, eds., *People in Transit: German Migration in Comparative Perspective, 1820–1930* (New York, 1995).
13 See Marion Kaplan's chapter in this volume, 37.

she had been very close to that brother, playing duets with him as they grew up together – he on the violin, she on the piano. Her reluctance was deeply private, largely springing from travel anxieties, neurotic in their intensity. How many women were there like her?

A second issue that invites the further attention of caterpillars is the question of how deep the shift from second sex to first sex went, and how permanent it proved to be. This will involve further interviews, further sifting of manuscripts, and, I suggest, considerable tact. Much of the deepest emotional gratifications and conflicts of refugee women – and of their men – has doubtless remained something of a mystery even to those most directly involved in them. But in a time of rising awareness of what it has meant to be a woman in history, this question remains an intriguing and as yet an unsolved one.

Finally, I come to a matter that requires the closest cooperation of the caterpillars with the butterflies. I am thinking of the relation between the experience of refugee women and the vast but, I believe, badly underrated influence of contingency on their fate. Of course, historians must generalize; even those offering the tersest autobiographies have done so. History is not a collection of biographies. Yet a grasp of the role of individual accident shaping the fate of refugees remains essential to our historical mosaic.

I know this is not a popular view of the historical enterprise nowadays. As I was working on the final draft of this epilogue, I happened upon the inaugural lecture of John Elliott, given in the spring of 1991 on his assuming the Regius Professorship of Modern History at Oxford. And I was pleased to see him asking historians to pay attention to what he calls "the baffling unpredictability of human affairs."[14] Of course, we must classify individual life histories and subject them to overarching explanations. Yet when the editor of this volume gave ample house room for autobiographical sketches, she was wise. And when the authors of these chapters that used statistics or made sweeping observations resorted to individual life histories to enforce their arguments, they were wise as well. We all know – it is a cliché of our shared experience, but it remains all too true – that the life story of each refugee has its unique shape and its unique fascination.

Again I want to call upon my mother to illustrate my theme. In December 1940, after nearly two years of waiting in Havana for visas to the United States, our number came up and my father, my mother, and I went to the American consulate for our medical examination and to have our affidavits

---

14   John H. Elliott, *National and Comparative History: An inaugural lecture delivered before the University of Oxford on May 10, 1991* (Oxford, 1991), 2. ·

checked. My mother came to the occasion drugged with stimulants, and her cheeks were painted a cheerful red, for she was driven directly from the tuberculosis sanatorium where she had been for over a year. As you all know, tuberculosis is one of those diseases that consular physicians were supposed to spot, to keep the United States as free from this contamination as possible. And tuberculosis appears to be one of the diseases easiest to detect. But that doctor passed her. I shall never know why. Was he one of those Graham Greene burnt-out cases who could no longer hear the telltale symptoms? Or was he a kindly man who thought it best to keep our family together? We all have stories of that kind of luck, good or bad, and they matter. I do not propose to recommend that we turn the past into a series of anecdotes. I do want to insist that contingency remain part of the story and that much remains to be investigated.

These, then, are the comments the invitation to address the conference and the chapters in this book have stimulated in me. If you disagree with me on this point or that, or on all points, that could only advance our enterprise. Nor would it surprise me. After all, unlike my *Tante* Hede, unfortunately I am not always right.

Index